MW00332259

THE STORY
OF
SIDONIE C.

The Story of Sidonie C.

Freud's Famous "Case of Female Homosexuality"

INES RIEDER AND DIANA VOIGT

TRANSLATED BY JILL HANNUM AND INES RIEDER

HHP

Copyright 2019 © Marlene Rodrigues and Raphaela Grabmayr

First German edition:
Heimliches Begehren: Die Geschichte der Sidonie C.
By Ines Rieder and Diana Voigt. Published by Deuticke, Vienna & Munich, 2000.

Second German edition:
Die Geschichte der Sidonie C.: Sigmund Freud's berühmte Patientin
By Ines Rieder and Diana Voigt. Published by Zaglossus, Vienna, 2012.

First English edition:
Translated by Jill Hannum and Ines Rieder

All rights reserved

Published in the United States by:

H▒P
Helena History Press LLC

A division of KKL Publications LLC, Reno, Nevada USA
www.helenahistorypress.com
ISBN 978-1-943596-12-6

Order from:
Central European University Press
11 Nador utca
Budapest, Hungary H-1051
Email: *ceupress@press.ceu.edu*
Website: *www.ceupress.com*

Copy Editor: Krisztina Kos
Graphic Designer: Sebastian Stachowski

Printed In Hungary by Prime Rate Kft., Budapest

TABLE OF CONTENTS

IN THE FIRST EDITION OF THIS BOOK (DEUTICKE, 2000), THE AU-
thors thanked a host of individuals who helped during its development
and writing, with particular thanks to the subject's close friends Andrea
Fingerlos, Ruth von der Maade and Lotte Wittgenstein. Thanks also
went to the staff of the following institutions: The Jewish Museum of
Vienna, the Puttkamer Family Archive, Nuremberg City Archive,
Austrian State Archive, Austrian National Library, Vienna City and
Regional Library and Vienna City and Regional Archive.

In the context of the second edition (Zaglossus, 2012), Ines Rieder
wrote: "I would like to stress that countless people are necessary to create and sustain a book. My heartfelt thanks to all the friends who accompanied and supported Diana and me through the years of creating
Gretl's/Sidonie's biography. I now add to the previous thanks, Raphaela Grabmayr, Diana's life partner, and especially Nicole Alceu de Flers
and Katja Langmaier of Zaglossus Press, who involved themselves actively and with great care in the preservation of Vienna's lesbian history in the twentieth century."

Translator's note: When Ines Rieder and I decided to collaborate on
a translation of Gretl's/Sidonie's biography into English, it had already
been published in French, Spanish and Portuguese, but English-language publishers showed no interest, often citing the cost of translation
as the rationale. After two years, we completed the translation, and at
the time of her death in December 2015, Ines was negotiating with a
publisher that had expressed interest but was demanding substantial

cuts, which Ines vigorously opposed. In her words: "Since the translations in French, Spanish and Portuguese also brought the complete version of the original text, it would be difficult to explain to English-language readers why they are going to be deprived of large sections of the original." After Ines's death, I made a promise to her friends and family that I would continue to look for a publisher that would respect the text in its entirety, and I am immensely grateful to Katalin Kádár Lynn at Helena History Press for recognizing the book's historical and scholarly value. Heartfelt thanks, too, to Marlene Rodrigues for her unstinting support, both logistical and emotional.

PREFACE

REAL NAMES OR PSEUDONYMS?
THE GENESIS OF "SIDONIE CSILLAG"

Preface to the second German edition,
Die Geschichte der Sidonie C: Freud's berühmte Patientin,
Vienna: Zaglossus, 2012

ALMOST EXACTLY TWELVE YEARS AGO, THE TWENTIETH CENTURY had just ended and the biography of Margarethe Csonka-Trautenegg was on its way to the printer. Margarethe—whose family and friends always called her Gretl—had died only recently, in August 1999. She was in her hundredth year.

Today, leafing through the original manuscript and rummaging around in the correspondence, I find myself reminiscing about the book's genesis. An issue that preoccupied us at the time and still raises questions that remain in doubt is the matter of "true identity." Throughout the years Diana and I spoke with Gretl about her life, she always said how proud she was that her biography would be published, but the matter of whether to use her real name or a pseudonym was of some concern.

She was aware that any interest in her was primarily in connection with Sigmund Freud. Through him she had become "such a celebrity in a grotesque way," as she put it, for she had always considered him a fool who had a filthy imagination. Freud anonymized the names of the patients about whom he wrote, and Margarethe Csonka was the nameless young girl who was in analysis for four months in 1919 and the subject of his 1920 essay "On the Psychogenesis of a Case of Female Homosexuality."

Gretl liked the idea that she had played a role in the writings of a world-famous professor, and she also wanted there to be a report of the long life she had dedicated, up until the last minute, to a quest for female beauty. She just didn't know whether she should do this under her maiden name, the name of her former husband, or a pseudonym. There was no longer any reason not to use her family name—the social circle on which she had always placed such great value no longer existed, all her great loves were also dead, and there was no longer any value in protecting her family members. What remained, however, was the question of aesthetics: shouldn't she choose a different name, maybe that of a Greek goddess, one that would make her something special?

When Diana and I listened to her mull over these considerations, we asked ourselves whether they were driven by vanity or by the old fear that having her real name known could have unpleasant consequences for her and/or her relatives and women friends. In any case, she never could decide on a name, and it remained for us to make the decision after her death. In the process of deciding, her voice was always in our ears.

That the name Sidonie Csillag is a pseudonym has likely been clear since the initial appearance of her biography. In the first edition we simply explained that we had used pseudonyms for the main character and her immediate family, but we didn't go into the circumstances that led to that choice.

After her death, Gretl no longer had any direct influence on the pseudonym we chose. I researched the most common names chosen for girls living in the Habsburg Monarchy in 1900, and we began experimenting with the list. None of those we tried out seemed to fit. To accustom ourselves to the sound of a pseudonym, I began writing the first chapter using the name Tilly Czurda. By February 2000 we had to make a final decision, and though less common than Margarethe, we agreed on Sidonie and the nickname Sidi. We chose a Hungarian family name, transforming Csonka to Csillag—Stern in German. Sidonie Csillag had become an autonomous person.

It was also important to change the first names of Gretl's parents and brothers. Instead of Arpad and Irma Csonka we chose the similar-sounding names Antal and Emma. Brothers Hans, Paul and Walter became Heinrich, Robert and Ernst. Gretl's husband Eduard Trautenegg became Ed Weitenegg. Her two great loves, Leonie von Puttkamer and Wjera Fechheimer, had both died and as far as we knew had no close relatives for whom their relationship to Gretl would pose a problem.

Both women are given their real names in the book, as are those in the circle of Gretl's close friends. As often as possible we discussed the matter with those relatives and friends who were known to us. When this wasn't possible, as in the case of the Weinberger family, we referred to the person in question only by his or her first name. For example, Gretl's friend Grete Weinberger married Willy Markl, to whom we refer only as Willy.

We also had reservations about whether to use Ellen Ferstel's real name, for that surname was and remains visible in Vienna's landscape. But Ellen's granddaughter Andrea felt that we should use the family name, and she had no problem with however we would portray Ellen. Andrea was also of the opinion that we should ignore her "Aunt" Gretl's wish for a pseudonym of her own; after all, she was now dead, and her remaining close relatives were far away. But that was precisely the matter on which we wanted to let caution guide us. In particular, one of Paul Csonka's wives was concerned about how we would portray the Csonka family. Naturally, we were aware that our representation of the Csonkas rested on Gretl's telling of the story and that hers was only one of many possible perspectives. Whether other family members would see things as she did is doubtful.

I often spoke with Diana about all this, even after the publication of the first edition of Gretl's biography, and it became relevant once again as the French translation was being prepared. EPEL Press was lobbying hard for its edition to use the name Gretl Csonka-Trautenegg. After going back and forth on this, Diana and I finally decided, again, on Sidonie Csillag. It was only after we decided to consign Gretl's estate—which was in our possession—to the Freud Museum in Vienna that the items were entered into the archive under the name Margarethe Csonka-Trautenegg.

I can no longer debate such questions with Diana, who died in 2009. While writing this preface, I reflect on our conversations and hope that both she and Gretl would agree with the approach I've chosen. To prepare for the new edition, I read the text once again and hear the voices and discussions that influenced the genesis of Gretl's biography, and it is Gretl's voice that remains the most decisive. We distilled what is most essential from her memories and left unchanged many references that still make sense today. To mention just one example: although today we no longer talk about domestic servants, in Gretl's childhood and youth their presence was taken for granted.

However, Diana and I helped Gretl out on several fronts; for example, when it came to placing her life in a historical context or providing a detailed description of her environment. This then is presented in the story's narrative voice, which Diana and I passed back and forth between us, patiently supported by our editor, Ilse Walter.

When Margarethe Csonka was born in Lemberg in April 1900, § 129 I b had been in force in the Habsburg Monarchy since 1852. As a young woman, Gretl found herself in the First Austrian Republic, a new form of government which had nonetheless adopted the monarchy's civil law code. When she returned to Vienna after the Nazi era (which she spent in exile in Cuba), the Second Austrian Republic had also adopted § 129 I b, and it wasn't purged from the criminal law books until 1971. For seventy-one years she experienced her yearning for women fully aware that the country of which she was a citizen—granted, with many absences—could sentence her to up to five years hard labor for the crime of "illicit sexual acts against nature."

Gretl was not a coward. She was also prepared to stand behind the people and things that were important to her. But on the one hand she didn't want to cause trouble for her family, and on the other she didn't want to be shut out of society, which was very important to her. To be charged and possibly convicted under § 129 I B would have banished her from society. Viennese families like the Ferstels, Schallenbergs, Mautner-Markhoffs—to name but a few—would have broken off all contact. Therefore, her longings were relegated to secrecy, and eventually she even broke off contact with her first great love, Baroness Leonie Puttkamer.

Only a few of her female friends knew about Gretl's passion for women. When I first met her, all the friends from her youth had died, though she maintained contact with their children and grandchildren. Diana was the granddaughter of Gretl's friend Sylvie Dietz von Weidenberg, and as such kept in touch with "Aunt" Gretl over the years. When Diana was preparing an anthology on the subject of "women and aging," she asked Gretl for an interview. Gretl started to tell Diana her story, and instead of coming home with information about aging, Diana learned of Gretl's great loves and her parents' unsuccessful attempt to "normalize" her with the help of the famous Professor Freud.

Diana knew about my biographical research on lesbians and asked me to collaborate in the interviews and research, provided, of course, that the subject was willing to speak with me about her life. Over the course of the next four years I met regularly with Gretl. Sometimes I recorded our conversations; sometimes we went out for a meal or to a movie; and often I simply sat with her and tried to gain an overview.

It took weeks before I could tell which of her three brothers she was talking about when she said "my brother," which girl or woman she called her best friend, second best, etc., whom she was thinking of when she said, "my great love." As soon as I felt confident about the players, I could delve into the time frame and contemporary history of her narrative and begin my research in libraries and archives.

So, for example, I would consult Vienna's address books for 1859 to 1942—the so-called "Lehmanns"—to research Arpad Csonka's home and business addresses, then take this documentation to Gretl and ask for details. She could give quite specific information about the family's various residences in Vienna, but her knowledge of her father's businesses was rudimentary. She recalled a few of her father's business partners, but since none of them had appealed to her personal aesthetic, she had paid them little further attention.

But since Arpad Csonka had business dealings with everyone who was anyone in Vienna, I was able to research the environment in which Gretl spent her childhood and adolescence. Their father's connections with the leading industrialists and bankers of the Monarchy gave the four Csonka children entree to their city's highest social circles. And many of these families had written down their business histories, making it possible for me to expand on Gretl's story.

Gretl's memories of her four-month-long analysis with Freud can easily be compared with his essay about her, and I was constantly surprised by how closely her memories coincided with how Freud described the course of her treatment. For as much as Freud suspected that Gretl didn't think much of him or his efforts to understand her, he had little awareness that she completely rejected him and his analytic process, and equally little that she found the whole exercise stupid and by the end thought of him as a blithering idiot.

There were other strokes of good luck in the process. The 1924 legal decision in the Puttkamer–Gessmann case was available in Vienna's City and Regional Archive, and it provided details, in police and legal jargon, to flesh out many of Gretl's stories and hints about Baroness Puttkamer. And also, Gretl's closest women friends, the daughters and granddaughters of her best friend Ellen Ferstel, willingly and generously provided information and set up contacts with others who had scattered to the far corners of the world.

Ines Rieder, Vienna, 2012

Sidonie Csillag as a young girl

CHAPTER

1

LEONIE

AN ELEGANT WOMAN PACES RAPIDLY BACK AND FORTH IN THE IN-
ner courtyard of a prison in Vienna, a fur coat draped loosely over her
shoulders. The fact that she's accompanied by armed guards doesn't
seem to bother her. The paint flaking off the enclosing walls in scrofu-
lous patches is the victim of damp and mildew. The first green shoots
are showing between lingering patches of snow, but the ground remains sodden, and the prisoner's shoes make a smacking sound on the
well-worn path. Stopping briefly to glance up, she looks straight into
the appalled eyes of her friend, who has, it seems, finally gotten the
long-hoped-for visitor's pass and is waving from a second-floor window. Waving back quickly, the prisoner shrugs and gives a tired smile,
as if none of this concerns her.

Spring 1924 has just begun in Vienna, and for the past few days the
city's newspapers have been slavering over the beautiful, and notorious,
thirty-three-year-old prisoner they've labeled "wild and sensation-
seeking." Baroness Leonie von Puttkamer, from Old Prussian nobility,
is married to Albert Gessmann Jr., president of the Austrian Farming
Association, and he has accused her of trying to murder him by poisoning his coffee. The couple is in the midst of vicious divorce proceedings, with both parties' lawyers hurling accusation upon accusation and
the police recording transcript after transcript, and now Leonie von
Puttkamer has finally ended up in jail.

On March 31, 1924, the *Neue Freie Presse* dissects the couple's marriage, which Albert Gessmann initially characterizes to reporters as

"exceedingly happy." A few days later, he acknowledges that, yes, there have been difficult moments; especially because his wife "has been under the disastrous influence of girlfriends who have been exploiting her." Leonie Puttkamer-Gessmann is rumored to have had an intimate relationship with the dancer Anita Berber, the newspaper points out, and "is said to have been interned repeatedly in psychiatric wards" during her youth.

The *Neue Montagsblatt* picks up the story the same day and focuses on Leonie's girlfriends. "When talking with a similarly inclined girlfriend, she [Leonie] is said to have remarked that her husband should be sidelined as soon as he has written a will."

According to the police, Mr. Gessmann has stated that his wife "has been so under the demonic influence of her lesbian girlfriend that she went after her own husband with genuine hatred."

On April 1, 1924, the *Neue Freie Presse*, hoping to one-up the other papers, states that Leonie Puttkamer-Gessmann is "a woman poisoned to the soul by gender aberration and the use of morphine and cocaine." Under interrogation, she has denied any involvement in causing her husband's poisoning symptoms, but, the paper stresses, "a human being with the notorious peculiarities of Baroness Puttkamer apparently cannot be made to take responsibility. Taking everything into consideration, including the police report, one cannot find any motive for such a serious crime, save Mrs. Gessmann's so-called aversion to men."

At this juncture, the police decided that due to the additional charge of illicit sexual relations, the baroness's circle of female friends—who refer to her exclusively as Leo—will also be questioned.

The baroness's young friend who stands at the window has also been mentioned in the media, although thanks to her father's influence, not by name. Her reputation in respectable society has already suffered greatly, and had her name found its way into print, she would have been ostracized permanently.

She is Sidonie Csillag, Sidi to friends and family, who will soon celebrate her twenty-fourth birthday. The daughter of an upper-middle-class family, she has never been to a jail before, and it has cost her considerable effort to come here. The pointed, derogatory looks the guards gave her when she signed in seemed almost compromising. The long, echoing hallways with their worn slate tiles, the stale smell of laundry room, latrine and cold meals all turned her discomfort into disgust. She has not been given permission to speak to Leonie, only to look at her from the window.

Leonie's face has grown so thin! See how she clutches her arms around herself and paces in an endless circle as if nothing could stop her! She seems to be looking at nothing, as if she has willed herself outside the walls and is already someplace else. Sidonie has to repress a laugh at the absurdity of the guards who stumble along behind Leonie with a kind of dull zeal. What is it they are trying to guard? What do they want to keep hold of?

She has been allowed to keep her fur coat, that's good; but underneath she is wearing a thin, grey institutional dress—and her shoes are so inappropriate for the slushy ground.

Sidonie looks at this beloved woman with a mixture of wistfulness, horror and disgust. How could her adored Leonie have ended up here? Where does the truth lie—in what the newspapers report or in what she herself has always seen in this elegant, beautiful woman?

Sidonie has never actually understood the baroness's strange appetites, or, more specifically, her contradictory, anchorless ways. At the age of seventeen, when she first met Leonie Puttkamer, Sidi had been an "innocent creature," a sheltered girl with no sexual experience who knew nothing about erotic affections. But the first time she saw the baroness, she felt as if she'd caught fire—not a sexual fire but a deep and burning desire to adore and to worship.

It was high summer 1917. Wartime rationing laws had just been passed. Foodstuffs got harder to obtain; the previous February, all gas-powered vehicles had been confiscated for the war effort; the number of trains had been reduced; and travel by ship on the Mediterranean was no longer safe. All this forced even the well-to-do to stay closer to the capital than usual during their annual summer escape to the countryside.

At the beginning of June that year, Sidonie's mother had given birth to her third son, a late comer after her three nearly grown children, and to recuperate she was spending time at a sanatorium. Sidonie, just turned seventeen, was tall, though still slightly plump, and pretty, with a cascade of long dark hair—the perfect image of an upper-class daughter.

She didn't yet know what to make of the newcomer to the family, but soon he would reduce even further the already small share of love Frau Csillag allocated to her only daughter. She adores all her sons but always keeps Sidonie at a certain distance.

Sidonie can recall that summer vividly. Having just finished school, she sees the summer as a time of transition, after which she will surely start a new stage in life. Her older brother has been drafted into the army, her father is away on business seeing to the affairs of his paraffin oil business, which is essential to the war effort, and so together with her younger brother and a governess, she is sent off to Semmering. This resort, traditionally favored by Vienna's bourgeoisie, isn't as beautiful as the Adriatic island of Brioni, which the Csillags and their circle preferred, but most of her girlfriends are at Semmering this year, though the young men are not.

The war is entering its fourth year, with an end in sight only at the Russian front, and the young men are away in war-related positions or on the battlefield—sacrificing their lives for the moribund monarchy. The voices raised against the war, and also against the ruling dynasties, have recently grown louder.

Three years earlier, on June 28, 1914, in the Bosnian capital of Sarajevo, a Serbian nationalist fatally shot Archduke Franz Ferdinand, the heir to the Austro-Hungarian throne, and his wife Sophie. A month later Austria-Hungary declared war on Serbia. Shortly thereafter, Czarist Russia, France and Great Britain—all Serbia's allies—declared war on Austria-Hungary and its ally, the German Empire. By the summer of 1914 most of Europe had been swept up in a tide of war enthusiasm. Confident that the war would only last a short while, many were willing to contribute to the cause: the wealthy bought war bonds and the general population participated in collections such as "give gold for iron." Few listened to the early voices speaking out against the war, but by 1915 their numbers had started to grow steadily. Karl Kraus, publisher of *Die Fackel* (the torch) and a staunch anti-militarist, started writing *Die letzten Tage der Menschheit* (the last days of mankind) during the summer of 1915. Sidonie had met the famous "*Fackel*-Kraus" several times while visiting his niece, her friend Marianne Kraus. Despite his fame, he hadn't impressed her.

The well-known Viennese merchant Julius Meinl II had invited like-minded business people to launch a peace initiative, and at Sidonie's home her father's guests and business partners had discussed Meinl's proposals seriously. They had been divided on the question of whether war or peace would bring them more profit.

Sidonie paid little attention to the on-going unpleasant events, but by late 1916 there was no escaping them. On October 21 she watched her father turn pale as he learned that Friedrich Adler, the son of Viktor Adler, a founder of the Austrian Social Democratic Party, had shot the prime minister, Count Karl Stürgkh. The new prime minister was to be Ernest von Koerber, who hadn't instilled much confidence in business circles. Exactly one month later, Emperor Franz-Joseph died of pneumonia, and his grand-nephew, Karl, took charge of the army two days after the funeral. Neither the army nor the industrialists nor the politicians put much faith in this devout young emperor. Then in the spring of 1917, Russia was inundated by the first wave of revolution. At the same time, the supply situation in Vienna was rapidly deteriorating, and even though Sidonie didn't have any personal day to day worries, she frequently had to witness scenes that she found quite unpleasant, and so she was glad when she passed her school leaving exams and was free to spend the summer—as usual—outside Vienna.

Sidonie's closest friend at Semmering is a cheerful brunette named Xenia Afenduli. The Afendulis are among the many Greek trading families that had settled in the harbor city of Trieste and accumulated considerable wealth. When war-time Trieste became problematic, the whole family—with personal effects and staff—moved into Vienna's Grand Hotel. Like their counterparts, they summered in the countryside.

SEMMERING

Two Semmering hotels compete for this upper-class clientele: the old, established Südbahnhotel and its rival, Hotel Panhans. The Panhans was enlarged in 1912 in a style reminiscent of the Riviera—a mighty central building is flanked by two large additional

Xenia Afenduli

buildings in a mixture of imitation Italianate styles that sport an opulence of little towers, gables, trim, carvings and other bric-a-brac.

The nouveau riche, Vienna's and Budapest's high society and by 1917 war-time profiteers and their pretty companions as well, all find accommodation in the Panhans's 400 rooms; but the hotel particularly prides itself on its titled visitors—this is noted on the hotel stationery— and each summer welcomes the German Imperial Chancellor, Prince von Bülow.

Great luxury is available here—giant suites, magnificent dining halls, a large café and separate salons for games, reading, conversation and the ladies. The luxury extends outdoors to private hunting grounds, fishing ponds, horse stables, tennis and croquet courts, and in the winter months ski slopes, ice-skating rinks and sledding hills. The Catholics among the guests can attend daily mass in the small adjacent church and ask for forgiveness for sins committed in the course of conducting secret transactions, profiteering, spreading malicious gossip and cavorting with concubines at holiday flings. For everyone's pleasure, there is also a spa in the forest, where, amid the sounds of chirping birds and the wind in the trees, one might take the waters, enjoy some hydrotherapy or a steam bath ... an idyllic spot, the Panhans.

A few hundred meters downhill, in the village of Schottwien, bitter people grumble because it has been months since they have had flour, let alone meat, while above them, refugees from the purgative "cures" at spas such as Karlsbad and Marienbad relax and refuel at culinary orgies. Their war is far away, and it is enough just to be alive ... who knows for how much longer.

Sidonie and Xenia soon grow bored with the daily routine. It is far more entertaining to escape their governesses, roam the neighborhood and gossip about the other guests. During their forays, they often encounter the same two women walking arm in arm; occasionally they are in the company of an older man, on whom they seem to heap flattery in a rather odd way. Sidonie dismisses as uninteresting the woman she thinks of as fat and ugly, but she is fascinated by the other—tall, slender, elegant and with an easy, somewhat swaying gait. When their paths cross, the girl admires the woman's beautiful hands, which always hold a pair of kid gloves, and her uncommonly short, slightly wavy hair style. The herbal scent of her perfume lingers after she passes by and always triggers a warm pull inside Sidonie.

But the sharp, almost hard look in her pale blue-gray eyes and the stubborn yet sensual set to her mouth are what make this stranger seem extraordinary. She is unlike any woman Sidonie has ever encountered.

The governesses close down whenever Sidonie asks about the oddly matched couple, in particular about the beautiful stranger. They let fall a bit of gossip but seem determined to keep Sidonie and Xenia well away from the women in question. The hotel doorman is more forthcoming. The two ladies often frequent the hotel. Klara Waldmann is the one Sidonie has dismissed; the other is Baroness Leonie von Puttkamer, from a quite noble Old Prussian family.

Sidonie is keen to concoct a meeting and drags the good-natured Xenia along at impossible hours to track down Leonie Puttkamer. The governesses grow more watchful; they reprimand the girls and repeat cryptic comments about the couple, mentioning dependency, depravity and triangles. They drop the word cocotte into the conversation.

Hotel Panhans at Semmering

Sidonie doesn't understand such outrage. What are Frau Waldmann and Baroness Puttkamer doing besides going for walks? "That's it exactly," is the governesses' snappish reply. Xenia, already eighteen and better informed about such secrets, enlightens Sidonie, who has always been attracted to women and now, finally, has a name for the tumultuous yearning she sometimes feels. Now she understands that she is not the only human being with such feelings.

Klara Waldmann and Leonie Puttkamer check out of the hotel before Sidonie can engineer an introduction. For the rest of the slowly passing summer Sidonie spends hours every day thinking about the baroness, writing letters and poems to her that she can never mail. She must see her again but has no idea how to make that happen.

The first time Sidonie visits Xenia at the Grand Hotel after returning from Semmering, she learns that the baroness has supper there every evening. No girl her age could show up there on her own without a good reason, so Sidonie has to concoct one. Perhaps if she offered to accompany her health-conscious mother on her daily walk around the Ring and then suggested tea at the Grand Hotel ...

Emma Csillag is a bit surprised by her daughter's sudden enthusiasm for exercise and her uncharacteristic display of devotion; but the hotel's panache and the comings and goings of its noble guests are a strong draw. The beautiful and quite spoilt wife of a wealthy industrialist, Emma likes to be seen and admired, and if she is in the company of her daughter, she can respond innocently to occasional glances from good-looking men.

She soon discovers Sidonie's ruse, but she plays along for some time before her daughter's pubertal puppy love and lingering glances at the outré lady begin to make her nervous. These women who use too much make-up, what is one to make of them? She doesn't like this one at all and announces that she has lost interest in the daily teas. Sidonie is again left to her own devices.

Sidonie's resourcefulness—fueled by her infatuation—proves boundless, and she positions herself by a tree outside the hotel, pretending to be on a walk or maybe waiting for the *Elektrische*—the then-current term for Vienna's streetcars. When the baroness emerges Sidonie stays close on her heels as she walks to the Kettenbrückengasse stop on the metropolitan railway and enters a modern, upper class building on Linke Wienzeile. It hasn't been a long walk, and now Sidonie knows where the baroness lives.

Whenever she has time—and she has plenty of it, having finished high school with no desire to pursue further studies or take a job, which is not befitting, given her social position—she investigates further by installing herself in a phone booth across the street from the house she saw Leonie enter and waits to see what she can find out. She has to leave the booth whenever someone wants to use it for its intended purpose, but otherwise she goes unnoticed. The Kettenbrückengasse stop is in the middle of the Naschmarkt, the city's biggest outdoor food market. It is busy day and night, crowded in the early morning with vendors and suppliers and later with noisy, aggressive shoppers.

Who has time to notice a girl in a phone booth?

Sidonie learns that the baroness leaves the house in the late morning, often accompanied by her wolfhound, and walks towards the tram stop on the Wienzeile. She remains unaware that the baroness lives with one Ernst Waldmann, a wholesale dealer in cooking fats and oils, and his wife, Klara. Their lovely modern flat lacks none of life's amenities, and rumor in Vienna has it that while Leonie shares the husband's bed, she prefers to share the wife's. This ménage à trois—as Klara Waldmann's lover and Ernst Waldmann's mistress—suits Leonie Puttkamer, who is accustomed to an extravagant lifestyle but has long since exhausted her own financial resources. For now, she is enjoying the financial security of this situation.

Whenever Leonie appears on the street, Sidonie scurries out of her observation post, gets on the same tram as the baroness and sits where she can keep her in sight.

Leonie is aware of this daily scrutiny and wonders if it could be accidental. Does the girl perhaps have lessons in the neighborhood? It is quite irritating. She can't be much older than eighteen and obviously comes from a well-to-do family: light-colored silk stockings mostly hidden by black lace-up boots with the obligatory low heels; a nice, dark-blue wool coat; long, wavy hair that is obviously brushed each morning by a servant, then topped off by one of those big silk or velvet bows. Leonie hated those bows when she was a girl. But this girl's gaze doesn't match the outfit—blue-grey eyes slope slightly downward at the corners, high, arched brows, an intensely serious stare and lips pressed together so tightly they almost turn white.

"No ... you're not going off to math class, young Miss," she decides, and is even a bit amused, because girls of that background are brought up never to look at anyone this way. Or is the young woman fascinated by her make-up? It does provoke stares and even the occasional remark. But why should she care? With a proud, nonchalant shrug, the baroness turns away.

Shy Sidonie doesn't dare to address the baroness until the day both women are waiting at the tram stop and shivering in a sudden rainstorm. When the tram arrives, Sidonie, who has watched her father defer to a lady, is first at the door and with a chivalrous hand flourish indicates that Leonie should precede her. She feels red-hot and can hear the blood coursing through her veins.

Leonie has to smile—the girl with the flaming cheeks wears a sailor dress under her coat and is acting like her squire. Touched and flattered, she says thank you and then asks if she attends classes nearby. Sidonie's response is quiet and constrained: "I'm only here for one reason: to see you."

The ice has been broken, first words have been exchanged, the object of her adoration has acknowledged her. Sidonie longs to repeat the experience as often as possible. She'll employ any lies or tricks that will let her escape her home for a few hours without supervision. The list of excuses varies—piano lessons, a visit to her best friend Ellen Schoeller, a visit to the museum with her second-best friend Christl Schallenberg—and once out of the house, she strolls about, loiters at street corners, waits to see the baroness.

It is rather easy to fool her parents. Her father spends most of his time in his office. In this fourth year of the war, he is busy with his Galician oil and solid paraffin companies, which bring in lots of money, since they keep the war machinery well lubricated. He is most concerned that the reversals on the Russian front—and not only those—could ruin everything; he has no time for his daughter.

Her mother, who has never shown any particular interested in Sidonie, is lenient to the point of indifference, and it doesn't even occur to her to keep a closer watch on her frequently absent daughter. Her older brother, Heinrich, used to watch over her like a kind of chaperone, but he has been at the front for several months. The household staff wields no authority, and Sidonie instructs them—rather harshly—not to wait tea or lunch for her.

And so she is free.

In the weeks following their first encounter, Sidi's "Puttkamer pursuit" changes tactics. No longer in hiding, she waits openly in front of the Secession building rather than at Kettenbrückengasse. Built a few years earlier, this building caused a bitter controversy because it was a concrete manifestation of a cultural revolution. "To every age its art, to every art its freedom" proclaims the defiant inscription over the entrance; and the Jugendstil ornamentation of the façade seems both too lascivious and too unambiguous. The Secession's golden dome has been dubbed "the golden head of cabbage," and few venture inside to inspect Gustav Klimt's famous friezes.

By 1917, however, the Secession, like so many other buildings in Vienna, has been transformed into a field hospital. Waiting for the baroness amid the bustle of those who've come to visit the patients exposes Sidonie to a whole new world. Wounded soldiers gather around the building, smoking and taking in the autumn sun. Some are missing limbs; some are heavily bandaged; crutches and wheelchairs are a common sight. Most of these men look haggard, as do their visitors. All this makes Sidonie feel uneasy and embarrassed, and soon she moves her reconnaissance to another corner, as much to avoid proximity to so much unhappiness and pain as to escape the rough talk. Nevertheless, before going to sleep these images sometimes resurface and unsettle her.

When the old emperor died the previous November, Sidonie had watched the funeral procession from the balcony of a friend's house across from the opera. It made her sad, but the endless parade of aristocrats' black six- and eight-horse carriages, women swathed in black, men in full dress uniform … that had been eerie, too. Since then, everyone has been talking about the collapse. Her parents, the Schoellers, the Schallenbergs, even the Afendulis, who have experienced the war first-hand, are all pessimistic about the future. Her father has even gotten a driver's license; and several packed rucksacks are stored in the pantry, just in case the communists take over.

In this regard at least, Sidonie will do whatever her father says to do; he will make the right decisions. "We are doing just fine now, and things will stay that way" … maintaining this conviction is how Sidonie pushes her fears aside and returns to visions of the baroness.

Every day around lunch time, Leonie appears near the Secession, having accomplished her errands in the inner city, and Sidonie accompanies her home. The baroness often wants to stop at Café Dobner to enjoy its somewhat threadbare splendor—the little chandeliers, the bentwood Thonet chairs, so practical and modern, the seat-sprung settees in the bay windows. This offers Sidonie an exciting whiff of the forbidden, for she has never been to a café before, and for two women to go there alone is like removing the keystone from the arch of her upbringing.

Afterwards they stroll through the Naschmarkt, since Leonie loves its bustle and the mix of people from all corners of the monarchy. Here there is no shortage of provisions. The baroness fingers a shiny apple or a golden pear with pleasure, examines lettuce and the piles of dark green spinach, wondering what she should buy.

"Sidi, look at those lovely carrots and mushrooms!" The baroness uses this nickname freely. Sidi giggles and points out that Leonie has

Leonie Puttkamer, 1919

used the High German rather than the Austrian names for these items. Most Viennese understand High German, but its use can be a source of amusement. Neither of them pays the slightest attention to the horrendously high prices.

These encounters become a treasured routine that continues for months. Sidonie is almost overjoyed to be near this woman almost every day. And Leonie has begun to grow quite fond of her young admirer. One day, however, they run out of luck.

When strolling with Leonie, Sidonie is always careful to avoid Antal Csillag's office, which is on Linke Wienzeile between the Secession and Kettenbrückengasse. He must already have picked up some gossip, because a few times he has insinuated that he doesn't want his daughter associating with "certain ladies." Leonie Puttkamer's reputation is not the best. True, she is well known for her beauty, but half the town also knows she is a cocotte, a high-class prostitute and in addition, an "invert," a lesbian.

Now, she sees her father across the street. He is walking with one of his business associates, then they pause, shake hands and part company. Sidi is certain that he's seen her, and before Leonie has a chance to ask why she's suddenly so fidgety, Sidi breaks away, mumbling, "My father, there …" and disappears at a run.

When she stops to look back, she is surprised to realize that her father is getting on a tram and doesn't seem to have noticed her. Filled with shame and embarrassed at having betrayed Leonie, she needs to explain as soon as possible. Leonie has moved on and she runs to catch up. Cool and remote, Leonie glances briefly at Sidonie, lifts an ironic eyebrow and keeps walking.

"You really got scared, didn't you, my little heroine?"

"You know … my father, he …," Sidonie says defensively.

"… doesn't want you to socialize with someone like me," Leonie finishes with frosty sarcasm. "Under the circumstances, ma chère, it would be best, if in the future you would spare me your half-hearted demonstrations of love. They just spoil my mood."

Sidonie feels as if she's been struck by lightning. Her mind in turmoil; she tries to figure out what to do. Father is going to make a row; she is sure about that. But what's the point in even listening to him do so, if the source of the quarrel doesn't want to have anything to do with her?

"Leonie, please, I want to be with you, always. I want to be at your side day and night, and everyone will know that, but …"

"This 'but' is precisely the reason why it is better that we are not seen together in the future. Run along, and goodbye." Baroness Puttkamer turns away and walks off quickly.

Dazed, Sidonie stumbles down Wienzeile, not caring who sees the tears streaming down her cheeks. Let them think what they like; with this war, so many people are crying over someone …

Does Leonie even realize that she is the sole focus of Sidi's emotions, that keeping their connection alive is essential to her survival? Nearing the metro station at Kettenbrückengasse, Sidi knows exactly what to do. Her father is going to punish her severely; her beloved no longer wants her around—why go on? Without hesitating, she throws first one leg then the other over the balustrade barring access to the tracks far below—not noticing that the rough plaster bloodies her hands. She has to hurry; she can already hear agitated voices behind her. Pausing for a fraction of a second, she inhales, squeezes her eyes shut and falls forward.

Sidonie regains consciousness surrounded by a noisy, excited crowd asking her questions that she can't understand. Two policemen—someone must have called them—push their way through and ask her name and address. Many hands lift her, carry her up the stairs, put her in a cab. The policemen are there. She feels nothing. The fear and desperation are gone; she's not in pain, though one of her legs does feel decidedly odd.

The policemen hand her over to her stunned parents with a brief explanation. They call a doctor, who puts her leg in a cast, tends to her broken ribs and orders bed rest. The feared row and the clarifying talk don't materialize. Her parents are just glad that their daughter is alive, and Sidonie is so relieved by her father's mild mood, that she never dares to ask whether he actually saw her with Leonie. Her mother's odd, indifferent tolerance of Sidonie's enthusiasms remains unchanged. Is it fine with her that her pretty young daughter is out of the running where men are concerned? Everything is cloaked in a mantle of silence, and everyday life goes on at the Csillags.

The household staff looks after Sidonie; her parents check in each day to make sure that her condition doesn't worsen. The pain in her leg soon stops, though her ribs still ache when she inhales. She's well enough to think about Leonie all the time and rack her brain for a way to get a message to her. Maybe a friend … someone her parents don't know well and who doesn't visit regularly. A friend with the courage to speak to a lady she does not know. Only one person would do her this favor and do it well: her school friend Christl Kmunke, a robust, masculine girl with a smart bob, a sharp profile and eyes that say she's ready for adventure. She never has a problem approaching people, particularly women—and she's "also so inclined."

Christl Kmunke in her father's hunting trophy room

In order to avoid suspicion, Sidi asks her friend Ellen to ask Christl to drop by for an impromptu sick bed visit. Christl appears two days later, and Sidi outlines her plan: Christl should wait for Baroness Putt-kamer in front of her building and give her Sidi's regards. She should then weave in the story of Sidi's desperate plunge and her resulting injuries. She provides the address and describes Leonie in exact detail. When the mission is accomplished, she should report back immediately. Christl soon returns with the news that the Baroness was quite distraught by the news. She had heard about the incident but hadn't had a clue that it was Sidi who was injured. She regretted having been so nasty, had never imagined that her rebuff would provoke such a reaction, wanted to know everything about Sidi's current condition. Sidi should take good care, have a speedy recovery and get in touch as soon as she is well enough.

Sidi is radiant. What more could she want—a dejected Leonie with a slightly guilty conscience and plans to renew contact, and on top of that, uncharacteristically attentive and caring parents. Without even having planned it, she has inadvertently killed two birds with the one stone of her reckless plunge, which easily could have taken her life. Sidonie will take this effective tactic to heart, and, likely only half-consciously, will use it again twice in the future in order to prevail against her father's oppressive authority.

As soon as Sidi is rid of her cast, her ribs no longer hurt and she's ready to go out again, she asks Christl to play *postillon d'amour* one more time and deliver this brief note: "Dearest, adored Leonie, may I see you as soon as possible? I really hope that you are not angry with me. Since I want to avoid running into my father at all costs, I suggest we meet in the Stadtpark—can you meet me tomorrow at 11 a.m. in front of the Kursalon?"

Leonie sends a positive reply via Christl, and Sidonie is beyond happy.

Sidi arrives in the Stadtpark an hour early, but the sun is already providing some warmth. She waits on a bench next to a big round flower bed bright with tulips and narcissus and has trouble containing her excitement. She glances constantly at her watch, tugs on her shawl, pulls back her long hair until her heart almost stops beating when Leonie arrives. She is on time but has brought Klara Waldmann along, chubbier than ever, dressed in an outrageous, too-long, dark winter suit and an ugly little hat with a feather. They are walking arm in arm. But upon seeing Leonie, Sidonie forgets everything else, even the nagging jealousy that always expresses itself as a snide remark. What binds these two women together will always be a mystery to her. Much taller than Klara and infinitely more elegant, the baroness sports a flared camelhair coat with wide lapels, the latest fashion in shoes and an extravagant hat. She approaches Sidonie, tilts her head slightly to one side and beams as Sidi plants a shy little kiss on her proffered cheek. After just a quick nod of acknowledgement, Sidi ignores Klara. At the nearby Meierei Cafe they sit at a table overlooking the river Wien and the conversation trips along lightly until Sidi tries to bring up the events of the past month. She wants to explain, excuse herself, reassure …

The baroness leans toward her with a look of amusement and warmth that leaves Sidi tongue tied. A gloved hand covers hers, a gloved finger touches her lips, "It's all right, my dear …"

During the next few weeks, Sidi sees Leonie almost daily, and they reestablish their routine of visiting cafés and strolling through the Naschmarkt. Then the summer holidays of 1918 separate them. Sidonie goes to Semmering and the town of Baden with her mother and two younger brothers because she couldn't find an excuse to stay in the city and didn't want to try her father's patience or make him suspicious.

STRIKES FOR BREAD AND PEACE

IN EARLY SEPTEMBER 1918 THE CSILLAGS RETURN HOME TO A CITY made miserable by war. Beginning the previous January strikes had broken out in every major town in Austria. Fueled by hunger, the strikers sought political rights for the working class. A new wave of strikes in June demanded an end to the war. There have been nearly 100,000 fatalities among the soldiers of the Imperial and Royal Army during its most recent offensive on the Italian front, and the Csillags fear for their oldest son, Heinrich. Finally, at the end of June, they get a field postcard from him reporting that he is well.

Kaiser Karl I is no longer in a position to prevent either defeat on the battlefield or the collapse of the Austro-Hungarian Empire. The situation intensifies: there are daily mass demonstrations in Vienna; the Social Democrats' demands for bread and peace are getting louder and louder; and by October everyone knows that political unity under the monarchy is a thing of the past. The Czechs, the southern Slavonic peoples and the Poles all terminate their collaboration with the Imperial Assembly. A Social Democrat, Karl Renner, now heads the provisional national assembly of the Republic of German Austrian, which demands recognition as part of the German Republic. On November 3, 1918, Austro-Hungary and the Allies declare an armistice. On November 11 the German Empire follows suit, the imperial government resigns and Kaiser Karl I abdicates. The monarchy and the war, which many history books will refer to as World War I, have come to an end.

The war had raged from Europe to Asia Minor, and 8.5 million young men lost their lives on the battlefields. Serbia and France suffered the biggest per capita losses. About 13 million civilians died between 1914 and 1918 from either direct or indirect consequences of the war. During its final year, a flu pandemic engulfed the globe, and particularly for those weakened by hunger and cold, whatever help there was came too late.

In the post war years, Europe will be caught between two ideologies: on the one hand, the new rulers in the Soviet Union postulate a socialist world revolution, and on the other, US President Woodrow Wilson backs the growing national movements in Europe with his vehement insistence that people have the right to self-determination.

The founding of the Republic of German Austrian on November 12, 1918, triggers daily mass demonstrations in front of Vienna's Parliament by the goodly number of Social Democrats who don't agree with comrade Karl Renner's moderate policies. They either join the newly founded Communist Party of German Austria or the Red Guards, and their banners and chants demand a socialist republic. There is a notably large number of red flags.

The majority of the working class, however, heeds Renner's tempering words: "Those who want socialism should not endanger our young democracy with rash, violent demonstrations of force." The workers' and soldiers' soviets retreat. News spreads of civil-war-like uprisings in Budapest, Berlin and Munich, but there are no copycats in Vienna, where keeping the political situation calm is almost second nature for both the haves and the have-nots, who prefer to weather difficult times with compromise rather than put the economic and political order on a completely new footing.

In contrast to the baroness and the besotted Sidi, who appear to be unaware of the changing political situation, Herr Csillag has been and remains seriously troubled by the unrest. His business is closely tied to the destiny of the Austro-Hungarian monarchy, and he's concerned about the future. The end of the war and the division of the empire into diverse Successor States pose significant problems. To be sure, he has already moved parts of his business to France and the Netherlands, but his wealth comes primarily from the solid paraffin mined in Galicia, a territory that the new nation states of Romania, Poland and Ukraine are fighting among themselves to control.

Upon returning from Semmering, Sidi haunts the familiar sites for days looking in vain for some sign of Leonie. Maybe the baroness has left Vienna for good? She doesn't dare to knock on the Waldmann's door.

The usually well informed Christl hasn't a clue. Then one day Sidonie's mother mentions having run into Leonie Puttkamer at the tram stop in Ungargasse, just around the corner from the Csillags' flat. All Sidi has to do is hang out in the neighborhood, and late the next morning she sees the baroness and greets her extravagantly, peppering her with questions. Why doesn't she live in Linke Wienzeile any longer? Did the Waldmanns treat her badly?

The baroness answers tersely that she has revived an old acquaintance with Count Apponyi, and he has put a flat at her disposal at Arenbergring 12. There had been a few disputes with the Waldmanns; it was best that she leave. She doesn't mention that Ernst Waldmann is no longer in a position to support her and had become jealous of her much closer relationship with his wife. (How much longer should a man who even supports his wife's lover be a cuckold?!) And so, it is fortunate that she was able to reconnect with the much wealthier Count Apponyi. He's a new source of financial support, and Leonie doesn't really care if she is his mistress or someone else's.

Now the baroness can invite Sidonie to her flat, and it's quite convenient for Sidi to visit every afternoon. She only has to cross the street, push open the big entrance door and run up a few flights of stairs. She never arrives empty handed. Food supplies have become distressingly scarce; few people can find anything to buy, and barter and illegal trade are commonplace. Even Count Apponyi can't maintain Leonie all that lavishly, and she herself certainly can't buy everything she needs—waiting in line for hours would be out of the question. And so Sidonie regularly ransacks her family's amply stocked pantry to supply Leonie with flour, sugar, rice and occasionally a salami, sent by her father's Hungarian relatives, or slices of his cherished smoked ham. The Csillags' table scraps provide daily meals for Leonie's wolfhound.

Of course, the Csillags' cook and maid notice that Sidi frequents the pantry and scrapes the dishes after meals, but as long as the master doesn't know and his wife just gives a tired roll of her eyes, everything is fine.

Sidonie also has enough pocket money to further spoil the baroness. Hoffmann's in Führichgasse is reputedly Vienna's best florist—also its most expensive—and Sidi often frets among the offerings, unable to decide. The splendid dark red orchids? Not tulips ... too vulgar. The white lilies with the heavy scent? Most days she chooses old Herr Hoffman's most beautiful roses and carries them to Leonie's third floor flat at about four—the classic time to pay a courtesy call for black coffee. Leonie greets her with a quick embrace in the long, dark hall and then brushes her cheeks with her lips, as is fashionable in Viennese society.

"Good day, my dear. Come, give me your coat and the flowers. You're an angel." The baroness is flattered—she has rarely been indulged like this. In her youth, in London, there was a man who showered her with flowers, but it has been years.

"Can I order a coffee for you, Sidi?"

"You know I don't tolerate coffee well. Juice would be just fine."

While Leonie instructs her staff in the kitchen, Sidonie goes into the parlor, where they will spend the next few hours and time will fly. Sidonie gazes pensively out the bay window at the late fall landscape in Arenbergpark. She will turn around only when the picture she will see is perfectly composed. She loves the beauty of this moment—the diminishing light in the room, the faint gleam on the old walnut furniture, the muted glow of damask on the walls and in the corner Leonie, stretched out among the Kilim and Turkish cushions on the couch, gesturing for her to come closer.

Sidonie sits at her feet—all she wants is to gaze at her and kiss the smooth, pale skin on the back of her hand. She follows the blue veins that she doesn't recall seeing on anyone else to the long fingers, past the ring set with two pearls to the slightly upturned fingertips, so suited to being played with. Devouring Leonie with her eyes and listening to her beautiful voice: this is Sidonie's world now.

Last year, she wrote poems to her beloved in secret, now she reads them aloud with romantic fervor. For her part, Leonie is impressed, and it feels quite good to let herself warm to the unconditional love, the delightful naiveté of Sidi's infatuation. Her own life is not so simple; it's difficult, this day-to-day business of accommodating and adjusting to the demands and perversities of her gentlemen friends. They think they can buy anything with enough money and remain untouched by a thing called love. And this business with women—sometimes it is just pure hell. It affects her more than she'd like it to, and it's draining, this addiction to that first rush of feelings. And then there are the inevitable scenes, the drama, the jealousies. And the money ... keeping her women in a good mood is really rather expensive.

Leonie knows that she can't involve innocent, inexperienced Sidi in any of this. She cannot seduce her, can't introduce her to the goings-on of the demimonde—and occasionally she regrets this, but she keeps her hands to herself and is satisfied with the hand kisses and ardent gazes.

Sidonie quickly catches on that she is the only "decent" female in her friend's otherwise lascivious circle. Occasionally she runs into one of these, these ... women, either leaving when she arrives or arriving when she's headed home. They are all ugly, and what's more, they are transitory. Her own love is something special and it will last. She feels that she occupies a special position at Leonie's, and she's making full use of it. She is not even insulted when the baroness lets slip that she passes Sidi's poems on to her own lovers and lets them think she is the source of this outpouring of emotions—as if she were still capable of such language after all these years. This makes Sidonie feel sort of proud. Her love is so

Leonie Puttkamer, 1919

strong that it is no problem to include all these ... others. The time will surely come when she will be deeply anchored in Leonie's heart.

At dusk, in early winter, the baroness likes to tell stories about her youth on her parents' estate, Schloss Schlackow in Pomerania. Unlike those knight's castles one could find in southern Germany and parts of Austria, it was a broad, triple-winged, red-brick building with a massive oak entry way. It was surrounded by an extensive garden and lawns bordered by boxwood hedges, and there was a wonderful sundial. She had been a rambunctious girl, and when her parents were fighting—this happened frequently, because her mother was beautiful and fun-loving—she would harness her two ponies to a carriage and take off into the vast, flat countryside to roam the birch forest or lie for hours among the reeds by one of the many lakes. Winter was her favorite time of year. There was ice-skating on the frozen irrigation channels, or sometimes, all wrapped in fox and wolf furs, a ride in a horse-drawn sleigh all the way to the Baltic Sea. The Schloss was heated almost all year round by burning peat that servants brought into the house in buckets. They also brought hot and cold water in big jugs because, unlike in Vienna, there was no running water. In the evening the rooms were lit by oil lamps. Her father's farm provided everything the estate needed, from sausages to butter, cheese and bread as well as plenty of vegetables and fruits. It was all stored in big larders, which her mother opened with an enormous key every morning, shortly before she and the cook made up the day's menus.

If Leonie had an ideal man, it would be her brother Agathon, a splendid equestrian even in his youth. Whenever he couldn't endure things at home, he'd flee to the forests on his dapple gray, go off to hunt and often not return for days.

Sidi hangs on every word and hopes Leonie will never stop talking.

On some afternoons the baroness gets a devilish notion to make Sidi blush and fidget in embarrassment. She likes to see what happens when her noble young gallant gets that prickling feeling in her tummy and between her legs and doesn't know what to do.

"Why don't you read to me from this book, ma chère? I'd like that."

Sidonie accepts the much-thumbed booklet and says, "*The Memoirs of Josephine Mutzenbacher* ... never heard of it."

Soon she is suffused with heat and thinks, "My God, whatever can Leonie want with that! This is ... terrible, this is disgraceful." And then, "Well, I'll clench my teeth and weather it. I'll read it to her painstakingly, like a schoolbook, the rest is of no concern to me."

Sidonie spends tortured hours reading this book aloud. She finds it hideous and feels ashamed, but to please Leonie she knuckles down to the task. And that little tug in her tummy and the heat in her throat—she prefers to ignore them.

Sidi loses her innocence to *Josephine Mutzenbacher*. The facts of life are explained in a way her parents never could have imagined. The ample range of meaty phrases and the inexhaustible descriptions of various sexual activities leave their mark. Now she can better understand the events in Leonie's life—the various men and the relations with women—and she can finally put a name to what drives her beloved.

Leonie is having fun, and maybe this is the only way these two women can live out what the increasingly sultry atmosphere in Leonie's oriental corner creates.

But once again Herr Csillag will disrupt their daily idylls.

With the end of the war, the return home of his eldest son, and the apparent consolidation of the new republic, he is now free to return his attention to his daughter. By now, her mother knows more than Sidi imagines, and she may have told her husband about the frequent visits to Leonie Puttkamer, which are bound to trigger a scandal sooner or later. Something has to be done to bring Sidonie back to her senses.

What are their options? Sending her abroad for an extended period is simply too difficult in shattered, postwar Europe. The only alternative is to seek medical help, and from someone proper Viennese society avoids like the plague—Professor Freud. His psychoanalytic method is not esteemed in their social circle, but Sidi's parents think it's their last hope to make her see reason and return her to normality.

CHAPTER

2

BERGGASSE NR. 19

IT HAS GOTTEN TO BE A ROUTINE. FOR WEEKS NOW SIDONIE HAS taken the same route every afternoon: leave the parental flat in Neulinggasse after lunch, walk to Ungargasse, take the O tram to Rennweg, transfer to the 71 going toward Schwarzenbergplatz, transfer again to the tram that circles the Ring, get off at Schottentor and walk to Berggasse Nr. 19.

Today the sun is shining, the sky is cloudless and Sidi is particularly vexed. Such weather is far better suited to going for a walk, but at least she can ride on the tram's outer platform and turn her face towards the sun. In fine weather, she quite likes Vienna—plump Maria Theresia on her memorial pedestal in the square facing the two museums, the lovely, majestic statue of Pallas Athena in front of Parliament. The latter offers some consolation for the fact that the flag of the young republic flutters above her. Red-white-red instead of black-gold. Her parents say this isn't good, this could lead to communism. Sidonie agrees that everything was better under the Kaiser, and she continues to support the monarchy.

Passing the Burgtheater, she feels that all is still right with the world, because the world's great, enduring plays are still being staged there. Her parents have a subscription, and recently she was allowed to accompany them to watch Else Wohlgemuth play Goethe's Iphigenia— she so admires this actress, even idolizes her, and by the end of the play, she even shed a few tears.

She gets off at Schottentor and hesitates before turning into Berggasse. Maybe she should go to Votivpark instead, sit in the sun and think about nothing. She would prefer to be in Stadtpark with Leonie, but when she started her analysis she had to promise not to see the baroness. This analysis takes up so much time! Five times a week, in the middle of the afternoon—the very best time of day—she has to lie down on Professor Freud's couch and be asked all kinds of nonsensical questions.

Sigmund Freud, 1922

But she has promised ... so, turn right. She starts to jog. She is late, and when that happens, the famous and quite controversial Professor starts analyzing and talks about resistance. Finally she reaches the tall, grey building where Freud has his offices. She actually knows very little about him and has only heard the rumors—he deals with crazies, can heal souls. Mentioning him to her friends' families has resulted in an embarrassed silence or a contemptuous glance, so now she keeps her mouth shut. Clearly, he is not highly esteemed. But he has to be competent on some level or her parents would not have gone to him several weeks ago to arrange for her treatment.

Afterwards, there had been a serious talk with Father, who announced in a tone that brooked no contradiction that he and her mother had tolerated her "acquaintance" with Baroness Puttkamer for far too long. Sidi's attempted suicide has been the final sign that Puttkamer's influence would destroy her reputation and had to end. Now that her leg had healed and her mind was functioning once again, it was time for treatment. Professor Freud, an excellent specialist, would get Sidonie back to normal and set her on the correct path for a woman. Given the high cost of the sessions, he emphasized that he expected her complete cooperation and a successful outcome.

She shed a few tears and put up a bit of inner resistance, but in the face of Father's stern resolve, there was really nothing to be done. She loves him, she wants him to approve of her, and she accepts that she must do penance.

On the first visit she was so nervous that she made a curtsey and was about to kiss Freud's hand before he rebuffed her. This was the first and

only time she saw him chuckle; since then he has been earnest and totally unapproachable, though not unsympathetic. She notices that his
eyes are soft but intense when he scrutinizes her before the start of each
session, but otherwise, she doesn't get to look at him, because part of
this particular treatment is that he sits behind her. In general, she finds
him uninteresting; an old man with a lovely white beard who poses
sticky questions and makes unbelievable assertions about her. On any
given visit she doesn't know whether she'll find the whole procedure
more boring or more obnoxious.

Professor Freud is preparing to start his consultation hours, always
held immediately after his lunch, taken punctually at 1 p.m. and followed by a walk to aid his digestion. Sometimes he feels so tired—all
this analyzing, peoples' sorrows and confusions. But he has a reputation
to uphold, and there are still a few mouths to feed, which has become
quite difficult. Food supplies are rationed and scarce, and at times he has
even accepted payment in potatoes or Havana cigars. The thought of
the icy temperatures in his study this past winter makes him shiver.
There isn't even enough paper to keep his records. The war is finally
over, though there is nothing left of Austria—it is all foreign territory
now. At this thought even he, hardly a patriot, feels some pain. Inflation is devouring the last of his funds, and he welcomes patients who
can pay in foreign currencies, ideally in dollars, and ten dollars per hour
definitely means something in this downtrodden country.

The father of the young patient who will soon ring his doorbell pays
in foreign currency, and the girl is a quite interesting case, even an exciting one. When the concerned parents sought him out the previous
February, he hesitated to accept the case, since the mental trauma they
described and the desire to effect a change appeared to originate entirely on their part, especially the father's. But he allowed himself to be
persuaded to make an attempt with the daughter for a few months, after which he would decide whether there would be ongoing analysis.

There was something touching about Sidonie Csillag; he'd felt it as
soon as she arrived for her first session—a shy, well-mannered girl on
the one hand, and on the other an intelligent young woman who simply could not see why she should give up her love for a demimondaine.
It would be a difficult case—precisely the kind that appealed to him.

Freud describes his young patient in his notes, published the following year in his only essay concerning female homosexuality—*Psychogenesis of a Case of Female Homosexuality*:

A beautiful and clever girl of eighteen, belonging to a family of good standing, had aroused displeasure and concern on the part of her parents by the tender passion with which she pursued a certain lady, about ten years older than herself. The parents asserted that this lady, in spite of her distinguished name, was no better than a cocotte. It was said to be a well-known fact that she lived with a married woman-friend, having intimate relations with her, while at the same time she carried on promiscuously with a number of men. The girl did not contradict these evil reports, but she continued to be none the less enamoured of the lady in question, although she herself was by no means lacking in a sense of decency and propriety. No prohibitions and no supervision hindered the girl from seizing every one of the rare opportunities of being together with her beloved friend, of ascertaining all her habits, of waiting for her for hours outside her door or at a tram halt, of sending her gifts of flowers, and so on. It was evident that this one interest had swallowed up all others.

...

Two aspects of her behaviour, in apparent contrast with each other, her parents took especially badly. On the one hand, that she did not scruple to appear in the most frequented streets in the company of her questionable friend, being thus quite neglectful of her own reputation; while on the other hand, she disdained no means of deception, no excuses, and no lies that would make meetings with her possible and cover them. She was thus as brazen in the one respect as deceitful in the other. One day it happened, as, indeed, was sooner or later inevitable in the circumstances, that the father met his daughter in the company of the lady. He passed them by with an angry glance which boded no good. Immediately after the girl rushed off and flung herself over a neighbouring wall on to the railway line. She paid for this undoubtedly serious attempt at suicide with a long stay in bed, though fortunately little permanent damage was done. After her recovery she found it easier to get her own way than before. The parents did not dare to oppose her so vigorously, and the lady, who up til then had coldly declined her advances, was moved by such an unmistakable proof of serious passion and began to treat her in a more friendly manner.

About six months after this occurrence the parents sought medical advice and entrusted the doctor with the task of bringing their daughter back to the normal.*

Today Sidonie tries to get comfortable on the stiff Persian rug that she considers a most unsuitable covering for Freud's couch. She allows her eyes to wander to the cabinets housing the tiny, apparently very old figurines that draw her eye in an eerie, almost magical way. Then she looks at a window, then at the huge overloaded desk, at another window, but she is not allowed to turn her eyes or her head to look at Freud. He sits behind her, invisible, and she can hear only his voice asking questions or saying "Ja" in a quiet monotone. She thinks, "It's as if he's breathing down my neck."

At the first session, he had explained that she was to tell him everything that came to mind, every shred of a thought, every memory, every association—no matter how absurd it might seem to her. In addition, she should write down her dreams, which were very important and would be discussed. He would elicit the rest by questioning her. She should feel neither ashamed nor afraid; she should talk about everything with total openness.

This in particular is what she finds most difficult, and today more so than ever. What is she supposed to tell him? Nothing happens to her and she cannot remember her dreams. So she keeps quiet, and so does he. As this silence becomes burdensome, she feels both a bit anxious and terribly bored. At last the Professor decides to break the spell and starts, once again, with questions about her family.

At first she didn't have a clue where these were supposed to be leading, but lately she has noticed that she has begun to observe her parents and brothers more closely. Scenes and events from the past, which had seemed completely insignificant, now push their way into her consciousness and preoccupy her.

---

* All quotations are from: Sigmund Freud, "The Psychogenesis of a Case of Female Homosexuality," *The International Journal of Psycho-analysis* 1, no. 2 (1920). https://www.lacan.com/The.Psychogenesis. of.a.case.of.female.Homosexuality.pdf

Antal Csillag, 1915

Emma Csillag, 1915

Yes, well—exactly what kind of a family *does* she have?

She tells Freud that she knows fairly little of her parents' past, no more really than the stories most families tell on special occasions. But during tea last Easter, she was again allowed to look at photographs of her mother in her wedding dress, and that had started her mother talking.

Emma Csillag is still a lovely woman, rather petite, with abundant dark hair and a fine, womanly figure that is also athletic and robust. Strong willed and vain, she always dresses in the latest fashions and painstakingly maintains the good looks that are the only capital she retained after a difficult youth. When Emma was eleven, her mother died of consumption. Her father, a civil servant with the railway with a secure but quite modest income, died four years later. Given their ill health, Emma's parents were unable to ensure her education, and she completed only the compulsory years at school. After her father's death, her eldest brother moved her and her sister, who was older by two years, from Vienna to Lemberg to live with relatives. There, she met young Antal Csillag, who was captivated by her beauty and soon started to court her. Like her, he came from a poor, religious Jewish family. He wanted to leave all that behind, and Emma wanted nothing more than to escape from her unloved relatives and the stale fug of poverty. She knew that Antal's status had already improved significantly from his beginnings as the penniless son of a salesman from Budapest. Immediately after graduating from commercial college at the age of seventeen he joined the petroleum branch of the Rothschild consortium's oil refinery in order to provide for his mother and younger siblings. As an eager-to-become-assimilated young Jew, he soon moved to Lemberg, then the capital of Galicia, where access to certain businesses—for example, the promising oil and solid paraffin industry—was easier than in other big cities of the Dual Monarchy. In Lemberg, he could continue to build a career, and he had an uncompromising drive to succeed.

Antal didn't much value the faith of his ancestors. While he still lived in Budapest, his love for his strictly religious mother had gotten him to temple on high holy days, but after he left the Jewish community, the only concession he was willing to make to his mother was the decision never to be baptized in another faith. However, he was determined that his children should not be marked as poor Eastern Jews, and when he and Emma married in 1897, he suggested that their future off-spring should be baptized as Catholics. Consenting, she asked in return for his promise to leave Lemberg behind and move to her native city as soon as possible. That was fine with Antal. He already had plans to start his own business, and Vienna would be a good place for him to move up the career ladder.

While still in Lemberg, Emma gave birth to Heinrich in 1899 and to Sidonie in April 1900. Antal and Emma had each infant receive what was then known as a "lying baptism," as distinguished from the baptism of Jews who embraced Catholicism as adults. Thus, as Sidi tells it, the Csillags bettered themselves ... and everything is going to be just fine.

Freud notes that his normally unforthcoming patient grows talkative regarding this detail. She has already told Freud the story of her Christianity on three occasions. An unusual emotional involvement with the topic is obvious, as is a touch of arrogance as well. He knows such people and the family context from which they stem only too well. It had been much the same in his own family. When he met the Csillags in person to prepare for Sidonie's first session, he had correctly assumed that despite their wealth and high social position, the Csillags were parvenus.

Shortly before beginning Sidonie's therapy, and quite by chance, he had learned a few most interesting details about Antal Csillag from a mutual friend, an internist who was treating a member of the board of directors of Antal's company. Although not particularly interested in industry and finance, Freud followed the young Austrian republic's economic development closely; so he did not turn a deaf ear to his friend's revelations. Of course, the Professor could not allow this information to influence his professional opinion, but still, such details could round out his image of the case in an interesting way.

Since the Csillags did not belong to any of the old, established families of note, Sidi's parents' social contacts would consist mainly of Antal's business acquaintances. To be precise, they would be *his* social contacts; for the beautiful but somewhat nervous and neurotic Emma also appeared to be shy, reserved and without any interest in socializing in society. But perhaps she simply lacked experience in organizing teas and dinner parties, ballroom dances and charity gatherings in the proper Viennese way. Or it could be that she felt she wasn't sophisticated enough, and therefore avoided such situations.

Antal Csillag, on the other hand, enjoyed a wide range of connections with affluent families, their businesses and banks through his activities in the oil industry. After starting his professional career with the Rothschilds' oil refinery consortium, he was quickly promoted, which was not, in itself, unusual. All the expanding branches of industry were interested in oil, and the promise of big money had quickly attracted numerous speculators, so it had been well known in Vienna for many years that the circumstances surrounding Galician oil production in particular were downright disastrous. But although the oil industry boom had had many negative side effects, Csillag, it seemed, had craftily cut himself a not inconsiderable piece of the pie.

In 1902, while still in Lemberg, he founded the Boryslaw Crude Oil Transport and Storage Company. Boryslaw was still a sleepy village when the new borders set in 1919 put it at the outer edge of the monarchy, in Poland. Nonetheless, it found its way into the newspapers again and again, either because of conflicts surrounding the oil cartel or for its deplorable social and working conditions, which were said to be so atrocious that they were almost unimaginable unless seen first hand. Day and night, derricks sucked crude oil from the rich deposits all along the northern incline of the Carpathian Mountains. For his part, Antal owed his large fortune to the extraction and marketing of the solid paraffin that was also found around Boryslaw. Extracting it required a huge work force, so early on no one paid it much attention; but when it proved valuable as a surrogate for the paraffin derived from crude oil, even small farmers suddenly started digging up their fields to look for it.

By the 1870s, the whole Boryslaw region had been randomly undermined. Thousands of "slave laborers" inhabited a chaos of tumbledown huts surrounded by the suffocating stench of sulfurous water. Even the bourgeois Professor Freud used the term "exploitation" to describe the state of affairs in Boryslaw.

During one of their first sessions, he asked his young patient about her father's business and was unsurprised by her ignorance—not just of conditions in Boryslaw but of any details regarding her father's work. Almost all the Professor's female patients, the majority of them from a

Boryslaw, 1902.

middle- or upper-class background, loved their lives of luxury but did not wish to know how it was financed.

The girl on the couch would probably never know anything about the appalling social conditions underlying her family's fortune, but Csillag himself was bound to know. The fact that it appeared not to bother him did not speak well of his character. But never mind. He was not treating the father, this case was rather inconvenient anyway, and he would concentrate on his patient and the emotional specifics within her family. In order to do so, analyst and patient would have to delve even more deeply into the Csillags' daily life.

THE LIFE OF JEWS IN VIENNA 1

LIKE SIDONIE'S FAMILY, TENS OF THOUSANDS OF JEWS CAME TO VI-enna at the end of the nineteenth century from all parts of the monarchy but in particular from Galicia, Bohemia, Moravia and Hungary. After what is generally referred to as the Compromise between the

Austrian Empire and the Hungarian Kingdom in 1867, the Jewish population throughout the monarchy was granted equal citizenship status. Many of them had experienced anti-Semitism in the East, often in the form of pogroms, and they never wanted to do so again, so they shed the dress, speech and even religious affiliations of the shtetl like an uncomfortable coat that no longer fit.

It didn't help. After the stock market crash of 1873, anti-Semitism increased again, fueled by the petty bourgeois Catholicism of the Christian Social Party. It reached an initial highpoint in the German nationalism of Baron von Vogelsang and Ritter von Schönerer, which sought to strengthen German-speaking Austrians' connection to Germany and was fueled by the open and popular anti-Semitism of Karl Lueger. Lueger became a member of Austria's parliament in 1885 and mayor of Vienna in 1897. Using anti-Semitism and German nationalism as his main ingredients, Lueger's friend and chief strategist, city councilman Dr. Albert Gessmann Sr., soon established what today would be called a right-wing party apparatus.

Lueger's oft-repeated anti-Semitic rhetoric became difficult to ignore. At the end of the nineteenth century, 10 percent of Vienna's population was Jewish, and the significant contributions many of them made to the city's cultural and economic life aroused considerable envy. Lueger said he wanted to prevent Greater Vienna from turning into Greater Jerusalem, but he was not thinking about exterminating the city's Jews. Rather, he was enthralled by Viennese journalist Theodor Herzl's Zionist ideas and wanted all Jews to emigrate to Palestine. Lueger remained mayor of Vienna until his death in March 1910. From his perspective, Antal Csillag was just one of the many Magyarized Jews who had come to Vienna from Hungary and were supposedly threatening the economic existence and cultural identity of the Christian Viennese.

The Csillags didn't talk about their Jewish heritage. Their children had all been baptized, and that was that. They didn't receive a Catholic education, but in school they were confronted with everyday Christian practices. In Sidonie's circles plenty of people thought of Jews as second class, and throughout her life she resisted being categorized as one. She was a good Christian, and that was that.

THE RISE OF THE CSILLAG FAMILY

ON THIS FINE DAY, THE PROFESSOR HAS, ONCE AGAIN, ASKED SIDI about her family, and she again has no idea what to say. Only two years of age when her parents moved to Vienna in 1902, she has no memory of their first flat at Wiedner Hauptstrasse 14 in the Fourth District, but she does remember the move to Strohgasse in the Third District. She was the shy little girl hiding in a corner watching big men use their muscles and wide straps to maneuver heavy wardrobes down the staircases to the street and heft them into waiting carriages. The horses, sweating and blowing hard, pulled many loads to the new flat, where they stayed for three years. After Sidi's second brother was born, Mother found more and more to criticize about the flat—it was no longer appropriate to their social status; a director and the president of a board of directors had to have something better. Whatever would people say?

Father rented a beautiful nine room flat—a whole floor—on Neuling-gasse in 1909, and they are still living there. Sidi loves this flat's beautiful rooms with big double doors and splendid ceilings heavy with plaster roses and vines so high overhead one could forget they're there. She used to practice hopscotch on the squares of the shiny parquet floors until she could balance like a stork and was the best in her class. She used to squeal with joy while playing hide and seek with her brothers. The windows of the parlor and dining room open onto Arenbergpark, and she prefers those rooms because they are bright and one can watch the leaves of the lovely old trees change color with the seasons—green, red, yellow, black-brown. Next to these rooms, but not facing the park, is Mother and Father's bedroom. The children are only allowed in there on special occasions. On the first day of Christmas, for example, when an exception is made and the children and parents breakfast there together, sitting stiffly on the edge of the bed while Mother puts sweets into their mouths and Father pats their heads. Sidi likes neither the heavy dark brown curtains nor the dark red brocade bedspread that make everything gloomy and depressing. And the smell of Mother's sultry perfume definitely makes Sidonie uneasy as it wafts up from her pillows, drifts over from her dressing table. Are all the children feeling equally constrained because they are not used to being with their parents, receiving treats or being petted? It's almost too much of a good thing, since ordinarily their nervous, abstracted mother, who would always prefer to be doing something else, looks after them only once a week on the governess's day off.

The stern and distant Csillag parents live in another world. One may not speak to them unless first spoken to; one is not allowed to eat at the same table until one has mastered good table manners. Nor may one laugh, make noise, romp about—that is possible only when the parents are not at home, when the servants, who seem to be the only truly alive grown-ups in the house, also take a break and romp with the children. If Father hears anyone making too much noise, he complains that it's "as loud as a Jewish schul." This is the worst thing Sidi can imagine, and she and her brothers quiet down immediately.

After the master bedroom come the children's rooms. Sidi has always had her own room, full of bright, flowered chintz and satin, and when she was younger, there were dolls and a doll's kitchen—a true girls' room, and one of the few instances in which her privileges surpass her brothers'. Across the hallway, vis-à-vis the children's rooms, are the kitchen, a big pantry and behind them two small rooms for the servants. Sidonie hardly ever goes into these parts of the flat.

They still have staff, despite the long war—a cook, two maids, a governess and for the youngest brother, a nanny. Also on the staff is Sidi's beloved "Fruli" (a peculiar pronunciation of Fräulein). A delicate person who walks slightly bent over and scurries around the flat monitoring everyone's work and tolerating no dissent, Fruli has been with the family for as long as Sidi can remember and is the only staff member she listens to. Her older brother once remarked, "I'm sure Fruli is as old as that baroque cupboard in the living room. It looks as chapped as her face and it squeaks like her shoes."

Mother oversees this eleven-person household, even though Sidi thinks that it doesn't need much supervision and functions on its own. While the family is still asleep, the domestic servants are up preparing breakfast, and they are the last to go to sleep at night, after clearing away the supper dishes and turning down the family's beds—in the winter they bring hot water bottles for everyone.

Heinrich, Robert and
Sidonie Csillag with Fruli,
1907

Mother gets up late, between 9:30 and 10:00, and has breakfast in bed. After she has finished her coffee—served in a tall silver pot with her monogram on it—Cook is allowed to enter, and they discuss the day's menu. Cook goes out to buy provisions, which errand boys carry up to the service entrance. After her morning toilet, the lady of the house dresses in the latest fashion, equips herself with a hat and umbrella against sun or rain, and is ready to go out. During her morning stroll she will buy any delicacies needed for the evening meal, then she often goes on to see her dressmaker, milliner or hairdresser if the fashion magazines have given her ideas. As the wife of a director, she can't afford to be out of fashion.

Sidi knows that all this costs a fortune, and she admires Father's patience and generosity regarding his wife's caprices. Recently, after the monarchy's collapse and more trouble with his business, there has occasionally been some tension during discussions at lunch, and he mutters about "exceedingly high household expenses" and "saving." At such times, Sidi looks eagerly at her mother, not knowing what to expect. Will there be a volcanic eruption enveloping Father in poisonous fumes, or will Mother get up like a gentle lamb and place a soothing kiss on his cheek? One way or the other, Father grows quiet; his wife is once again wearing the pants in the family.

How she strings him along, how much he is willing to endure! This is what Sidi thinks at such moments, though she admires her mother's mix of subtlety, entitlement and fickle tyranny when dealing with men. Men are drawn to her, and she can get so much from them! Yet Sidi also finds all this repugnant in a way that stabs her in the heart—especially the way Mother interacts with her brothers.

When Freud interrupts Sidi's so-far fluent flow of words to ask for more details on this last remark, she tenses a bit and pulls herself back from the stream of images she's been narrating. Then her shoulders twitch and her whole body is racked with sobs. It is the only time during her four-month analysis that she is so deeply affected that she cries. "I think my mother is so beautiful, and I do everything for her, but she only loves my brothers."

Still weeping violently, she describes how funny and tender her mother is with her three sons, romping with them often, tussling with them, rolling on the floor. When she is with her boys, her daughter doesn't exist. With them, she's indulgent and anything goes; with Sidi she is harsh and often unfair. She brings her mother gifts, pampers her with flowers, surprises her with her favorite chocolates, but Emma Csillag remains distant and cool.

Sometimes, seeing Mother reclining on the couch after lunch, she thinks she's wonderfully beautiful. Despite the pain it causes, she takes Mother's hand, presses a kiss on it. Somewhat disconcerted, slightly amused, Mother looks up, lifts an eyebrow, but never has she embraced her so very needy daughter.

Sidi likes her brothers ... well, not Heinrich so much. He is only eleven months her senior, but he knows that he has special status as the first-born and takes advantage of it. He can do no wrong; and if Father does get angry with him, Mother protects him. He is a know-it-all who patronizes his siblings and is a bit of a hypocrite—very popular among his friends and a spoilt tyrant at home.

She prefers funny, artistic Robert, who is five years her junior. Right after starting high school, he began skipping classes and spending his time in cafés and parks or playing billiards. Father found out and gave him a good scolding, but Robert just laughed and said simply, "I can't do it, Papa." Father accepted that and sent him to a commercial school.

Sidi can't say much about the youngest boy, Ernst, who has just turned two, still wets his pants and smells bad. She is not interested in him.

What really nettles her is that her brothers are given so much more license because they are boys. They can go out on their own, to the theater, even to cafés, and if she wants to join them, she must appeal to their good will. If she and Heinrich attend together, she is allowed to go to parties and balls given by their friends, but her own family never entertains. Mother socializes with no one, except when she is taking a cure.

Ernst Csillag, Sidonie's youngest brother

The doctor orders these cures because Mother is often terribly nervous and dissatisfied and full of the most absurd fears—of thieves, fires, floods. There is nothing she doesn't think is dangerous. But somehow, while taking the cures at various spas, Mother is transformed from a fearful, anti-social woman into a vamp, and Sidi must watch, embarrassed and repulsed, as she plays the coquette and draws men to her like bees to a honey pot. She doesn't want to know what else her mother does with them, but she sees her being wined and dined and promenading with her admirers as if she were free and unmarried. Last year, Sidi and Mother were together at Semmering—Father had stayed in Vienna—when something utterly humiliating happened. She heard Mother tell one of these men that no, Sidonie was not her pretty, well-behaved daughter but the child of an acquaintance. She disowned her own daughter in order to seem younger, to divert the man's interest away from Sidonie. It hurt so deeply that Sidi began sobbing and ran to her room. She spent the following days roaming the forest alone and avoiding Mother—a terrible woman who found her own gender so distasteful that she saw every female as an enemy and competitor ... even her daughter.

Sidi also sees this behavior as a terrible disgrace for Father, a kind man whom she loves very much. Sidi would like to tell him he is being deceived by his wife, but she respects him too much to do that and doesn't want to hurt him. But she really doesn't understand why he endures, pampers, supports his wife with such a show of patience and devotion. He is an angel.

Mother even intervenes in Sidi's cautious but tender relationship with Father. On the rare occasions when he comes home from the office a bit early, settles in the living room and pours himself a cognac, he sometimes calls for Sidi to come and keep him company and tell him about what she is doing. This makes Mother get really unpleasant and obnoxious. She turns flippant and snappy and tortures her husband and daughter with her moodiness. It has gotten so that Sidi has stopped even going near Father in order to avoid the resulting conflict with Mother.

Sidi is sorry to have to say it, but though the Csillag children have inherited some of Mother's good looks, that's the sum of it. All their human qualities are thanks to Father, even though he is small and rather corpulent and not at all handsome. She just loves Father, doesn't want to cause him any pain and will do everything necessary to make him happy and pleased with her; and that is why she is willing to do her best in the analysis.

Freud is aware that he has arrived at a central point in his anamnesis, and he now has a clear understanding of his patient's relationship with her mother. In his essay he writes:

> The mother's attitude towards the girl was not so perspicuous. She was still a youngish woman, who was evidently unwilling to relinquish her claims to charm by her beauty. ... She had suffered for some years from neurotic troubles and enjoyed great consideration from her husband; she was very erratic in her treatment of her children, rather hard towards her daughter and overindulgent to her three sons, the youngest of whom had been born after a long interval and was not yet three years old. ... The girl we are considering had little cause in general to feel affection for her mother. The latter, still youthful herself, saw in her rapidly developing daughter an inconvenient competitor; she favored the boys at her expense, limited her independence as much as possible, and kept a strict watch that the girl should not be too much with her father. A yearning for a kinder mother would, therefore, have been all along quite intelligible, but why it should have flamed up just then, and in the form of a consuming passion, is not comprehensible. ... Since there was little to be done with the real mother, there arose from the conversion of feeling ... the search for a mother-substitute to whom she could become passionately attached.

In light of her behavior with Baroness Puttkamer, Freud has his suspicions regarding Sidonie's wild devotion to her father, her idealization of him. He'll have to take a closer look at this, but not until one of the next therapy sessions. He announces that today's session is over, sees his patient to the door and says goodbye with a brief nod.

They'll see each other again after the weekend.

"How was it this time?"

"Outrageous."

In a fury, Sidonie tosses her handbag onto the green marble table in one of Café Herrenhof's bay windows, where Leonie Puttkamer has

Café Herrenhof in Vienna

been waiting for her. Leonie catches the bag before it slides to the floor and watches her flustered young friend slump into a chair and shove angry fingers into her long, dark hair.

For the past three weeks, the two women have been meeting just as they do today, a Monday. Despite her promises, Sidi can't and doesn't want to do without Leonie. Who else can she open her heart to? Who else will offer a bit of consolation? Besides, her only promise was to do her very best in her analysis, and she has been doing that. And she'll continue to prove to both Father and Freud that she is truly an innocent regarding this beautiful woman. And meetings in coffeehouses are also something quite innocent. And meeting immediately after an analysis session is ideal, because nobody will notice if she gets home half an hour late. She can always say that the Elektrische was delayed.

They have chosen Café Herrenhof because it is centrally located: Sidonie just has to walk down Herrengasse and she's home, and Leonie can do all her errands beforehand and then relax with a cup of coffee. In addition, Café Herrenhof attracts bohemians and writers; not a likely place to accidentally run into Herr Csillag. It offers comfy nooks among its booths, and its urban-liberal clientele cares little if two women flirt with each other.

"Go on, tell me, ma chère!" The baroness watches Sidonie eagerly. Today there is no flirting.

Sidonie crosses her arms on the table and bends over them until her head almost touches its surface. "Just imagine! For some time now he has been asking me in great detail about my parents and my brothers. He was particularly keen on the youngest one in the last session. And do you know what he told me today? That I would have liked to have a child with my father, and because my mother had the child, I hate her and my father as well, and *that's* why I turn away from men altogether! It is completely outrageous!"

Her rings clatter as she bangs her hand on the table, startling a few patrons, then she turns abruptly towards the window so no one will see her tears. Across the street, two Atlases flank the entrance to the baroque Palais Caprara-Geymüller. Their stony expressions look as desperate as if they truly did carry the weight of the world on their shoulders and were also well aware of all its ills. This is how she feels at Freud's, and it is unbearable.

Leonie breaks into peals of laughter, and again a few heads turn toward their table.

"I've heard all kinds of tales, but never that a nineteen-year-old girl wants to have a child with her father and therefore hates her mother. Admit it Sidi, you are a bit perverted."

She should not have said that. Sidonie winces and threatens to dissolve into tears. A tender caress of her hand and some reassuring words calm her down, but a few minutes later she starts again.

"He is such a creep. A disgusting brute. He has the dirtiest fantasies a human being can have. Always talking about this subconscious!" She puts both hands over her eyes for a moment. "By now he ought to realize that I'm as innocent as a five-year-old. I don't understand why he has gotten so famous …" And so it goes for several minutes more.

Leonie is both amused and touched. She has never seen Sidi so angry and so hurt. This well-behaved girl has a temper, and she likes that, although it still takes a bit more effort on her part to calm Sidi down.

"Come on, ma chère, let's get some fresh air—a walk through Burggarten, it is beautiful outside." Cups clink as the waiter clears them away; coins clink as they're placed on the table.

"He's now at the very bottom of my list!" Sidi finds it necessary to make this final, fierce pronouncement before the two women, both of them quite elegant, leave the café and are absorbed into the late afternoon bustle.

It is raining a few days later when Sidi is once again on her way to see Freud. She had to make a real effort even to go to her piano lesson that morning, and she definitely has to force herself to go to Freud in the afternoon. His most recent interpretations have hit her hard, even though she doesn't want to show it and is still trying to pretend that his treatment is having some positive results. She wants to do it right in order to stop her parents from worrying, and in particular to placate Father. If only the Professor would tell Father that nothing has happened between her and Leonie, that she is still an innocent! That would mollify him, and she could leave the couch behind. And then, in due time, she'd somehow arrange everything with Leonie.

Maybe she'll endure until the summer holidays; then she could enjoy her stay on Brioni. But she isn't there now; and, for the umpteenth time, she climbs the broad staircase at Berggasse 19.

Freud senses Sidonie's aversion and reluctance regarding his analytical treatment. This is based more on an instinct he has acquired during years of analyzing patients than on any clear evidence of resistance. The Csillag girl chats cheerfully and seems rather detached. And yet … he cannot get a handle on her. But this doesn't surprise him—she is not sick, hasn't come to him on her own and never complains about her condition. And if she doesn't want to change, then changing her version of sexuality into a different one would be as difficult as turning a fully developed heterosexual into a homosexual.

After having explored her family, Freud wants to build a bigger picture of her milieu, and at the beginning of this session he asks about her schooling and her female friends. Once again, she sets off talking at a mile a minute.

During her first year of elementary school she was home schooled. The teacher was boring and dry; he smelled bad and had sweaty hands.

Then she attended a nearby elementary school. She enjoyed being together with so many children for the first time. In the afternoon, there were regular French and English lessons—native speakers of those languages would come to her home to talk with the children, a common practice in high bourgeois households. It was important that one be able to speak those languages. After elementary school, she attended the Schwarzwaldschule for a year. She has no fond memories of the well-known reform pedagogue Frau Doktor Eugenie Schwarzwald ... everyone had crowded around her much too much, even though she was certainly no great beauty.

She took her secondary education at the girls' lyceum Wiedner Gürtel and stayed there until her recent school-leaving examinations. That's where she met the daughters of those long-established Viennese families with which her parents did not socialize. One of them was Ellen Schoeller. She noticed right away—she is in the habit of noticing things—that Ellen was one of the best dressed among the crowd of schoolgirls. She started to go into raptures over Ellen's plaid dress with its wide collar, and soon Ellen became her best friend.

The only daughter of Robert von Schoeller and his wife Mimi, nee von Seybel, Ellen, too, is the only girl among three brothers. The Schoeller's large traditional family is highly regarded in Viennese society. They are Protestants, which is a bit unusual in Vienna, and come from the Rhineland. They used to be based in Brünn, where people said they were held in the same regard as people in Vienna hold the Rothschilds. Ellen's father's family has been very successful in the iron and sugar industries, and that's the source of their wealth. Herr Schoeller is a leading figure in the sugar industry; her mother, a very affectionate person, comes from a family that grew rich on vinegar.

And Ellen is not only very pretty and well dressed, she is also good at tennis, skiing and ice skating. She herself participates in sports only because her parents want her to, but Ellen does so with a passion.

They always walked to school together. Ellen could easily have walked there on her own, but she was always accompanied by her governess. On the whole, Ellen's parents are much stricter than the Csillags. Ellen is only allowed to socialize with the children of families her parents socialize with. They made an exception only for Sidi.

The Schoellers have a busy social life, with constant comings and goings at their house and visits from friends and acquaintances and myriad relatives, including many elegant society ladies. She found Mimi Schoeller's sister, Lini, particularly attractive. She had watched Lini's wedding to Friedrich Franz Ringhoffer, a wagon-making industrialist from Prague. They were married in Vienna's Dorotheerkirche, and with her slim figure and fabulous red hair Lini had surely been the city's most beautiful bride.

She is also friends with other girls from her school. Christl Kmunke, for example, who has been such a valuable messenger to Baroness Puttkamer. She's such a tomboy type, and she doesn't hide her attraction to girls and women. That's just terrible! Christl has tried her luck with her, but her kisses and wistful touches left her cold. She just doesn't find Christl attractive. Everyone already knows about her inclinations, though. One summer both their families were in St. Gilgen, and Christl, whose family was staying in a nearby villa, came over for a visit. Not finding Sidi at home, Christl went for a walk with her brother Heinrich, and one of Mother's friends saw them walking towards the forest and made the snide remark that it was lucky Christl had gone with Heinrich and not with Sidi …

And so Sidonie goes on and on recounting one little anecdote after another, piece after piece of society gossip, so there can't be any debilitating pauses or any talk about Leonie Puttkamer, and also so the Professor will see that she's showing an interest in her treatment.

But as session follows session, she eventually runs out of stories and has no idea what else to talk about. Moreover, she doesn't dream, and Freud insists on dreams. Does the Professor suspect that she meets Leonie regularly? She hopes not, but perhaps she can give reality a helpful tweak and distract him from any inconvenient ideas. And so she presents her meetings with Leonie as if they were dreams, adding a few details to complete the fiction of a good girl who yearns for her beloved but is sticking bravely to her promises.

Freud notes at this juncture:

Warned through some slight impression or other, I told her one day that I did not believe these dreams, that I regarded them as false or hypocritical, and that she intended to deceive me just as she used to deceive her father. I was right; after this exposition, this kind of dream ceased. ... With our dreamer, the intention to mislead me, just as she used to her father, certainly emanated from the preconscious, or perhaps even from consciousness; it could come to expression by entering into connection with the unconscious wish-impulse to please her father (or father-substitute) and in this way it created a lying dream.

It doesn't occur to Professor Freud that he might have been lied to on purpose.

Sidonie's folly and her slyness have continued unabated. A few days before this particular session her desire to see Leonie had been so strong she'd forgotten to be cautious—as if a malicious little devil inside her was testing the strength of her boundaries ... until they crumbled.

Quite boldly, she had gone to pick up Leonie at Salon Geppert where she has her hair done twice a week. Ironically, she shares a preference for this salon with Frau Csillag. Hugo, the maestro who crafts the ladies' curls, is a blabbermouth, and he has told Emma Csillag about having met her daughter—such a pretty, elegant girl—who left his salon arm in arm with the lovely Baroness Puttkamer. Her mother passed this gossip on to Sidi that evening, sounding cool and piqued but relaxed, and saying only, "You know we don't want this. In the future you might want to take care. In particular, Papa and Freud won't be pleased to hear about it."

Now Sidonie has to take the bull by the horns, because she can't trust her mother not to tell the Professor. And so she trots out the "dreamed" half-truth at her next session, not knowing if the Professor believes her, but at least she has gotten herself out of a tight spot.

Otherwise, she is just counting the days until the summer holidays and Brioni. In two more weeks, at the beginning of July, everyone will have left Vienna. As for what will happen after Brioni ... she doesn't want to think about that right now. Maybe she can talk her father into letting her stop this analysis. As far as she's concerned, it's already over, and she is dreaming about the South. Her family will pack their trunks and head first to Strobl on the Wolfgangsee and then on to Brioni again, where it will be hot.

BRIONI

PAUL KUPELWIESER, SON OF THE BIEDERMEIER PAINTER AND FRANZ Schubert enthusiast Leopold Kupelwieser, turned fifty in 1893. For seventeen years he had been a manager of the Witkowitzer Iron Mill near Moravian-Ostrava and had accumulated a handsome fortune. He had only one desire: to retire in the South. For 75,000 Crowns he bought the Adriatic island of Brioni from the Francinis, a family of Venetian aristocrats. Stone from Brioni, offshore from Pula on the Istrian Peninsula, had been used to build Venice, and the island was known primarily for its quarries.

Together with his family and friends, Paul Kupelwieser embarked on the tedious task of transforming Brioni into a holiday resort. The island was reforested, an orchard and vineyards were laid out, the roads were improved, the harbor was deepened and a simple inn with fourteen modest rooms was built. A mail boat from Pula took care of communication with the mainland, and later a telegraph line was installed. People arrived in customized motorboats or on steam powered ferries.

The influx of summer guests increased the demand for fresh water, but Brioni didn't have its own source. So Kupelwieser bought several caves with good quality water north of Pula and had a system of pipes installed to pump water to Brioni. Part of the system was under the sea, and this engineering feat alone gobbled up a small fortune.

During its first years as a resort, the island harbored another problem: malaria. In 1900 Kupelwieser turned to the bacteriologist and later Nobel Prize winner Robert Koch for help. Koch traveled to Brioni, examined all its resident inhabitants and treated their malaria with quinine. In the following years the incidence of malaria dwindled to zero, and only then did Koch allow Kupelwieser to drain the island's swampy areas. By the time of tourism's heyday on Brioni, malaria was a thing of the past.

In 1903 Brioni began to morph into a health resort. The owners took out loans to build hotels named Neptune, Riviera, Carmen and The Grand. They built a sand beach and a swimming pool, sun terraces and playgrounds on the eastern shore. Visitors could hire motor cars, cabs and motor- and sail boats. There were two polo fields, an eighteen-hole

golf course, eighteen polo ponies and several tennis courts. The guest
register read like a directory of Austro-Hungary's aristocratic and high
bourgeois families. Only 10 percent of the guests came from outside the
boundaries of the Empire.

Paul Kupelwieser's friends and former business colleagues from the
iron and steel industry were frequent visitors—among them gentlemen
named Wittgenstein, Weinberger, Feilchenfeld, Kestranek, Skoda and
Wolfrum. At first, they had been skeptical about the whole enterprise
but soon were enchanted by the island. They bought lots and built their
own villas. They also put Kupelwieser on several boards of directors in
order to strengthen his financial position. After all, one hand washes
the other, and a piece of property on the Adriatic coast bought for a
good price deserved a service in return.

Another, perhaps more quirky, guest was Carl Hagenbeck, an animal breeder and circus director from Hamburg, Germany. In 1911 he
started the transfer of about two hundred exotic birds to the island,
among them African ostriches, flamingoes and wild geese. His dream
was to transform Brioni into a paradisiacal zoo with animals from all
over the world, and he fulfilled it.

Throughout World War I the entertainment on Brioni continued
uninterrupted. After 1918 and the defeat of the Austro-Hungarian
monarchy, Brioni became part of the Italian Kingdom. The following
year, at the age of sixty-six, Paul Kupelwieser died, and his sons Karl
and Leopold inherited the island. Karl took over the administration,
and Leopold managed the by then well-developed facilities for tourism and viniculture.

Throughout the 1920s, tourism and social life on Brioni changed
little, and even though the island had become Italian territory, most of
the guests continued to come from Austria and Hungary. The stock
market crash of 1929 and the ensuing world economic crisis, however,
were to have far-reaching negative consequences for the island. The
number of hotel guests dropped dramatically, the Kupelwieser family
couldn't make the payments on a loan, and in November 1930, Karl
Kupelwieser committed suicide. His three nieces inherited the deeply
indebted island, but in the end, Brioni fell into Italy's hands. After
World War II, Istria, and thus Brioni, became part of the republic of

Yugoslavia, whose first president, Marshall Josip Tito, turned it into his private retreat.

But in 1919, despite the end of the Austro-Hungarian monarchy, pampered vacationers like the Csillags do not note any changes in their privileged life on Brioni. The day-to-day habits and rituals unfold as they always have, with a strong orientation toward leisure and recreation. Sidi is drawn, like most of the ladies, to the Saluga, a pool connected to a clubhouse that doesn't have a beach but a beautiful terrace where patrons can sit above the sea, enjoy the slight breeze and watch daring divers balance on the rocks in oddly contorted pre-plunge poses.

But regardless of how one spends the day, at dusk elegant evening dress goes on public display. It is understood that the ladies must wear a different creation each evening, and these are usually a topic of conversation during next day's Kaffeeklatsch.

After dinner comes each day's highlight: dancing. There is always waltzing, and the young people go wild over the music imported from the USA: the Blues, the Shimmy and the Foxtrot with its slow–quick–quick steps that let couples float across the dance floor. There's also the lascivious Tango, but it is preferably reserved for the very late hours.

Christl Schallenberg, Sidonie Csillar and Grete Weinberger on Brioni

These evenings offer the younger generation the best opportunity to establish contact with their peers among the "best families." Sidonie is less interested in the young men than in their dance partners, who she watches intently in an effort to satisfy her insatiable thirst for female beauty. Every summer she finds at least one woman worth falling in love with, and those women take notice, as do the other guests. For the past two summers there has been gossip about whether the Csillag girl is developing in the right direction. These are crushes, however, and they remain quite harmless.

Brioni is where Sidonie has met many of the friends with whom she will remain in close contact over the coming years; some will be friends for life. In Vienna, their parents' homes are the centers of Sidi's social life: Maria Kupelwieser, known as "Pussy," is one of Paul Kupelwieser's granddaughters. She will marry beer baron and arts patron Manfred Mautner-Markhof in a noisy, very high-fashion ceremony in 1926. Grete Weinberger, the daughter of a long-established Viennese family, will become a sculptor and her family's country house in Katzelsdorf near Vienna will serve Sidonie as a restful hideaway in the 1920s. And the third party in Sidi's Brioni-summering crowd is Christl, the young Countess Schallenberg, who Sidi will always characterize as her "second best" friend.

Only Ellen Schoeller is never at Brioni. She spends her summer vacations with her family in St. Gilgen and hears the Brioni gossip only after the holidays are over.

AT BERGGASSE NR. 19 FOR THE LAST TIME

PROFESSOR FREUD ALSO LONGS FOR THE SUMMER HOLIDAYS. HE WILL go to his favorite spa, Bad Gastein, and his sister-in-law Minna has agreed to come along. He hopes Martha, his wife, will be well enough to join them, but she still hasn't fully recuperated from a terrible flu. At the end of the summer, he might go to Italy or Switzerland. Two months without shop talk and not a word about analysis—that is true relaxation.

Only his youngest daughter, Anna, will not join them this year. She has plans to spend the summer with the Rie family on Königssee, and he doesn't want to spoil her fun. The mother of that family, the lovely Melanie Rie, has been a motherly friend to her during these past months, and Anna is also very close to their daughter Margarete.

Anna is his joy. He has been analyzing her for the past six months, and she will follow in his footsteps and continue his life's work. Love is the only thing that hasn't been working out for her, and there are no men in her life—almost like that Csillag girl. But he doesn't want to let the disagreeable thought underlying that idea come to the surface.

He will close the Csillag case. There is no point in continuing to struggle with the girl. She has built up a strong resistance, which he failed to notice for the longest time, and he can't get through to her. It's obvious that this parallels her behavior with her father, and it's quite obstructive. On the one hand, there's the compliant good girl who is trying hard to please, but behind that is an iron will determined to get her what she wants in life. He will suggest that she continue her treatment with a woman, if the parents wish. This has been an interesting experience for him, however, and it will be incorporated into future research and writings. For now, he just has to note the outcome of her analysis:

> The analysis went forward almost without any signs of resistance, the patient actively participating intellectually, though absolutely tranquil emotionally. Once when I expounded to her a specially important part of the theory, one touching her nearly, she replied in an inimitable tone, "Oh, how interesting," as though she were a *grande dame* being taken over a museum and glancing though her lorgnon at objects to which she was completely indifferent.
>
> ...
>
> In the case of our patient, it was not doubt, but the affective factor of revenge on her father that made her cool reserve possible ... In reality she transferred to me the deep antipathy to men which had dominated her ever since the disappointment she had experienced through her father. ... So I broke it [the treatment] off as soon as I recognized the girl's attitude to her father, and gave [the parents] the advice that if it was thought worth while to continue the therapeutic efforts, they should be carried out by a woman doctor. The girl had in the mean-

while promised her father that at any rate she would not communicate with the "lady," and I do not know whether my advice, the motive for which is obvious, will be followed.

Freud tells Sidonie of his conclusions during their first session following the summer holidays, and she heaves an inner sigh of great relief. She has done what was required of her and shown her father that she was well intentioned; but not everything can be changed. If the Professor will make that clear to Father, and if he adds that Leonie has never knocked her off the straight and narrow path and into her bed, then Father will be reassured and will leave her in peace. If that happens, everything really will have turned out for the best once again.

As they are saying their goodbyes, Professor Freud remarks, "You have such shrewd eyes. I would never want to have you as my enemy."

For the rest of her life, Sidonie will remember that that is what the famous Professor Sigmund Freud said to her when she was just nineteen years old.

3

ARSENIC, COCAINE AND LONG NIGHTS

"Put me through to Dr. Saxl in the Third District. Yes, the physician. Hurry."

It's very late at night and the sharp voice on the trunk line is clearly used to giving orders. The switchboard operator hastens to plug the jacks into the outlets and make the connection.

"Saxl? Gessmann here. She has tried to poison me. I feel ghastly. Come quickly."

The line goes dead.

Dr. Saxl sighs and glances at the clock on his nightstand. Half past one. He has had a hard day with a never-ending flood of patients. It is spring, everyone is sick, and those who can afford it consult with an internist. He would have liked a bit of sleep, but Albert Gessmann is a special patient. A hypochondriac with a constant focus on his minor ailments who is also distrustful, bossy and intolerant. Basically, an obnoxious type, but it's best not to mess with him. His connections in the highest ranks of politics and business could do one some harm.

All the lights are blazing on the second floor at Sebastianplatz 7, and despite the late hour, the housekeeper is there to let Dr. Saxl in. Gessmann rushes into the hall.

"Saxl. Finally! I feel nauseated, and I've been in a constant sweat.

Look at me." He opens his paisley silk dressing gown and shows the doctor his stomach.

A check-up carried out in the salon reveals nothing concrete. A slightly elevated pulse rate, enlarged pupils, the abdomen somewhat distended and taut, a coated tongue. It doesn't look like poisoning. The greedy pig probably just has an upset stomach, Saxl thinks.

But Albert Gessmann doesn't relent and insists on describing the previous evening's events in detail.

He and his wife Leonie had been to the Ronacher Theater and returned home around eleven p.m. The housekeeper served them a late-night meal of fish, potatoes and some peas; as a starter they'd had a bit of caviar, and there was a wine chaudeau for dessert. Nothing to make one sick; and besides, Leonie had eaten exactly the same thing.

Then they started arguing, just as they had at the beginning of their marriage, because once again his wife had been monosyllabic and dismissive, had been acting moody and cold. It was impossible to talk to her. At such moments she lets her contempt for him be felt, lets him know that she finds him repugnant and that she is a cut above him. And then she rejected his sexual advances, even though she knows that he must sleep with a woman once a day. At that point, he lost control, banged on the table and cursed her, then stormed off to his room. After some time, Franziska, the maid, brought him coffee and tried to calm him down. He often found it easier to talk with her than with his wife. Soon, he started to feel nauseated.

"And Saxl, I tell you, that was the only thing I didn't share with Leonie. I'm sure she sneaked into the kitchen after our fight, and when Franziska wasn't looking, she put poison in my coffee. Given her perverse hatred of men, I can believe she'd do such a thing. You're my friend, Saxl, I want you to have the coffee tested."

I don't know that we're friends, the doctor thinks, but nevertheless he lets himself be talked into taking samples from the coffee pot and coffee cup and promises to send them to the lab first thing in the morning. He'll send word as soon as he has the results. He's dismissed and can return home to resume his interrupted rest.

March 26, 1924, starts quietly for Leonie Puttkamer-Gessmann, who had spent a rather pleasant weekend after Albert calmed down following their fight and almost lovingly suggested that they spend a couple of days at his country house, Gut Haarberg in Edlach. Driving there in his car, he mentioned en passant that he had felt so nauseated after their fight that he called for his internist. There must have been something in the coffee. She had responded with a bit of compassion and caressed his hand. She knows how sensitive he is about nearly everything that has to do with his health and his body.

The late morning also proceeds nicely. She meets Sidi in the Stadtpark, and together they drive to the police station in Landstrasse in her electromobile—a possession Leonie enjoys immensely. There aren't many such vehicles in Vienna, and it usually attracts attention. Also, it is nice to be a bit protected from the cold and to move along so quickly. At the station, Sidi picks up her new passport and puts in an application for a new one for Leonie. Albert had torn hers to bits in one of his rages. Sidi is really very good at dealing with authorities, because she knows how to manipulate the typical Austrian state functionary and turn his mind toward actually achieving something concrete. This is something that Leonie—having come from Prussia—has never mastered. Then she picks up Albert at his office and they return home in time to prepare for lunch.

From this point on, things escalate quickly.

Leonie enters the dining room to find Albert and Dr. Saxl standing rather stiffly at the window, as if they had to present a united front, since either would be too weak to face her alone. Albert informs her in measured tones that poison, to be precise arsenic, has been detected in his coffee and Dr. Saxl must file a complaint with the police. Saxl nods assiduously, knotting his fingers together. He is far too embarrassed to look at her. Albert waits for his words to sink in. The food on the table is still steaming but starting to cool … a still life that imprints itself on Leonie's mind. At first, she doesn't understand what this is all about, this ridiculous tribunal organized by two weaklings. Then it dawns on her—Albert's hints in the car, his recent friendly detachment. He wants to doom her. As her outrage builds, she turns to ice, a response she learned as a child.

"You are mad, Albert. How dare you accuse me of such a thing? Maybe instead of orchestrating your own murder by poison you should get busy writing your next unsuccessful play!" The words "perverted pig," can be heard as she storms out, slamming the door behind her.

At the Csillag residence, the phone rings just as lunch is ending. A most inconvenient moment. The maid, aware of this, scurries around the table to whisper in Sidonie's ear that she should go to Baroness Puttkamer immediately, something has happened. Sidonie swallows her last bite, tosses her napkin on the table and leaves the dining room. Her parents have given up commenting on Sidi's affectations, and they imagine that only Leonie Puttkamer could have instilled such a sense of urgency in their daughter—still, this breach of good manners has left them speechless.

Arriving at Leonie's a quarter of an hour later, Sidi finds the older woman pacing nervously and smoking, something she hardly ever does at home. Summarizing the situation, Leonie curses, gesticulates, carelessly flicks the ashes off her cigarettes and mumbles an incoherent monologue of repetitive questions and answers. Sidonie has never seen Leonie this agitated.

It's enough to have to deal with his constant harassment; she knows she married a mad man, but to claim that she tried to poison him! Oh, she often wanted to poison him, but she would never actually do it. Though, really, why not? It wouldn't be any great loss. But now he's trying to ruin her, to have power over her, to control her.

Gradually, Sidi calms her down and coaxes her to sit beside her on the couch. Leonie has absolutely no idea what to do. Sidi, being a practical sort, knows exactly what the next step should be. Since they first met in 1917, Sidi has matured from a love-struck young woman into one of Leonie's closest friends and confidantes, and this turn of events has truly alarmed her. She suggests that Leonie pack some of her things and whatever money she can find.

Sidi quickly arranges an immediate appointment with an attorney, and by three in the afternoon both women leave Gessmann's flat for Dr. Klemperer's office in the Ninth District. He advises that, given Gessman's suspicions and the insults she has already suffered, Leonie should not return to the conjugal flat. She promptly decides, with a certain amount of relief, never to spend another night under the same roof as the man who is still her husband.

One of the office girls suggests that Pension Reiter, right around the corner at Ferstelgasse 5, would have suitable temporary lodgings. They prove to have an acceptable room available, and the Baroness decides to stay there while Sidi and the office girl go to the flat to pick up her suitcases. While she waits, Leonie counts the cash she has on hand and calculates how long it might last, given her lifestyle. On March 15 Albert had given her 15 million crowns as pin money, and after having paid for an expensive suit and a few odds and ends, she has just 4.5 million left. It won't last long, but she doesn't want to worry about that.

When Sidi returns, neither of them can think about dinner or sleep, so they try to bring a bit of order to the inner and outer chaos—but with little success. The suitcases remain half emptied, toiletries clutter the bathroom, and only the beautiful bouquet Sidi got hold of somewhere manages to perk up the room. Eventually they sit together on the edge of the bed like two exhausted birds on a perch and deliberate. Hours later, they decide that it would be best for Leonie to return to Germany, where she'll be safe. Carola Horn, Leonie's current lover, lives in Munich, and she'd be more than pleased by an unexpected return. But in order to leave Austria, Leonie will need the new passport she recently applied for. Sidi will pick it up at the police station the next day. Despite the difficult circumstances, they breathe a sigh of relief and feel a kind of edgy happiness now that there's a plan in place. Everything will work out, one way or the other; the main thing is that the Albert chapter is closed, Leonie is free, and she will soon be safe.

At the police station the next morning, Sidonie is dismayed to learn that Dr. Saxl has already filed a complaint regarding the attempted poisoning, and until that matter is cleared up, the passport cannot be handed over—particularly not to a third party. Baroness Puttkamer herself will have to appear—preferably by tomorrow.

Leonie is now in danger on several fronts. Gessmann's attempt to pin a felony on her is one of the ugliest things she can imagine, and he's sure to air their dirty laundry in public and testify in court about her numerous affairs with women. Unlike Germany, Austria classifies lesbian relations as a crime, on a par with intercourse with animals, and revealing this is Albert's trump card.

Goaded by her indignation at Gessman's tactics, Sidonie tries frantically to come up with a defense strategy as she heads back to the pension. The previous day, when Leonie told her about his accusations, Sidi had to try not to laugh out loud at his absurd, superficial tale. She's sure he put the traces of poison in his own coffee. It is rather easy to buy arsenic in a pharmacy, and men like him keep it handy to increase their sexual potency.

She does find one thing thought-provoking—Albert's obsession. Even more thought-provoking is that she can almost understand him. Since they first meet in 1919, he had wanted utter and complete possession of Leonie. He tried with money, with sexuality, with dependency, and he never succeeded. Leonie can't be captured; there is always something about her that is elusive, distant, unattainable and free—despite the morass she's found herself in these past years. Sidonie has had to learn this the hard and painful way, and she has become Leonie's best friend. But Gessmann—what new role could he decide to play? His helplessness and humiliation certainly make him dangerous.

Leonie's temper flares when she hears about her passport and the summons for tomorrow.

"What should I do now? I can't leave, I have very little money left, and I have no claim on him. That pig will be the death of me."

"Calm yourself, dear. I'll arrange an appointment with Dr. Klemperer for tomorrow morning. I'm sure he'll think of something; and I have a few ideas, too. We'll just turn the tables."

"What do you mean, turn the tables?"

"You've already said it—he's staged his own poisoning."

Hours of heated, agitated discussion follow, during which the two women invent, develop, throw out and reinvent campaigns, lines of defense and attack strategies. Finally, Leonie is exhausted and Sidonie decides to be reasonable and make an appearance at home. A close embrace, a few more encouraging words, and then Sidi says, "We'll see each other at the attorney's tomorrow morning at nine, my dear," and is gone.

March 28 is a foggy late winter day, and Leonie gathers her fur coat tightly around her on the short walk to the attorney's office. The route takes her through the square behind the Votivkirche. She usually likes it there—one could almost be in Paris behind Notre Dame. But today the neo-Gothic monstrosity Kaiser Franz Joseph had built after a failed assassination attempt on him just seems eerie. "Murder complot on Friedensplatz," Leonie thinks grimly. And this, of all places, is where her attorney had to have his office.

Sidi is already waiting in the lobby when Leonie arrives, but their talk with Dr. Klemperer is not encouraging. Yes, the Baroness has to obey the summons; yes, she'll have to answer all questions relating to her husband's charges. It would be best if he were to accompany her so he can intervene if necessary. And so Leonie Puttkamer, Sidonie Csillag and Dr. Klemperer proceed to the police station in the Third District.

The barren interrogation room has yellowed walls, a high ceiling and ancient file cabinets along the wall. Two big desks sit back to back in the middle so the functionaries can keep an eye on each other at all times. Only the tall, light-filled windows provide a spot of beauty and a glimpse of the trees in the courtyard. At least they give the extremely nervous Leonie something to look at in order to escape the disgusting inevitability that is about to take place here.

The room suits her two would-be interrogators. The skinny one, who will take notes, clenches his jaw and wears dark sleeve protectors. The other—a bit more corpulent, an un-buttoned frock-coat, a sloppily knotted tie—will ask the questions.

"So, this vision of loveliness is going to interrogate me. I'm accustomed to something better," Leonie muses, having reclaimed her habitual sarcasm. Aloud, she says, "Let's precede, gentlemen. Let's get this over and done with. I'll tell you everything you want to know."

The note-taking begins:

Father: Günther von Puttkamer, landowner
Mother: Anna Luise von Alvensleben
Married in 1885, divorced since 1903.
In 1904 the mother married Count Ludwig Holnstein of Bavaria, resides with him in Tralhausen near Freising.
I attended a private secondary school for middle- and upper-class girls in Gotha and continued my studies in London for the next five

years. Upon returning from London in 1910, I lived with my mother in Munich until 1916. Then I came to Vienna, where in 1917 I met Paula Gessmann, the first wife of my husband. I socialized with the family, and in the following years my husband grew attached to me. He divorced in 1921, and for a year before our marriage—that is, from January 1921 until our wedding on February 4, 1922—we lived in the same household. Due to some minor differences, we divorced in August 1922, and because my husband wished it, I signed a paper at the notary renouncing my right to alimony. At first, I moved in with the actress Fedy Ferrard, Fourth District, Gusshausstrasse 3, and six weeks later I left for Berlin. In March 1923 and upon the request of my husband I returned to Vienna for six weeks, but because of various disagreements I left Vienna and returned to Berlin. At the end of August 1923, I went to Munich, where my husband—with whom I had been exchanging letters and who I had met with in Salzburg in January—picked me up on March 15, 1924. We were completely reconciled and arrived in Vienna on March 16 at 7 a.m. The evening of March 17 we spent at the Chatham Bar, First District, Dorotheergasse, and on March 19 we were at the Ronacher Theater.

Leonie knows that under the circumstances she mustn't let herself say anything unconsidered. Thank God her interrogator shows considerable lack of imagination. There's no need to give him a whiff of anything he doesn't actually ask about. She focuses on her relationship with her husband, answers concisely and reveals only what's absolutely necessary.

She doesn't reveal details about her family's history and avoids above all mentioning her many affairs and relationships with women in Germany and Austria over the past several years. In later interrogations, she won't be spared having to talk about them—in great detail.

THE PUTTKAMERS

BOTH OF LEONIE PUTTKAMER'S PARENTS ARE FROM OLD AND NOBLE Prussian families. The Vietzke-Pansin branch of the Puttkamers, Leonie's ancestors, was first documented in 1436—there was a big estate in Schlackow near Saleske (its wealth was generated by agriculture and forestry) and the corresponding political influence at court. Leonie's father, Günther, was born in 1861 and was a major in the Royal Prussian Army. Her mother, Anna Luise, née Alvensleben, was born into one of northern Germany's oldest and most influential families. Described as a beautiful, erotic, energetic and vain woman who knew how to please men, before her marriage Anna Luise apparently influenced her future husband as much with her lineage as with her beauty.

They married in 1885 and had three children: first a daughter, Julianne Anna Erika, then their son, Agathon, and on January 10, 1891, Bertha Hermine Leonie. After the birth of the children, the difficulties in their marriage increased: Günther felt overburdened; Anna Luise felt neglected and started having affairs with men and women.

When Leonie was nine years old, she saw her mother with one of her male lovers, but out of pity said nothing to her father. Anna Luise fell in love with an Italian diplomat in 1902 and followed him to Rome, which was more than Günther von Puttkamer would tolerate. He went to Rome, and after a dramatic encounter, he filed for divorce. Soon after her move to Rome, Anna Luise's Italian companion died, and she had to provide for herself. Given her affairs and divorce, she was no longer accepted by the archconservative Prussian nobility and thus was no longer acceptable at court. She worked in Paris as a lady's companion for a short time before meeting Ludwig, Count von Holnstein of Bavaria. They were married in London in 1904 and moved together to Partenkirchen.

Soon after his divorce from Anna Luise, Günther von Puttkamer married one Dolly von Planckenburg from Linz. At first, the children remained with their father, but soon Agathon was sent to the military and both daughters went into boarding school. Günther von Puttkamer was having trouble keeping his head above water financially. First his father and now he had neglected to pay attention to worldwide economic developments—particularly in agriculture—and they hadn't adjusted their practices accordingly.

There was already a serious agricultural crisis in Prussia by the late 1870s. The new North American market was no longer quite so far away as it had been, and its producers had become a real threat to the historically stable market for Prussia's agricultural output. Many of the smaller estates held by noble families had to be sold after the first big crisis. Other aristocrats forged alliances with the rising bourgeoisie and adapted to the changed economic conditions.

The Puttkamer estate, Schlackow, had 5,889 hectares in 1879, and Leonie's grandfather, Julius, was Prussia's second largest landowner—the German Kaiser owned 15,453 hectares. At the time of his divorce, Günther von Puttkamer still owned nearly 5,000 hectares, but by 1910 he had sold off the estate and moved with Dolly to Baden-Baden, where he died in 1921.

One can assume that the sale of the estate allowed Günther von Puttkamer to lead a comfortable life until the outbreak of World War I. One can also assume that he behaved like many good German patriots and invested most of his wealth in war bonds and that whatever was left at the end of the war was likely eaten up by the rampant post war inflation. Any hope his children might have had for an inheritance must have evaporated by the beginning of the twenties.

But to return to the year 1902: eleven-year-old Leonie was sent to boarding school in the town of Gotha, where she stayed for five years. A good student who caused no problems, she was diligent, engaged and good at sports—she enjoyed riding, biking and gymnastics. She was also particularly taken with one of her teachers, a Frau Salzmann, then perhaps thirty years old. With her Leonie had her first erotic experiences, and their tender friendship lasted throughout Leonie's years in boarding school.

In 1907 Leonie chose to go to Weimar to study piano, languages and literature. That was also the year her father tried to marry her off to a cousin, but Leonie refused point blank. On the one hand, she considered Nuschi, the intended husband, boring and superficial, and on the other hand she had a new girlfriend in Weimar, Lucy, a young English woman with whom she shared both a pension and a bed.

While Leonie did have a great love for the English language and English literature, Lucy was certainly the reason both young women moved to London that same year. Well supplied with her father's money, Leonie lived for four trouble-free years at the home of Mrs. Fox, Lucy's mother, becoming involved in the then very active suffragist movement.

Leonie reestablished contact with her own mother during one of Anna Luise's frequent visits to London. She decided to move in with her and her husband, and during the next three years, mother and daughter traveled often, especially to Italy and France, and spent long stretches of time in Paris.

In consequence, Leonie's already tenuous connection with her father weakened steadily. In 1911, while Leonie was visiting him and her stepmother, for whom she felt no affection, the latter claimed that Leonie was mentally disturbed and asked a specialist in Berlin to give his medical opinion. The examination was a humbling procedure, and the specialist concluded that while Leonie was mentally healthy, she was sexually "abnormal." Her father stopped providing her with a subsistence allowance, and in response Leonie filed a legal claim for reinstatement. This was the last straw: Herr Puttkamer renounced his daughter.

By 1914 Leonie von Puttkamer had started traveling on her own, her preferred destinations being Munich and Berlin. Her family background gave her access to aristocratic circles, where she was most welcome, but she also circulated in what was then called the demimonde— the lesbian meeting places in Europe's major cities—and she had many affairs. She usually met the women at spas or private parties and gatherings at places like the plush Pension Elvira in Munich. That's where she met the French countess who supposedly taught her everything there is to know about lust and sexual gratification between women. And during a stay at a spa in Partenkirchen, she met Fräulein von Benke, a trim, witty brunette four years her senior, who had beautiful eyes and a melodious voice. Leonie thought her a true woman of the world and their relationship lasted—at times through letters—for a year.

From August 1915 to March 1916 when Leonie again resided at Pension Elvira in Munich, her stay coincided with that of a certain princess and her lady in waiting. Because she herself was no longer accepted at court, Leonie's mother forbade her daughter to socialize with the princess, but that didn't stop tender relations from budding between Leonie and the tall, slim, sporty lady in waiting. Leonie found the end of that affair quite painful, but the pain dimmed after she moved to Vienna and found consolation in Klara Waldmann's arms.

THE TRAPPED BARONESS

LEONIE HEAVES A SIGH OF RELIEF AS THE QUESTIONING FINALLY comes to an end. The two officers seem to have bought what she said, but as she rises to leave, the corpulent one says, almost as an afterthought, "Frau Gessmann, we have been told that you took a cure with arsenic a little while ago. Unfortunately, we have to arrest you."

While Leonie is in the interrogation room with her attorney, Sidonie sits tensely on one of the long, wooden benches in the hallway listening to the echo of passing footsteps bounce off the vaulted ceilings and disappear down the endless corridors. She will have to testify as well. Then footsteps approach, fall silent, and Albert Gessmann is standing in front of her. Unbelievable! He places a kiss on her hand, sits down beside her and launches into a lament about his wife.

Really, this is going way too far! "You have made a huge mistake. How could you possibly come up with such an accusation against her?" is Sidonie's angry response.

Albert seems oddly disoriented. He says, "Shush, one mustn't talk about that," then becomes quite friendly and invites Sidonie to visit him on Sebastianplatz after her testimony so they can talk things over calmly and maybe work out all their differences. He plans to do all he can to shift suspicion away from Leonie. When Sidonie coolly refuses his invitation, he turns surly, hisses "But she did it," and walks off, leaving his wife's utterly dismayed friend behind.

Soon a pale and harried Leonie and her lawyer emerge from the interrogation room accompanied by two police officers. They stop briefly near Sidonie, and while Dr. Klemperer diverts the officers, presumably by talking about the next judicial procedures, Leonie whispers, "Sidi, they are arresting me, and I'll be transferred to the regional court. I'll have to remain in custody. I beg you, rush to Sebastianplatz, you have to be there before six p.m. They'll execute a search warrant. Clear away my correspondence and any other written stuff you find. Look in my secretary to the left of the door, the second drawer in the middle. Please, you have to get everything from Carola, Anita, all the letters written by women, everything that looks suspicious."

She grasps Sidonie's hands and squeezes them in desperation. The officers pull her away and lead her off.

Shaking off her shock, Sidi rushes to Sebastianplatz. She doesn't have a key to the flat, and at first the housekeeper tries to keep her out, but all it takes is a bit of money and a few words about how much the poor lady is suffering and absolutely must have a few things from her wardrobe. In Leonie's room she snatches up a leather folder, yanks open the appropriate drawer, and within minutes has put everything that could possibly be incriminating into the folder. Leaving, she passes by the resident Cerberus with her head held high and a self-assured air, then runs down the stairs and out onto the street with a deep sigh of relief.

When the police arrive after six p.m., they find all kinds of lovely literature, packages of nice family correspondence, a box with childhood photos. There are no traces of medications or insecticides containing arsenic in the flat.

Sidi's family has taken note of Baroness Puttkamer's arrest. Her father is scandalized that his daughter has received a summons to testify at the police station. He makes a few phone calls but can't get it revoked, so he drums it into her that every question put to her must be answered only "yes" or "no." Her good reputation is at stake, and the slightest carelessness could mean exclusion from society.

He has misjudged his daughter.

The next morning, March 29, it is Sidonie's turn to be interrogated, and she's not going to restrain herself. Gessmann is vile and she's going to put a stop to his game and liberate Leonie from this humiliating detention center.

She tries to cover for her friend as much as possible and to lay a specific trail for the police to follow. Her line of defense is clear:

I've known my friend Leonie Gessmann for about seven years. I know her so well, that I'm her only confidant and she keeps no secrets from me. I'm in a position to assert that this woman is not the perpetrator; I don't think that she is capable of such a deed. On the other hand, I consider her husband's behavior rather odd. Albert Gessmann called for one of his friends to be present while he informed his wife about the results of the chemical analysis. These were the circumstances in which his suspicions about his wife were expressed conclusively—even though he didn't actually phrase it like that. … It was also quite striking that because his pain was so intense, Gessmann asked the doctor to take two samples of the coffee, one from the coffee pot and one from the cup, given that it is rather difficult to put such a tiny amount of poison into a cup unnoticed. One would take rather too much than too little.

My friend has told me, and I believe her one hundred percent, that Gessmann told her after they remarried that a few people had warned him about her, saying that she would make attempts on his life. Then he added this remark: "Imagine, if something actually did happen to me, it would be easy for people to believe that you were behind it."

It seems especially odd that this happened just two days after their reunion. It would have been sheer madness for the woman to carry out an attack immediately after hearing that she would come under suspicion for it.

I make the following assumption, which may not even be provable: Albert Gessmann is very much in love with his wife, and he wants to bind her to him. Evidence of this is that during their divorce proceedings he twice urged her to come back to him.

Because of his work in agriculture, he frequently experiments with chemicals, and he knows about the effect of poisons. Thus, it is possible that he put bits of arsenic into his own cup. The suspicion falls on his wife, and then he will try with all his might to prove that she isn't guilty; as a matter of fact, he has already started doing that. On the other hand, he is also fueling suspicion of his wife, in private with me (but also with other acquaintances) and with strict instructions not to talk about it. He wasn't comfortable with the doctor's complaint to the police, and if it had been possible to retract it, he would have done so.

Obviously Gessmann believed that if he campaigns in favor of his wife and she is free again, her love for him will double and she will be drawn to him out of gratitude.

In her solitary cell in the Regional Courthouse—known locally as the "Grey House"—Leonie has plenty of time to reflect. That final sentence from the police interrogator, her arrest, all the pushing and shoving until she was in her cell—all this still chills her to the marrow. At least it is quiet here, and thank God it's dark and she doesn't have to notice how wretched this place is.

Tomorrow and the day after tomorrow and for many days thereafter—she is sure she'll be here for a while, given the accusations—there will be plenty of time to contemplate the blotchy walls, the narrow cot and the nauseating item behind the short curtain, which must be a toilet. She has already moved the only available chair to face the cot, so at least she can put her feet up.

Exhausted, she leans back and rests her head on the wall behind

Albert Gessmann Jr in the 1920s.

her. She'd like to smoke now, but that is only allowed during yard exercise; so she just stares at the small, barred window or into the darkness.

This is what it has come to—a woman of her social rank in a prison cell! It will be the end of her here in Vienna. On the other hand, what are morals anyway? She has already given up living according to the strict rules of so-called "good" society, and it has never really harmed her. She has always been able to find a man who will adore her and be willing to support her. They are all liars; but she never would have thought that this is how it would end with Gessmann.

When they first got to know each other, things looked promising. She noticed Albert Gessmann soon after her arrival in Vienna because their paths often crossed in bars and smoking theaters, particularly at the Tabarin. He was rather good-looking, obviously a few years her senior, with a lively face, thinning hair, a big nose and a firm mouth beneath a heavy moustache. He had a deft and charming way of dealing with the people around him, particularly the many and ever-changing women. This was proof of his self-confidence. Besides, he seemed to have some money, which he spent freely in those bars. She liked that. She often encountered Albert's first wife, Paula, at the Waldmanns and through her was eventually introduced to Gessmann. He then began to court her, always bringing flowers and often small gifts. At the end of 1919 he sent a letter suggesting an affair. Had he known about her financial situation?

At any rate, he promised to pay for anything she desired, anything to which a woman of her background was entitled. He painted a vivid picture of his generosity—a beautiful flat, dresses from the best fashion houses, luxury vacations. He invited her to dine at his flat on Schleifmühlgasse to discuss the details of the arrangement with Paula present.

The only thing that seemed odd was that Paula seemed to be positively pushing her to accept Albert's proposal. Did she want to be rid of him? Was he so difficult that she needed some relief? Leonie didn't find any answers, but since she had no real need for men at that time, she put such unsettling thoughts aside.

She was still living with the Waldmanns then and was well taken care of, but Ernst Waldmann was rather jealous and choleric, and she was already thinking of looking for other lucrative offers so she could move out. She had plenty of lovers, all of whom had more to offer than Albert, and she neither needed nor wanted to give in to his pressure. But Albert pursued her persistently throughout the following year, during which she had two lovers: Count Apponyi, an elegant, refined man, whom she appreciated but who, after July 1920, couldn't afford her any longer; and then a wealthy, stay-at-home industrialist, one Herr Fleischer, who maintained her but never appeared in public with her.

Bertschi, the nickname Leonie soon gave Gessmann, had fallen very much in love with her. He kept an eagle eye on her affairs, and he proved frightfully jealous, which put a lot of pressure on her. From the first, he kept trying to make it clear to her that she was his destiny and she absolutely had to move in with him. She wasn't particularly impressed, knowing from long experience that men had to be kept on the hook—the greater their desire, the higher the price. She was beautiful, noble and wicked—and she had her price. She calmly let him wait for her decision and used the interval to find out more about Albert. Without a background check, she didn't even want to get as deeply involved as just playing mind games.

The smitten Bertschi Gessmann was a bigwig. His father used to be Mayor Lueger's right hand man; a leading Christian Socialist and once an advocate of clericalism, he would later become Minister of Labor. He had probably smoothed the way for his son, who started a banking career after university and in 1911 was appointed director of the Bau-Kreditbank and also held a leading position in the Erste Österreichische Beamten Creditanstalt. Albert certainly didn't get those positions only by virtue of his diligence.

Soon bored with banking, he started to write plays and was obviously still proud of this years later. After one of their dinners together, his expression grew serious as he presented Leonie with a signed copy of his play *Das Fremdvolk* (The foreign people). Reading it later, she could barely stop laughing at the grandiloquent yet didactic descriptions of noble Greek men and corrupted Phoenician women. Well, perhaps she didn't like it because she just wasn't interested in literature, or the play's elaborate phrases couldn't appeal to someone with her own concise, Prussian prose style.

After that, Albert used his privileged position in order to speculate in real estate, a venture that discredited him and ruined his father's career. The elder Gessmann very much would have liked to be Vienna's major, Karl Lueger's successor, but his aspirations were destroyed by a combination of his son's dubious business dealings and his own image as a quirky party strategist who didn't even understand that he had to make public appearances.

Shortly before Leonie met him, Albert had gotten into agriculture. He founded ARA, a company that sold agricultural supplies and later added a sales department for agricultural equipment. He has a fancy office in the First District and a country house in Edlach near Reichenau, where he keeps busy with his favorite project: building a cable car on the Rax, one of the mountains in Vienna's backyard.

Maybe she shouldn't reject this one—that was her thought at the time.

Albert and Paula divorced in January 1921. That same month Leonie ended her affair with the industrialist, took up with Gessmann and soon moved into the Schleifmühlgasse flat with him, but they didn't stay there long. He arranged an exchange, and in March 1921 they moved to Sebastianplatz 7. Paula had disappeared from the scene quickly and completely and was said to be living in South America. This seemed odd, and rumors persisted that Albert had blackmailed her and shunted her off almost violently. Leonie heard the rumors, but she wasn't concerned.

On February 4, 1922, after living together for a year, Albert and Leonie got married. She knew exactly what was in it for her—marriage to a bourgeois was a survival strategy, as all her liaisons with men had been. She was not in love, but Albert had worked hard to talk her into marriage and though he had used every trick in the book to cut Fleischer out, his tolerance of her relationships with women counted in his favor. Even during their early encounters at Tabarin, he had offered her his cocottes. There was nothing to fear in that arena, except maybe a randy husband who wanted to watch.

At the beginning of the marriage, Albert had been quite nice, though on the condition that she not contradict him. However ... as far as everything related to sex was concerned, he was really a quite bent. He flaunted his prowess with all the women with whom he supposedly had had affairs. He loved to describe every inch of various women's bodies and to detail the ways he had had intercourse with them. He was particularly proud that he was known as the daddy of all Viennese whores; because actually, that's what it came down to—he preferred whores to decent women. To document his astounding success with women, he had even kept count and claimed to have slept with more than two thousand women since the age of fifteen.

Gradually, his narratives became more and more jaundiced and sardonic. It drove Leonie crazy, and she also found it disgusting. Eventually, all he talked about was venereal diseases such as the clap and syphilis. On a bad day, he went so far as to say that all the women he had been bragging about had been depraved and diseased. He even accused Leonie and her mother of harboring venereal diseases.

Of course Leonie wouldn't tolerate that, which triggered violent invective on Albert's part that always ended with the accusation that she had infected him. He even went so far as to break off the base from cigarettes she lit for him, fearing contagion.

For Leonie, the studio in his photo cellar was the worst. He had set it up before they met, and it was still in the building on Prinzenallee where he'd had his previous flat. He considered it his pride and joy;

Leonie considered it thoroughly perverted. The studio was even used by professional photographers, who lined up to work there because it had Vienna's most modern lighting equipment, which could be used to produce special effects. Albert took nude pictures there of many of the women he slept with—most likely while he was carrying on with them. He acted as if it were all quite serious and maintained that he was always discreet and covered the women's genitals. But Leonie knew what he kept in his drawers. His reputation as a photographer of nudes spread quickly, and soon so many women were knocking on his door that it got to be too much, and he stopped taking pictures altogether.

Correspondingly, their sex life as a couple has always been strange, and intercourse was never easy, since Leonie was not in love with Albert. Over time, she found him increasingly nauseating—his skin was covered with blemishes, and she thought he gave off a sour smell. She didn't like to go into his room, the air was always stale because he kept the windows closed—he lived in constant fear of getting rheumatism or a cold—but copulating with him there kept her own room free of his smell. The whole endeavor was no fun at all, and though she knew all kinds of tricks to convince men how wonderful she thought it was to sleep with them, even that was nearly impossible with Albert.

And the things he demanded of her!

He wanted her to dress like a whore and brought her tight, low-cut chemises with ridiculous embroidery, which she absolutely refused to wear. He demanded that she perform what he referred to as *Minette*, the word his circle used for oral sex. If she refused, he would beat her on the buttocks with a strap, a whip or his hand. Leonie allowed these beatings and even endured it when he spat on her, because it obviously turned him on. But for him to tie her to the bedpost or bring young men to the house for her to have sex with while he watched and then plowed into her after they were done—that was going too far and was deeply humiliating.

His efforts at conventional sex with her were unsuccessful. His rheumatic joints were stiff, so she had to help him get on top of her and then she was not allowed to move. After arduous pushing and shoving, he tumbled off her like a log and displayed the condom he always used (ever dreading infection) so the volume of his semen would prove his manly prowess.

Albert also started to exhibit other traits that Leonie found creepy. His combination of peculiar eating habits and paranoia made life difficult both for her and for their housekeeper. Like a predator, he devoured large quantities of meat in a hurry. If doing intellectual work, he ate dark bread, because of its higher phosphorous content, and drank great quantities of coffee. All his food had to be prepared at home because anything prepared elsewhere might be poisoned. When he had still been with Paula, she had watched as she served him cake from a confectioner, and he had clearly believed that it contained poison. Furthermore, he was convinced that he always needed to be armed, because Paula's lovers might want to kill him.

He became increasingly unbearable, and Leonie was through with him after only six months of marriage. His generous financial arrangements on her behalf couldn't offset her growing repugnance. She also became increasingly aware of their class differences, and eventually reached a point where she so despised him that she just wanted out.

Ah, yes—and that was also the time of Anita Berber, the famous nude dancer with the dreamy body, whose "Dances of Vice, Horror and Ecstasy" had both thrilled and disgusted half of Europe. Oh, God, Leonie would prefer to forget about that! The frenzy, madness and lust Berber had aroused when they met on a film set in Vienna in 1922. She was another reason for leaving Albert in the summer of that year and then traveling to famous/infamous Berlin a few months later in order to immerse herself in its demimonde of ladies' bars, butches, femmes and lesbian relationships.

Reconnecting with Albert after that was her own personal kind of madness, and she can only blame herself for that. She should have known better, and now she has to think of some way to dig herself out of the hole that her relationship with him has plunged her into.

ALBERT GESSMANN'S POINT OF VIEW

ALBERT GESSMANN HAS BEEN RESTLESS OF LATE AND GOES TO HIS office in Babenbergerstrasse earlier than usual. Maybe working more is a good diversion. Sitting at his massive oak desk with the carved griffons at each corner, his gaze wanders to the window looking out on the museums on Ringstrasse and finally comes to rest on the distant Kahlenberg hills. One of Vienna's most beautiful views is laid out before him, and he notices it less than he ever did.

He has given his initial testimony at the police station and learned that Sidonie Csillag had botched things and told the police about their earlier talk in the corridor. She seems to be trying to incriminate him by asserting that he staged the whole thing ... or at least the questions the officers asked had led to that conclusion. He has to change his strategy if he doesn't want his poisoning accusation to lose some of its punch. He has already told the court in great detail about his wife's lesbian relationships, and dual accusations—attempted murder and illicit sexual relations—will ruin Leonie more quickly than one.

But still this doesn't really satisfy him, rather, it leaves him increasingly restless and tense, and his anxiety peaks at night, when he can't stand to be alone in the big, empty flat. So he returns to the familiar nightclubs, in particular the Femina-Bar and the Tabarin, where beautiful young women who know him well greet him with radiant smiles and lend him more than just an ear. The clubs are his second home these days; but he's still plagued by rage, still constantly weighing the pros and cons, still feeling clueless.

He never would have guessed that Leonie would leave so abruptly and even seek the protection of an attorney. He's sure that was the wretched Csillag girl's doing. She has been at his wife's side for ages, offering help and advice and regarding him with cool mistrust. Clearly, with her in the background it won't be easy to teach his wife a lesson she won't forget and get her back again.

Lately, Albert has been trying to understand why, more than any woman before her, the baroness has enslaved him. He had been quite attracted to Paula, but she lacked Leonie's class and allure. He married Paula because it seemed to make both their families happy, but she hadn't known how to turn him on sexually, and after a while she bored him.

But Leonie! He gets weak just looking at her, even after all these troublesome years. He had loved her so ... no, he loves her still and has done everything for her—in his own way. And for a man in his position, her noble background was also important. He could show her off with pride, and his business partners and political allies were green with envy. She upstaged everyone with her flawless manners and air of nonchalance, which she could turn on and off at will. So different from the countless dames he'd met in bars and couldn't even remember anymore.

Actually, he had met Leonie in a bar and under circumstances that made her particularly attractive. Her changing array of male companions indicated that she approached sexual matters rather casually. Most likely she could be bought, if her lascivious smile and bold coquetry were any indication. This made his fantasies of conquest and success run wild.

The older Gessmann got, the more his health deteriorated and the more he yearned—in almost unimaginable ways—for arousal. Everything he'd taken the trouble to learn about the baroness promised precisely his brand of excitement, and he had to have her at any price.

It wouldn't be so difficult. He was an impressive looking man; he enjoyed both patronage and some renown in the highest circles; add to that his money, real estate and extravagant lifestyle—those were the things that counted with women; that was why everyone admired him.

He made sure Leonie was aware of all this, and he didn't hold back on the tales of his sexual experiences. He had had numerous women and was eager to prove that he was the best in all Vienna. Leonie was going to be his masterpiece.

After many months, he had her. He got rid of Paula just in time by filing a complaint alleging she'd had sex with underage boys, thus speeding up the process. Perhaps that wasn't a particularly classy thing to do, but she had quickly gone off to join her sister in South America. He cut Leonie's latest paramour out of the action with gifts, jealousy, pressure and more gifts. He spent too much money and wrote far too many letters in those days, but he finally did convince her to marry him.

During their first weeks, he had been happy for the first time in ages, and he showered her with attention, expensive meals out, visits to the bars they both liked. And making love with her was intoxicating. For the first time in years, he felt potent and gave his fantasies free rein. Leonie wasn't fastidious. He had suggested all the things that excited him, and she hadn't refused. He loved it when she performed *Minette*, loved the games in which he imagined his noble wife as a whore and

paid her for sex ... incredibly satisfying. A few times he ordered cocottes—he preferred them buxom—from the Femina Bar and played
around with them while Leonie observed. That she allowed this made
him feel like nobody could constrain him, he could do everything,
own everybody. A man at the peak of his power.

Naturally, in exchange he had to be a bit tolerant regarding her lesbian inclinations, that was self-evident. He knew what he was getting
into; it shouldn't cause any problems. He knew of enough cases where
the wives had those tendencies, and they were all good companions for
their husbands. Besides, it turned him on to imagine Leonie in the arms
of a woman, even though she didn't let him watch when she was with
women.

But something was missing. It was as if they were separated by a
glass wall and Leonie was retreating farther and farther behind it. In
conversation she was often abstracted and didn't bother to listen. When
speaking to him, she was curt, often snippy and derogatory. She knew
how to let him know that he was nothing special, a little bourgeois
who, despite all his money, would never have the class or the taste to offer her a suitable life. After all his efforts and the enormous amounts of
money he spent on her! He felt diminished. She simply didn't want to
understand that he loved her. Though he had possessed her body hundreds of times, he had never gotten through to her soul.

Once they began living together, he also realized that her interest in
women went much deeper than he had assumed. She was not just attracted to women's bodies, all her emotions belonged to women—
emotions she never felt for him. This pained him deeply, and he tried to
put a stop to it by forbidding her to be with women openly in public.
Of course she didn't listen and instead took great pleasure in driving
women around in his car all day looking for places where they could
amuse themselves. And to make a public show that he was a cuckold.
For surely such behavior made everyone think his wife had to go after
women because he, president of the Farming Association, wasn't able to
satisfy her. The humiliation!

And then came the madness with Anita Berber. He had never seen
Leonie so animated. After seeing Berber's picture in various magazines,
she pestered him for months to organize a performance at the Tabarin

for that morphine-addicted syphilitic—and he had been stupid enough to try. Thank God it hadn't worked out.

But Berber came to Vienna anyway, for a film shoot, and suddenly he either didn't see Leonie at all or only very late at night, drunk, with the half-naked Berber on her lap as she announced that they were going to sleep together.

She was clearly out of her mind. One evening after a dinner at Sacher, where she had flirted with a stranger and made him look like a fool, she confronted him, saying that she found him disgusting, he could shove his money up his ass, she never wanted to see him again. When he moved forward to hit her, she threatened him with his own revolver.

The next day she was gone. Then she got a separation decree and disappeared to Berlin with another cocotte from Berber's circle. She had pawned all the furniture, silver and jewelry he had given her, and she had left with the incredible sum of one billion crowns—he couldn't even blackmail her. The divorce went through in August 1922 and he was alone again.

He still feels angry, shamed and nauseated when he thinks about it today. Even more shaming is that he simply couldn't get her out of his mind. His longing for her had resurfaced quickly, and he felt lonely and old. He wrote many letters to Berlin, tried to engage arbitrators, and whenever Leonie showed up in Vienna for brief visits, he tried to talk to her.

Finally, in March 1923, she agreed to return to Vienna on the following conditions: he would never again send investigators to spy on her; he would provide her with enough money; and she could travel whenever she wanted to in order to have some peace and privacy.

He kept a copy of the letter he sent to Berlin that had finally turned her around, and he reread it many times soon after filing his attempted murder complaint:

I, who have been courted and desired by so many women, must cling to the one woman who can't stand me! And I must work to do that; to do that I must provide for this woman!

No, Leonie, that can't be what you think. And even if you did think that at times, those times were aberrations, and, once done with, they were replaced with better and more reasonable feelings towards me. Isn't that true? But tell me, what do you have in mind in terms of finances? How can I secure your financial future from a distance? You are a pampered woman with rather lofty affectations. And providing for your upkeep also means keeping Frau Carola. If you aren't to come up short, I would also have to provide enough for Frau Carola as well. For you would share with her anything I were to send you.

Naturally, when you are far away from me my expenditures on other women are not inconsiderable, for your absence will make me rather unhappy but not impotent. The more unhappy I feel, the more I'll play around with other women. That's the sad realization I've come to in the course of the past year, and the women I tend to enjoy typically cost me a fortune.

Particularly in light of the constant turnover ... But where am I to find the funds to lead the life you have forced me into, that of a man about town, and also to keep you and Carola in a manner befitting your social status? Leonie, you know that I have a rather large income, but even it has its limits. It would be enough—and in these times that is a lot—to keep you in style and comfort as my wife. And along with you, your girlfriend Carola would also fare well. In exchange, it would be your duty to make me happy and thereby make it possible for me to work happily.

That's how it should be! After so many odysseys, let us come to an amicable agreement and settle in peace. It's high time! You and I have reached an age where we should finally stop this mad bouncing back and forth. If we don't spend the coming years—and they could be the best and most beautiful of our lives—together sanely and with tender goodness, then our lives will definitely be wasted! That would be such a pity for both you and me!

Anxiously awaiting your reply, with longing and love,

Your Bertschi

Leonie did go to Vienna with her new girlfriend, Carola Horn. Their visit didn't last long, for Albert immediately fell in love with Carola and made such pointed and indecent propositions that the situation became intolerable. Carola left after two weeks. Leonie stayed six weeks then returned to Berlin and in the fall of 1923 moved to Munich with Carola.

Albert continued to write conciliatory, love-struck, pleading letters, but he didn't see Leonie again until an encounter finally took place in Salzburg in January 1924. During this meeting Albert both confessed that he had indeed fallen in love with Carola the previous year, though she had rejected him, and arranged with Leonie that she return to Vienna and to him. He also suggested another attempt at marriage. There are no records of whatever financial proposal he made, but it must have been so enticing that Leonie couldn't pass it up.

In March Albert went to Munich to fetch Leonie, and he invited Carola to follow in about four weeks—they could enjoy life as a threesome. Carola refused the offer but said she would come in about six months, time enough for Albert's and Leonie's relationship to have strengthened. The remarriage in Vienna took only a few hours, and a new beginning seemed possible.

THE WAR OF THE ROSES

ON MARCH 19, THE DAY LEONIE ALLEGEDLY PUT ARSENIC IN Albert's coffee, she seemed quite overwrought. During the performance they attended at Ronacher, she had a bout of the shivers, which, according to Albert, always happened when her hatred of men grew more pronounced than usual. Everything that followed is already on record.

The testimonies given by Leonie and Albert Gessmann and Sidonie Csillag on March 28 and 29, 1924, are duly submitted to the district attorney's office in Vienna, which, that same day, charges Leonie Gessmann-Puttkamer with the attempted murder of her husband. The district attorney further decrees:

> 1. The defendant shall be interrogated as to how, when and where she had sexual intercourse with Anita Berber, Carola Horn, Bebi Becker, Susanne Wanowski and Gisela Spira (each case to be heard separately).
>
> 2. A decision shall be made regarding the petition for release (bail set at 250,000,000 crowns[*]).

---

[*] Equivalent, at that time, to about 35,000 US dollars.

3. Leonie Gessmann shall undergo psychiatric examination.

4. Anita Berber and Susanne Wanowski shall be investigated according to 38/3 Code of Criminal Procedure respective to their personal data giving the location of their current residence. Also the personal data of Bebi Becker as well as Carola Horn, who allegedly had sexual intercourse with Gessmann only in Berlin, shall be established.

The prosecution has a great deal to do to collect all the data, and as a first step it interrogates the Gessmann's staff, hoping to shed some light on this confusing situation that is rife with contradictory claims.

On April 8, 1924, Gessmann's current housekeeper, Franziska Waschke, is questioned by the police. She is not very talkative, and her answers are brief:

She has been working for Gessmann only since January 1924, so she cannot recount very much. When she took up her post at Gessmann's, there was a Frau Elfriede Hörmann living with him. She left the flat at Gessmann's request and left Vienna for Berlin before Madam returned to Vienna. On the evening of March 16, Herr Gessmann had been more talkative than usual, and late one night, when she was serving him coffee in the study, he told her that he had been warned about Leonie as early as just before Christmas. He had heard rumors that she was planning to kill him little by little. He also told her about one Carola Horn, who was waiting in Munich to be informed of his demise.

For additional information, the housekeeper recommends that the police officer get in touch with her predecessor, one Bertha Schramböck, currently residing at the Hotel Auge Gottes.

That same day, the police call on Bertha Schramböck. Having worked for Albert Gessmann for several years, she was in a good position to describe in detail the conditions inside the flat and the spouses' dealings with one another.

She took her post as parlor maid at Gessmann's in November 1919 and worked for him until the middle of January 1924. Bertha Schramböck remembers that shortly after the first wedding in 1922, the baroness's girlfriends were already coming to the flat. She remembers Anita Berber and Bebi Becker very well but not fondly. She frequently heard about other girlfriends, such as Klara Waldmann or one Susi Wanowski, but she didn't see them in the flat.

Herr Gessmann usually spent the weekends at his country house in Reichenau, while Leonie Puttkamer preferred to stay in Vienna. She often invited her girlfriends to spend the nights with her. But Albert Gessmann had been very mistrustful and often made a surprise return from Reichenau. The Frau Baronin tried to erase all traces of the women's visits, but with the help of private detectives, Mister quickly found out who had spent the night with his wife. Of course, they were constantly quarreling about the girlfriends, and the spouses were quite rude to one another. Then the baroness would turn vulgar, and she never wanted to hear soothing words from her, Bertha.

She said she hated him, she called him a cretin, a mangy dog, at best a skeleton. Another time she stated to the housekeeper that she planned to ruin her husband and added, "Generally one has to exploit men. My heart is with women; I'd give the whores the shirt off my back."

In addition, she, Bertha, learned a bit later from the lady's companion Gisa Spira, that the Frau Baronin had once said, "First Gessmann has to write a will, and then I'll poison him little by little."

She, Bertha, is convinced that the baroness married Albert Gessmann only because of his wealth and in order to devote herself in peace to her perverted inclinations. At any rate, she was glad when the baroness left the house. When she learned that Puttkamer was returning, she resigned her post.

Soon, Gisela Spira is also questioned in detail. She acts as a ladies' companion to the vaudeville actress Bebi Becker, who was Leonie Puttkamer's lover for a short time in 1921.

The witness statements get increasingly wild and over the top and turn the proceedings and all future interrogations of Leonie towards an additional charge of illicit sexual relations.

Leonie's fears have come true. She is not only accused of trying to poison Albert Gessmann but also, and this is nearly impossible to deny, of having lesbian relationships.

A new round of inquiries begins, and the two opposing parties and their respective attorneys keep the courts busy. One petition after the other, primarily from Gessmann's attorney, Dr. Khittl, is filed in court. Each accusation—with its inherent absurdity—turns the screws a little tighter.

For his part, Gessmann focuses on his wife's madness, instability and addictions:

> Contrary to her claims that she is addicted neither to morphine nor cocaine, I have been convinced by many people, that she is an addict. Many years ago, her father had already ordered a psychiatric examination because her behavior had given him cause to suspect that she has a mental disorder. My wife is homosexual and occasionally experiences such a strong desire for a beloved woman that it triggers a great hatred and disgust for men. ... Before remarrying my wife, all I wanted was to take her back, just her, not along with Carola Horn. But in her incurable state of mind and due to her maniacal love for Carola Horn, my wife was consumed with such hatred for me that she fixed on the idea of returning to me in order to acquire lots of cash quickly upon my death, in order to be able to continue a luxurious life with Carola Horn.

Even Leonie's choice of reading material is cited as evidence.

> I was really afraid of her at that time. Her holy bible was a novel about Theodora published by Rikoha;[*] she particularly enjoyed the passages where Theodora kills the men she had sexually abused.

Leonie Puttkamer, on the other hand, knows exactly what kind of accusations will hit her husband the hardest. She describes him as impotent and perverted:

> He suffers from rheumatism, can't stand up on his own, can't bend over, can't wash himself or put on his shoes. This is also the case during copulation, as described earlier. He must stiffen his member with continual onanistic manipulation and after entering the vagina it collapses and he

---

[*]   Gessmann is referring to Alma Johanna König's *Der Heilige Palast* (The Holy Palace).

has to use his fingers. ... Soon after our marriage, he asked me to have another woman once a month because that alone would complete the happiness of a marriage. In fact, he brought home a "brothel whore," as he called her, who had to do *Minette*; then he played with his genitals between her breasts until he finally ejaculated there. After such scenes, these women had to come to me, kiss my hand and ask for my forgiveness. ... Then he would come towards me on his knees, his hands in the air and ask for my forgiveness. During these proceedings, which I thought disgusting, I sat in an armchair and smoked. While on his knees he would cry out: "Dearest wife, don't be angry! I ask you to forgive me."

Albert Gessmann can't let that stand, and he counters with the allegation that Leonie wanted to force him to carry out sadistic acts:

Her sympathy for me also expressed itself in the fact that she not only allowed but asked me to have sexual intercourse with women she fancied. ... It is true that two years ago I had intercourse about five times with other women in the presence of my wife; those women were strangers. My wife took great pleasure in it. ... Sadistic acts such as beatings demand that the arm muscles and genitals be used simultaneously, an activity for which I was always too lazy. ... She berated me for my deficient sadistic activities and told me several times ... that I was some kind of sexual swindler, and that I should be ashamed of my lack of perversity. She was particularly angry that I didn't fulfill her demand that before intercourse I drag her through the room by her hair, then trample her and make love to her on the floor.

And he also could not let Leonie's accusation that he enjoyed sex with colored women remain uncontested:

My tastes focus on intellectually superior women of cultured European background, and I even consider black hair, black eyes and yellowish skin to be thoroughly unappealing. My sexual desires lean toward racial inbreeding; I'm attracted only to blondes or brunettes with blue or grey eyes and pink skin. I can't abide negresses or even mulattas or Creoles, not even for social interaction.

Such petitions continue to be filed one after another almost until the hearings come to an end. All that aside, however, the forensic report filed on April 5, 1924, established that the amount of arsenic found in both the cup and the carafe was insufficient to cause either discomfort or illness; and in addition, the time elapsed between consuming the coffee and the first appearance of symptoms had been much too brief to indicate arsenic poisoning.

This finding absolves Leonie of the murder charges and undermines Albert's accusations. She immediately files a petition for release, which is initially denied.

Still hanging over the baroness's head is §129 I b—illicit sexual acts—and that is where dear Bertschi now concentrates his efforts to effect his wife's downfall. In preparation, he cleverly moves to get the upper hand and keep her dependent on him by posting her bail of 250 million crowns on April 8. When Leonie is released, Albert immediately has her sent to the Löwy Sanatorium in Sulz-Stangau in the Vienna Woods, where he tries not only to confine her in the psychiatric ward but also to make her his ward.

Leonie Puttkamer cannot refuse this; she is destitute and therefore dependent on her husband, and she also has two pending exams by a court-appointed psychiatrist. Once again, she is imprisoned.

To top things off, Albert launches an open attack on Leonie's attorney. Apparently, his strategy is to remove both her legal counsel and any possibility of resistance. He tries to convince Leonie to get rid of her attorney herself, pointing out that attorney Klemperer was responsible for getting her into such a mess. He also writes threatening letters to Klemperer, and on May 25 files a complaint with Vienna's bar association alleging abuse of power and exerting undue influence on the client.

In his dealings with the interrogating authorities, Albert Gessmann has his hopes set on §129 I b. His trump card is the Anita Berber story, and he lets it unfold in full detail in the weeks to come.

4

DANCES OF VICE, HORROR AND ECSTASY

As early as 1921, Leonie Puttkamer began to notice newspaper and magazine articles about Anita Berber's scandalous dance performances. The pictures showed a small woman with a beautiful body and lascivious, kohl-rimmed eyes set in a deathly pale face. She was either completely nude or wearing unconventional costumes and striking unusual poses, and the baroness fixated on her. She sent letters and telegrams to the dancer's Berlin address but never received a reply—likely because they never got past Berber's jealous private secretary, who was also her lover.

In the summer of 1921, when Albert and Leonie were taking a course of treatments at a spa in Gastein, Leonie learned from another hotel guest that Anita Berber and her companion, Susi Wanowski, were in Carlsbad. Leonie besieged Albert with requests to leave this ugly resort and go to beautiful Carlsbad for follow-up treatments. When Albert refused, she changed tactics and proposed a few weeks in Berlin. It would be good for Albert to cultivate his business contacts there. The director of the German Potash Syndicate had come to Vienna on several occasions, it would be tactful for Albert to pay a return visit. She herself wanted to see how the political and economic scene there had change since the end of the monarchy.

But Albert had been forewarned. His wife had been mooning over Berber for months; it was getting worse, and he was jealous. He did indeed have some business to take care of in Berlin, but nonetheless he vetoed her travel plans.

Leonie then announced that she would go to Berlin on her own and returned to the argument of wanting to see firsthand the effect that inflation had had on life in Berlin. She had read that people from all over the world were going there to profit from the enormous social changes underway, and such a large, diverse gathering could mean only one thing: a wild, exciting life day and night.

Albert tried to frighten her by painting a dark picture of the profiteers and thieves who might victimize her in Berlin. But this tactic failed. Then he had the brilliant idea of suggesting that it might be possible to bring Berber to Vienna, surely one of the many vaudeville theaters there would book her. He thought he would have a better chance of controlling his wife on their home turf. Urged on by Leonie, he approached the director of the Tabarin, who sent an offer to Berlin, but it was refused. Frau Berber had far too many other engagements.

Then, in June 1922, Berber arrived in Vienna to act in the silent movie *Die drei Marien und der Herr von Marana* (The Three Marias and the

Anita Berber, 1922

Lord of Marana). Leonie deduced that the actress would likely be staying near the studio on Rosenhügel and started calling hotels in that vicinity. Berber, it turned out, was staying at the elegant Parkhotel Hietzing, located next to Schönbrunn Castle and convenient to the studio.

Berber's long-term girlfriend, Susi Wanowski, was also her manager, private secretary and bouncer and, for reasons of self interest, she kept the dancer's numerous male and female admirers at bay. So it wasn't particularly surprising that in response to one of Leonie's frequent phone calls Wanowski announced in no uncertain terms that Anita Berber had neither free time nor interest in making the baroness's acquaintance.

Leonie continued to find excuses to go to the cafes and bars in the Hietzing district to look for Berber. She even included Albert in the search. Then one evening Berber, clad in an outfit that showcased her perfect body most favorably, flowed elegantly into the Parkhotel bar with the boyish Wanowski in tow. Knowing everyone's eyes were on her, she made her way to the marble bar and ordered a large, stiff drink. Despite the din, Leonie knew how to attract Berber's attention and signaled her with a wink to follow her to the vestibule. There, they began a private conversation.

Albert quickly sensed that an erotic storm was brewing. Susi Wanowski, too, set out to put an end to the encounter. Attacked on two flanks, Leonie whispered an invitation for the next evening into Berber's ear and beat a quick retreat, thus missing the row between Berber and Wanowski. Everywhere they went, Wanowski shouted, Anita engaged in at least one—no, not just one, countless such escapades. She was fed up! Anita must cancel the appointment with Leonie.

More or less indifferent to Susi's scenes, Anita didn't plan to miss out on the experience of having Leonie's noble beauty at her fingertips or, better, at her bedside. One day more or less wouldn't matter.

Somehow the two women managed to meet behind the backs of both Gessmann and Wanowski for a few days, then, after a week, Anita arrived at Leonie's for her first official visit. They dined together with Albert, who tried to put a good face on a basically bad situation and made an effort to keep the conversation going. But he had never before felt as superfluous as on that evening. The two women left their food nearly untouched, though the diners emptied four bottles of the best champagne. Leonie was delighted by Berber's tales of her countless amorous adventures and couldn't hear enough about night life in Berlin. Eventually it got so late that something had to happen, and with a charming giggle Leonie pointed out how much easier it would be if Anita spent the night at Sebastianplatz … Leonie would take her back to the Parkhotel the next morning. Berber grinned and nodded her agreement.

The baroness ignored Albert's rage. She hadn't made a secret of her fantasies about Berber; and this close to her goal, she didn't want any man, even her man, to keep her from reaching it. Tortured by jealousy and curiosity, he retreated to his room but barely slept and got up frequently to listen at his wife's door. The snippets of conversation he overheard confirmed what he already knew: Leonie detested any kind of sex with him and endured him only because he paid very well for her services.

Gessmann's jealousy turned to hatred, and he tiptoed back to his bed intent on revenge.

On the rare occasions when husband and wife encountered one another after that, their conversation was both insipid and tense. If Gessmann mentioned Anita, his wife would leave the room without another word. Leonie spent most of her time at the film studio or the Parkhotel, where there were some serious rows with Susi Wanowski. To make Anita jealous, but also because she was genuinely interested, Wanowski made a move on the actress Bebi Becker, and after a fight with Anita one morning, she moved to the Hotel Bristol. This eased the situation considerably, and relations among all those concerned promptly improved. At some point, all four ladies even started going out together in the evening.

Then came two weeks that proved utterly intolerable for the Gessmanns and included a failed attempt to vacation on Mendelpass in Südtirol and at their country house at Edlach. At the beginning of August, right after their return from Edlach, Leonie told Albert that she wanted a divorce.

She packed up and went to Fedy Ferrard, an actress living in the Fourth District. The separation, on August 24, 1922, took place just seven months after their wedding. The divorce was amicable, though the real reasons were known to insiders.

Anita Berber was well known in Vienna. After her first dance performance there in 1918, she returned in 1921 to make films. That year, she partnered as the female lead in *Verfehltes Leben* (Failed Life) with father and son Burgtheater actors Carl and Philipp Zeska, then made *Lucifer* and *Die Nacht der Mary Murton* (Mary Murton's Night). By 1925 she had made four more films in Austria, which she managed to do despite having been put under an Austrian exclusion order in early 1923.

By August 1922 Anita Berber was exhausted after the rigors of filming, and she wanted to take a short break before devoting herself to her true passion, dance, and preparations for a scheduled performance at the Wiener Konzerthaus, where the program included *Dances of Vice, Horror and Ecstasy*. She moved into the Hotel Bristol, which was opposite the Opera and in close proximity to her aristocratic new girlfriend and the places where after-dark amusement could be found.

In September 1922 Sidonie Csillag returned to Vienna from her summer retreat and immediately sensed that Leonie was being consumed by a kind of fire that seemed impossible to contain. She hadn't noticed this with Leonie's previous women, and, afraid she might fall victim to the flames, Sidonie instinctively despised Berber from the outset. Her initial impression was confirmed when she and the baroness visited Berber at her bedside at the private clinic preferred by Vienna's wealthy, the Loew Sanatorium in the Ninth District.

Berber had a lot of time on her hands while she was there—ample for writing to Karl Kraus, publisher of *Die Fackel*, to inform him that she had heard that rumors were circulating in town that she had gone crazy and been sent to the psychiatric hospital at Steinhof. In truth, she was in quite a good mood and was in the women's ward at Loew recuperating from a minor case of peritonitis, which she likely caught while filming in the park at Schönbrunn Castle. She'd be fine in a couple of weeks and will go on tour to Italy, Spain and Paris with her dance partner, Sebastian Droste.

On November 14, 1922, Droste and the well-recuperated Anita Berber performed at Vienna's Konzerthaus. Sidonie attended the event, and despite her dislike of Berber, she couldn't help being impressed by her art. She was less impressed by Droste—very theatrical but nothing compared to Anita's wild, erotic fire.

Shortly thereafter, the newspapers reported that Droste was involved in some shady deals and would be deported following his Vienna performances. To delay deportation, he successfully secured additional performances, but he ended up signing contracts with several theaters for concurrent appearances.

According to the December 28, 1922, issue of the *Interessante Blatt*: "The dance pair was considered an attraction only after Anita Berber risked a few dances completely in the altogether and two critics locked horns regarding the performance's artistic value. Three theaters that allow smoking, the Apollo, Ronacher, and Tabarin, all offered contracts. The impossibility of fulfilling all the contracts led to conflict among the competitors ... that ended at the district court."

That the irregular contracts triggered arrests and clashes with the police provided Berber with an ideal situation—she loved scandal and her cheeky remarks were always picked up by the media. This was the best kind of publicity; it both aroused the public's curiosity and sent them to the theaters in droves. Every performance sold out.

But then Droste was suspected of having pilfered cash and jewelry from two German countesses, and although the matter was never clarified, he was extradited to Hungary nevertheless. Berber stayed in Vienna for a few more performances on her own. But after her fist connected with the doorman's face during a brawl in the Tabarin, she, too, was extradited to Budapest and put under an exclusion order.

THE TENCH

WHILE ANITA BERBER WAS DUKING IT OUT WITH THE PUBLIC AND the police in Vienna, Leonie sold her furniture and carpets in Vienna, packed up and went to Prague, where she sold her household silver for Czechoslovakian crowns—the most stable of the Central European currencies. She then headed to Berlin.

During her final weeks in Vienna she had gotten to know Susi Wanowski, and after their initial antipathy turned into cordial affection, they became lovers. Affable, witty Susi was up for all kinds of fun and was at the hub of every social event. For a short while the previous year, Susi's amour, Bebi Becker, had been bedded by both Albert and Leonie. Susi lost interest in Bebi rather quickly, and their affair was brief. Before Bebi had time to make a jealous scene, the new lovers decided to clear out of Vienna and, as a prank, take Bebi's lady's companion with them. Susi talked Leoni into promising to take said companion, thirty-four-year-old Gisela Spira from Budapest, to Berlin, which convinced Gisela to quit her job with Bebi.

By early December 1922, when Leonie was still ensconced on the mezzanine of Vienna's Hotel Bristol, Gisela was already employed as her maid. Gisela had been a delighted observer of Leonie's affair with her previous employer, and she knew that Leonie became Leo when she was with a certain circle of female friends. She also knew that Leonie threw her money around—some valuable gifts had landed on Bebi, who had her own income as an actress and had also profited handsomely from a lusty Russian prince.

On December 16, 1922, Susi, Leonie and Gisela took the night train to Berlin, where the lady and her maid took up residence at the Hotel Eden and the lover moved into the Hotel Zoo. Leonie Puttkamer got to know all the Berlin bars and restaurants of interest and preferred the Comobar, where it was easy to meet women. She took a different one to her hotel room every night.

Anita Berber was already nothing but a memory, and soon so was Susi Wanowski—who had a beaver fur coat and a pearl ring as keepsakes. Leonie's new woman was Carola Horn, who was then living with Lotte Oeltjen, the gynecologist for whom she worked as an assistant. Leonie had met Lotte first and even spent a night with her, but her girlfriend Carola was much more attractive. There were many stormy scenes when Carola started spending night after night at Leonie's, but in the end, Carola decided to stay with Leonie.

Once again Leonie became Leo and in true butch style bought her new love dresses, jewelry and even a motorcycle with a sidecar. Outfitted with leather helmets, goggles and mufflers, the two women explored the beautiful, flat countryside around Berlin on the motorcycle, which Leonie had paid for by selling her diamond solitaire. On one

Leonie Puttkamer and Carola Horn on their motorcycle

particularly dissolute night, she had almost handed the solitaire over to a barmaid, but Gisela had restrained her. Gisela, too, appreciated Berlin's women's bars.

Leonie's savings were disappearing quickly, however, and she started to accumulate debts. The love between Leonie and Carola was flourishing, and they spent many a steamy night together, but someone was going to have to pay the bills. If necessary, it would be a man. Gisela, who was many things in her capacity as lady's maid, but never a chaperone, received a detailed tally each morning—or so she recalled during interrogation two years later—of the number of times the lovers had had sex the previous night. With each account—the total was always in double digits—she was assured that that one had been "a good fuck."

But the lovers' erotic repertoire was apparently in need of expansion, and Gisela—taking her job title literally, though not in a conventional manner—arranged for some "companionship."

One day she returned to the hotel with a big pickle jar of water containing two rather bewildered looking small grey tench.

"Look what I got for us! My sister recommends it highly. Much in vogue with the ladies here in Berlin."

"Come on, tell us what those icky creatures are for," Carola urged.

"Ladies, please follow me to the bathroom," Gisela said, laughing so hard she had to be careful not to drop the jar.

Carola and Leonie followed, one bursting with curiosity, the other a bit reserved—after all, one really shouldn't be so chummy with the help.

Gisela filled the bidet with water, emptied the tench into it and watched them began to swim around more freely—little did they know it wouldn't last.

"My ladies, would you please undress."

By now Carola and Leonie understood. Giggling, blushing slightly and uttering mock protests, they undressed and listened as Gisela explained what to do: a tight grip on the gills, head under water, tail up, insert with caution. This was a new experience for the tench as well, which doubtless had no idea how much pleasure its struggle for survival was imparting.

When the initial protests turned to soft sighs, there was some pushing and shoving to be next in line. When the first fish grew exhausted and stopped thrashing its tail, the other provided new energy and new orgasms. (How, precisely, one puts a slippery fish to use as a predecessor of the modern vibrator shall forever remain a mystery.)

These and other pleasures of the ladies' wild life in Berlin in January and February 1923 were dulled only by Albert Gessmann's almost daily letters and telegrams from Vienna as he pulled out all the stops in his bit to convince Leonie to return. Reading these, Leonie usually let slip a few derogatory remarks then put them away in a drawer, but her lack of funds eventually moved her to give in.

At the beginning of March, a threesome left Berlin for Vienna. Instead of Susi Wanowski, this time Carola accompanied Leonie and Gisela. Their first stop was Munich, Carola's hometown, where they stayed for a few days before going on to Vienna, where Leonie quickly managed to get into debt and Albert refused to pay. There were rows because of Carola, and she and Leonie moved first to the Hotel Bristol and then back to Germany in mid April, when it was clear Leonie wasn't going to get what she's expected from her former husband.

The former spouses immediately began a voluminous correspondence, in which Leonie unambiguously informed Bertschi:

In my opinion you always have been and always will be a pathetic weakling. You are by nature dishonest and subservient, and in accordance, you excuse your beastliness toward me by lying to yourself. I regret every hour that I forced myself to spend in your disgusting, phony, petty bourgeois milieu. It was beneath me. In addition, your refined and "gentlemanly" attempts to ruin and blame me will lead nowhere, given that my personal style, even if arrogant and reserved, is more valued than your trite vulgarities, which will only redound on you.

For some things, be it keeping one's word or even effectively carrying out an act of skullduggery, one needs more breeding, class and wit than you ever had or ever will have… The 15 million that you still owe me is yours, together with my deepest contempt. Maybe you'll use it to support your faltering marmalade factory or that odious sauerkraut plant (which, by the way, I would chuck into the Danube along with your "authentic" Chippendale). I forbid you to harass me with further letters, since I'm happy to have escaped from your endless, tedious utterances, and since, for me, the curtain has fallen for good on this obnoxious and dishonest comedy. Mileonie.

Gisela Spira stayed behind in Vienna, in possession of a bundle of letters from Albert Gessmann to Leonie. Leonie later recalled that she had entrusted the letters to Gisela with a request to hand them over to Sidonie Csillag. Spira recalled that Leonie had advised her to publish the letters in order to make Bertschi seem laughable. Looking to make more money than working for Frau Puttkamer-Gessmann could provide, Gisela instead took the letters to Albert Gessmann and offered her services. To show his genuine gratitude, and of his own free will, he gave her 3 million crowns.

In May, Albert commissioned Gisela to go to Berlin to make enquiries about Leonie and ferret out additional slander for his "collection." She returned with tales of Leonie's alleged abnormal relations with her dog, which she had so overstimulated sexually that a veterinarian had to be called in to help.

During the summer Leonie and Carola had moved to Munich, where they lived on Kunigundenstrasse and frequently spent time on Tegernsee with Carola's mother. Albert commissioned Gisela to seek out Leonie there and negotiate her return to Vienna. Leonie came straight to the point: she would return to Vienna only if she got a lot of money in return.

And obviously, the money materialized. In mid March 1924, after their "reconciliation"—or should one say, after signing an agreement in Salzburg?—Baroness Puttkamer returned to Vienna and to Albert Gessmann.

THE END OF EVERYTHING

THE INTERROGATING AUTHORITIES ARE QUITE IMPRESSED WITH Albert Gessmann's revelations, and they continue to uncover many more details through intensive questioning, but there is little they want to or can do. Most of Leonie Puttkamer's "acts against nature" happened in Germany, where same-sex love between women is not criminalized; besides, Gessmann is a bigwig, and throwing his wife into an Austrian jail because of §129 I b might not be advantageous.

Therefore the regional court does what the Austrian bureaucracy has done since the old Imperial days: it bides its time. At this point, that means waiting for the results of the Frau Baronin's psychiatric assessment, and then they'll go from there.

On May 5 and 20, 1924, the two court-appointed medical examiners have two long talks with Leonie and then write a very long report, from which the following are excerpts:

Regarding the erratic nature of the accused's various psychological complexes, which one refers to scientifically as a psychopathic inferiority complex: these are revealed in particular in the considerable superficiality of her knowledge base and her sober, seemingly old fashioned and typically northern German decorum, which is barely masked by manners that are appropriate to her class background. By no means does she possess an "extraordinary mental gift" … that is rooted in reality. There

are no symptoms of pathological mendacity, as Herr Gessmann asserts
… She can be quick and even funny. Occasionally, she lets slip vulgar
slang expressions or commonplace sayings, surprising for someone in her
social position, making her seem vulgar and indicating that she must
have spent a lot of time in déclassé company and has already lost any
sense of womanly tenderness or never had it to begin with. The latter is
probably correct, since her female gender characteristics are physically
underdeveloped, and the "poised, bossy, headstrong, tolerates-no-dis-
sent demeanor," love of sports, heavy smoking, lack of desire to carry
out expressly female tasks, and "great agro-cultural technical knowledge" attested to by Herr Gessmann reveal a more masculine type,
which is also demonstrated in the form and content of her correspondence. Gessmann may have been suffering under a delusion, and like
many men he attributed more to the woman than she really has in her.

The uranian or the lesbian will have a particularly hard time with-
drawing from such a compulsion if the sex drive manifests especially
strongly at times and if the occasion presents itself and facilitates its use,
as was the case for the individual in question to a high degree in Gessmann's milieu. Since, as the husband, he tolerated her lesbian sexual activities, and since, even though he is an exceptionally intelligent man,
he didn't see or take into consideration the meaning and consequences
of this, then one can expect even less from this degenerate, morally unstable, weak willed and homosexual woman.

She is not insane, but her mental life is crucially disturbed, and
therefore she is unable to have a sense of culpability for her offenses.
Added to this is the fact that in Germany, in contrast to Austria, only
same-sex acts between men are crimes, not those between women, and
this must have additionally influenced a loosening of the restraints.

Determined to regain her freedom whatever the cost, Leonie is busy
preparing her counterattack. With the help of her attorney, she turns
the tables on Albert and accuses him of the same crimes he accused her
of—barring murder—and adds a few small details.

On May 31, 1924, Leonie Puttkamer-Gessmann files her complaint
at the regional court charging her husband with libel, blackmail, incite-
ment according to § 129 I b and deceiving the authorities. She also

requests an order to have Gessmann committed to a psychiatric ward. Numerous grounds for this request are cited.

Now needing to prove his own mental health, Gessmann consults one of the best-known authorities in the field. On June 17, 1924, a hand-written medical report attesting to Albert Gessmann's mental state is submitted to the court by psychiatrist and later Nobel Prize winner in medicine Professor Julius Wagner-Jaurgegg. And of course, nothing is found to be amiss with Bertschi.

A specific, particularly extensive consideration of Herr Präsident's sexual life has revealed that his views concerning sexual matters are rather liberal and that, perhaps in accordance with his virility, it is possible to call him hypersexual. But there are no indications that would prove that Herr Präsident Gessmann "himself" has any perverted sexual tendencies whatsoever. If he engaged in minor deviations from normal intercourse, he did so only in response to the explicit demands of his partners, who wanted to increase their sexual pleasure. Such matters cannot lead one to draw an adverse conclusion regarding Herr Präsident's mental health.

The whirl of activity over the past months finally ends in a stalemate. Even the authorities seem to have lost their appetite for further interrogations, concluding dryly: "Difficulties—because both husband and wife accuse each other of being mental ill, their statements must be taken with a grain of salt."

On July 5, 1924, Leonie is released from the Löwy sanatorium and returns to Pension Reiter in the Ninth District. By mid July she has decided to go to Achensee in the Tyrol for three to four weeks to recuperate beside a lake surrounded by beautiful forests. She has had no recent news from her faithful friend Sidi, who informed her at the beginning of July that she was going on summer holidays with her parents, maybe to St. Gilgen for a while and then, as always, to Brioni.

On July 30, 1924, while Leonie is in the Tyrol, Gessmann rescinds the bail he posted for her before having her committed to Löwy. After her return, Leonie will have to fend for herself if she's going to stay out of jail. She will offer two fur coats and a platinum wristwatch set with

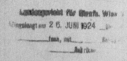

Landesgericht für Strafs. Wien
Eingelangt am 2 6. JUNI 1924

191

Aerztliches Gutachten!

Der Gefertigte hat am 17. Juni 1924 in einer längeren Unterredung Herrn Albert Gessmann, Präsidenten der öst. Landwirtestelle, über seinen Wunsch in Bezug auf seinen geistigen Zustand untersucht und kann feststellen, dass er nicht den mindesten Anhaltspunkt gefunden hat, der es rechtfertigen könnte, an der vollen geistigen Gesundheit des Herrn Präsidenten Gessmann zu zweifeln.

Eine specielle besonders eingehende Erörterung des Sexuallebens des Herrn Präsidenten hat ergeben, dass derselbe zwar in geschlechtlichen Dingen ziemlich liberalen Anschauungen huldigt und vielleicht seiner Potenz entsprechend, als hypersexuell bezeichnet werden kann; dass aber keinerlei Momente vorliegen, welche beweisen würden, dass Herr Präsident Gessmann "selbst" in irgend einer Richtung sexuell pervers veranlagt ist, sondern sich zu geringfügigen Abweichungen vom ganz normalen Vakter nur über Wunsch seiner Partnerinnen herbeigelassen hat, um deren sexuelles Empfinden zu steigern.

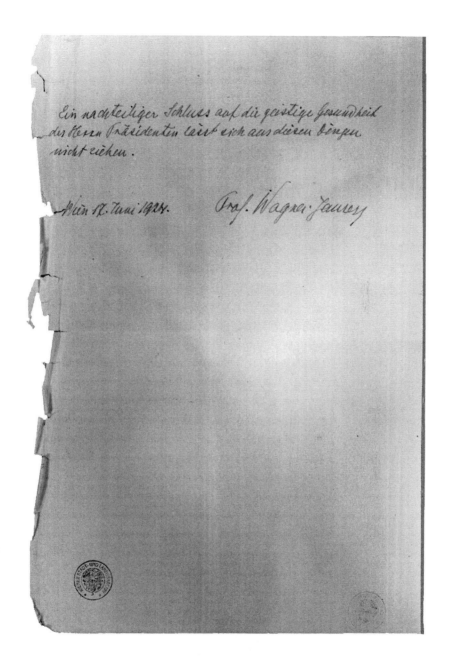

Expert opinion report from Professor Julius Wagner-Jauregg

brilliants as bond. The wristwatch will be accepted, but the police cannot guarantee that they will be able to prevent moths from getting into the fur, so the coats are rejected, and Leonie will have to come up with an additional 20 million crowns to buy her freedom.

THE TELEGRAM

"Request you cease all contact with my daughter. Antal Csillag."

Stunned, Leonie has already reread this one-line telegram several times. Returning to her pension from the Tyrol, where she had almost been able to put the recent past behind her, she had eagerly picked up her mail. And now she wants to cry, but tears don't come easily to the Prussian landed gentry. In all these years, stern old Csillag has never before addressed her personally or stopped his daughter from seeing her. Now he expresses his contempt for her by constraining his daughter and didn't even think Leonie is worth looking in the eye or talking to face to face. It's as if this scrap of paper has slapped her face.

The telegram was sent from Brioni, there is no doubt that it is genuine. Now Leonie does dab a handkerchief to her nose. She'd like to write Sidi a few lines, but Antal Csillag would surely be intercepting his daughter's mail. Best to consult her attorney. Maybe he can circumvent the father.

She can't lose her best friend and closest confidante who has been on her side all these years, no matter what, even when she was accused of a capital crime. Never before had she been loved so unconditionally.

Two days later she asks her attorney, Dr. Klemperer, to intercede and send a letter to Fräulein Csillag.

Dr. Klemperer reads the telegram several times before replying in his cultivated Viennese, "I don't know, Frau Baronin, if I were you, I'd keep my hands of that girl."

"But this was written by her father," Leonie protests. "I'm sure she wants to hear from me."

"That might well be. But you know, she is young and she should be given a chance in society. She should marry well. If she continues to be involved in this case, her reputation will be ruined. Look at it this way, Sidonie Csillag has been really very good to you all these years, why don't you oblige her and let things be."

Resigned and again close to tears, Leonie thinks the attorney may be right. Sidi had risked a lot for her, but maybe she'll manage to find a husband after all. Leonie can't really imagine what it will mean not to see Sidi again, but in the name of friendship she has to give her this chance.

At Brioni, the afternoon sun is bright and piercing and the blue-grey sky shimmers like stained glass. The recent sirocco brought some rain, so today is a bit cooler, and Sidi has retreated to the Saluga to sit in the shade of a big pine tree while everyone else is having a siesta. Finally alone, she can mull things over.

The past months, actually, the past three years have been exhausting. And the name for her tension, for the emotional flux has always been: Leonie. Because of the terrible court case, the baroness had desperately needed her help, and nothing could have kept her from providing it—within limits. But she is utterly drained now and needed Brioni in order to find some peace.

Is Leonie really the person Sidi has always considered her to be, or is she a worthless exploiter? She will never find the answer, and the uncertainty has triggered a merry-go-round of crazy thoughts. Since such questions aren't going to silence her heart, she will have to let reason prevail.

She has risked a lot for Leonie, planning the defense strategy with Klemperer and helping them through all those embarrassing interrogations. Her father had implored, had ordered her to answer only "yes" and "no" when questioned in order not to endanger her social position; and he had used all his connections to keep compromising information out of the press. She had disobeyed because she thought Gessmann's accusations were outrageous, but what came out in the course of the interrogations opened her eyes a bit more with respect to Leonie.

Sidi's first inkling that she was going to have problems in society came during the preparations for the wedding of one of her best friends, Countess Schallenberg. Sidi's inclusion among Christl's bridesmaids would once have gone without question, but the bride was being oddly hesitant, and gossip had it that Sidi's involvement with Puttkamer, particularly during the scandal, was the stumbling block.

Her best friend, Ellen Schoeller, now Baroness Ferstel, came to Sidi's rescue. Recently married, Ellen lived with her husband in Andritz near Graz and was expecting her first child. In a touching letter she wrote, "You are suffering quite a bit at the moment, why don't you come for a visit…?" Unsurprisingly, news of this invitation made its way to the other important families, and what was right for a Ferstel couldn't be wrong for a Schallenberg, so Sidi was invited to be a bridesmaid.

But clearly, she had to be more careful in the future.

For the longest time, she hadn't been able to articulate what she had hoped to gain from her relationship with Baroness Puttkamer, but now, if she's honest, she has to admit that she had wanted to have Leonie all to herself. She wanted to be loved by her, not have to watch her squander herself on disgusting men and women. She had been able to pretend for a while that because she was concerned only for Leonie's wellbeing, she was better, more noble than the others, the ones she had looked down on … such sleazy creatures. But in the long run, it hadn't been enough just to be the confidante while Leonie lived out her passions elsewhere.

After the baroness left for Berlin in December 1922, Sidi, desperate, once again seriously considered ending her life. During a dance performance, she stole a poison capsule from a friend. In those days, many people in her circle carried such capsules as a failsafe in case the communists took over. In her despair, she swallowed the capsule one night, but though she felt miserable and nauseated for several hours, death eluded her.

The baroness had stayed in Berlin for over a year that time, with only a short interval in Vienna, and each of her unselfconscious letters about how terrific Berlin was brought Sidi new pain. She burned them immediately and wrote stiff, forced chitchat in reply. She didn't bother to write that she had tried seeing men—just in order fill her days and also to give in to pressure from her father. She mentioned only in passing that a certain Klaus was courting her, and then penned a few words when he asked her father for her hand in marriage—the topic prompted no response from Leonie.

It wasn't until March 1923 that Sidonie had an opportunity to see the baroness again, however briefly. Leonie had arrived from Berlin with her new girlfriend, Carola Horn, who wasn't an actress and wasn't as bad as Berber, but her appearance and her behavior were not at all ladylike. After only six weeks, Leonie boarded the train for Berlin, and Sidi knew it would be a long time before she saw that beloved woman again.

She agreed to Klaus's proposal and mechanically endured the engagement preparations—the meetings with the dress maker, the plans for the honeymoon—but in her heart, she didn't really care. There was no longer any communication with Leonie. She felt indifferent to Klaus, though she didn't break off the engagement. She just went on living, feeling dull and very sad, and was sustained—or imprisoned?—by the daily routine with her parents and a few of her women friends. Slowly, she recovered. The days became brighter, she made plans, sometimes she even laughed, and there were moments when she enjoyed life again.

Then one morning in March 1924, Leonie phoned. Laughing excitedly, she announced that she had arrived in Vienna a few hours earlier in the company of Albert Gessmann, and despite everything, Sidi's heart leapt with joy. Maybe there was a chance to have Leonie in her life again? Would the joy quickly be replaced by disappointment? Would those sleazy women materialize again to exert their terrible influence?

That afternoon, holding Leonie in her arms, hearing her voice, looking at her again, Sidonie felt euphoric, felt once again that there really was a heart beating inside her body. There *would* be some kind of a future for the two of them.

And then, two weeks later, came the accusation of attempted murder, and the madness started.

A sharp wind off the sea startles Sidi out of her ruminations. The shadows beneath the pines have grown long, the sun is almost down, and she finds that she's surrounded by summer visitors, romping children, much splashing in the water. She hadn't noticed any of it. She gets up a bit stiffly, pulls a shawl around her shoulders and returns to her room to sit at the desk by the window. The wooden shutters let in only narrow strips of light as she writes the single sentence she will telegraph to Leonie tomorrow: "Request you cease all contact with my daughter. Antal Csillag."

It is August 4, 1924, and one phase of her life has come to an end.

On October 7, 1924, the Vienna public prosecutor's office will decide to end all criminal proceedings against Leonie Puttkamer-Gessmann due to lack of evidence. The baroness will have her bail money refunded, and there is nothing to keep her in Vienna. With 50 million crowns in her pocket, she packs everything, leaves Vienna for good and returns to Germany. For her, too, a phase of her life has come to an end.

The charges the Gessmanns lodged against one another in civil court remain active well into 1925. Neither the court files nor the media reveal the outcome of those proceedings. The baroness had left Vienna, and the delicious scandals that fueled so much vicious society gossip left with her.

5

WAY STATIONS: 1922–26

THE HANDSOME, DARK GREEN ROADSTER HUMS ALONG REASSURingly despite the murderous heat. What a blessing that young Georg Strakosch had put the car's top down and one could enjoy a bit of breeze. He'd come close to insisting on leaving it closed for fear of the considerable fuss Strakosch pére would raise should the family's sacred cow be damaged—or even if the red leather seats got dusty. In the front seat, Sidonie's elder brother Heinrich is telling another one of his pompous jokes. Strakosch gives a short laugh—his left hand barely touches the steering wheel, his right nonchalantly holds a cigarette, both are encased in pigskin driving gloves. The fellow's a bit too brash, Sidonie thinks, leaning her head out the window to catch the breeze. Georg's younger brother, Hans-Friedrich, dozes between her and Hans, the elder son of the Wunsch family, who intermittently gives terse directions to his family's cottage on the shore of Lake Wörthersee outside the village of Velden.

Sidonie hadn't wanted to make this trip, but Heinrich has been close to the Strakosch family since his years at the Gymnasium in Wasagasse, and as she had been included in the invitation, he almost forced her to accept. "Better than hanging out all grumpy in Vienna," he kept saying. Yesterday afternoon, after a long train journey, the Strakoschs had served them a welcoming repast of homemade blackcurrant juice and a

Sidonie Csillag, 1922

delicious apricot cake, served on the veranda of their pretty villa just off the Velden Promenade—the rather grandiose name of the narrow road through the village.

It's summer 1922 and today was already steaming hot when Sidonie woke up. She hates to sweat and not feel fresh, especially early in the morning, when tortured thoughts of Leonie threaten to overwhelm her, and all she wants is to pull the blanket over her head and not wake up at all. Not in the best of moods, she had put on the roomiest linen dress she could find and shoved a straw hat on her head. She doesn't know Heinrich's friends very well, and she's not at all inclined to make conversation.

She had gone downstairs to find the breakfast table already nearly cleared, but she had no appetite anyway and all she wanted was to feel the morning breeze on her skin and avoid seeing anyone.

Ten minutes later, Heinrich popped around the corner shouting, "Come on, Sidi, let's go, let's go. We're off for a swim!" In the group of young men behind him she recognized the two Wunsch sons, who were also at Wörthersee every summer. Father had some business connection with their father, Hans Wunsch, the director of the Floridsdorf oil factory. She'd been introduced to the boys at a luncheon—and promptly forgot them.

Grumbling, she had packed her beach bag and climbed into one of the two cars idling by the driveway where her brother groused, "You always take ages to get ready," and Georg Strakosch and one of the Wunsch boys grinned stupidly.

Prone on the jetty, Fritz Dietz von Weidenberg squints into the harsh light glinting off the almost-still lake and contemplates the southern shore, where forested hills front the glorious panorama of the Karawanken Mountains.

The jetty's wooden planks are burning his back, and his black tricot smells as if it had just been pressed with a red-hot iron. He slides into the water.

When he returns to the jetty, there are the new arrivals from Vienna. His best friend, Klaus Bäckström, told him about them yesterday— the young Csillags, supposed to be nice, and one of them is a girl; there's a shortage of those here, unless one counts his sister Sylvie, who is already married.

He watches the tall, slender young woman standing three or four meters away. "My God, what a beauty!" One forearm is propped, as if casually, on her hip, the other rests along the back of her neck, where her long, dark hair is gathered into a knot. She shifts her weight onto one leg and the artful tilt of her hips accentuates her small waist. She knows how to have an effect, and nothing in this tableau has been left to chance. Fritz knows women too well not to be aware of this.

When she looks at him, her gaze lingers for just an instant too long, very serious, very dark. Fritz senses in her a wistfulness or sorrow that makes her seem almost eerie and raises the small hairs on his arms. This is not a woman for a light-hearted flirtation.

"Come on, Fritzl, don't stare yourself blind." A wet hand lands on Fritz's shoulder and two bony knees and a mop of white-blond hair materialize in his line of sight. Lofty Klaus Bäckström, who looks like some Nordic giant, has lowered himself into a crouch beside Fritz, a

Sidonie Csillag at the shore

mocking smile on his face. "You like her, don't you? But it's my turn. Don't even think of getting in my way."

Jumping to his feet, Klaus heads towards Sidonie and will introduce himself with a slightly crooked bow. Only later, during lunch, will Sidonie and Fritz be officially introduced to one another.

The Dietz von Weidenberg siblings, Fritz and Sylvie, are the Wunsch brothers' cousins, and like them come from Floridsdorf. Their father is an architect who has designed quite a few buildings in Vienna, primarily the homes and factories of the Mautner family, whose products are known to every child in Vienna. Fritz is a few months younger than Sidi and is said to be studying something or other. She hasn't found out what, but he seems to be rather easy going, quite in contrast to Sylvie, who is three years younger. Sylvie has just started taking a photography course at the graphic institute in Vienna, and Sidi catches herself thinking that's a fairly unusual step for a girl from the better circles. Maybe the siblings are not from one of the finest families, but they are so nice that they have already won her heart. She wants friends like this.

The weeks fly by in a blur of swimming, tennis and hiking with these new friends, and Sidi's melancholy seems to have flown. Whenever she sees Fritz, her heart makes a tiny leap, and she has to admit to herself that she has fallen in love. To make a special occasion of the night before they must all go their separate ways, the group decides to have a nice dinner together and then visit the only dance club on the Velden Promenade, which is open on Saturday nights for the "better" guests.

They arrive at the club rather late and already quite merry after having consumed a few bottles of a fine Rhine Riesling. The Strakoschs haven't exaggerated; this really is one of the nicest places in the village. Tall glass doors open onto a terrace directly above the lake. Colorful Chinese lanterns illuminate the deck chairs and comfortable wicker chairs that ring the dance floor and invite the guests to sit, to observe, to drink. Sidi feels Klaus garb her arm and pull her onto the crowded dance floor, where he attempts to waltz with her without causing serious collisions. She hadn't dared to turn him down, but would have much preferred to dance with Fritz, or just to be in his arms, dancing or not. After the waltz, there's a foxtrot, then a shimmy, and still it's Klaus.

Dizzy, she heads for a chair to wait for Klaus to bring the cocktail she will sip with a gracious smile.

Fritz is dancing with an extremely attractive older woman he obviously picked up at the bar. He's an idiot! He approaches her only once, beaming and leading her into a slow foxtrot as if nothing were amiss. He does not hold her as closely as Klaus did, and when she snuggles up to him, he corrects her position with the very next turn. Confused, her mood sinks to rock bottom and deep inside there's an almost imperceptible pain. A little later, she is standing on the terrace and staring into the lake when Sylvie comes up and links arms with her.

"You like him, eh?"

Sidi gives a barely visible nod.

"We'll do something about it, don't worry. I'd be very glad if you could come to see us in Vienna soon. What do you think?" Sylvie laughs in such a kind way that Sidi finds herself close to tears.

Late that night, as they are saying their good-byes in the street, Fritz puts his arms around her, briefly, lightly, and kisses her on the cheek.

Klaus Bäckström at Wörthersee

"See you soon," he says, and Sidi answers inwardly, "Oh yes, please, see you very, very soon." She has taken his words at face value and, as ever, rejoices prematurely.

The next day the Csillag siblings will go to Brioni, where their parents await them; Klaus is off to the Baltic States to visit relatives; the Dietz brothers return to Vienna. The brothers Wunsch and Strakosch will stay until called back to their duties in another fortnight.

Back in Vienna from Brioni, daily life engulfs Sidi once again. It is only the beginning of September, but clouds veil the sky and the weather has turned cold and wet. The outlook for the coming months doesn't seem promising. Leonie is still the leitmotif of life in Vienna and that causes constant unhappiness. She has no idea how to escape that. True, Leonie has finally separated from her unpleasant husband, but it is general knowledge that there is nothing better on the horizon.

On top of this, for months Father has been urging her not to stay at home doing nothing. Doesn't she want to choose a career? She's talented, she graduated with very good marks. If she can't manage to find a husband and doesn't want to work, she should at least learn something useful, stenography or cooking or whatever, something that could come in handy in the future.

He wouldn't want to hear her say that she has no interest at all in having a career. But after Wörthersee, she finally has something to tell him that might placate him and grant her some peace and quiet for a while.

Shortly after her return, when he is sitting in his massive leather armchair distractedly flipping through the daily paper, she sits down to tell him how nice Wörthersee had been—the wonderful hosts, their two charming sons, the many new friends, the outings to the countryside! They had even gone hiking and proven themselves to be quite athletic! This latter detail will earn her extra points with her nature- and sports-obsessed father.

"Just imagine who I got to know there, Papa—young Klaus Bäckström!" From somewhere in the back of her brain she has managed to pull the information that this name has some business connection with her father—not that most of the young men around her aren't knotted together in one or another way through their fathers. That is how it is in their circles.

"Oh yes, Bäckström. Indeed, I know the father well—done some work together more than once. He's a director with Alpine Montan, a real gentleman. Also saw the young one once—seems to take after the father. That's lovely, Sidilein, really lovely…"

Whenever her father calls her by her pet name, when his words are wrapped more thickly than usual in his Hungarian accent, Sidonie can be sure that he is pleased with her and is about to soften.

"Please, Sidilein, turn on the gramophone and let me hear the Vivaldi."

This is the signal that the hostilities and, simultaneously, the conversation are over and he will shake open the newspaper and, feeling reassured, disappear behind the business section.

All she has to do is feed him more stories about men now and then, and the grip of his displeasure will surely loosen a bit.

HOW THE YOUNG REPUBLIC IS COPING

As a matter of fact, Antal Csillag really does have other things on his mind these days.

Throughout the turbulent years of political change he'd been concerned for his family's safety, but now the fear of yet another political turnaround has diminished. Surprising how the young republic is coping. The borders are stable and so are the governments in the various states of the former Austro-Hungarian monarchy. Not that everything is quite the way industrial giants such as Csillag and those who pull political strings would like it, but under the newly created conditions, it's not yet possible to make changes.

The propertied classes have already adapted, and in truth, things aren't going at all badly. Even before the war they had known that they couldn't trust the nationalist movements among the Italians and in Bohemia—the word Czechoslovakia would never cross their lips. But was this a reason to give up the sugar refineries in Bohemia, to sell the oil and bitumen wells in Poland or to drop a deal with a business partner in Trieste? Hardly. Political events might shake up the old business and family ties a bit, but in the end, it is in everybody's interest to limit the losses and either minimize unwelcome political leverage, mainly from the left, or, perforce, accept it.

Antal Csillag has managed to hold on to his shares in the various companies he founded. The Galician mineral oil industry was now Polish, and the Polish state preferred to find its business partners in the West, so those interests were transferred to banks in Belgium and France. Csillag has recently bought a bitumen processing factory outside Paris because he'd been made to feel a bit insecure about his various market speculations, both by Austria's galloping inflation and by the

March 1919 decree that all one's stocks, shares, jewelry and savings accounts had to be reported. So why not invest in a factory? After his brother-in-law Victor, Emma's brother, was killed in the war in 1916, there was really no one left in Poland who he could trust with the bitumen processing there; and anyway, he preferred to locate the factory in a country to which he plans to send one of his sons. He still does some of his business through Austrian banks but generally relies on a Dutch bank that knows how to adjust matters to his personal expectations in an extremely satisfying way. In the long run, the Austrian banking situation is much too unstable.

In 1914, the eight largest of Vienna's 500 banking establishments held more than two thirds of Austria-Hungary's total available capital. The 1914 market value of Credit Anstalt was 60 million US dollars; in 1920 it was 2.4 million. This astonishing decline made Austria a paradise for international speculators who could invest a small sum and own a whole bank. The financial instability also seduced many into founding their own bank, and by spring 1924—at the time of the currency reform—Austria hosted some 1500 banking companies.

Despite having cleverly spread his interests all across Europe, as a patriot Antal Csillag has, of course, also invested in Austria. And haven't his business partners Camillo Castiglioni, Paul Goldstein, Friedrich Wagenmann, Philipp Broch and Adolf Popper-Artberg done so as well? From a political perspective, none of these men thinks much of the way the new republic is structured, but from a business perspective, they're still in good shape. Production and consumption go on, they continue to grow their fortunes and live their privileged lives.

Only one thing troubles Antal Csillag's thoughts in such quiet evening hours, the increasing number of demonstrations against Jews. Almost every week thousands of people from the nationalist movements march around the Ring carrying anti-Semitic banners. Probably one had to acknowledge this—just not take the trouble to ignore it, to put it the Viennese way. This, too, would pass, once the economic situation stabilized at last.

Still, just this summer on a hiking trip to the Salzkammergut it had left a sour taste in his mouth when he discovered that the Alpenverein (Alpinists' Union) and the Austrian Tourist Club had started to apply an

Aryan clause that banned Jews from using the groups' cabins. Csillag was an avid mountain climber who routinely read the Alpenverein's magazine, which now bragged that places such as Windischgarsten in Upper Austria and Mattsee in Salzburg province had turned away Jews who wanted to stay there on holiday. Csillag wonders bitterly how the wretched riffraff think they're going to recognize them. Well then, he'll take his money elsewhere.

What a blessing that this will not afflict his children. Their Catholic baptism has freed them of that irksome stigma and all its attendant inconveniences. He is rather glad his children aren't really interested in politics. Since the end of the monarchy, the high bourgeoisie had been playing in a significantly smaller political arena, and it would be better for his children if they kept out of party politics. It does worry him that Sidi remains totally indifferent to the idea of a professional education. Of course, a woman of her class would not have to work, but Antal Csillag is not sure that's how things will always be, whether from a political or a personal perspective. Sidi has shown no interest in men at all, so where is an affluent husband supposed to come from? Perhaps her stay at Wörthersee has awakened something ... one should never give up hope.

Soon after her talk with her father, Sidonie receives an unexpected call from Sylvie Dietz, who invites her for tea at her parents' home the following Saturday. Fritz will be there. Sidi is touched that her new friend has been true to her word.

This good news adds some zest to the monotony of Sidi's daily life, which is interrupted only by visits to Leonie, who is staying at her cocotte's flat in Gusshausstrasse. Sidi is sorely in need of something to counterbalance Leonie and all the pain and futility associated with her, and she daydreams about how pleased Fritz will be, how they might even get to spend some time alone. Maybe, for a change, reality is going to be an improvement on fantasy.

Sidonie dresses with care on Saturday—a brightly colored wool suit, a smart little black hat, some perfume, powder, gloves, and off she goes. She barely arrives on time because, and this is the worm in the apple vis-à-vis the Dietz siblings, they live at the end of the world. In

Floridsdorf! Not only is it a rather unrefined neighborhood, Sidonie has never before set foot in it, but getting there takes more than an hour and several transfers. When the number 31 tram finally saunters across the Floridsdorfer Bridge, she lets her excitement build. It has been more than a month since she last saw Fritz.

She gets off at "Am Spitz" across from the Dietz family's pretty, sprawling, old house. Just two stories tall, its yellow façade and green shutters prove that generations of Viennese homeowners learned a thing or two from examining Schloss Schönbrunn.

Since nobody responds when she rings, Sidonie enters the courtyard and looks around shyly. To the left are old stables, now apparently storage for everything no longer of any use in the house. Next to it a staircase leads to a second-floor balcony with beautiful Jugendstil glazing at the corners. The surrounding evergreens host noisy sparrows, but otherwise it is quiet. Sidonie has just decided to climb the stairs when the door suddenly flies open and a radiant Sylvie emerges to take her into her arms. Behind her is an older man with sparkling eyes and a big white moustache, and behind him an elegant, delicate and apparently rather shy woman—obviously Silvie's parents.

"Ah, young Miss Csillag, it's my pleasure." Herr Dietz bows and kisses her hand. Given their age and class difference, Sidi responds with a blush. "The most beautiful lady in a bathing costume in all of Wörthersee, I've been told—and, I must say, not only in a bathing costume."

Sidi can't stop blushing, and now she knows where Fritz got his charm.

She is led down a frightening hall where stuffed wood grouses and dozens of stags' heads stare down from the walls—sad witness to her host's passion for the hunt—to the living room, where a sumptuous meal awaits.

Herr Dietz talks about his work as an architect, talks about the latest plays at the Ronacher, where he has a permanent subscription to a box, goes on to talk about duck hunting and the horses he once owned and used to ride along the flood plains of the Danube, the nearby Donau-Auen. Now, things are getting built everywhere, all the wetlands are being drained—but that's because of people just like him! And he roars with laughter. These days, he goes hunting in Hungary and takes the train there every weekend, much to the delight of his wife and daughter, he says mischievously.

Fritz has not shown up, and Sidi doesn't dare ask about him. Sylvie seems to have noticed that she is looking distracted and whispers to her while serving the next round of cakes that Fritz has called to make his excuses, one of his acquaintances is not doing well. He'll get in touch with Sidi.

Her heart plummets. She swallows, stares out the windows at the passing clouds and doesn't hear the next few sentences. Then she clears her throat and with the utmost self-discipline attends once again to the elder Fritz's jokes and the solicitude of his wife and daughter.

After the minimum amount of time has passed that is proper to an afternoon visit, Sidonie begins to take her leave, apologizing for her quick departure and saying that her mother has a cold and she must stop at the pharmacy. Poised stiffly in the doorway, she even forgets to invite Sylvie to visit her in turn. Sylvie sweetly assures her that she'll be welcome again and adds that she plans to box her irresponsible brother's ears. In any case, they'll see one another next weekend in Katzelsdorf, where the Weinbergers are giving a tea dance. Sidi knows nothing about this but says "yes, yes" mechanically and shakes hands all around, then escapes the scene of her defeat. Back on the number 31 tram, she sheds a few tears and lets the by now familiar blue-grey veils engulf her soul again.

The Weinberger abode in Katzelsdorf near Wiener Neustadt is more than just a house, it's a country estate. This isn't Sidonie's first visit, but every time she turns into the driveway—without a car, the place is difficult to reach—she is impressed all over again. Broad, raked-gravel paths bordered by lilacs and standard roses lead to a status-conscious entry capped by an overlarge family coat of arms in sandstone and flanked by Ionic columns. The big, asymmetric structure boasts a semicircular veranda off of which an arcade leads to a romantic stone bench. From the courtyard, curved stairs lead down to a gigantic garden with a tennis court. Above the main entrance, the terrace doors stand open and the Roman blinds sway a bit in the light afternoon breeze—an indication that this is a particularly warm fall day.

The Weinberger's country estate at Katzelsdorf, near Wiener Neustadt

This is where the tea dance is to take place. Fritz will be present, and despite a yearning anticipation, Sidonie doesn't know if she should look forward to it or be afraid of it. She clambers out of the car after Heinrich, her brother and chaperone, and goes to the reception line where she hugs Grete Weinberger and curtsies to her mother, Muni, who looks so very much like Grete. Papsl, the grim-looking father who always has a half-smoked cigarette in his mouth but is actually quite good natured, is not interested in this adolescent stuff and is nowhere to be seen.

Everyone else has already arrived. Punch glasses in hand, the guests stand about in the parlor or on the veranda or stroll about on the terrace and in the garden. The Wunsch boys are there, the Schallenbergs, the extremely handsome Egon Jordan, a superb bridge player who is starting an acting career and is not interested in women—a fact Sidonie can definitely appreciate. Grete Weinberger's husband Willy is there, talking animatedly with Sylvie Dietz's husband, and over there, leaning against the balustrade, are the Dietz siblings. Sylvie greets Sidi with a kiss on each cheek, while Fritz, to her regret, only shakes her hand and smiles at her mischievously. His shiny hair is brushed back with pomade, and his double-breasted summer suit looks rumpled, but somehow without seeming sloppy.

Sidi smiles insecurely and soon goes to the buffet, hoping distance will rescue her. To her embarrassment, she has overlooked Klaus, who was standing not far from Fritz.

A few hours later, Sidonie has fixed her burning gaze on the dance floor, where Fritz is waltzing with her friend Grete. Only two more hours until midnight, and Fritz has asked her to dance only once. He held her rather stiffly and not as close as he is holding Grete. Encouraged by alcohol, she has been casting overt glances at him all evening, but he pretended not to notice. Klaus is approaching her again, and she can't think of another excuse to refuse to dance with him. She follows him sullenly to the dance floor, thinking maybe she should change tactics and behave as if she were in love with Klaus; maybe then Fritz would pay more attention to her.

She positively clings to young Bäckström. He's not all that bad looking, if only he weren't so serious and stiff. He can hardly think of anything to say, and their conversation is stilted, but he pulls her close and holds her tightly for a slow waltz. She has drunk enough to feel fine, but she is bothered by the hard object in his pants pocket.

"Tell me, do you carry a key in your pocket?"

This Klaus denies vehemently.

"But there is something hard in your pocket; it is unpleasant while dancing," she insists.

Only when the young man turns beet red, abandons the dance early and almost runs away, does she realize that she has said something wrong. She commits an even worse faux pas when her favorite song, Little Japanese Man, begins and she spontaneously goes up to Fritz and asks him to dance. The fruit in the punch has absorbed a lot of strong alcohol, which helps them both get over the accompanying tension, and the next dances are theirs. Sidi's new tactic, combined with her—unintentional—indiscretion, seems to have had the desired effect. Fritz is funny, charming and very attentive. Klaus is completely forgotten.

It's no surprise that rumors have been flying behind her back. During a break, while Sidi, exhausted, sweating and happy, stands on the sidelines, Grete approaches and asks, "Is it true what everyone is saying, you tried to finesse the cards on the dance floor?" (In bridge, a finesse can be the soul of the game: the Jack is led, the Queen takes a trick, but only in order to acquire the King or the Ace.)

Playing the giggling naïve, Sidi babbles, "What do you mean? I'm just amusing myself; you should be happy about that." And her eyes search the room for her most recent dance partner.

Sidi really is an innocent. She has had no experience flirting with young men, hasn't gotten any sex education at home, and the little she knows is theoretical and came from reading *The Memoirs of Josephine Mutzenbacher* to Leonie. To date, she has never even been interested in young men. She finds Heinrich's friends too childish; the brothers of her school friends didn't interest her; and her father's business partners are too old and ugly—nothing there for a woman in love with beauty.

Fritz Dietz (with pipe) and Christl Schallenberg

Occasionally she has risked a glance at one man or another while on summer vacation, but her mother's sharp, admonitory glance always signaled, "Hands off, *I* want him."

With Fritz, things are different. He amuses her a great deal, and deep inside she is suddenly full or mirth and has no defense against it. Her seriousness and melancholy are gone, her blasé attitude and arrogance have vanished. He's good for her; she wants him. But this is not mutual because—and this is something Sidonie doesn't know—her encounters with Fritz und Klaus have been part of a pre-arranged game. Despite his youth, Fritz has had plenty of experience with women and has gone through all the initiation rituals typical for young men of his class and generation. He knows the bars in the red-light district, and he has learned a lot in the arms of the high-class prostitutes on Kärntnerstrasse. He enjoys putting this knowledge into practice, but it certainly wouldn't do with Sidonie.

He has, of course, noticed the signs of puppy love, the dark glances from beneath her lashes, her soft, supple moves while dancing. He is flattered that this beautiful woman is letting him know her intentions … but a relationship with her? Good heavens, no! Too much work, too many restrictions and too much dependence.

Weeks later, Muni Weinberger, who enjoys being Sidi's confidante because it makes her feel young again herself, pulls Fritz aside and asks, "Tell me, why don't you have an affair with Sidi?" To which he replies, "With Sidi? Never! With the others yes, but not with her. She is such an aesthete, and there are no aesthetics in bed."

Soon after their first encounter at Wörthersee, Fritz had thought Sidi might suit Klaus, whose soulful glances and air of romantic sadness couldn't be overlooked. So, over beers at a bar back in Vienna, the two quite dissimilar friends had discussed who was going to have her. In the beginning, Klaus feared that, once again, Fritz was going to thwart his intentions with the usual easy-going charm that he himself lacked and wished he had, because then it would be so much easier to win women over. His resentment made Klaus both aggressive and insecure, but then Fritz smiled, put a hand on his shoulder, and said, "I don't want her, my friend. Such romantic follies are not for me. She is all yours. And … be careful you don't get hurt. You know the rumors about her."

The gossip had been going around Vienna for years that Sidi Csillag had a noticeable penchant for women, but the two young men, so self-confident, were sure this usually didn't last with women. She just needed the right man, and surely that was Klaus. Out on the street, a euphoric Klaus hugged his friend again and again, danced around him and gave him a good slap on the back. Extricating himself, Fritz sent the blond dreamer home to bed to dream on.

THE PROSPECT OF MARRIAGE 1

SIDI BEGINS TO FEEL THE EFFECTS OF THIS DEAL SOON AFTER THE TEA dance, which lasted late into the night, and she had left feeling happy and full of hope. But Fritz doesn't get in touch, and her one or two cautious attempts to run into him via Sylvie prove futile. Her pride forbids any further chase, and she hides her love and sorrow behind a stiff and silent façade. To make everything worse, her beautiful baroness has now left Vienna "for good" and gone to Berlin.

With the launch of the 1923 ball season, Klaus finds many opportunities to meet with Sidi and show her how attractive he finds her, how much he likes her. She endures this, and Klaus reads her forced, absent-minded smile as a sign that he hasn't been rejected.

One February evening, Klaus escorts Sidi home in a cab after a masquerade ball in Palais Auersperg. He hadn't been able to keep his hands off her all evening, and sitting next to him in the back seat, she feels his hot breath beside her ear and the occasional soft touch of his lips. Outside the entrance to her building, next to a tall mound of snow, he wraps his arms around her, presses her tightly to him, and—just a few weeks before her twenty-third birthday– Sidonie Csillag is kissed by a man for the first time. It is an experience from which she will never recover; and even well into old age she can still recall, with a cringe, his tongue in her mouth, his hot, labored breathing and those intrusive hands moving beneath her coat from her waist to her breasts.

Standing there in the snow, what she feels is disgust—this is bestial— and she quickly turns her face and body away and pushes Klaus away.

Flabbergasted, embarrassed, hurt, he mumbles an apology, presses a swift good-bye kiss on her hand and consoles himself with the thought that she needs time … things will work out.

They never will.

Sidonie can't get this episode out of her mind, and it confuses her. Is this how it is between men and women—the men excited, eager and demanding, while the women just apathetically accept it? Maybe this is nature's way, and it's quite normal that women do not enjoy men. Or is she not normal? Playing doctor with both her elder and younger brother many years ago comes to mind. They were keen to see her naked and to touch her between her legs, but she was unimpressed by it all and by the bit of meat between their legs. Those episodes had made her uneasy and ashamed, and all she wanted was to get dressed again quickly. She envied the animals that at least had fur to hide their nakedness and any evidence of lust.

Sidi has always only experienced deep feelings for women, but she's never felt a desire to be undressed by them or have them cover her with wet kisses or touch her body. If anything, she likes it the other way around.

Why have her girlfriends never said a word, never warned her about how terrible it is with men? They'd just giggle and cackle, wiggle their butts and behave as if they knew all about it. By now all of them have gotten married or are engaged. Ellen has married Paul Ferstel; Christl Schallenberg will be next. Sylvie Dietz married Rudi Mumb when still really young, just eighteen. Sidi doesn't like Rudi Mumb, who is not from Sylvie's social class and whose numerous affairs are known to everyone but Sylvie. Grete Weinberger is married to a man everybody says has affairs with men, which doesn't seem to put a damper on Grete carrying on her own affairs. Only Christl Kmunke doesn't seem to have been infected with the marriage virus. Maybe Sidi should ask her why, but she doesn't really need to bother; the answer is in the longing she sees in the mischievous glances Christl sends her way.

Maybe men and women share some secret that everyone else in her circle is privy to—a secret so powerful that it has become a pact around which everyone arranges their lives. It must be normal to live according to this pact, and it must be normal that it is no fun. So she should just accept it and forget about her dreams.

Given Sidi's mood, Klaus's solicitations fall on prepared but barren ground. Then one day he asks if she might not want to marry him, and she shrugs, smiles cryptically and answers coquettishly, "Why not?" Klaus doesn't know that the price she's paid for such casual ease has been deep sadness and great pain. Her true loves have slipped through her fingers. Leonie loves other women and took off for Berlin overnight because of them. Fritz is also having fun with other women, and he avoids her. They are inaccessible, there is nothing left for her, so why not Klaus? He is gentle, good-natured and crazy about her; he will do whatever she tells him to do. If one day a beautiful woman touches her heart—she is hoping and praying for this because it would mean an end to her boring everyday life—that's a pill he will just have to swallow. From Leonie she has learned how easily a social façade can hide a life tailored to suit one's own desires.

Klaus also brings one big advantage: he is a good match, and her parents will be more than welcoming. Marriage would mean the end of their nagging, and she'd be out from under their control.

Well then, let it be Klaus.

When Sidonie announces to her parents early one afternoon in the late spring of 1923 that Klaus Bäckström is going to ask for her hand in marriage, they are overjoyed and want all the details. In a few words, Sidi says that as Father already knows, he comes from a good family. He is going to finish his studies soon; he can expect a promising, well-paid position in a bank, thanks to his father's connections; she has met him frequently over the past months and his behavior has been impeccable and attentive; he is very much in love with her. It would be best to delay the wedding until after he graduates, but one could at least start the preparations.

The prospect of having Klaus Bäckström as their future son-in-law exceeds Sidi's parents' wildest dreams. They would also have been pleased if Sidi had been courted by one of the Wunsch sons, because their father was Antal Csillag's close business associate. Fritz Dietz would also have been a welcome son-in-law, though his family was rumored to be heading downhill because Dietz senior was busy enjoying life and living beyond his means. But money isn't a deciding factor; the most important thing about Sidi's marriage is simply that it take place. They suggest inviting the young man for tea the following week. Sidi should call him right away and set a date.

When Klaus arrives at the Csillags a few days later, the flat seems to positively vibrate with happy anticipation. There are beautiful flower arrangements everywhere; Sidi's brothers all wear their best suits and perhaps look more elegant than the future groom; her parents greet Klaus almost as if he were already a family member.

The formal request for Sidi's hand is over in a matter of seconds, and Sidi's parents ask Klaus no additional questions. Klaus has fulfilled his dream … his great love, the beautiful Sidonie Csillag from a wealthy, reputable family, will be his wife—till death do they part.

In their conjugal bed that evening, Antal and Emma Csillag—each quite satisfied with the afternoon's events—exchange more than a few sentences for the first time in years. Klaus strikes them as a serious sort, and obviously he is in love with Sidonie. But it is Klaus's father who carries the most weight with Antal. Heinrich Bäckström served as the technical director of the Alpine Montangesellschaft for many years and became its director after the early death of Oskar Rothballer. The Alpine Montangesellschaft has since become one of Austria's most important industries, maybe even the most important, and its influence extends far beyond the country's borders. This guarantees a secure future, one in which their daughter will continue to be able lead a life of luxury. Is she happy and does she love him? Well, appetite comes with the eating, old Csillag thinks as he turns out the light.

In the Bäckströms' world, too, everything is pure bliss when Klaus reveals his marriage plans. He is their only child, much loved and pampered. His parents know that his sensitive, rather too-serious nature has made it a bit difficult for him to make friends. An adoring wife could look after his tender soul. That she is Jewish and there have been rumors about her in society—so what. The Bäckströms are liberal-minded, and a daughter-in-law—even a Jewish one—will be welcome in their house as long as their only child is happy with her.

It's a foregone conclusion that the official meeting of all four parents at the Csillag's home will be a success. Similarly dressed in morning suits and each with a glass of Port in hand, the fathers lean against the fireplace mantle and talk about their shared business interests—they have found common ground. The mothers occupy opposite ends of a settee and nip at their coffee, showing off their rings and gold and platinum bracelets. They talk excitedly about the guest list, wedding dress styles and arrangements for the wedding banquet. On the opposite settee, Klaus and Sidonie sit holding hands, silent pawns in the chess game of marriage politics in Viennese society.

Antal Csillag and Heinrich Bäckström discuss the latest hot topic at the Vienna stock exchange: the speculation in French Francs. Because that currency is weak and getting weaker every day, almost all Austrian investors were gambling with Francs. One of Antal's close business partners is Kommerzialrat Paul Goldstein, president of the Depositenbank, which is heavily involved in such speculation, and he has convinced Csillag to invest part of his fortune in Francs. Heinrich Bäckström has also speculated a bit, and both are now wondering when they can reap the profits.

They will wait in vain. Within a year, Vienna's Creditanstalt and Bodencreditanstalt will sell off their Francs because they receive timely information that J. P. Morgan & Company in the United States plans to support the Franc. But the Depositenbank is not informed in time and on May 5, 1924, will have to close due to heavy losses.

After the end of the Franc speculations many stocks are cashed out abroad and returned to Austria: from the beginning of March to the end of July 1924, almost 30 percent of the foreign currency holdings in the Austrian national bank flowed out of the country. This was the beginning of the First Austrian Republic's big stock market crash, and between 1924 and 1926, 37 joint equity banks and 136 private banks were dissolved, stock prices plummeted and the market grew insecure. Gentlemen like Csillag and Bäckström lost a great deal of money.

And so, beginning in the fall of 1924, the Csillags will have to look after their money a bit more carefully, and the wedding might not be as opulent as the vain Emma Csillag is envisioning.

But the outlook still seems blissful when the engagement is announced. A small but elegant reception at Bäckström's allows Viennese

Depositenbank, corner of Schottengasse and Teinfalt-strasse, Vienna I

society to digest the news and congratulate the bride and groom. Sidi looks lovely, and Klaus is elegant, stiffly formal and happy. Sidi likes him as a friend—almost like a brother—but she wonders how she is going to endure being married to him. So soon after the engagement, however, she has little time to think about her future alongside a man.

In March 1924, Leonie returns to Vienna—unexpectedly and in the midst of the wedding planning. The ensuing scandal and police investigations consume most of Sidonie's energy and almost cost her her position in society. The whole episode reopens the barely healed wound in Sidonie's heart, and the pain of not being wanted returns, together with a deep longing to have a fulfilling love life. These feelings have names, they are called Leonie and Fritz, and Sidi is growing increasingly aware that she cannot marry Klaus.

By October 1924 the wedding gown has been ordered—a dream in white and to Sidi a symbol of her desperation. Klaus gushes about the honeymoon plans, tracing the route for her on a map, detailing the stays in Venice and Florence, the museum visits, the nights in the best hotels. Sidi panics. But she'll find a way out—a radical one, as always when she has her back against a wall and is afraid to tell her father the truth.

Isn't there always the ever-faithful, most understanding Christl Kmunke? Isn't her father obsessed with hunting and collecting weapons? Through Christl, it ought to be easy to get a revolver—she'll tell her it's to be a gift for the groom.

And Christl comes through.

The following weekend, a small group of friends has plans to meet at the Weinbergers in Katzelsdorf. Sidi has agreed to join them, but Klaus won't be able to make it.

At the Weinbergers, Grete, Sylvie, Hans Wunsch and Sidonie pass the first afternoon strolling around and drinking punch, then enjoy a sumptuous dinner. Even Fritz has joined the party, and though they haven't seen each other in a long time, Sidi still can't feel indifferent towards him—he radiates something that attracts her. But he is somewhat pale and seems to have lost weight ... he doesn't look well. They stay in the parlor until late, drinking wine and talking about events during the months since they'd lost touch with one another. It is obvious to Fritz that she isn't happy, for when the talk turns to her imminent wedding, her eyes well up and she breaks off the conversation. Not wanting to press the issue, he soon bids her good night. Sidi stands, and in an unexpectedly direct and inexplicable move, she puts her arms around his neck.

"Goodbye, Fritz. I'm still very fond of you ... to this day."

Alone in her room late that night, when everyone is asleep and the house is dark and quiet, Sidonie turns on the light, opens her handbag and reaches in to touch the cool metal of the revolver. Slowly, she takes it out, checks that all six bullets are still in place. The caliber is large enough to kill a good-sized animal, she has made sure of that.

Holding her breath, she caresses the fine-grained walnut butt, it feels soft, comforting. She is not afraid of the grey barrel—maybe death is something soothing. Her mind is made up. She can't marry a man she doesn't love while also having to give up the woman she loves so deeply. And she is causing her parents so much shame.

Slowly she turns the barrel towards her, embraces the butt with both hands and places the muzzle over her heart. With all her strength, she pulls the trigger.

The shot reverberates throughout the house and brings all the guests out of their rooms. Excited and disturbed, for the moment nobody knows what happened. Maybe thieves broke in, a murderer went berserk? But soon Sidonie is discovered lying across her bed, drenched in blood, unconscious, with a bullet wound in her chest. But she is alive. Muni Weinberger is trying to stanch the bleeding and yells at her husband to fetch the car so they can rush Sidonie to the hospital in Wiener Neustadt. Grete must telephone and inform the surgeon on duty. Sidonie's pulse is weak and each breath rattles in her chest. They put her on the back seat of Papsel's big Steyr-Coupe and speed off.

After several anxiety ridden hours in the hospital waiting room, the friends are told the good news in the early morning: the bullet lodged in her lung, and because she chose—probably unwittingly—a bullet with a full metal jacket, it hadn't fragmented inside her body and torn apart her organs. And thanks either to divine providence or her lack of experience with a gun, she missed her heart by two centimeters. She is going to survive, but she has been greatly weakened by the blood loss and will take weeks to heal.

After a period of deep unconsciousness followed by hours of restless sleep, Sidonie opens her eyes and is aware that once again she has failed to end her life. Her third suicide attempt hasn't worked—obviously that's not the way she is meant to say good-bye to the world. When the worst of the pain has passed and she can breathe again, the veil has finally lifted from her eyes. The first thing she does is take off her engagement ring and give it to Heinrich with instructions to return it to Klaus. She doesn't send any message or letter along with it. Unconcerned for her finance's feelings, she is happy just to be rid of him.

To be sure, there is something she'd like to tell Klaus, something she should have said before their engagement: she likes him, she considers him a brotherly friend with whom she would like to stay friends as long as she is alive, but that isn't enough for a marriage. But though she had the courage to turn the revolver on herself, she lacks the courage to say this to his face. And so first poor bewildered Klaus receives the terrible

news that his beloved Sidi has tried to commit suicide, and then shortly thereafter the return of her engagement ring announces the end of
their relationship. He will never recover from this, will never court another woman and spends the rest of his short life as a bachelor. At the
age of forty-two, while waiting for his new suit in his tailor's fitting
room, he falls from the chair and is dead.

The man who is actually at the center of all this does not come to the
hospital during the weeks Sidi spends there. This is a painful confirma-
tion of what she has known all along: Fritz is avoiding her.

Sidonie's appearance changes as her body heals. She sheds all vestig-
es of the young girl she was, and now, slim as a wand, she projects the
serious, noble beauty of a grown woman, and her face reveals that she
has suffered greatly. All of a sudden, Fritz finds that he is drawn to her,
and one evening, shortly before her twenty-fifth birthday he invites
Sidi to the movies. It turns out to be an evening of misunderstandings,
over-sensitivity and ambivalent communications.

After the film, they go to a small restaurant where Fritz tells Sidonie
that he has been thinking about getting serious about a relationship …
he wants to get married. She feels a pang in her heart. She wonders why
he is telling her this, why he wants to hurt her, because this announce-
ment wasn't made with her in mind. She asks rather sharply how he can
think of getting married when he hasn't graduated from university yet.

Fritz gives a start and says bitterly, "Yes … I don't believe you really want to marry me."

Sidonie can't believe what she's hearing. He has avoided her for so
long, and now all of a sudden he is making an implied proposal? Is he
really talking about her or about someone else? Why did she mention
his graduation? Now she can't take it back. A voice inside her is crying
that she doesn't care about his graduation, she wants him, only him and
could he please repeat his question.

But Fritz keeps silent, his head bowed, withdrawn and tight-lipped.

And she starts doubting again—well-founded doubts because of her
experiences with him in recent months. Maybe he is asking for her
hand now, but in a few weeks he'll reconsider … particularly after what
she has done to his best friend. If he really wants her, he'll have to ask

again, later, when she has finally weathered all that has gone on with Klaus, with Leonie and with herself.

And so love and spontaneity drown in a bitter lake of doubt, mistrust and past injuries. And neither Sidonie nor Fritz will have a chance to emerge from this impasse.

Fritz will not live long enough to graduate and perhaps propose to Sidonie once again. Shortly after his twenty-sixth birthday, at the end of March 1926, he is hospitalized to be treated for a venereal disease. Apparently, something goes wrong with the treatment, and within days he dies of sepsis—so quickly that there wasn't even time for Sidi to have paid him a visit.

The younger Wunsch brother, one of Fritz's cousins, doesn't have the courage to tell Sidonie on the phone and asks Antal Csillag to relay the sad news to his daughter. Silenced by pain and dismay, Sidi absorbs the information. The funeral at the Stammersdorfer Cemetery is very difficult for her, and by the end of the ceremony she feels almost like a young widow. Twice a week over the course of many months, she visits Fritz's grave on the outskirts of Vienna. It takes almost the whole day to go there and return, but what else does she have to do? The dead Fritz is a more reliable anchor than the living one had been, and maybe she can tell his serpentine gravestone all the things she was unable to say to the man when he was alive.

These past years have brought too many separations. First the farewell to her beloved Leonie, for there was no future in it and it would have broken her heart. Then the separation from Klaus, which almost cost her her life. And now Fritz's death. So many deaths and farewells, so much unfulfilled love. Everything around her has changed, and she doesn't know how to go on. All she knows is that her life has to change.

CHAPTER

6

WOMEN'S BODIES, MEN'S BODIES

SIDONIE HATES THE SPRING OF 1926. THE CHESTNUTS AND LILACS went into full bloom shortly after Fritz died, and she is repulsed by their beauty, the colors of the opening buds, all those shades of white and lilac, the vitality, the sweet smells everywhere. She avoids the streets and the memories that assault her wherever she goes—here a path she took with Leonie, there the Wunsch family's house where she last danced with Fritz, a movie theater, a park bench, a tree ...

With the exception of her frequent visits to the Stammersdorf Cemetery, she spends her days at home, sitting silent and abstracted in an armchair. She stares out the window or at the ceiling, dreaming, dozing and unapproachable. Her parents and brothers tiptoe around her, spellbound and touched by her pain as she silently endures recurring waves of emotion and memory. For weeks she can do nothing else.

Sometimes she is tempted to write to Leonie in Berlin, but then she smothers that desire. Nothing will come of it other than rekindling old emotions.

Unexpected rescue comes in the form of a small, pale blue letter: Marianne Kraus has written to her from Prague.

A friend since childhood, Marianne is the niece of the famous writer Karl Kraus, publisher of the journal *Die Fackel*. They have never been all that close, but Marianne is among the group of pretty, endearing young women whom Sidonie likes and has seen regularly over the years. Her family lives nearby in the Third District, on Mohsgasse, and particularly during the war Sidonie often visited to chat a bit with Marianne and observe the comings and goings of their international guests. Occasionally she would run into the uncle, "Fackelkraus" as he's known in Vienna. He would regard her sternly from behind his rimless glasses, then turn away coolly with his head held high, and she had found this rather unsettling. Obviously, he was interested neither in her nor in any of the women present. He was always surrounded by a small circle of serious and important-looking men whose animated discussions about the political situation were accompanied by fierce gesticulations. He was known to be an adamant anti-militarist and war opponent who wrote actively on those topics.

A short while ago, Marianne had gotten married—unfortunately, to a man of whom Sidonie did not approve. She had several reasons for this, the most important of which was that he was Jewish; the second most important was that she thought him unattractive.

The Kraus family hasn't distanced itself from Judaism as explicitly as the Csillag family has. Sidonie had been taken aback when Marianne told her that her family had introduced her to a wealthy Jewish lawyer from Prague, with the idea in mind that she should marry him. Eugen Winterberg was considerably older than Marianne, heavy-set and not very attractive. At first, she didn't feel anything for him at all, but then she made the effort and talked herself into an infatuation she did not really feel. In the end she agreed to marry him.

The wedding had been opulent, and afterwards as Marianne said a tearful goodbye to Vienna and to her friends, she asked them all not to forget her and to visit her in Prague, often and at any time.

And now here's Marianne Kraus-Winterberg's first formal invitation—spring in Prague is wonderful, there are many families one can visit, many opportunities to play bridge and to enjoy life.

The silence of the past weeks weighs heavily on Sidi, and she knows she won't be able to stand it much longer. Maybe it would help if she went back to having some fun. In addition, her parents won't think twice about letting her go to Prague.

She packs her suitcases, buys a first-class train ticket, and quite enjoys the journey through the Waldviertel and the Bohemian forests—travelling on her own suits her.

INTERLUDE IN PRAGUE

AN EXCITED MARIANNE WELCOMES HER AT THE PRAGUE RAILWAY station and has a cab waiting to take them the short distance to her flat in the center of the old city, not far from Na Příkopĕ Street (On the Moat), an almost exclusively German-speaking neighborhood. The elegantly furnished flat contains a splendid series of rooms connected by tall double doors, and each is as grand as any in her friends' flats in Vienna. In the parlor, where Marianne offers her a sherry, walnut shelves house an impressive library, and Sidonie has her choice of seating from among the various suites, each upholstered in heavy silk. There is a coffered ceiling with heavy chandeliers and enough Persian carpets that her feet never have to touch the parquet flooring.

"Just like home," she thinks and leans back and relaxes. When she looks up, it's into the sparkling eyes of her friend, who is outlining their

The livingroom of Marianne Kraus-Winterberg's flat in Prague, 1926

plans for the coming days. Marianne is extravagant and imaginative, and she comes up with more to do than could be done even if Sidonie were staying for a month. "She must be rather lonely," is what Sidi thinks to herself.

After the sherry and a short rest, they set off. Though Marianne has only been in Prague for a short time, she already knows her way around and also seems to know someone everywhere they go, whether in the elegant stores on Wenceslas Square or in the various cafés. Soon they are invited to join a bridge game—in Vienna Sidonie plays at peoples' homes, but in Prague the cafés are the place—and end up staying at Café Continental on Na Příkopě for several hours, winning one game after the other. The mostly German-speaking regulars call it the Café Conti, and Marianne is almost magically drawn to the place, which, she tells Sidi with a wistful smile, feels almost like Café Herrenhof in Vienna. She and Sidi will play there daily for the next several days.

Sidonie's only problem is with Czech, which, in her rather snide opinion, is vulgar, a servants' language. She is impressed with Marianne's skillful Czech but can't get used to the sound. Also, she simply can't like it that Marianne says Vaclavske Namesti instead of Wenceslas Square and that this ungrateful country has broken from the monarchy and gotten rid of everything reminiscent of Old Austria. Walking through the old town the following afternoon, she is surprised to notice that Prague seems to be suffering far fewer aftereffects of the war than Vienna. Everything seems better kept; the people are more tastefully dressed and seem to be in a better mood. Her judgmental mood lifts a bit; she might be able to find this atmosphere infectious and perhaps even feel free and easy in disloyal Bohemia, now known as Czechoslovakia.

Then one afternoon something happens for which, even hours later, Sidonie cannot find an explanation. The previous evening they had been out visiting and had not returned home until the wee hours. The morning routine chez Winterberg took its usual course, but after lunch, instead of having coffee, an afternoon nap is proposed. A friend of Marianne's is visiting, and the three women retire to Marianne's bedroom.

Sidonie is, indeed, tired, and she is the first to sink onto the pink silk coverlet on the extra-large bed and doze off. She wakes as the sound of giggling, whispers and soft sighs grows louder. Irritated, she turns her head and can't believe that what she has longed for for years, has fantasized about, is happening right next to her. She would only have to stretch out her hand to take part in the women's game. But she is frozen, mesmerized by the beauty of the situation, the appalling nature and vibrant eroticism of the moment, and her own indignation.

The two women kiss wildly until—gently, passionately—Marianne pulls her girlfriend closer and lowers her lips to her neck. Long, dark hair cascades around them, both covering and revealing the intensity of their desire.

At first unaware that they're being watched, when they do notice, there are a few light-hearted remarks, an invitation, a joke, some come-hither glances.

Propped stiffly on her elbow, Sidonie remains immobile and just shakes her head.

The girlfriend slowly pulls her hand away from Marianne, gets up, smooths her dress and says, "Show her." She throws one last glance at Sidonie, gives a deep, soft chuckle and closes the door behind her.

Slowly, Marianne turns towards the still frozen Sidonie and stretches out her arms. Her unbuttoned blouse opens to reveal large, soft breasts beneath a lacy camisole. As Marianne reaches out to embrace her friend, Sidonie thinks for just a moment that what she is seeing—this pale, fine skin and thick hair, this sensuous mouth already pressed against hers—is beautiful.

Then, suddenly, Leonie is there, and Sidonie is stabbed by an intense, sharp pain. In order to ward off thoughts of what never was, Sidonie responds to the kisses more vehemently than she intended—they definitely taste better than Klaus's.

But all the while she feels lost and small and doesn't know what to do with the longing that's focused on her. Marianne is experienced, and what she is showing her she can't have learned with her husband. In no time Sidonie is embracing a naked woman who knows how to direct Sidi's hand, who knows what she wants. But when Marianne tries to reciprocate, her hands are pushed away. Sidonie allows no touching, no caresses; her desire ebbs and turns to fear when it's her turn. She lives only in her devotion to others.

As Marianne heaves a final sigh beneath her and falls back onto the pillows, Sidonie feels like laughing, as happens so often at the most inappropriate moments.

"This is what everyone goes so crazy about? We are just like animals. All the effort, the sighing, the longing—how absurd." These are the thoughts running through her head.

How did she ever get involved with someone who doesn't think as she does, whose husband sleeps in another room down the hall, who suddenly seems to be melting with desire for her?

Lying beside her, Marianne pulls Sidonie's hand to her lips and covers it with kisses. There is happiness in her eyes, and she seems to be laughing quite softly.

Sidonie is touched, shy, uncomprehending ... she cannot return these feelings and is afraid of their power.

Sidonie gets up, smooths the disheveled dress she had never taken off and quickly leaves the room, the rumpled pillows, the heavy peonies in a blue Chinese vase, and the afternoon light falling on the naked body of a happy woman.

The following evening adds a special touch to the whole experience. The Winterbergs are giving an early summer costume party, and the participants will find themselves party to a game, some with foreknowledge, others unsuspecting.

Sidonie dresses as Rosenkavalier, slender and androgynous in silken knee breeches and a baroque frockcoat with broad lapels. With the three-cornered hat pulled low on her forehead, she feels daring and allows herself to look deeply into other women's eyes and put her lips to their hands as well as to their lips. She can even press harmless kisses on Marianne, who is dressed as Pierrot Lunaire. She makes quite a cuddly Pierrot in a shiny white costume with heavy black pompons on the jacket and a tulle ruff. Assuming her role, she dances around Sidonie, tenderly clowning with her.

When Eugen Winterberg appears awkwardly on the scene, Rosenkavalier almost falls out of character—from laughing too hard. A heavy-set Hungarian Marischka, has entered through the parlor door, balled up newspaper breasts swell beneath a lacy blouse and are barely contained by a tight corset. An apron covers the traditional

Sidonie Csillag as Rosenkavalier, Prague, 1926

Marianne Kraus-Winterberg as Pierrot, Prague, 1926

Eugen Winterberg as Marischka, Prague, 1926

skirt (and Marischka's beer belly), and long black braids frame the thickly made-up face.

Sidonie takes the opportunity to pat Eugen's behind with her dagger and poke fun at this Hungarian beauty, who is embarrassed by her shameless flirting with Pierrot. Eugen feels, rather than knows, that the change in gender roles is a mighty tool that makes him look like a fool—and not just for this evening.

Sidonie stays for another week, enjoying the spring days on the Vltava and, a little, also Marianne's embraces. But although Marianne waits for her with longing every afternoon, Sidonie maintains her emotional distance by turning to irony and by constantly reminding herself that she is not in love. And she is happy that all of this is happening in Prague—a place she can leave, a place that's far from her father's stern watchfulness and far from Austria, where the state has criminalized such a love.

Sidi's departure on the following weekend finds a saddened Marianne standing on the railway platform. Sidi will visit her several times over the next two years, but both women know that theirs will never be more than an afternoon's affair, though the pompon from Pierrot's costume that Marianne slipped into Sidonie's handbag while saying good-bye will always be a reminder.

Sidi doesn't tell her girlfriends in Vienna about her experiences in Prague. At times, she'd like to talk to Ellen Ferstel about it, but Ellen is busy with her two little daughters, and their conversations are limited to the topics of diapers, nursery food, suitable entertainment for the little ones, or perhaps the husband who is rarely at home and works far too much. Ellen lives just around the corner from Sidonie on Pfarrhofgasse, and Sidonie visits regularly but often finds that her best friend is absent-minded and overburdened. She also complains of frequent severe headaches, which not even the best doctors can explain. How would Ellen be able to understand the confusion and emotional turmoil of Sidi's first sexual encounter with a woman?

But even though they don't discuss Sidonie's inner life, at least this friendship provides some outdoor entertainment. Almost every Sunday, the Ferstls and some of their friends go for an outing in their own car, with a driver. Someone always comes along who owns a country house outside Vienna, where, depending on the season, the entertainment will include bridge or lovely walks, mushroom hunting, skating or just afternoon tea.

During the 1926 summer holidays, spent as always on Brioni, Sidi's father again had a serious talk with her about getting training in some profession—when they return to Vienna, she absolutely must go back to school. And so, until the end of December she attends the Weizmann Academy on Wollzeile daily, taking courses in various commercial subjects, starting with accounting and moving on to bookkeeping, trade law, and office procedure and correspondence. She excels in all these subjects and also learns to type. Her skill and industriousness when dealing with various typewriting machines are attested to in the certificates she earns.

But Sidonie doesn't have the slightest desire to make use of these new skills, and she even refuses her father's offer of work in his own office under the guidance of his best secretary. She does, however, enjoy using the typewriter, and from this point on she takes a small one along most everywhere she goes. An avid letter writer, she uses it for her private correspondence.

On weekdays with no classes or Ferstls, Sidonie doesn't know what to do with herself. She walks around Vienna, takes care of errands and spends a lot of time at home, where she does what pampered women do to pass the time: she reads avidly. She doesn't read those pompous women's novels, however, but books on geography and animals. Adventure stories about places where one can feel free and where everything is different from life in this small, miserable remnant of greater Austria, which she imagines the Socialists will take over, making the streets unsafe and endangering her world with their protests.

She had not witnessed the anti-Semitic demonstrations by the National Socialists, German Nationalists and Christian Socialists who were trying to disrupt the Zionist Congress that took place in Vienna in the second half of August 1925. She also missed the other rally protesting the Zionist Congress, which was organized by the Austrian-German Peoples' Federation. Held on Rathausplatz, it was also in support of Austria's annexation to the German Empire.

Sidonie doesn't want to know what is still going on out there every day, and in addition to reading, she indulges passionately in games of solitaire and the assembly of jigsaw puzzles. She is able to forget everything when sitting over the hundreds, often thousands of pieces until the early morning hours, only realizing how much time has passed when the blackbirds start singing in Arenberg Park. Another day gone and a new one ahead of her.

Her favorite brother, Robert, is the only person who can always shake her out of her lethargy, and it's thanks to him alone that Sidonie takes any note of Vienna's political changes. Robert spends a lot of his time in cafés; he reads the newspapers and magazines, talks with people and is generally observant. It doesn't matter how many business schools their father sends him to, Robert just laughs off the idea of account balances and ignores the secrets the courses reveal about correct business correspondence. He does, however, have a finely developed sense for the hidden mechanisms of political power. Now, he takes his sister along when making the rounds of the cafés and points out the brown shirts, whose numbers are steadily growing, and explains why there are recurring confrontations between two growing paramilitary organizations—the Social Democratic Party's Schutzband and the conservative Christian Socialist's Heimwehr.

Brother and sister now often get into verbal altercations over political issues and end up sitting in Café Herrenhof, red-faced and yelling at each other. Robert doesn't understand why Sidonie continues to keep company with her old friends; for quite some time, he himself has deliberately neglected to stay in touch with them. He directs his attacks against the Weinberger and Wunsch families in particular but derides the lot of them as smug archconservatives. His derogatory name for them is "political ostriches," and alas, he is right.

The young men around Sidonie are quite open to the rising tide of National Socialism. When Grete Weinberger's older brother Hans returns from one of his now frequent trips to Munich, his eyes shine at the memory of having heard Adolf Hitler deliver shrill speeches in some smoky cellar or pub or beer tent. And even though the Weinberger family has Jewish roots, Hans has even managed to sweep his father along on the tide of his enthusiasm. Together father and son have gotten caught up in some sort of Hitler tourism, and they go to Munich almost every weekend.

Hans Wunsch, the older of the two brothers who had so idolized Sidonie at Wörthersee, is also among the dubiously bedazzled—he is even trying hard to change his appearance in order to conform to the heroic blonde ideal of the National Socialists.

And in the middle, there's Sidonie: a Jew who doesn't want to be one, clueless and politically ignorant. Not understanding Robert's position, she tells him, feeling offended, that they all treat her so very nicely.

"One refuses to have anything to do with such people," Robert says venomously and finishes off the last of his coffee.

Sidonie feels attacked and cornered. It is all very well for Robert to talk. He had secretly married a Jewish woman at the age of nineteen and divorced her a year later, though they are still seeing each other. He certainly knows how to polemicize against her friends, even though they really are right about a few things.

She is hurt and so lets her guard down, telling him in an unchecked flow of words that she doesn't like Jews, they are a second-class people, they are cursed and that is why it would be better if they were gone from this world.

Jews are still "the other," the poor, ragged figures who came from the East at the beginning of the century and undermined the reputation of all those who had been in Vienna for a long time—like the Csillags. Why should families like hers be subjected to anti-Semitism or treated like second class citizens when they were baptized long ago and have assimilated so well? It's because of those people who speak Yiddish and behave as they do and look the way they do. She won't have it.

Robert is speechless. Such vehemence coming from his otherwise quiet sister has taken him completely by surprise. How can she negate her own family's origins? What's causing her so much pain? Furiously he puts down his cup, pushes back his chair and leaves the cafe, taking long strides and holding his head high.

He is not going to be told whom to meet and whom to avoid, particularly not by his anti-Semitic sister. He genuinely loves women—women and music—that's the life he will lead and damn the conventions. He will lead it despite his father, his society and the frightening closed-mindedness that is spreading through his social circle like a disease.

Robert first met his ex-wife where he feels most at home, in the world of music and dance. He is particularly attracted to dance and has gone to see all the well-known performers. He never misses Grete Wiesenthal, and was fascinated by her two most recent appearances, one at the opera and the other at Hagenbund. And he has been following Tilly Losch ever since her first solo performance in 1924, though now it's particularly difficult to get tickets to see her because all Vienna wants them—last time, he had to stand in line overnight.

In 1927 he even went so far as to buy a figurine based on his adored Tilly. Designed for the Augarten porcelain factory by Mathilde Szendrö-Jaksch from the Wiener Werkstatt, it had been horrendously expensive and now holds a place of honor on this nightstand.

By mid 1927, the political situation has escalated to a point where even Sidonie can't look away—not from the smoldering embers of the Palace of Justice.

SCHUTZBUND AND HEIMWEHR

Two days before her birthday in April that year she casts her vote in the First Republic's third national election. Her father has been particularly concerned about the rapid growth of the Social Democrats. At the previous elections in 1923 they gained 68 seats, this time they will gain even more. The Christian Socialists meanwhile have grown closer to the Greater Germans and don't always distance themselves from the National Socialists. To be sure, her father doesn't approve of that at all, but as long as the conservatives hold a majority in the government, business will do just fine, so he has been willing to accept some brown spots. The elections of 1927 don't bring much change: the Christian Socialists and the Greater Germans get 85 seats, the Social Democrats 71 and the Landbund, which also supported the Anschluss, gets 9. Prelate Ignaz Seipel, the head of the Christian Socialists, is once again charged with the task of forming a government.

On January 30, 1927, armed conflict broke out between the Schutz-bund and the Heimwehr in Schattendorf in South Burgenland. The Heimwehr shot and killed a child and an old man and injured five more people. When the Schattendorf trial begins at Vienna's Regional Court on July 5, the Csillags are on summer vacation in St. Gilgen in Salz-kammergut; but even there, the vacationers could read the newspaper reports from Vienna, so they learn that on July 14 the shooters were ac-quitted. The next day's papers inform them that the Palace of Justice, right next to Parliament, is burning.

Just hours later it becomes clear that not only did the Palace of Jus-tice go up in flames but demonstrators had also clashed mightily with the police. On July 16, the newspapers report the details: 89 dead, 600 seriously injured and 1000 with minor injuries. A crowd of furious So-cialists had stormed the Palace of Justice, smashed the windows and then set fire to furniture and files. There were so many obstructions at the site that the fire department couldn't get to the fire to extinguish it. Socialist functionaries, including Mayor Karl Seitz, had run to the scene but could not calm the furious crowd or convince the demonstra-tors to go home, at which point Johann Schober, the chief of police, or-dered the use of firearms and provoked the ensuing blood bath.

For days no one in Salzkammergut talks about anything else on the beaches and private verandas, in the pubs and salons. A peculiar appre-hensive tension fills the summer air. People don't know whether to be aghast, frightened or just curious about what will happen next. No one in Sidonie's circles wants to believe the news at first, and there are fierce discussions during the afternoon bridge games. The gentlemen, who sport Styrian loden-cloth suits or linen jackets with green collars over smart leather shorts, and the ladies in their dirndl dresses or light-weight linens split into various factions. There are those who think the police were wrong to fire into the crowd and those who think it the only way to deal with Red rabble. A few claim that Schober never gave the order to fire and the police acted on their own. Gone are the usual lethargy and shallow conversation, now every gathering hums like a beehive.

Sidonie is distressed by the news, but as a bridge fanatic she is more annoyed by the fact that talk about the political scandal in Vienna tends

The Palace of Justice on fire, July 1927

to slow the pace of the game. Impatiently, she asks the other players to concentrate on their cards and postpone other discussions until dinner.

But once back in Vienna, Sidonie finds that she can't escape the all-pervasive air of agitation and political hypersensitivity. The sight of the gutted Palace of Justice causes an unfamiliar shudder, and a fleeting vision of a dark future for herself and her country. But she shoves her premonitions aside, pulls herself together and quickens her pace through town. Eventually, any urge she might feel to go for a walk in Vienna will be quashed by the unending tension.

How nice, then, that for someone in Sidi's position there are plenty of opportunities to get sidetracked. One evening, when sorting through her clothes to decide what to discard, she finds an old riding outfit. Smiling, she recalls a time, years earlier, when her father was still forcing his children to go on excursions into the mountains, pressuring them so hard that Sidi would vomit before they set off and her brothers became heartfelt enemies of mountain trips. This had been a skiing outfit back when women still wore wide, dark skirts over thick woolen stockings and came down the slopes like scarecrows on wooden planks, using only a single long pole. When she was finally old enough to refuse to participate in the excursions, she had remodeled the outfit into riding attire—very smart and tight fitting—and secretly took riding lessons in the Prater.

Her friends Grete Weinberger and Sylvie Dietz have been riding for years and have become real amazons —in every sense of the word. Sylvie is already divorced and raising her small daughter on her own while working as a photographer. Grete took classes at the academy and has become a sculptor, and she often leaves her husband and two little boys and goes off to enjoy life in equestrian circles to the fullest. Sidonie envies their carefree independence and disregard of convention and wonders whether some of that might rub off on her if she goes riding with them.

And so she arranges to rekindle her riding career, and her pleased girlfriends promise to find her the best teacher.

Ever since the 1760s, the Prater has been Vienna's favorite place for people and horses to stretch their legs on the miles and miles of chestnut-lined avenues and in the riparian forest. The training grounds lie right behind the baroque stables and consist of a well-groomed lawn with small boxwood hurdles and several paddocks, where the horses' feet sink into soft sawdust up to the fetlocks.

Sidonie has her riding lessons in the late mornings and finds she has forgotten everything she once knew and has to start from square one, beginning with relearning how to sit one of those ghastly side saddles. She fights with her skirts and the stirrup when mounting; then she fights with the two stiff leather straps intended to keep her legs modestly together on the left side, then with the muddle of the reins, her gloves, the crop, all of which must be in proper order along her horse's mane; and most of all she fights when the animal starts moving.

While she is trying to sit her horse's trot, tense and cursing her weak thighs, Grete dashes by on her lovely little Arabian mare, followed by Sylvie on her a big brown gelding called Fritz, just like the men in her family. Sylvie is training for a dressage competition and executes delightful passages and traverses.

Sidi still grits her teeth just going through the simplest steps and doesn't really notice how patiently her riding teacher repeatedly calls out in his raspy voice: "Soft hands, steady the thighs, knee down."

Grete Weinberger on her
Arabian mare

One day he tells her that he can only give her lessons at seven in the morning as has to train for the next Concours Hippique. The bitter pill of having to switch is soon sweetened by the appearance of an exceedingly elegant rider who is obviously training for the concours. Her instructor identifies him as Herr von Weitenegg, who used to ride for the Spanish Riding School and whose mastery of dressage has earned him numerous prizes.

Since Fritz's death, Sidi hasn't taken a second look at any man, but she is exceptionally pleased by this one. All of a sudden, she has no problem getting up early each morning; she wants to be at the training ground before he arrives. She is embarrassed to have von Weitenegg see how inexpert she is on horseback, while he looks like a god in custom-made breeches as he trots by, bolt-upright yet totally relaxed. He dominates his horse with no apparent effort and dismounts after two hours, looking as fresh as if he had just come from the dressing room—once he has dusted off his boots with his doeskin gloves.

Sidonie feels a tingle whenever she sees him, and she is particularly attracted to his confident, authoritative attitude and distanced reserve. For several days running she arranges to finish her ride just as Herr von Weitenegg is dismounting. Then one day she drops a riding glove as if by accident and smiles delightedly when he immediately picks it up and returns it.

"You haven't been riding long," he says, scrutinizing her. It is more a statement than a question.

Sidonie, very much the lady, raises an eyebrow and with a slight nod toward her glove says, "Thanks," then, "Not as long as you have."

He is not prepared for this answer and is suddenly aware that, distressingly, he has not yet introduced himself. He bows and says, "von Weitenegg." Even though he officially lost his title with the founding of the Austrian republic, he and most of his associates continued to use the noble "von."

"Csillag," Sidonie responds cheerfully and extends her hand. In perfect form, he pulls it towards his lips, provoking a shiver in Sidi. She was right, even up close he is a very attractive man—perhaps around forty, a chiseled face, sharp nose, well-defined cheeks that could be the result of exercising those muscles while clenching his teeth. "A real gentleman," is the thought that flashes through her mind. If she had combined that with his preferred leisure activity, she would have been closer to the mark: "Gentleman rider."

After their formal introduction, the two see one another almost daily and exchange a few inconsequential words when dismounting. Then one day von Weitenegg asks Sidonie if he might drive her back to the town center in his car. She declines the first offer, it's best to come across as proper and indifferent, but she accepts the second and glides into the passenger seat of his Steyr-Coupé. This drive together is soon a frequent occurrence, and Sidi finds that she enjoys being seen beside this man, about whom she has already learned more than just his name.

Eduard von Weitenegg was a high-ranking officer and a pilot in the Habsburg army, and on their drives he talks enthusiastically, yet almost wistfully about the war, spinning frightening but romanticized tales about his own audacity. He confesses that he still longs for the experience of flying and everything associated with it. In those days, an officer was really somebody, and pilots wore a special nimbus of daring, courage and loyalty to the emperor. But, he concludes with regret, all of that has vanished, and honor, patriotism and manly virility have disappeared.

He neglects to mention that during the final years of war the officers continued to live well while the troops, the simple soldiers, survived on rations of grain or polenta so meager that their hunger pangs were stilled only briefly before they were sent back into meaningless battles.

And he doesn't talk, because recalling it makes him cringe, about the looks the starved soldiers gave the superiors they had learned to hate. The soldiers who survived until 1918 started to take revenge for the years of humiliation, and he remembers with horror scenes in Vienna's railway stations and on the streets when returning soldiers ripped off officers' cockades, when officers were beaten and abased by their own bat man.

Nevertheless, former Habsburg officer Eduard von Weitenegg mourns the lost monarchy and the time-tested hierarchies he had been born into. His father, Eduard Rzemenowsky, was of Polish origin and had started his career in 1867 in the infantry regiment of Archduke Carl Ludwig. Beginning in 1884, he was employed at Vienna's military college and by the time he retired in 1906 he held a leading position at the Military Geographical Institute in Vienna. He was knighted in 1902 and changed his name to Eduard Rzemenowsky von Weitenegg.

The first son, named Eduard after his father, was born in 1886 and in September 1905 joined an infantry regiment as a cadet. His younger brother, Franz, started as a marine cadet in 1907. At the beginning of the war, Eduard was a senior lieutenant, and in 1915 he started training as a pilot. At the end of the war he was discharged with the rank of captain and was awarded numerous medals.

In 1918 the entire family took Austrian citizenship, dropped the Polish name and took their title of nobility—Weitenegg, without the von—as the family name. A difficult to pronounce name like Rzemenowsky seemed like a bad idea if one was going into business, which the two brothers planned to do.

Sidonie is impressed as this story unfolds, though she has been almost certain from the first moment that Eduard had been in the

Ed Weitenegg at a dressage competition

military. His posture had been the clue, and that was what had most attracted her. She has heard the stories about philandering officers who look to marry rich society women for their dowries, but those days are gone, and to Sidi, Eduard von Weitenegg seems serious, quiet and confident. And he must have money of his own or surely he couldn't afford his big flat in the Third District, the car and his horse. Sidi hasn't yet discovered what kind of business earns him this money.

Given all his positive attributes, if she could introduce von Weitenegg to her family, her father might abandon his ingrained distrust of all officers.

Sidi doesn't mind at all that Eduard Weitenegg had once been married to a Hungarian noble woman. They had a daughter in the spring of 1919 and separated shortly thereafter. Some time ago, his former wife had taken their daughter to live in Hungary with her new husband, a Hungarian count.

Sidi finds it exciting to be courted by a man who is experienced in marriage and exudes finesse—very much in contrast to the young men of her own circle.

He continues to invite her out: for dinner, or to the movies or a concert, and occasionally on the weekends for an excursion to the Wienerwald. For the longest time, he treats her with great reserve and sensitivity. From time to time he holds her hand—nothing more.

Sidi hopes that she will be more comfortable being close to him than she had been with Klaus, whose desire for her had been so pressing it had forced her onto the defensive. Maybe this time she will feel and can maintain a little spark of excitement, like that rudimentary spark she has felt with women.

Soon she becomes more open and trusting with Eduard, whom she has started to call Ed, and he interprets this as a signal. During a weekend outing on Sophienalpe, while sitting in a sunlit meadow, he no longer just holds her hand but pushes her onto the grass und starts kissing her fiercely. As once before, Sidi becomes stiff and wooden and turns away.

Ed immediately apologizes for having rushed her. "You have to understand me properly," he says, "I like you very much. You are the first woman I've been really pleased with since Maria left me."

"Oh, indeed," Sidonie responds with the apparently phlegmatic composure she usual shows under such circumstances. Surreptitiously, she tidies her somewhat disordered hair. It is so hard to accept this whole kissing thing; having a strange tongue in her mouth triggers an inner tumult of disgust and aversion.

But it can't go on like this—she is going to have to think of a way to pay tribute to "normality" or she'll remain an unmarried outsider, scrutinized with suspicion by the others in her circles. And she doesn't want to be an outsider; she is already sufficiently endangered by her secret love of women and by being Jewish. She wants to belong, to be like everyone else and play by their rules. What her body tells her doesn't need to be taken into consideration. And a quite inner voice tells her that she is soon going to lose her virginity. She is twenty-eight, why wait any longer? Ed is not the worst; he knows what he is doing, and besides, she is a bit enamored.

One morning after that kiss, she allows him to convince her to accompany him to his flat after they've finished riding. It's a harmless invitation—just for a cup of coffee to counteract the fatigue of the horseback ride. Morning is a good time, Sidonie thinks. Nobody at home
will be prompted to ask curious questions, there will be no outrage, as
there would be if she were to stay out all night. Both guest and host
know that it won't be just for coffee.

Ed lives in the better part of the Third District, on Reisnerstrasse,
not far from the Csillags. His flat is large and dark and lacks the elegance and order Sidonie is used to in the homes of people in her circle.
He doesn't really seem to have much money, she thinks, before she is
otherwise preoccupied with her beating heart and demonstrating the
coquetry and signs of affection that she thinks are necessary under the
circumstances in order to turn a man on.

Ed himself makes the coffee, and she doesn't dare tell him that she
never drinks it because it makes her feel horrible for hours afterward.
As soon as he has put the tray with the silver pot and milk jug on the table, he starts to caress her leg. She finds this rather pleasant. Legs are
somehow above suspicion, not a target for erotic attacks and therefore
unencumbered by associations. If only he had stopped there.

Then there is kissing again, which is much more demanding today.
The brittleness of her response seems to make no impression on him.
"Come on," he whispers, "you want it as well. I'll be very careful, and
you'll see, you'll enjoy it." He has already unbuttoned her dress and
slipped it off her shoulders. He doesn't say anything else, just buries his
lips in her neck. As soon as she begins concentrating on one point of reference, he's already busy elsewhere. All of a sudden, her clothes are off,
and later she will find it impossible to reconstruct how he was also able
to get rid of her undergarments, how his hands seemed to take possession of her whole body.

When he himself gets undressed, she quickly closes her eyes. She
has never seen an excited nude man, and what she does see, frightens
her. From this point on she keeps her eyes closed, which has the added advantage of keeping him from seeing in them either that this is
making extraordinary demands on her or that she completely lacks
enthusiasm.

When he enters her, she sighs loudly because of the hot, sharp pain. Then all she does is wonder what all the groaning and fidgety doings are about and when it will be over. Soon Ed drops down beside her, sighing deeply. She stares at the ceiling feeling empty and disappointed. This had nothing to do with love. Surgery without anesthesia couldn't be worse.

Ed looks at her lovingly, caresses her cheek and calls her "my little woman." He mumbles that it has been wonderful with her, her beauty excites him terribly, he wants to do it with her frequently from now on. She gets up from the settee quickly, gathers her clothes, and spends several minutes in the bathroom, where she can't seem to stop cleaning between her legs with a wet cloth. She returns fully dressed to the hall, with a half-hearted excuse on her lips that she doesn't want to be late for lunch. She can't prevent Ed from seeing her to the entrance, where he takes her tenderly in his arms and says happily, "See you tomorrow."

Out on the street, she sucks in fresh air like someone rescued from drowning and almost runs to her parents' flat. Dazed and harboring a grudge against the whole world, she climbs the stairs. Her mother hasn't prepared her for this! Why had her girlfriends never told her anything? They should have known. They let her walk straight into a trap. Sidonie never wants to be involved in this gross thing between men and women again and decides to send Ed a message in the morning informing him that she never ever wants to see him again.

Pretending to have a migraine, she goes straight to bed and falls into a leaden, exhausted sleep of denial. When she wakes, the tumult in her brain hasn't abated and she turns onto her tummy and scratches pensively at the red of the water lilies on her silk coverlet, digging into their pale yellow calyxes.

What's wrong with her? Maybe she isn't normal—well, that's for sure. But she does know about passion and excitement; it's just that she feels them at moments that others don't find very exciting. To watch a beautiful stranger in the streets or take Leonie's hand and kiss it—these have kindled a fire in her body. And it had taken her breath away just to look into Fritz's eyes. How much she'd like to feel that same fervent glow for Ed, but she can't seem to transfer those moments of adoration and being in love to real life.

Leonie never had to come down from her pedestal, because she never became a reality. Fritz had died before anything could happen.

"As soon as something starts going well, it's over. That's how things are with me," she thinks bitterly.

Beauty, that's her criterion, that's her aphrodisiac. And longing is what drives her. Fulfillment, reality—they just crush her.

The next morning she is still too shaken to write to Ed, and when he calls her, she doesn't know how to respond to his deep, tender voice in a way that will avoid another encounter. She agrees to a dinner date, at which all her resolutions dissolve into nothing. She still finds him attractive, and she gets bogged down in passivity and silence and endures his caresses. Only when he invites her to his place after dinner, does she refuse, using the pretext that she wants to make sure she doesn't get pregnant. With a placating pat on her arm, he says she should leave that to him and arranges their next meeting. She hasn't managed to tell him how repugnant that first experience was or that she never wants to see him again. Refusal has become half-hearted consent, and half-hearted consent becomes an implicit agreement, and all at once Sidonie is caught up in a relationship.

She learns, over time, how to keep intimate relations with Ed to a minimum. This seems to increase his interest and intensify his longing for her, which paradoxically gives her a certain sense of satisfaction. With respect to all other matters, she manages to convince herself that he is a good friend with whom she likes to pass the time.

Sidi tries to keep Eduard von Weitenegg a secret from her parents. They will find out about her Prater acquaintance soon enough, and most likely they won't be pleased.

Antal Csillag has already heard that his daughter has often been seen with a divorced officer in recent weeks. Yet he doesn't even ask her about it. Maybe he has gotten old and lenient, or perhaps he's simply worn out. In any case, he has given up trying to understand how his only daughter manages, with supreme single-mindedness, to enter into the worst imaginable alliances. He can't find a reason. Has he not given her enough love and support, or has he been too lenient? He should have forced her to marry the son of one of his business partners—that would have saved him and his wife a lot of trouble.

But he couldn't have managed to do that. He knows how difficult it is to spend one's life with another person, even when it's someone you love. There is nothing for him to do but support Sidi no matter what she does, whether he likes it or not. He won't be able to change her; he can only love her.

Besides, he has other problems at the moment. He knows he is no longer young, and the worsening political situation disturbs his sleep, and that robs him of strength. His middle son Robert recently came home from the opera in a state because the Nazis had organized protests against the opening performance of Ernst Kreneks' "Jonny spielt auf." Antal Csillag anticipates changes and feels threatened. Maybe it is time to make sure his estate is secure, and with it Robert's and Heinrich's future.

He should definitely get Robert away from his senseless love of music as well as shield him as much as possible from hostile attacks in the uncertain future. Best to send him to more liberal Amsterdam, where he could gain some experience working in a friend's bank. And Heinrich can go to France and work at the solid paraffin factory there.

When he tells his sons of his decision, Robert is aghast and resists the idea of leaving Vienna, while Heinrich looks forward to a change of scene. For some time now he's been having an affair with his best friend's wife, and he'll be glad to put some distance between himself and that rather complicated situation. The youngest son, Ernst, isn't included in his father's schemes for his sons' future. He has just started Gymnasium and will stay with his parents for several more years.

THE PROSPECT OF MARRIAGE 2

THE YEAR 1929 OPENS WITH ENORMOUS AMOUNTS OF SNOW AND A blanket of freezing cold that will last into March. In hindsight, Antal Csillag will wonder if the icy winter had been a symbolic herald of the coming economic debacle. By early October, the Austrian government has forced Creditanstalt, the Rothschild's banking house, to merge with the bankrupt Boden-Creditanstalt, and only a few days after the merger, the New York stock market crashed. Soon, the whole world begins to feel the dramatic impact of the economic crisis.

Ed Weitenegg is aware that new economic winds are blowing, but at first he doesn't grasp their significance. So far, he has always been able to make ends meet. After working as a sales representative for Zeiss and Michelin, he joined his brother Franz's company, which produced iron and metal products, eventually taking it over. Franz had founded the company, but after his marriage to Thea Kuhlemann, he wanted to pull out of the smaller business and concentrate on his father-in-law's well-established firm, Imperial Feigenkaffee.

In this crisis year, Ed starts to look at Sidonie with new eyes. Maybe it wouldn't be a bad idea to marry her. Her father would give her a reasonable dowry, and maybe he could follow in his brother's footsteps and join his father-in-law's firm. The longer he thinks about the situation, the more he realizes that it would be silly of him to refuse to marry again, even though originally that had been his intention. The finances in her background would make Sidonie an ideal future wife for a decommissioned officer, and given her beauty, the idea seems even more appealing.

And really, she ought to be happy if he were to ask for her hand in marriage, thus ruling out any other offers. He has already rejected the advances of some ladies from the Mautner-Markhof clan, whose parents had come right out and asked him. The main candidate had a considerable dowry, but she didn't conform to his ideal of beauty. Even he can't imagine living with a woman he finds ugly.

The only serious cause for concern is that he would be marrying a Jew, albeit a convert. Not a very clever step, given that he is an officer in the Heimwehr. He has avoided mentioning to his future wife that he has been actively involved in the development of the Heimwehr ever since the burning of the Palace of Justice in 1927. True, he belongs to the monarchist-Catholic wing of the Heimwehr, not the petty-bourgeois anti-Semitic wing, but he still has to plan carefully when it comes to his career. And he doesn't want to disappoint his many friends from the former Habsburg army, whose weapons and military know-how have been put at the Heimwehr's service.

Despite his reservations, at the beginning of 1930 Ed proposed to Sidonie, explaining that in such times he thinks it would best if they sealed their relationship with the bond of holy matrimony.

Sidonie is a bit surprised and refers Ed to her father: after all he's the one responsible for business in the family. Obviously, it isn't much more than that for both of them. Ed's proposal hadn't included the word "love," and that's fine with Sidi, because ever since they became physically intimate, she has stopped feeling even the least bit enamored.

Yes, she likes him—the way she likes her father, her brothers or certain close friends. A marriage of convenience would make sense. After all her infamous escapades, it would be advantageous for her to be tied to him. She would be accepted as a full-fledged member of the "better" social circles, and behind that façade she'd have enough freedom to do as she liked.

And so, one Sunday afternoon Eduard Weitenegg makes his way to the Csillags to officially ask for Sidonie's hand. He is received with cool formality. This time, the flat has not been filled with elaborate flower arrangements; there is no joyful air of excitement because the only daughter has made the right choice. Sidonie's parents have known their daughter's future husband for almost two years, but they don't care for him. The mother is a bit more positively inclined towards him because she can never resist the appeal of a beau. But Antal Csillag is icy. He dislikes Herr Weitenegg's vain posturing. That he is a former officer and divorced only makes matters worse. And a sales representative and "small iron dealer," as Antal characterizes Ed to his wife, is not the husband a baron of industry envisions for his daughter.

The men sit opposite one another as if they were negotiating a hostile business take-over. Antal obliges Eduard to promise to look after Sidi particularly well and to reliably lend her his support in these turbulent economic times. For his part, Antal promises to start the young couple off financially. In addition, the separation of property has to be arranged legally.

Only after these formalities are concluded is Sidonie drawn into the discussion. First, like Ed, she must convert to Protestantism, because that is the only way it will it be possible for them to marry. The Catholic Church allows neither divorce nor a second marriage for divorcees. Antal also agrees to rent a flat for the couple, and all the household goods, including silver and linen, will be part of the dowry. After the wedding, Sidi will continue to receive a monthly allowance from her father, but this money will be exclusively for her private use and is not to be spent for joint household expenses.

Ed smiles stiffly and pretends to be satisfied. But deep inside he's angry—because clearly, there's no chance that he'll be joining his father-in-law's business. And as long as the old man is alive, there is no chance he'll get anywhere close to Sidi's money.

Upon parting, the two gentlemen exchange a brief handshake and an implied bow. Ed places a mannerly kiss on Sidi's mother's hand and another on his wife-to-be's cheek. Once he is out the door, Antal tenderly takes his daughter's small hand and holds it between his two larger ones.

"Oh, little Sidi," he says wistfully, and even Sidonie has tears in her eyes. "I wish you all the happiness on this earth, more than anyone else, but do take care of yourself…"

And both of them know that under the circumstances, happiness is something that will be relative.

Through his office, Sidi's father arranges to rent a flat in Weyrgasse, on the other side of Landstrasser Hauptstrasse and still in Sidonie's beloved Third District. By the time they're married, in May, it should be all renovated and put in order.

Ed owns some old pieces of furniture, but he thinks that some of the money put at their disposal should be used to have a cabinetmaker make a few additional, rather extravagant pieces. Sidonie is a bit put out that he doesn't care for the Old German furniture that is part of her dowry, but since she doesn't understand much about cabinetmaking, she lets her fiancé's wishes prevail.

Antal Csillag begrudges his future son-in-law the very air he breathes, but he nonetheless wants to please his daughter. Through some business partners he hears about a special event at the Dorotheum auction house and takes Sidi there to show her a set of fine china that once belonged to the Burgtheater actress Katharina Schratt and had originally been commissioned by Kaiser Franz Josef. There had originally been 36 place settings, but some plates and bowls hadn't made it through the years, and that might have been why this rare and precious china was up for sale. It is still terribly expensive, but it makes Sidi's eyes shine, and that pleases Antal beyond measure. He had been afraid that shine was gone for good, and seeing it again opens his wallet. For a few moments, father and daughter are happy together.

On May 18, 1930, Sidonie and Ed are married in the Lutheran Church in the Third District. Only the immediate family is present; it is definitely not a social event.

While Sidonie and Ed are making their private pledge before an evangelical minister, thousands of Ed's fellow travelers, among them Julius Raab, later a chancellor in the Second Republic, are taking the Korneuburg Oath, a pledge to the Heimwehr. They affirm their desire to take over the state and restructure it. They explicitly reject the Western democratic parliamentary system, which they want to replace with a more autocratic, corporative state. Everything is to be subject to the new Austrian-German patriotic ethos, based on belief in God, one's own will and the orders of a leader.

In 1930 almost 300,000 people in Austria are officially registered as unemployed, and it is against this backdrop that general elections are held on November 9. They will be the last free elections of the First Republic. Once again, the Social Democrats get the most votes: 72 seats. But the bourgeois block, consisting of Christian Socialists, the National Economic Block, the Landbund and Heimatblock, closes ranks, and the Social Democrats remain in the opposition. The National Socialists get 3 percent of the vote but do not gain more seats in Parliament.

As ever, Sidonie is not interested in politics; and although by now Ed talks openly about the Heimwehr, the subject bores her utterly. She's glad that he's spending lots of time with his war comrades because it gives her time to herself. She doesn't want to know about the grand plans these men have for Austria's future; her concerns are about very different issues. She is, for example, horrified by the fact that she has to make do with just one person to provide household help, because Ed doesn't earn enough to hire more. He seems to have a rather nonchalant attitude about work, and the industrious activity that Antal and Heinrich Csillag always exhibit seems to be foreign to him. And while Ed has used her father's money to furnish the flat, it was done according to his taste, which she doesn't share. The expensive new pieces are all in

Antal Csillag (right) on the Grossglockner with climbing friends

his study, and no matter how much he tries to portray it as their shared parlor, Sidi points out bitterly that he has egoistically overruled her.

At least she has insisted on separate bedrooms, a tactic she learned from Leonie. Being well away from an intrusive husband is highly advantageous. She never ceases to wonder how married couples like her parents can endure spending every night together in one bedroom. It's enough that Ed comes to visit several times a week and she has to put on her "act."

Just as Sidonie is starting to get used to married life, an unexpected event precipitates profound changes in the lives of all the Csillags.

In early April 1931, Sidonie answers a late-night phone call from her distraught and weeping mother. At first Sidonie can't understand her, but then she hears, "Papa is dead." Her heart plummets. Her kind and beloved father is dead! Far too young! Why couldn't he have waited? Given her more of the love and security she surely won't get from Ed?

She goes into the study and snaps at Ed that he must take her to her parents' home immediately. She gets her coat from the wardrobe, and only when they are out on the street does she start to cry and tell her clueless husband what has happened.

At home she learns that Antal Csillag had returned in the late afternoon from a skiing trip to Rax Mountain. Wind-blown, sweaty and happy, as he always was when he had been to the mountains, he took a long bath then sat in his reading chair listened to the radio. He picked up a book. Then the book dropped, and he stopped breathing. On April 17, 1931, a few days before Sidonie's thirty-first birthday, many mourners—friends and business partners alike—gathered at the Zentralfriedhof crematorium to lay Antal Csillag's ashes to rest. Between sobs, Sidonie realizes that she's now a bit more alone, more on her own, and no one is going to reach out a protective hand to shelter her anymore.

CHAPTER

7

WJERA

THE LADIES ARE MEETING FOR AFTERNOON COFFEE CHEZ FERSTEL one Friday in November 1934. Ellen Ferstel's two daughters are with their nanny, and for the first time in ages she has invited a number of friends and society ladies to her elegant flat on Pfarrhofgasse. She has also invited her husband to stay at his office, and the fifteen guests have the parlor to themselves. Sidi, Ellen's closest friend and almost a member of her household, sits in a big red leather armchair, smoking a cigarette and scrutinizing the arriving guests. Two white-gloved maids wearing lace-trimmed white aprons over their dark blue uniforms bring in trays of petit fours and little cheese pastries, place them on the buffet and quickly return to the kitchen to pour coffee into silver pots.

Sidi is tired and had considered taking a nap instead of attending this party. She'll know all of the guests and had wondered if it might be less boring to stay home with her idle husband, who spends his days poring over old military maps instead of working.

But now she's quite comfortable at the smoking table by the warmth of the fireplace. Two new guests enter as she is stubbing out her cigarette. She pulls the filter from the holder and looks up, wondering if she knows them.

Sidi has seen the somewhat stout older woman before. The slightly tilted eyes and small mouth remind her that it's Helene Rothballer, whose rough charm and original wit have drawn Sidi's attention at other social gatherings. She always wears a flower in the buttonhole on her right lapel, and today her camel hair suit sports an orange gerbera.

Sidonie doesn't recognize the woman with her but is enthralled. Something in her eyes and smile reminds her of Helene. Her daughter, perhaps? No, she's much too pretty. A tall, erect figure in a dark, calf-length suit, she wears an arctic fox stole across her shoulders that flatters her light eyes and calm, reserved face. Wearing a slight smile, the stranger stands in the middle of the room, unsure where to sit and revealing a few moments of insecurity.

The lovely woman gives her a brief nod and chooses a seat nearby. Sidi is captivated.

After the first cups of black coffee have been emptied and the conversation has settled into a quiet hum, Sidonie goes over to the buffet, ostensibly for more pastries, but actually, she has been waiting to talk to Ellen privately.

Grasping her by the arm, she asks, "Who is she?"

"Whom are you talking about?" Ellen replies, surprised. Has she neglected her duties as hostess and forgotten to introduce all the guests?

"Over there. The one with the short dark hair and the fox stole."

"That's Wjera Fechheimer. She lives in Nuremberg now. Helene Rothballer's daughter. You must know her; in the early twenties she got married in Vienna to one of the Gutmanns. She's a beauty, isn't she? Though rather an austere beauty."

Sidonie summons a vague memory. Right after the war was a long time ago, when she only had eyes for Leonie Puttkamer. She must have overlooked Wjera then, but for the rest of this afternoon she has to try hard to avoid staring improperly. As good-byes are being said in the hallway, Wjera struggles to put on her coat and Sidi seizes the opportunity to help her into it. The evenly clipped hairline at the nape of Wjera's neck makes Sidonie want to kiss her there. As a warm ripple spreads through her body, she barely manages a few meaningless words before wishing Wjera a pleasant evening.

As soon as she wakes up the next morning, Sidi, her hair loose and still wearing her nightgown, throws a warm mohair shawl around her shoulders and phones Ellen, who always gets up early.

Ellen was going to bet that the first call in the morning would be Sidi, wide awake and demanding at an unusually early hour. Tucking the heavy, black receiver between her shoulder and cheek, Sidi lights another cigarette, sits on the parquet floor, settles her back against the wall and fires off a string of questions. She wants every detail.

Ellen is surprised that Sidi doesn't remember Wjera but patiently tells the whole story, and Sidi discovers that she has more connections to Wjera than she realized.

THE ROTHBALLER-GUTMANN-FECHHEIMER INTERCONNECTIONS

As a young man, Wjera's father, Oskar Rothballer, came to the attention of Karl Wittgenstein, then the owner of large iron-producing factories in Moravia and Silesia and the main competitor of the Rothschilds and Gutmanns. Karl Wittgenstein took the ambitious Oskar under his wing and sent him east to take care of some of his business dealings with Russia. Wjera was born in December 1896, toward the end of her parents stay in Moscow, which had lasted several months. The family soon relocated to Prague, where Oskar Rothballer became the managing director of the Prague Iron Industry Society.

In 1906 Anton Kerpely, then the general manager of the Alpine Montan Society, one of the Habsburg monarchy's biggest industrial enterprises, convinced Oskar to take a position in Vienna. That summer, the family moved into a beautiful flat on Brahmsplatz in the Fourth District, and Oskar worked first as an authorized signatory and soon as managing director of the Alpine Montan Society. In 1914 he succeeded Anton Kerpely as general manager of the Society, which not only met domestic needs but also exported to neighboring countries, and this was the capacity in which he had had dealings with Sidonie's father.

Rothballer guided the Society through the war years and the first years of the new Austrian republic and was esteemed in industrial circles for his profound knowledge of the iron industry. Also, he was always the chief negotiator for larger stock transfers. The *Neue Freie Presse* often quoted his vehement statements opposing both the exorbitant price hikes that crippled consumption and the profiteering that was popular in industrial circles.

In 1921 Oskar Rothballer became seriously ill, and the managing director, Eugen Herz, and the then technical director of Alpine Montan,

Henrik Bäckström, took over for him temporarily. Bäckström's son
Klaus had been Sidonie's finance. After Rothballer's early death in 1922,
Herz became Alpine Montan's general director.

Wjera Rothballer spent her youth in Vienna, married Ernst Gutmann in 1921 and lived with her husband in Vienna's Cottage Quarter
in the Eighteenth District. From the mid nineteenth century until the
Aryanization by the National Socialists, the Gutmanns—who owned
large coal mines—were one of Vienna's wealthiest families, to which
their former palace on Ringstrasse between Schubertring and Beethov-
enplatz bears witness.

Around 1850 Wilhelm Gutmann founded the family's wealth with a
mining enterprise in Witkowitz and coal mines in Orlau-Lazy. He was
very involved in Jewish community work, financing charitable institutions that included hospitals and the Israelite Girls Orphanage.

Max Gutmann, Wilhelm's son, joined the family enterprise in 1883
and served for many years as president of the Industrialists' Associations

*Wjera Rothballer at the
time of her marriage to
Ernst Gutmann, 1921*

and on the board of various other organizations. He married Emilie Hartmann, daughter of Ernst Hartmann and Helene Schneeberger, both actors in the court theater. Ernst Hartmann, originally from Hamburg, was a very successful member of Vienna's Hoftheater, and his statue and one of Helene Schneeberger now grace the halls of the Burgtheater.

Max and Emilie Gutmann had three daughters and two sons. Ernst, the older son, was born in Vienna in 1898, and like many young men of his generation was drafted into the army right after graduating from gymnasium. He and Sidonie's older brother, Heinrich, spent almost a year together on the Italian front. After returning from the war, Ernst started looking for a bride and paid several courtesy visits to Ellen, then still a Schoeller. His charm and winning personality made an impression on her, and they were said to have made a lovely picture together on the dance floor. But one day Heinrich informed Ellen over cocktails that Ernst suffered from some incurable disease and wouldn't be able to father children, suggesting that she had better look elsewhere for a husband.

Ernst Gutmann married Wjera Rothballer in 1921. According to strict Gutmann family rules, the females could convert to Christianity or marry into Christian families, the males' wives could come from Christian families, but they themselves were obliged never to leave the Jewish faith.

Soon after the marriage, Ellen learned that Wjera was pregnant and was left wondering if Heinrich's information had been wrong. Months later, she was dismayed to hear that Wjera had given birth to stillborn twins.

In October 1925, after only four years of marriage, Ernst Gutmann died of leukemia. Had this been the disease that first announced itself during the war?

After her husband's death, Wjera went on a cruise, where she shared a table with a tall blonde man and his beautiful blonde companion, who she assumed was his wife. Only upon debarking, when he asked her for her address, did she learn that the woman was the sister. Soon, the flowers and letters started to arrive, and eventually, Hans Martin Fechheimer came to Vienna in person to propose to the young widow.

The Gutmanns would have liked to keep their daughter-in-law in the family. The famous violinist Bronislaw Hubermann once said of Wjera, "If this woman also had charm, she'd be irresistible." True, Wjera could be a bit stern at times, but this was counterbalanced by her beauty, and she had started to attract admirers and suitors quite soon after Ernst's death. Hans Martin Fechheimer was from an upper-class Nuremberg family, owners of the Vereinigte Margarine-Werke, and he was certainly a suitable match. When Wjera met him, he had just gotten his law degree and was working as a lawyer in the family business. The Fechheimers' wealth didn't have as diverse a base as the Gutmanns', but Wjera's life in Nuremberg would be just as comfortable as it had always been in Vienna.

Wjera married Hans Martin in Dresden in April 1928, and the young couple went to live in his parents' villa in Nuremberg until moving into their own home a year later.

The name Fechheimer surfaces frequently in the history of Jews in the city of Nuremberg, which didn't have a good relationship with its Jewish inhabitants. While neighboring communities, particularly the city of Fürth, put no restrictions on where Jewish families could settle, Nuremberg refused to allow them to live within the city limits. The main synagogue was consecrated only in 1874 and was torn down in August 1938.

At the end of 1935—just before the Nazis' anti-Semitic madness set out on its path of unlimited destruction—21 percent of the businesses in Nuremberg and Fürth had Jewish owners, and many of the cities' private banks were partially in Jewish hands. The National Socialist Party's measures against Jewish citizens and the Aryanization of businesses were in many ways similar in both Germany and Austria. This can be attributed to the fact that *Stürmer* editor Julius Streicher, who lived in Nuremberg and wanted his city to set an example for the rest of Germany, dictated the Reich's anti-Semitic policy. Streicher suggested in November 1938 that all of Nuremberg's Jews be interned in order to solve the city's housing problems.

The Fechheimers must have started feeling the first gusts of the sharp brown wind fairly early, because Hans Martin and Wjera left Nuremberg in June 1935 and moved to Munich. Hans Martin's parents stayed in Nuremberg until March 1939, when they moved to Berlin-Charlottenburg, where Hans-Martin's sister had lived since her marriage in 1933.

The Fechheimers had all become Protestants long ago, but according to the Nuremberg Racial Laws they were Jewish, and as of January 1, 1939, they, like all Jews, were forced to use Israel and Sara as their middle names.

In 1928, at the time of Wjera and Hans Martin's marriage, the National Socialists' ascent was still in the future; and even by late 1934, when Sidonie rediscovered Wjera in Vienna, Austria's world, too, still seemed to be in somewhat reasonable order.

Satisfied with the information she has just gotten from Ellen, Sidonie wraps up their phone conversation the moment Ed appears at the living room door—vain as ever in the silk pajamas that he insists that the maid iron with a perfect crease in the trousers. He doesn't need to know that she has finally developed a crush again, one that's already burrowing into her heart—or that, once again, it's on a beautiful woman.

The last bit of information she secures from Ellen is where Wjera usually stays when in Vienna: Hotel Sacher. At the breakfast table, while Ed hides behind his newspaper, she eats an egg, butters her bread and starts to plan an encounter with Wjera.

Hotel Sacher is an ideal place to run into someone by accident, and she is thinking along the same lines as in the days of Leonie Puttkamer. Of course, she'll go about it differently this time; after all, she's no longer seventeen years old and is now often referred to as one of Vienna's most beautiful women. The meeting should seem casual—two elegant acquaintances encounter one another while doing errands in the city center.

Inside, however, Sidonie feels like an agitated teenager. Nothing has changed—the pounding heart, the excitement, the joyful anticipation of meeting a woman she adores. And Sidonie is delighted that she hasn't lost that tingling feeling after so many years.

"I'll always have this," she thinks cheerfully.

The next morning she leaves the house early, having decided that buying something at Demel's confectionery will provide an excuse to go to the city center. After making her purchase, she takes up a position among the opera house arcades where she can keep Hotel Sacher's entrance under surveillance. Such antics had been better suited to September 1917 than to November 1934. The cold creeps into Sidi's fur-lined ankle boots, and even the ample collar of her mink coat can't insulate her well enough. Just as she is thinking, "I'm too old for such nonsense," with a hint of self-directed irony, Wjera emerges from the hotel. Sidonie is well schooled in the art of crossing unobtrusively to the other side of a street, walking absentmindedly towards her objective and then feigning overjoyed surprise.

She takes Wjera's arm and steers her towards a white-draped table in one of Café Sacher's dark wooden booths. They exchange trivialities, talk about the afternoon tea at Ellen's, the weather ... Wjera talks a bit about her life in Nuremberg, deploring the city's provincialism, mentioning the party meetings—all those men in black leather boots and brown shirts—that do not make life there any easier.

Hotel Sacher, Vienna

Sidonie doesn't seem to get the message, maybe because she can't take her eyes off Wjera's hands. Lost in her own thoughts, her eyes follow them as they move from the sugar bowl to the spoon and back, then to the cup and up to her mouth. Everything has to seem innocuous, and so Sidonie's eyes rest only briefly on the fine, sensitive mouth, the straight nose, the bright, playful eyes, the white neck graced by a string of luminous pearls. Her glance can linger on those hands with less fear of detection. They look soft but are also broad and firm, sometimes animated by the flow of the conversation, sometimes resting beside her cup. Sidi adores them as a stand-in for the woman whose soul she's sure they express.

A brief, "Sidi, I have to say good-bye," pulls the dreamer back to reality. The ladies stand, allow the waiter to help them into their fur coats, glance in the mirror to put on their hats and are back on the street.

"I return to Nuremberg tomorrow," says Wjera. "I'm sure we'll meet again during my next visit."

Two kisses on the cheek and Sidonie is free to go home with her Demel purchases. But first, she goes to her favorite flower shop in Führichgasse and chooses the most beautiful orchids she can find. She writes a little poem she has already prepared at home on the enclosed card and leaves both at Sacher's for Wjera. She doesn't sign the card, after all they are both married women, but she'd pay a small fortune to see the surprised and puzzled look on Wjera's face as she reads it.

Sidonie hadn't dared to ask if she could write to Wjera in Nuremberg, but after a week she realizes how much she wants to have some connection with, some message from that beautiful woman. She needs a plan—something discreet, she can't act as impetuously as she did in her youth.

In the silence before going to sleep at night, she mulls over all the people who might connect her to Wjera and remembers that Grete Weinberger's mother, Muni, is friends with Wjera's mother, Helene Rothballer, and because they live in the same neighborhood—one in Schwindgasse, the other in Wohllebengasse—the mothers are likely to meet frequently.

She phones Muni Weinberger a few days later and mentions Wjera and Helene in passing. Muni takes the bait.

Ed Weitenegg and Sidonie Csillag

Yes, she'd like to see Helene, what a good idea; she will invite her to come to Katzelsdorf next weekend. Sidi and Ed should also come. One can easily drive there; the first snow of the season has melted in the Rosaliagebirge and reaching the country house won't be a problem. The second step in Sidonie's plan is going to work.

Sidonie has to make sure that her husband doesn't notice her recently improved mood. Yesterday he caught her humming to herself and making faces in the bathroom mirror. He asked if she had premature spring fever, then sidled up behind her and pressed against her to signal that her spring fever had been contagious. The familiar ice age enveloped her once again.

Sidonie isn't happy with Ed. They have been married for over four years, and things have settled into a state of permanent equidistance. At the beginning she had imagined things very differently, but the only positive thing about this marriage is that she is living with a man and thus fulfilling social expectations. Even her closest friends don't like Ed and make fun of him behind his back. As a former army officer, he isn't particularly welcome among those who themselves had only recently risen to the status of minor nobility. The men make slighting remarks because he doesn't work and sneer at his man-about-town mannerisms and dandyish vanity—of which the crisply ironed silk pajamas are but one example. And his harsh, domineering attitude doesn't exactly make him easy to be around, particularly since it is all just hot air—Ed is the master of the house only because Sidonie supports him. Since the beginning, her money has been the primary contributor to his comfortable lifestyle: the furniture, the new car, the horse's upkeep, his bespoke wardrobe, which is not cheap, all come out of her purse, which is to say, from Antal Csillag's purse via his estate. Ed is particularly thrifty, however, when it comes to funds not destined for his personal use. This recently led to a row when Sidonie decided to hire a second maid in order to escape having to do any housework, to which she is unsuited.

She does still try to keep up appearances and pretends to the outside world that they are a happy couple. Who knows, maybe Ed actually thinks they are perfectly suited for each other, because she carries the play acting all the way into the bedroom, where she allows him the illusion that he is a perfect lover who takes her *au point* to ecstasy. And—unbeknownst to him—even in this he is an object of ridicule, because, with the redemptive bitterness of the unsatisfied, Sidonie can revel in the thought that it is she who chooses the moments to enact her comedy and thus can take him for a fool.

But at the moment, given the grave political events, Sidonie's personal problems are rather fading into the background.

AUSTRIAN POWER PLAYS 1932–34

ON MAY 20, 1932, CHRISTIAN SOCIALIST ENGELBERT DOLLFUSS became the Austrian chancellor and formed his first coalition government with his own party, the Landbund and the Heimatblock. While Dollfuss had a specific political plan and was able to put his own people in key positions, he was unable to prevent the Nazis from holding a Gau

[Regional] Rally in Vienna at the end of September. Joseph Goebbels and Ernst Röhm were among the participants.

Dollfuss and his people also couldn't improve the bad economic situation. In 1932, 362,000 Austrians were unemployed and an additional 150,000 were "Ausgesteuerte," people who had lost all their state benefits. And the numbers kept increasing. Alpine Montan's iron and steel works had already been shut down three times and the workers sent home. The number of negotiated debt settlements and insolvencies in 1932 was double the number in 1929, and the average income of a Viennese household had decreased by 34 percent since 1930.

On March 7, 1933, the National Council president and two vice presidents resigned in order to be able to cast their votes as parliament members, thus rendering the National Council incapable of acting. Dollfuss declared that the National Council was unworkable and announced that the federal government was unaffected by the parliamentary crisis and would continue to govern based on the Kriegswirtschaftliche Ermächtigungsgesetz (Wartime Economic Authority Law) of July 24, 1917. Among other things, this law banned public meetings, prohibited the massing of troops and enabled pre-censorship of publications. During the course of the year, Dolfuss's Christian Socialists and their various organizations continued to take actions against the Social Democrats and those allied with them. The police barred deputies from entering the parliament building, the Republikanische Schutzbund was dissolved and the traditional May Day parades were prohibited. Government social insurance programs were restricted and federal employees who didn't agree with the government were fired.

In May 1933 Italy's Fascist leader Benito Mussolini gave money to the Heimwehr to organize a celebration to commemorate the 250th anniversary of Vienna's liberation from the second Turkish siege. A quarter of a million people participate in the festivities. In June 1933 Austria outlawed the National Socialist German Workers' Party (NSDAP). Detention camps were opened and the death penalty reinstated.

At that point there were only fifteen companies left in Austria that employed more than a thousand people; 44 percent of all industrial workers were unemployed. The government tried to cope with this situation by commissioning large public works projects, including the Vienna

Höhenstrasse and a road crossing the Grossglockner, as well as a new Reichsbrücke bridging the Danube.

In February 1934 the conflict between the Christian Socialist Heimwehr and the Social Democrats escalated to civil war-like confrontations that left about 1500 dead and many more wounded. There were mass arrests, and in addition to the Social Democratic Party, all cultural organizations and unions were dissolved and their finances confiscated. Many of the reforms and programs that had been implemented by the Social Democrats were abolished or revoked.

On July 25, 1934, the National Socialists attempted their "July Putsch," assassinating Chancellor Dollfuss but failing to effect a coup d'état. This did nothing to change the official government line. President Wilhelm Miklas asked then-Minister of Justice Kurt Schussnigg to form a new government.

As Sidi struggles through the fourth year of her loveless marriage, Austria's economic situation continues in decline. (Eventually, in 1936, even Phönix Insurance—which financed the Heimwehr over the years—will declare bankruptcy. At which point, the Austrian state will assume its debts.) The number of the unemployed and Ausgesteuerte only keeps increasing, and many are no longer included in the statistics. Those who still have work receive an average salary of 60 to 120 Schillings a month. The city's pubs display posters with witty sayings such as "Eat your fill and drink your fill, but talk of politics should be nil" and offer three course lunches—soup, main dish and dessert—for 1 Schilling. Those who decline the soup can make a phone call instead.

The much-anticipated excursion to Katzelsdorf is planned for the coming weekend. Ed agreed to this visit to the Weinbergers even though the weather forecast bodes ill for his lovely dark blue Steyr automobile—the combination of rain and dirt roads will splash mud everywhere. But Sidi has been so happy recently that he doesn't want to spoil her plans.

An hour's drive takes them to the big lattice-work gate at the entrance to the Weinberger's estate. The servant who comes running to open it shivers in the cold. A bell is rung in the main house to announce the guests and call all the servants to attention while the

Weiteneggs make the short drive down the conifer- and beech-lined drive to the house.

Once there, Sidi almost leaps out of the car, paying no attention to Ed, and rushes into the open arms of Muni Weinberger, whose loud cries of "Sidi, Sidi!" vie with yelps of the two Pekinese dogs that cavort about, tails wagging.

Sidi is in a hurry to get to the grand salon, where the guests are gathered and meet with Helene Rothballer, her only hope as a source of regular information about Wjera. But first she has to stop to greet two friends, who rather seem to be blocking her way: Sylvie Dietz with her little daughter Dorli and Grete Weinberger, busy trying to tame Peter

Grete Weinberger with her husband, Willy, and sons Peter and Rolf; Ed Weitenegg in the background

and Rolf, her two sons. For a change, Willy Weinberger is helping out with the boys today—Grete has divorced him, but they still live together. He is a small, hardy man with jolly features behind which lurks a dreaded and choleric temper.

Finally Sidonie cuts through to Helene Rothballer, whose grey lapel features a yellow rose today. She greets Sidonie with a mischievous smile and accepts two kisses, one on each cheek.

The lady of the house summons the guests to lunch. Her face flushed—despite her large staff, she is passionate about doing her own cooking—she emerges from the kitchen and tosses her large apron onto a chair in the corner only minutes before taking her place at the head of the table. The meal features a pork roast with dumplings, and everyone enjoys the lusciously greasy food. As usual, there is lively discussion around the table. The men are talking politics. Papsl and Hans Weinberger, father and son, declare themselves satisfied with the situation in Germany and express their hope that Austria will soon follow. Willy, who is strongly anti-Nazi, voices his opposition. Ed, a moderate Austro-fascist, tries to accommodate both sides, and the discussion culminates in a huge shouting match, with some guests throwing napkins and banging their glasses on the table.

As ever, Muni puts an end to the yelling with her resolute friendliness and asks everyone to adjourn for coffee. Her words carry weight, and a good-natured calm returns. Everyone is friends again.

Sidi chooses an armchair next to Helene Rothballer's and starts making small talk, in the course of which she extracts some useful information. Wjera comes to Vienna regularly to see her mother—mostly just not to feel guilty, Helene says with a laugh. Her next visit will be later in the spring. Also, Helene is fond of ice-skating—another possible way to meet up with her to obtain news of Wjera. Sidi skated a lot in her childhood, and with three more winter months ahead, she is thinking of unpacking her skates and trying the sport again. She even makes a date to meet Helene at the rink.

In the late afternoon, after the coffee, shop talk, small talk and teasing, the party starts to break up. Ed and Sidi offer Helene a ride, since the Weinbergers plan to stay at the country house and no other car is going back to Vienna.

After much cheek kissing and other farewell rituals, Sidi decides that this very agreeable afternoon has given her much hope for the future.

In the following weeks Sidonie increasingly seeks out Helene's company, and she proves to be a very nice, fun-loving woman whose task, since being widowed at a young age has been to enjoy life. She is flattered by this young, beautiful new friend's interest in her and is never disinclined to accept an offer to do something. Nor is she averse to a subtle flirtatious suggestion. Nevertheless, it strikes her as a bit strange that Sidi prefers her company rather than that of men. To be on the safe side, she asks Muni Weinberger if Sidi has a happy marriage. Muni, long Sidi's confidante, can provide many details and also passes on the information that Sidi is mainly interested in women.

Helene Rothballer feels even more flattered. She is past the age when she'd consider a woman's interest in other women to be dangerous, and she enjoys the little frisson caused by the attention she thinks is directed towards her.

Almost half a year passes before Sidonie learns that Wjera will soon return to Vienna. In the first flush of excitement, she tells Helene that she will be overjoyed to see Wjera again, and Helene finally realizes that Sidi's attentions have been on behalf of her daughter all along. She can laugh at her own vanity, which has certainly led her to draw the wrong conclusions and is not angry with Sidi. She promises to arrange a few gatherings so her young friend can spend some time with Wjera in Vienna.

Their first encounter will be a dinner at the Weiteneggs, for which Sidonie starts making detailed plans at the beginning of April 1935. Normally, household activities are at the bottom of her list, but in this special case, she plans the menu, the table settings and the choice of wine. The invitation she sent to Nuremberg a while ago has been acknowledged with a card bearing a small engraving of the Church of Our Lady on the front and a message on the back in an energetic hand accepting the offer and closing with kind regards. The only drawback is that Wjera won't be coming alone but with her husband, Hans Martin. But this will at least give Sidi the opportunity to observe their relationship and assess her chances with Wjera.

April 28 is the big day. Early in the morning Sidi sends the maids to the Naschmarkt to buy the ingredients for dinner. She has "borrowed" a cook from her friend Ellen for the evening and has planned a delicious meal starting with a light vegetable soup, followed by poached trout and then cream puffs. She has learned that these are Wjera's favorite dessert, and it will take the cook most of the afternoon to prepare them.

She sets the table with her father's wedding present to her, the china that had once belonged to Katharina Schratt. She adds heavy crystal glasses and places a small, pale pink rose on Wjera's plate.

Despite the warm weather she has chosen a snug dark dress for the evening—it highlights her figure and her elegant, austere beauty. Shortly before the doorbell rings at seven, she rearranges the flowers in the window alcoves—lush callas, colorful anemones and dark aconites that she ordered from Hoffmann in Führichgasse.

Sidonie herself answers the door, and a quick glance confirms that she still finds Wjera both beautiful and enticing. But Hans Martin is a surprise. Her condescending prejudice had led her to expect a "Jewish looking" man, but he is tall and blond and could have been from northern Sweden. He meets with her approval, and the positive impression is reinforced at dinner by his casual, rather ironic manner and the caring way he interacts with his wife.

After the starter course, Wjera rather abruptly excuses herself and asks Sidi to tell her where she can reapply her powder. Taking advantage of this opportunity, Sidi soon leaves the table to follow her. Ed looks up quickly, as if smelling something unusual on the wind.

In her boudoir, she finds Wjera standing before the mirror rouging her cheeks. She turns to reveal a lovely profile framed in short, unruly, reddish curls. Unable to restrain herself, Sidi reached Wjera's side in two swift strides, takes her in her arms and kisses her passionately. Wjera's respond is briefly soft and yielding, but then she startles, stiffens and pushes Sidi away.

Speaking firmly, as if wanting to undo what has just happened, Wjera asks, "How can you do this to your husband?"

Sidi smiles and shrugs. "He has the woman he loves. And I don't."

"If that's the case…" Wjera mumbles. "I didn't know that." Embarrassed, she looks at the open compact that's still in her hand, closes it and says with a look that mixes softness, seriousness and sadness and touches Sidi deeply, "I don't know, Sidi … I don't know where this is going to lead us."

She turns and leaves the room, wondering if she should let the old, well-suppressed inclination emerge again. She has always had a fancy for women, and Sidi does have something special, something that has preoccupied her since they first met. She had thought that this peculiar attraction to women was just part of her adolescence; it wouldn't do any good if it resurfaced.

Unaware of these thoughts, Sidi soon follows Wjera back to the dining room, where both women rejoin the conversation with practiced ease—their husbands' lovely, versatile wives, nothing more.

But in Sidonie's head there's room for only one turbulent train of thought: "I'll kiss her, kiss her again, hold her in my arms until she wants me. Even if it takes years."

On her way home, Wjera finds that it is her turn to feel confused. She has known Sidi only fleetingly and has heard all the rumors about her predilection for women. She had concluded from her mother's letters that Sidi had been courting her, and that had been the only reason Wjera agreed to dine at the Weiteneggs—she wanted to put Sidi under the microscope. And now this!

In the days that follow, Wjera finds herself growing restless and unable to concentrate. She hardly talks to her husband and won't let him touch her. At night she vacillates in her dreams between fear and lust in the arms of various women. Eventually, the dreams and the experience that triggered them recede, and she does everything possible to avoid their return. She sees Sidi only two more times during her time in Vienna. They go for a walk through the Stadtpark together with Wjera's mother, whose presence eases the tension. At another time, they sit smoking in the sun on the terrace at Café Meierei, and it almost seems as if the talk they are having is an easy, casual one. When saying goodbye, perhaps Wjera presses herself to Sidi for a bit too long before Sidi draws both her hands to her lips and kissed them with all her heart. Then Wjera is on the train, Hans Martin by her side, Nuremberg ahead, and all the visit's strangely unreal events disappear behind her as if in a fog.

Sidonie Csillag, Wjera Fechheimer, Helene Rothballer in the Vienna Woods, 1936

When Sidonie returns from her summer holidays in September 1935, she learns from Helene Rothballer that Wjera and her husband had moved to Munich at the end of June. Sidonie is disappointed that Wjera hadn't told her personally but ignores the small pain. All the trifles of her everyday life give her enough to cope with.

She's pleased that Ed hadn't noticed much, maybe not anything, of her wooing of Wjera, because this frees her to dwell undisturbed in a Wjera dreamland. Though she thinks about her a lot, she forces herself not to make contact. Now that she is older and knows that the excesses of her youth are no longer appropriate, she consoles herself with the thought that the mills of a god, who is not hers, grind slowly but steadily.

When she hasn't received any news from Wjera by Christmas time, Sidonie relents and decides to send flowers to Munich, accompanied, as before, the by an anonymous poem.

Wjera sends a well-mannered thank you note for the flowers to her Viennese ex-brother in law, who had always courted her a bit, and is baffled when he denies having sent them. Her next letter is to her mother, asking her to make inquires; and an apprehensive Helene Rothballer goes straight to Sidonie. With a small smile, Sidi confesses.

In Sidonie's everyday world, things go on as usual—excursions on the weekends, bridge games at various locations, invitations from Ellen, Grete, Sylvie, and more recently from Ed's relatives.

Like her, Ed has three siblings: two sisters and one brother. The sisters, both of whom married before Sidi and Ed did, mean Sidonie well and make an effort on her behalf. Irene, the older one, is a primary school teacher, married and with a young daughter. Socially very active, she is a member of several welfare organizations and convinces Sidi to donate some of her time to a good cause.

Sidonie doesn't think much of all this "do-gooding," but she doesn't want to disappoint Irene. Besides, it looks good for a lady in society to spend some of her husband's money—actually, her own—on the world's poor, even if one doesn't know why they are poor.

She agrees to help at the Elisabeth Table once a week. This is an organization of society ladies who prepare and serve lunch for widows and orphans. Sidi lets everyone know that she is useless at cooking and has no intention of learning that skill, but she is willing to set the tables, serve food and talk a bit with the poor.

Some of the charitable ladies give Sidi a cool reception and remain standoffish despite her attempts to engage them in conversation. They turn away haughtily when she enters the room, and once in passing she overhears the word "Jewish." She immediately pushes this aside and resolves to ignore these women arrogantly from now on.

Sidonie gets along better with Ed's younger sister, Grete. Like her, Grete tends to be melancholy and is very fond of animals. Grete had married an older man who worked at a government ministry—she didn't seem to have cared for him particularly. Once, in the Rathauspark, Sidonie had accidentally run into her walking in the company of a tomboyish woman. It had been too late to avoid the mutually quite embarrassing encounter, and for a moment Sidonie had been tempted to patronize her sister-in-law, but taking her own preferences into consideration, she decided to let her know that she approved of her companion. Grete's husband died a year after that episode, and she now gets a nice widow's pension that lets her face the future without any worries. She no longer hides her attraction to women and to the tomboyish lady, Olga, who has moved in with her and is always at her side. Ed is unaware that he has a second lesbian in the family.

Sidi simply cannot relate to Ed's younger brother, Franz. As vain as her husband, he is also ambitious, and his ego craves validation. This is probably why he married Thea Kuhlemann, whose father owns the Imperial Feigenkaffee Company.

Franz and Thea have been very busy elevating their social standing, and they constantly entertain guests who they think will further their company's interests. Sidonie and Ed are included in their invitations, which Sidonie enjoys at first, but eventually she finds that the nouveau riche get on her nerves. Social climbers of all sorts attend these soirees, hoping to meet people who are already established in society and whose very presence in the same room will let the newcomers think that now they "belong." But mostly they just run into more people like themselves, among them men with swastikas on their lapels who sport the same little moustache as their idol.

In 1936 Franz dies shortly after having undergone an appendectomy, and soon Ed and Sidonie stop visiting the Kuhlemanns. Sidonie doesn't mind; the pro-Nazi atmosphere and attendant anti-Semitism had gotten to be too much even for her. For a while she was afraid that Ed might take the same line, but these fears prove unfounded. Ed is more of a fellow traveler, someone who doesn't want to rub anyone the wrong way. He just doesn't want his siblings to know that his wife's origins are Jewish, and before getting married he had impressed it on Sidonie that she had to keep her mouth shut on the topic. Though for very different reasons, both spouses are in complete agreement about keeping silent.

ST. GILGEN

TO SIDONIE'S GREAT RELIEF, SUMMER 1936 FINALLY ARRIVES AND with it hope for a break in the monotony of her life. As they do every year, she and Ed will go away for the summer, and once again they have chosen St. Gilgen am Wolfgangsee for their retreat.

By 1880 St. Gilgen had already started its climb into the ranks of most-preferred summer vacation spots for the Viennese bourgeoisie. Many well-to-do families bought property and built villas there, including the

Viennese doctor Theodor Billroth, in 1883, and factory owner and banker Max Feilchenfeld, who would later build on Brioni. Feilchenfeld had a villa in St. Gilgen that, at the turn of the century, was considered to be one of the most ostentatious in all of the Salzkammergut.

In order to make the whole area accessible for the increasing number of tourists, hundreds of Russian prisoners of war were put to work building a new road in 1916. They also built a footpath from Fürberg to St. Gilgen via Brunnwinkl.

During World War I, summer vacationers were not made particularly welcome there because the lack of milk, butter and meat made it hard to provide food for so many people. But after the war and into the twenties and now the thirties, the summer social life of Vienna's bourgeoisie once again migrates to the Salzkammergut. The Salzburg Summer Festival, founded by Max Reinhardt in 1922, creates a lively atmosphere and attracts lots of international guests. The tennis courts, bowling alleys, riding stables and other outcroppings of the luxuriously equipped villas fill with life. And for vacationers who lack their own villas, the locals have built summer houses that they rent out.

Now more than ever before, the Austrian tourist industry depends on attracting Austrian tourists. In 1933 the German Reich implemented the Tausendmarksperre (thousand Mark barrier), a fee of 1000 Reichsmarks that German citizens had to pay if travelling to Austria. This cut the number of annual visits from Germany to the Tyrol from 1.25 million to just 130,000. Bargain rates were offered in order to make it possible for Austrians to vacation in their own country. In Carinthia, for example, in the off-season one could book two weeks, all meals included, for just 80 Schillings.

Thus, the von Weiteneggs have found quite reasonable lodgings at Schöpkes this year. The owner of this villa on the lakeshore is a grumpy old German man, but it's his cousin who runs the establishment and takes care of the guests. A tiny one-room house in the garden offers a rustic setting where Sidi and Ed can enjoy playing at country life for a few weeks. They accept the fact that they have to share a bed, there is no running water and they have to wash at the fountain in the garden.

The loveliest thing about the place is the view. The lake is just outside their door, and while they sit on the bench outside the house to watch the ever-changing colors on the lake for hours on end, Sidi doesn't even mind Ed's company.

When it is sunny and warm, the Weiteneggs go swimming or rowing. When it is overcast, they go hiking or visit friends, among them the Imhofs, who are staying across the lake in Fürberg. Sidonie quite likes this merry family. The father and one of the sons are heavyset men who laugh loudly and frequently. The mother is a beautiful, slim and elegant woman who Sidonie likes for quite other reasons. And best of all, the Imhofs are always ready to engage in a positively excessive game of bridge.

Ellen's parents, too, have rented a villa in St. Gilgen, and all their children and grandchildren are welcome there. As in Vienna, they host social gatherings almost daily—here they feature swimming, tennis, hiking and, when it is raining, bridge parties.

When hiking here, if one runs into people, one takes the time to greet them and often stops long enough to gossip about those who are in residence and those who are not. The high aristocracy continues to meet in Bad Ischl, where the Imperial Family used to spend its summers.

Ellen Ferstel and Sidonie Csillag in the cabriolet

The artists gather on Attersee—where everyone meets at Schloss Kammer, which is owned by the wealthy Berlin heiress Eleanore von Mendelssohn. Her guest lists read like an international "Who's Who" of gays and lesbians. The bourgeoisie, business people, industrialists and their family all gather around Wolfgangsee.

When it is raining—a frequent occurrence in the Salzkammergut—the Weiteneggs drive to visit Ellen's family across the lake. During their endless card games, any chance reference to Ed's dark blue Steyr can get the men talking about cars. Ed is among the 10,000 privileged Austrians who own a car in the mid-thirties, which makes many men jealous—even those with the financial means to buy one.

Uninterested in cars, Sidi wonders how men can discuss their various merits for hours on end. This summer she much prefers to spend her time at Count Almeida's castle on Mondsee, which her brother Robert has rented for himself and his opera company, the Salzburg Opera Guild.

Robert's musical career has taken off nicely, and he's become quite successful. Shortly after Antal Csillag's death in 1931, he informed the family that he was going to give up the job in Amsterdam, which he hadn't wanted, in order to study music at the Neues Wiener Konservatorium. He had already talked with Josef Reitler, founder and head of that conservatory, who would be happy to accept him as his student. Also one of the co-founders of the Salzburg Festival, Reitler knew Gustav Mahler personally and was in contact with Europe's most important conductors, directors and singers.

The family was surprised but not averse. Emma Csillag thought everything her sons did was wonderful. Sidonie was happy to see her favorite brother doing what he wanted to do, which had never been business; so let him be happy with his music. Only prudent Heinrich urged Robert to think this decision over; their father would have wanted them to keep music just for pleasure and have a solid profession.

But Robert was immune to all objections and brought an enthusiasm to his music studies that no one had seen him exhibit before. He had lots of ideas for new compositions and hoped to become a successful conductor. After separating from his first wife, he met Herta Glaz, a singer at the conservatory. Her voice was a beautiful contralto, and she was on the brink of establishing a career in Germany when the National Socialists came to power and she had to change her plans. Shortly after returning from touring through Germany in the spring of 1933, she and Robert married.

Robert finished his music studies in 1935, at a time when it was difficult for him to establish a career in Europe as the important German stages were closed to artists of Jewish descent. So he decided to start his own business and put Herta's good contacts to use. In the fall of 1934, she had very successfully presented Ernst Krenek's *Reisebuch* at his New Austria Studio, a venue for modern classical music. She had also sung in other Krenek concerts—once it was Lieder by Adorno, another time it was popular Austrian music.

The Ernst Krenek/Herta Glaz collaboration continued to be a success. In November 1935 they were in London to record for the BBC. Then there were concerts in Geneva, Lausanne and Lugano. But though

Herta Glaz and Robert
Csillag, 1934

the Austrian musicians were appreciated while on tour, even many months before the Anschluss their concerts in Austria had been cancelled, including one of Herta's in Graz because neither her religious affiliation nor her ethnic origins were to the promoters' liking.

In 1936 Robert had an idea he thought it made sense to follow through on—he would found an opera company that would tour the United States performing selections from various well-known operas. For publicity reasons, the company was called the Salzburg Opera Guild, and during its first summer it was housed in Count Almeida's castle on Mondsee, not too far from the well-heeled and culturally interested Viennese bourgeoisie and the many international visitors vacationing in the Salzkammergut.

Sidonie is hardly the only summer resident who goes to Mondsee to hear Robert, Krenek and Glaz's new company. The castle is not very comfortable, but it is big and there is room for everyone. They perform *Cosi fan tutte*, Monteverdi's opera *Poppea* (directed by Krenek), a combination of short operas by Rossini, Ibert's *Angelique* and Milhaud's *Le pauvre maltelo*. Robert is firmly convinced that operas should be sung in their original language, and he doesn't seem particularly concerned that not everyone is able to follow them. Herta has been chosen to sing all the female leads. An attractive young soprano is also part of the company, and she will become Robert's third wife in a few years' time.

The pay is meager, but the prospect of making more money in the United States makes this less of an obstacle. An invitation to make an extensive U.S. tour has already been extended, and the company is scheduled sail from Le Havre in October 1937.

When Ed and Sidonie return to Vienna at the end of August 1936, neither is aware that Ed will soon make a decision with far reaching consequences for both of them.

At the beginning of the 1930s, Ed was theoretically job-hunting— though to be more exact, he was sitting in his wife's living room. That is, he was unemployed. And after his brother Franz married into the Imperial Feigenkaffee Company, that joint enterprise with his brother ceased to exist. Like many other former Habsburg army officers, Ed had good connections and good manners, but in troubled economic times, such skills were not in demand and couldn't guarantee either business success or finding a job.

Finally, in November 1936, Ed's comrades from the Heimwehr come to his rescue and offer him the directorship of an institute. He doesn't know a thing about the job, but the prospect of secure employment offers redemption for both his problematic social position and his difficult financial situation.

After its victory over the Austrian working class in February 1934, the Austro-Fascist regime had started to dismantle all the institutions belonging to or affiliated with the Social Democrats. On April 5, 1934, the Gesellschafts- und Wirtschaftsmuseum had been given its orders to dissolve. It had been founded in 1925 by the philosopher Otto Neurath, who had made a name for himself as the organizer of the post World War I settlement movement—an attempt to provide badly needing housing at the time. The Gesellschafts- und Wirtschaftsmuseum was designed to illustrate complex social and economic relationships in a simple, understandable manner. Together with the graphic artist Gerd Arntz, Neurath developed the Viennese Method of Pictorial Statistics, also known as isotypy, which is still widely used today.

To avoid being arrested, Otto Neurath emigrated to the Netherlands in April 1934. The process of dissolution took until the fall of that year, when an administrative council was established. It was led by several Heimwehr majors and one captain, and they changed the name to the Austrian Institute for Pictorial Statistics.

One of the majors was recently sacked for embezzling 10,000 Schillings from the Institute, and another of the majors has remembered Ed, who is asked to step in and lead the Institute as the representative of the new era and new spirit. Ed gladly accepts, and in the coming years he will indeed have to come up with all kinds of new ideas in order to keep his job. Times are hard, and one has to stay flexible and do what one is asked to do.

Sidi has been growing increasingly frustrated by Ed's excesses. One day during lunch he suggests that it is time to purchase a new automobile. Not really interested, at first Sidi retreats into silence, then she snaps to attention and listens in disbelief as he explains that he'll need some of her money to buy the car, and if she doesn't have enough, she

Ed Weitenegg, Wachau, 1930s

should ask her brother Heinrich for a loan. This is too much! She can feel her anger build until the feelings she's bottled up over the past years come spewing out—everything that's made her angry, the things she despises, the nausea she's felt. Her voice cracks as she yells that he shouldn't be so vain as to believe that he is a fantastic lover, he has simply been too stupid to notice that she doesn't enjoy it at all. No, worse, she finds it disgusting. He has been taking advantage of her only to satisfy his vanity and indulge his laziness. But this is going to come to an end. She is packing her suitcases and leaving him today.

Ed is completely taken aback. None of this can be true. He has been a careful and affectionate lover. Maybe now and then he has asked her not to wash too often, because he loves her natural smell more than all the perfumed soaps in the world. But he has never forced himself on her. He is experienced with women and knows how to distinguish between those who pretend to like it and those who really like it. He had never doubted for one minute that her feelings for him were genuine. She can't just shove him aside. He talks to her in his most soothing voice for so long that she forgets why she yelled at him in the first place.

He asks her to be understanding, says he has this new job and soon everything will be different. Surely she knows how difficult his situation has been, that he is no longer young, that former Habsburg Army officers have a hard time in this new republic. She should trust him; soon he'll be able to carry the whole load and will repay everything she has done for him over the past years.

Sidi calms down, pushes her anger even deeper inside and decides to give Ed yet another chance. Still, the atmosphere between the spouses remains tense in the coming months, while the atmosphere outside their home grows even more tense.

THE LIFE OF JEWS IN VIENNA 2

MANY PEOPLE ARE WATCHING THE DEVELOPMENTS IN GERMANY with increasing concern, wondering how much longer it will be before the brown tide inundates Austria. Sidonie and her women friends are not particularly worried and think that none of this is going to influence their own little world; but her brothers remind her again and again of her Jewish origins and try to explain that the Nuremberg Racial Laws of 1935 will also apply to her.

A chain of decisive events begins in early 1938. On February 12, the Berchtesgardner Treaty is signed, sealing Austria's fate. On March 11, Austrian chancellor Kurt Schuschnigg says good-bye to his country, and the next day the Anschluss to Hitler's Germany is suddenly a reality. Shortly before the first German troops march into Austria, high-ranking Nazis Heinrich Himmler and Reinhardt Heydrich arrive in Vienna to suppress any opposition. Adolf Hitler makes his own appearance there on March 15. Driven by curiosity, Sidonie visits a friend who lives opposite the Staatsoper; from there she can watch the Nazis parade around the Ring from a safe distance. The jubilant cheers reach her from the Heldenplatz, and as much as she would like to close her ears, the sound of these new times is beginning to give her an eerie feeling.

The Nazis have prepared for Austria's annexation in minute detail, and everything goes like clockwork. At a rally on March 26, Hermann Göring declares that within four years the city of Vienna must be "cleared of Jews." By April 1, the first transport of "Schutzhäflinge"— prisoners in protective custody—is on its way to the concentration camp at Dachau. On April 10, the Nazis hold a plebiscite to ratify the Anschluss, and as expected, 99.75 percent of the votes are reported to be in favor.

Ed and Sidonie exchange hot words about what they are going to do under these new political circumstances. However much she tries to push the thought from her mind, Sidi might have to consider leaving her beloved Vienna. Ed is willing to go anywhere with her. Her brother Heinrich in France would take them in for sure. But the thought of being abroad with Ed makes Sidi break out in a cold sweat. He doesn't even speak any useful foreign languages. Although he knows some Polish, Czech and Hungarian from his army days, these have no value in Sidi's opinion; and his English and French are a catastrophe. Also, he has never learned not to treat almost everyone the way he treated his subordinates in the army. With such limited social skills, he would be sure to encounter significant problems abroad. Besides, Ed already seems to be well taken care of. He is busy planned Austria's future with his old comrades, who are sure to shield him; and as long as he doesn't stick out, nothing is going to happen to him.

By now, however, one of Ed's friends, a lawyer, has already pointed out that in the Third Reich he won't be able to keep his job if he is married to a Jewish woman, so he proposes to Sidonie that they get a pro forma divorce. She is not averse to the idea; indeed, it might kill two birds with one stone. So she tells him that she has no desire to hinder his career and tells herself that she almost feels relieved, because this is one way to get rid of him.

The court, however, refuses to grant them a divorce and decides instead that the marriage must be annulled. The annulment order is supported by a long brief that arrives on September 13, 1938, and reads, in part:

> The plaintiff claims that he didn't know about his wife's Jewish origins at the time of the marriage. This assertion seems believable, since the respondent has been Roman Catholic since her birth in 1900. Upon interrogation, the respondent has stated that neither at the time of the marriage nor subsequently did any talks about origins take place and that there was no other way for the plaintiff to learn about her racial

Der Kläger behauptet,dass er anlässlich der Eheschliessung über die jüdischer Abstammung seiner Frau keine
Kenntnis hatte.Diese Behauptung erscheint nicht unglaub-
würdig,da ja die Beklagte seit ihrer Geburt,seit 1900
römisch katholisch war und die Beklagte selbst als
Partei vernommen glaubwürdig angegeben hat,dass bei
der Eheschliessung und auch in der Folge irgendwelche
Erörterungen über Abstammungsfragen nicht gepflogen
wurden,und auch sonst dem Kläger keine Kenntnis über
ihre Abstammung zugekommen ist.Es kann daher mit Recht
angenommen werden,dass der Kläger bei Abschluss der
Ehe in einem Irrtum über einen die Beklagte betreffenden
Umstand befangen war,welcher ihn bei Kenntnis der
Sachlage von einer Eheschliessung abgehalten hätte.
Nach den glaubwürdigen Angaben der Parteien ist dieser
Umstand erst nach dem politischen Umbruch hervorgekommen
als die jüdische Rassenangehörige gesetzlich zur
Vermögensanmeldung verhalten wurden. Wie aus den bei-
geschafften Akten des Bezirksgerichtes Landstrasse

1 Nc 137/38 hervorgeht,haben die beiden Parteien
aus ihrer rassischen Verschiedenheit sich bereits
zur einverständlichen Scheidung von Tisch und Bett
entschlossen,deren Erwirkung aber mit Rücksicht
auf die Einführung des neuen Scheidungsrechtes
unterblieb. Sie haben hiedurch zweifellos zum
Ausdruck gebracht,dass einer der beiden Teile
die Ehe fortsetzen will.

Nach dieser Sachlage sind dem Gerichte die
Voraussetzungen für die Aufhebung im Sinne § 37
ÖLGBl.244/38 gegeben.
Kostenentscheidung entfiel mangels Verzeichnung.

Das Landgericht ZRS Wien Abt.17,am 13.September 1938
                    Dr. Karl Paschinger

Annulment order for the marriage of Sidonie Csillag and Ed Weitenegg, 1938 origin. One can therefore assume that the plaintiff had no knowledge of the circumstances and that if he had known, it would have prevented him from getting married. Both parties state convincingly that these circumstances surfaced only after the political change and after all people of the Jewish race were ordered to file reports detailing their assets and properties. As stated in the file from the Landstrasse Court, the two parties have already decided on a legal separation because of their racial differences. Due to the new divorce laws, the divorce decree hasn't been granted yet, but it is without doubt that neither party wants to continue the marriage.

Instead of being candidates for a legal divorce, Sidi and Ed, in the eyes of the new rulers, have simply never been married. According to the racial laws of 1935, Sidonie is considered a "Volljüdin," fully Jewish. Her Catholic baptism as an infant—of which she has always been quite proud—no longer counts. Ed is no longer officially "jüdisch versippt" (closely related to a Jew), and the Civil Servant Act of April 7, 1933—which states that "civil servants who are married to a Jew or to a first degree Mischling (person of mixed race) will also be retired"—no longer applies to him. His career has been saved.

Ed does not, however, join the Nazi Party. He cites personal, family reasons, but most likely it's just that he is at heart an Austrian monarchist and therefore dislikes the German Empire—no matter who is in power. And so he must have had very good connections indeed in order both to keep his position and keep the Institute for Pictorial Statistics from disintegrating. Before being confirmed as the director of an institute or an association, an applicant had to have references from the Nazi Party's regional leader, the Party itself, the Gestapo and the Security Service (SD) of the Reichsführer SS. Only the approval of each of these entities certified a person as appropriate for appointment to a position.

Just three days after the German Wehrmacht enters Austria, Arthur Seyss-Inquart is nominated as Reichsstatthalter, or governor of Austria. The following day, Gauleiter Josef Bürckel orders a halt to all organizational activities until April 10, the day of the plebiscite. On March 18, Albert Hoffmann, a party member from Munich, is appointed as

Stillhaltekommissar (Standstill Agreement Commissioner) for associations, organizations and unions. In this function he is responsible only to Gauleiter Bürckel.

On March 31, Hoffmann sends a letter to all of Vienna's associations stating that no personnel, organizational or financial changes can be implemented without either his or Gauleiter Bürckel's explicit permission. The permission must be in writing.

On May 9, party member Professor Dr. Anton Haasbauer, acting in his role as head of the NS-Culture Community, certifies that Ed Weitenegg may continue in his post as acting director of the Institute for Pictorial Statistics. Hoffmann, however, has appointed a long-standing party member, a graphic artist who has been working at the Institute, as provisional director. In the middle of May, said graphic artist arrives at the Institute accompanied by two SS-men. But in the long run, it seems that Ed von Weitenegg's connections were the most influential—the graphic artist doesn't prevail, and Ed remains the Institute's director.

On May 17, Bürckel and Hoffmann—eager to maintain the fiction that the rule of law exists—introduce a law codifying all future procedures for those operating under their jurisdiction. All the approved associations must change their statues and in many cases their name as well. As far as Bürckel is concerned, it's of only secondary importance that such actions will stifle independent thinking and independent associations in Austria, now called Ostmark; both men are concerned primarily about safeguarding the various institutes' and associations' assets.

While Ed prepares in his own way to survive the coming months—surely the Nazi chimera isn't going to last long—Sidonie tries to find her own path. Her brothers are pressuring her to organize a quick departure; but Vienna is her home, and nothing in the world is going to make her leave it.

CHAPTER

8

"... ANYWAY, I'M NOT ONE OF THEM."

INSIDE THE RAILROAD CAR, EMMA CSILLAG LOOKS LIKE A PALE AND fragile little owl with her head thrust through the open window, gazing out at the platform. A white enamel destination placard stands out against the side of the black iron car. It reads: Paris. Emma smiles and waves and blows kisses as if a crowd of admirers were on the platform envying the glamorous holiday she's about to embark upon. But this is February 16, 1939, and she is going into exile—though she seems to have suppressed all thoughts of that.

Standing on the platform, Sidi feels her heart constrict. There's her mother, toward whom she has long since buried any positive feelings, once again behaving out of line, clinging to her vanity, though there no longer seems to be a reason to do so, and it looks as if she might break down after all. Watching this white-haired woman, Sidi notices for the first time how much her mother has aged. Emma wears a black hat with a little veil and a wool dress cut to reveal her collarbones; and despite the cold her black coat is open, exposing a string of much-too-large black wooden beads around her creased neck. The little handbag she refuses to let go of swings wildly each time she waves. But, Sidi thinks, what's most outrageous are her round, black, horn-rimmed spectacles—a style usually worn only by men. As Emma gazes at the small huddle of close friends waiting uneasily on the platform, her eyes seem watery and blurred, as if the lenses were made of old crown glass. Or are those tears?

Enough! Sidi hugs Ellen one last time, quickly climbs the steep steps into the train and closes the door with a thud. She will accompany her mother all the way to Kehl on the German border with France. From there, the old lady will be safe from the Nazis and can continue on to Paris, where Heinrich is waiting for her.

For the first time, Sidonie feels older than her mother, responsible for protecting her as best she can; and, also, for the first time in years, a bit of tenderness toward her emerges. The idea that she might have to protect herself as well hasn't yet entered her head. When the train starts to move, Sidi watches the cast iron pillars of the Westbahnhof disappear behind her and knows that she'll return to Vienna and continue her life there. She is not going to give in to those interlopers; and she will not be branded as "one of them," the ones whose destroyed shops now bear a prominent six-pointed star.

A few days after Austria's Anschluss to the German Reich in March 1938, Heinrich took a few days off from managing the solid paraffin factory near Paris and took the train to Vienna, hardly able to believe his eyes. It seemed as if one big folk festival was underway everywhere, with bonfires on mountain tops, cheering crowds in the towns, church bells ringing. In Vienna pictures of Hitler were everywhere, and the media praised him around the clock. A euphoric fellow passenger told Heinrich that the Führer had distributed twenty thousand Volksempfänger (cheap "peoples" radios) in Vienna so everyone could hear his speeches.

On the evening of his arrival, all the Csillags except for Robert, who was touring in the United States, had gathered in Emma Csillag's flat for a talk. She was still living in the nine-room flat on Neulinggasse, and although some of the rooms had been rented out, the main rooms were still their mother's domain. Sidi lunched there at least once a week, but the current circumstances somehow made being in the flat feel strange. Little had changed since her childhood—the plaster roses still bloomed at the height of four meters, the sofas were a bit sprung, but the yellow damask upholstery had been renewed, even her father's old reading lamp hadn't been moved. It's good that he doesn't have to experience this, she thought, he would have felt sick to death. It was a cold March evening, and everyone's face reflected the turmoil of the past few days.

Heinrich hadn't changed in twenty years. Typical of the eldest, he had taken on all the responsibilities and acted as head of the family since Father's death. The first to speak, his opinion was that it would be best if the whole family left Vienna quickly and quietly. Now a French citizen, he could help them settle there. Money was not an issue; the family had enough; the factory in France was doing well. But it was important to act decisively and quickly. He planned to tell Robert not to return to Austria. Sidi should help her mother dismantle the household and then go to Paris with her.

Ernst was still doing his military service, but Heinrich thought that, as a Jew, he would soon be kicked out, so he might just take Ernst along to Paris right away.

When Heinrich finished, everyone fell silent. It had grown dark outside, but no one turned on the lights. The brothers rested their hands on their knees and stared at the floor; Emma gazed toward a photograph of her husband on the opposite wall. It was too dark to read one another's faces, but each could gauge the others' feelings.

Sidi was the first to break the silence. No, she was not going to leave Vienna. This Nazi-trouble would last for one or two years and she'd survive that. A few days ago she and her husband had talked about emigrating together, but this proved impossible, and they

Ernst Csillag before emigrating

had decided to get divorced instead so he could keep his job and his connections. He would be in a better position to help her than if they stayed married. She'd continue to live with him; other divorced women among her friends had made the same sort of arrangements. However, it was clear that Mother had to leave, and she would help her make all the preparations.

The terrible business of packing consumed the summer and fall of 1938. Sidonie moved in with her mother to facilitate things, though living with her day in and day out drove her crazy. And even being in the flat brought back memories of her childhood and youth that she would have preferred to forget.

As the two women made their orderly progress from one room to the next, Emma frequently complained about how horrible it was to have to pack her whole life away and often cried uncontrollably when deciding what to pack and what to throw away. Standing in front of her closet, arms full of twenty-year-old fashions, she whined that giving them to charity would be like giving away parts of her life. She wanted to take all the furniture, even though Heinrich, wringing his hands, had asked that only two or three really important pieces be sent. He already had everything she would need in Paris and had little space for more. He also didn't want to pay the 25 percent Reichsfluchtsteuer (Reich flight tax) imposed in 1931 on rich Germans who wanted to settle elsewhere. The Nazis used it to expropriate the assets of Jewish citizens who were persecuted into exile. After many heated discussions with Sidi, Emma agreed to take only her Biedermeier desk, a dressing table with a large mirror and her beautiful altdeutsch matrimonial bed. Big white labels bearing the Paris address were affixed to these pieces.

Emma found a bit of consolidation only in the fact that she planned to take all her jewelry with her, despite the Nazi ruling that all Jewish property be declared and registered. Having it along would at least be a way to safeguard her memories. In the final days and nights before emigrating, she spent countless hours sewing the jewelry into appropriate seams, linings and folds. The remaining furniture went either into a large cellar at the Ferstels or to Sidi and Ed's flat. Sidi was certain Ed would acknowledge that the furniture was not his and would return it to her family when asked.

Organizing Emma's emigration papers proved much more complicated than dealing with the flat. One had to line up for days on end at the emigration authorities' main office in the former Rothschild Palais on Prinz Eugen Strasse. The bureaucrats in charge combined typical Viennese crossness with a snide and derogatory attitude stemming from their newly acquired sense of superiority, and they tormented the anxious Jews seeking to emigrate. After going through this procedure, it took several weeks more to get the necessary papers from the French embassy and to obtain Emma's visa.

After all this had been taken care of, Sidonie could finally buy their train tickets and set a departure date. To make the trip somewhat endurable, Sidi decided that on her way back from Kehl she would stop in Munich for a few days to visit her beloved Wjera. In times such as these, nobody could know when they would have an opportunity to meet again. She wrote a short, carefully worded letter to Wjera and quickly got an answer welcoming her visit. In the midst of all the horror, Sidi felt happy.

The furniture movers arrived to take everything away in mid December 1938. For Emma, this was the saddest chapter in the whole story. She didn't want to witness the dissolution of her Viennese life and went out shopping, but her shock on returning to the empty flat was worse than if she had stayed to watch. Seeing that the rooms she had lived in for thirty years now contained only the three big trunks that would go to Paris with her, Emma broke down and sat weeping on one of the trunks. Sidi clasped her mother's hands and waited for her to calm down, but when Emma could speak again, she only sat shaking her head and repeating again and again, "I don't understand this. We have all been baptized." Sidi put an end to this by calling a cab to take her mother to Bösendorferstrasse, where she would stay until her departure. In a few days, the new tenants, surely Nazis, would arrive to start their new life in the flat where Emma Csillag had just ended hers.

Now Sidonie and her mother sit side by side in a first class compartment on the Paris-bound train a few hours from Kehl and have no idea when they'll see each other again. What can one say under such circumstances? Sidi tries to be optimistic and talks of all the nice things awaiting Emma in Paris, particularly the reunion with Heinrich. It will be the best possible place in the world for her. And Paris is definitely *the* city of beautiful, fashion-conscious women, like her mother, and she won't know where to put all the new clothes she's going to buy there. She should be happy to leave provincial Vienna behind. Emma nods, says occasionally, "God grant that you are right."

At the German–French border the train enters the station at Kehl, and alert German inspectors and security police jump on board. Their stiff, aggressive demeanor and the exacting border controls keep Sidi at her mother's side until all her papers are in order and the continuation of her journey is secured.

When it is time, their farewell is quick and seems almost casual. Emma and Sidi step out of their compartment into the corridor, embrace briefly, and Emma caresses her daughter's cheek tenderly.

"May God protect you my child," she says, adding very softly through her tears, "You have always been so very good to me."

Dealing with her own emotions, Sidi says hastily, "I'll write to you, and I'll come to visit you soon. You'll see, soon this will be over." Then she hurries off the train in order not to miss her connection to Munich. Ten years will pass before they see each other again.

Wjera and her husband are waiting at Munich's central railway station when Sidi arrives. Although the two women haven't seen each other in a while, the warmth and closeness they share hasn't changed. Wjera can tell from Sidi's solemn face how difficult the past weeks have been for her. They embrace, and Sidi rests her head on her friend's shoulder for a few moments, then collects herself, in part because she doesn't want Hans Martin to feel left out.

Sidi feels so welcome in Wjera's large, lovely flat and is so enchanted by her company that she is able to forget everything and sink beneath the waves of her renewed infatuation. But it is impossible to ignore reality completely. Walking through Munich the next day, Sidi acts like a true tourist and lets herself be charmed by the old houses and the gothic city hall at Marienplatz; she finds the two round towers and beautiful main altar of the Marienkirche quite moving; even eating Weisswurst with Wjera is fun. But at the same time, she sees brown and black uniforms and massive displays of Hakenkreuz flags everywhere.

It's not until they reach the Englische Garten, empty of people today because of the icy cold, that Wjera relaxes the cautious tension she's been exhibiting, and the two bundled-up women begin to speak freely. And what they tell each other about political realities is mutually disillusioning. Wjera's husband has been attacked and threatened by the Nazi regime over and over again. His father's company has just been, as it is officially termed, "entjudet"—cleansed of Jews. In order to escape the hostilities, he lives almost as if he had gone underground. Only his marriage to her, a non-Jew, has saved him from what one hears whispers about: deportation and a concentration camp. His parents are thinking about leaving Nuremberg and moving to Berlin, where their daughter lives. She is married to an Aryan from the higher ranks of the aristocracy; maybe this will protect the two old people.

Sidi is aghast. Until now, she hasn't been aware of the scale of the threat, and she admires Wjera's obvious courage. Strolling along the bank of the frozen Eisbach, Sidi waits until they reach a secluded spot before taking Wjera's hand and telling her own story. Now it's Wjera's turn to be shocked. She hadn't known that Sidi's marriage had been annulled by the Nazi bureaucrats or how badly Ed had behaved. She is particularly alarmed to learn that the other Csillags have gone into exile, leaving Sidi in Vienna without protection.

"Sidi, you have to save your own skin," she insists. "Leave, find a safe country before it is too late ... although it won't be easy for me to know that you are far away." Embracing, they seal their mutual fear and concern with a kiss.

During supper with Hans Martin that evening, the talk turns again to emigration, and he, too, urges Sidi to leave Vienna quickly. He rants against the Nazis; dislodged strands of blond hair fall over his eyes, and he leans across the table to take Wjera's hand and declare that his life has been saved thanks to her. Sidi understands that he truly seems to love the woman she loves, and that Wjera returns his love. They make a good couple. She should be distressed by this, but she is comforted that Wjera is in good hands, even though, regrettably, they are not her hands.

After a few days, Sidi returns to Vienna, only to learn that according to the language of the Third Reich, she—baptized Catholic, converted to Protestant—is now a "non-Aryan." She clings to this term, even though in everyday life everyone just talks about Jews and Jewesses. But even Sidonie can't fail to see that since the big pogrom on November 9, 1938, everything has changed. The new rulers have let their true face show. The laws have gotten stricter. Daily life has been filled with hurdles.

THE LIFE OF JEWS IN VIENNA 3

As of June 16, 1933, 499,682 Jews lived in the German Reich, while, according to the Nuremberg Racial Laws, the number of Christians was estimated to be about 340,000. In addition, there were 50,000 baptized Jews, 210,000 so-called "Halbjuden" (half-Jews) and 80,000 so-called "Vierteljuden" (quarter-Jews). According to the census of May 17, 1939, 213,930 Jews were still living in the so-called Altreich (Nazi Germany in its pre 1938 borders), as well as 19,716 non-Jewish "Rassenjuden" (racial Jews), of whom 3,025 were Catholics. In 1939 almost all Jews—regardless of their religious affiliation—were forced into the "Reichsvereinigung der Juden in Deutschland" (Reich Association of Jews in Germany).

The same measures that had targeted "non-Aryans" in Germany since 1933 were implemented by the National Socialists in Austria in May 1938, just two months after the occupation began on March 12. In Austria—or rather, Ostmark now—those measures affected a large number of Catholics, and the Jesuit priest Georg Bichlmair responded by starting a rescue operation for them in Vienna. This was a forerunner to the Erzbischöfliche Hilfsstelle für nicht-arische Katholiken (Archepiscopal Aid for non-Aryan Catholics), which was established in December 1940. Many persecuted Austrian Jews who emigrated to neighboring countries were supported by Bichlmair and later by the Erzbischöfliche Hilfsstelle.

In Germany, as of 1935, laws were already in place defining the "crime" of "Rassenschande" (racial defilement). To be considered a crime, sexual intercourse had to take place outside of marriage; meaning that a Jewish man divorced from his Aryan or "quarter-Jewish" wife, could be punished if he continued to have sexual relations with her. Only men were held responsible, participating women were not punished.

The National Socialists constantly passed new regulations. An order issued on August 17, 1938, stated, among other things, that, as was well known, many "assimilated Jews" liked to take on the first names of German heroes and heroines so they couldn't initially be identified as Jews. Therefore, as of January 1, 1939, all male Jews were ordered to use the middle name Israel and all female Jews the middle name Sara when dealing with the authorities. In addition, Jews would have to use "Jewish" family names. What is to be considered a Jewish family name would be determined by popular interpretation, taking into consideration that there are family names of German origin that are generally considered to be "Jewish family names."

From now on Sidonie Csillag is to be known as Sidonie Sara Csillag.

Since her mother's departure, Sidonie feels increasingly like a stranger in the city she loves. Her marriage has been official annulled, and having spent the recent months with her mother, it would be simply impossible to live with Ed again. He thinks only of his job at the Institute and of maintaining his contacts with various colleagues from the Heimwehr, all of whom are trying to be as accommodating as possible toward the new powers. His opportunism and servility towards the Nazis both seem limitless, and this disgusts her.

Ed is still in his post as director of the Institute for Pictorial Statistics, though he hasn't joined the Party. As its first big gesture of genuflection before the new rulers, the Institute has organized an anti-Semitic propaganda exhibit—titled "The Eternal Jew"—in the huge entrance hall of the former Nordwestbahnhof. This stretches even Sidonie's patience to the breaking point, and she no longer wants to have anything to do with Ed, who doesn't want any connection with his Jewish ex-wife either, although he certainly doesn't mind staying in the flat her family's money bought and furnished.

At the end of 1938, Sidi moves out and sublets a room in a friend's flat on Stubenring. She's happy to be rid of Ed, but without her own furniture or any personal items she feels like a foreigner here, too—a guest who's just passing through. And the Nazis are too close. The office of the

Construction of the exhibit "The Eternal Jew," Nordwestbahnhof entry hall, 1938

Deutsche Arbeiterfront (German Workers Front) had taken over flats in the same building, after having driven out the Jewish tenants. Inside the building and along the surrounding streets there are posters proclaiming the "Honor of Work" or "The Beauty of Work." They provoke a tired smile from Sidonie. "Only the Nazis could call work beautiful," she thinks—but only to herself.

By the end of February 1939, Sidi no longer likes to leave the house. Particularly since there are Nazi flags and posters of Hitler on every street corner, and aside from the ideological madness he preaches, which she refuses to pay attention to, she finds him laughably ugly—a little man with a belly who parades before the masses like a cockerel. She cannot comprehend how he is able to evoke such enraptured enthusiasm in both women and men.

And she can no longer force scenes like one she witnessed shortly after the Anschluss out of her mind. In the city center, on her way to see her seamstress, she stopped briefly at the edge of a tumultuous crowd to see what was going on. Several men and women were kneeling on the sidewalk, scrubbing at it with little brushes and rags and being overseen by sneering men in uniform and ordinary Viennese men wearing Nazi Party armbands. People like her, Jews—men and women in suits, some just in shirt sleeves, so cold that their fingers were already red and chapped—were being forced to scrub the sidewalk. Seeing their humiliation made her recoil in horror, and she had to struggle to control herself enough to walk away calmly, so she could continue on unnoticed.

Soon after that incident, in the spring of 1938, Heinrich urged, indeed ordered their youngest brother, Ernst, to get to Paris as quickly as possible. Paris would be a safe first stop; from there, they could figure out how to proceed. Ernst has been in a hurry to comply ever since. The initial plan was for all three brothers to work things out together. Robert was soon due to return from his second successful tour of the States with the Salzburg Opera Guild. The ensemble had made optimistic plans for future engagements and even started to figure out who would sing which parts. Then, while at Carnegie Hall in New York City—almost while they were performing onstage—all the Austrian company members had learned that their country had been annexed by the German Reich.

The company fulfilled the rest of its contract under great strain, and some members immediately began trying to secure residence and work permits in the United States. Robert filed a petition for himself, Ernst and Sidonie to be placed on the quota list for US immigration but learned that the quota for Austrians had already been filled. Only Sidonie had a chance, since she had been born in Lemberg and thus was entered in the Polish quota.

Robert returned to Europe bearing this news. Knowing that he couldn't return to Vienna, he stayed with Heinrich in Paris; then both brothers traveled to Venice, where they called for another family conference. After some heated discussion, the two elder brothers came to an agreement regarding the family's future. Heinrich would stay in Paris, as would their mother. Robert had heard only good things about Havana, which was relatively secure, and he suggested Cuba as the place where he, Ernst and Sidi would wait for their turn to immigrate to the United States. It seemed quite possible, he said, that pressure on the United States would increase so dramatically that it would open its doors to all those fleeing racial persecution. Robert has always been an optimist, and he is not going to let an unimportant little house painter from Braunau change that.

Only Sidi—stubborn and ignorant—still chooses to remain behind in Vienna. She will not give the everyday madness and the hunting down of the Jewish population any space in her life. Why should she bother about such things? She has her circle of friends and she is welcome everywhere. For her, this is security, and she doesn't want to do without it.

But by the spring of 1939, the new rulers' repressiveness has penetrated even into the circle of her most intimate friends, and there is no protection anywhere.

S129 I B

LATE ONE MORNING IN MARCH 1939 SIDI'S PHONE RINGS. STILL busy with her breakfast, she reluctantly lifts the receiver, shouts "Yes," and hears a moment of silence. Grete Weinberger's subdued voice asks, "Sidi please, can we meet? It is urgent; something has happened." On the brink of tears, Grete can barely speak.

Aware that the telephone is no longer a safe medium for exchanging information, whatever it might be, Sidi replies, "In half an hour in Stadtpark, on the promenade by the River Wien. Would that be okay?"

Grete agrees in a whisper, and the line goes dead.

Sidi downs her roll and hot milk, slips into felt-lined boots and an old mink coat and leaves for Stadtpark, walking quickly and softly cursing the terrible times that force one into the deep recesses of a park in the freezing cold just to hold an unobserved conversation.

Grete is already waiting and clearly has been crying. She looks even smaller and more pinched than usual.

She embraces Sidi and says how relieved she is that Sidi could come right away; she desperately needs someone to talk to and simply has no idea what to do.

Gently disentangling herself—it would be terrible if they were noticed—Sidi takes Grete's arm and like ordinary strollers they walk along the promenade below the art school.

After a few steps, Grete exclaims, "Can you believe it?! Willy has been arrested."

Sidi is stunned. She's been so busy arranging for her mother's emigration that she hasn't had time for her friends.

"He was denounced. You know, because of his little adventures. They arrested him at his office on January twenty-seventh."

Sidi, like everyone in the Weinberger's circle of friends, has known for years that Willy has an invincible weakness for his own gender. Grete has always taken it in stride, and often laughingly repeated the story of how she had found out. Sometime in the mid 1920s, her hairdresser had telephoned to announce indignantly that he would report Willy if he laid a finger on his son again. "He really ought to," Grete had observed drily to Sidi, who thought this reaction very odd; but then she had never understood Grete's attitude towards anything having to do with sex. For her part, Sidi couldn't begin to imagine sex between two men.

At the time of the hairdresser's call, Grete and Willy's marriage has already fallen apart, largely because of his fits of bad temper and his intense, driven personality and inability to relax. The union formed in 1921 was dissolved in 1932. They continued to live under the same roof, in particular because of their two sons, whom Willy idolized, and they had found a way to do so amicably.

Calming, Grete tells everything she knows, including what she has learned from Willy when visiting him in jail.

At the beginning of January, Willy had been approached on the street in front of their building by two young men who said that if he didn't pay all their expenses for a trip to Munich, they would denounce him to the Gestapo. He capitulated and met them at Westbahnhof the next day, where he bought their tickets and gave them cash.

Under Grete's continued probing, Willy admitted having had a relationship with Friedrich, one of the blackmailers—the other was Friedrich's friend Günther. After their return from Munich, both young men were arrested in a Gestapo roundup and confessed to having had sexual relations with various men, among them Willy. Friedrich was from the German city of Dusseldorf, Günther was from the Vienna district of Meidling, and both earned their living as rent boys.

Friedrich preferred to find clients in the baths, while Günther worked mostly at the public toilets.

That's all Willy has been willing to say. When Grete told him she needs to know everything in order to find him a good lawyer, he rebuffed her with a gruff, "Leave me alone," and sent her home. She has been going mad with worry, because it is unclear what the Nazis will do to Willy. She needs more information in order to prevent the worst.

Sidi shakes her head. What a mess! First the Nazis force Jews to scrub the streets and now they are rounding up homosexuals. This puts her in increased danger, but her inner voice immediately downplays the implications—after all, she is a woman and as such nothing could happen to her; she doesn't do the perverted things men do.

"You know what?" Grete says, grabbing Sidi's arm. "We should ask Egon Jordan; he's queer, maybe he knows something. Do you think you could talk to him? I'm not in any condition to do it."

Sidi, too, has just thought of Egon, known as "Exi" to his intimate friends. He had gone to school at the Theresianum and had spent lots of time with them before leaving Vienna ages ago for professional reasons.

One of the few from "the other side" who admits it, he is, at least in Sidi's eyes, one of Vienna's best looking men. He, in turn, considers her to be one of Vienna's most beautiful women. Whenever they run into one another—perhaps two or three times each year—he bustles about her in a sweet, adoring way that makes it clear that they share the same aesthetics and can rely on each other's sympathy. When it comes to good-looking men, Egon should know all the gossip, and Sidi promises to get in touch with him. Grete seems relieved by this sliver of hope and finally stops crying. They bid each other a somewhat more relaxed good-bye.

When Sidi telephones Egon Jordan, he is delighted to hear her voice and easily picks up on the hint that she needs to see him urgently in person.

At his apartment the following afternoon at four, Exi receives Sidi with a strong embrace, something she allows from no other man. His apartment is filled with light, antiques and outlandish flower arrangements, and little chocolate cakes have been set out in the living room. He looks more serious than usual but still resembles a beautiful, lascivious deity in a silk dressing gown.

Shortly before her marriage to Ed, Exi had returned to Vienna after a five-year stay in Berlin. He had come to say good-bye to all his friends, for he had just signed a five-year contract with Goldwyn Mayer and was off to Hollywood.

His letters from there revealed Hollywood to be a big disappointment—especially the way its puritanical attitude masked hidden licentiousness. The moment his contract expired, he took the next boat to Europe and by January 1933 was back in his beloved Berlin. But when one of his queer friends was hospitalized after taking a beating from the SA, he fled back to Vienna, where he was hired first by Theater an der Wien, then, in 1935, by the Volkstheater. He married Cecilie Mattoui as a "preventive measure" to both forestall unpleasant questions and protect society in general from too much awareness of sexual alternatives. The marriage, therefore, was welcomed by all. He was also in several films; with his best role being that of a gorgeous singer in *Ein Stern fällt vom Himmel* (A Star Falls from Heaven).

At the moment, however, none of his ravishing charm is evident; he listens to Sidi and grows serious and concerned.

He has heard about this particular affair and has even been indirectly affected by it because Hugo Wazlawek, a close friend, was arrested at the same time as Willy. The police had been systematically intercepting all the men who went to Hugo's building looking for him, and he himself had been warned off just in time while on his way there.

It started when Sebastian Blumenauer was mugged on January 13, 1939; that is all he has found out so far. That old monarchist with an eye for beautiful boys was well known to the Gestapo. Only a few days after the Anschluss he had been arrested because of his monarchist activity as the unpaid secretary of the Reichsbund der Österreicher, an organization working actively since 1932 for the restoration of the monarchy. He was transported to Dachau four months later and released two months after that, on September 20, 1938. He immediately returned to Vienna.

Blumenauer's preference for men is common knowledge, but most everyone agrees that his frequent visits to the city's many public toilets are due to kidney and bladder problems. But police officer Heinrich Rojnik begs to differ. He doesn't like Blumenauer and sees it as his mission—even when off duty—to have him rearrested. He often follows Blumenauer, hoping to catch him in the act in a public toilet. Rumor has it that after interrogating young men in the parks, Rojnik was able to establish that Blumenauer had invited them to perform "unnatural acts."

Blumenauer adamantly refused to talk about his January mugging, which prompted the hot-tempered Rojnik to ordered raids on the well-known OK Inn on Kärnterstrasse, as well as at the nearby public toilets. And that is how Willy and Hugo ended up in jail.

Unbelievably, even old Blumenauer has been jailed—turned from victim into offender in a society where even a sixty-year-old man is not safe from the Gestapo.

Now in a state, Exi gesticulates wildly as he lays out plans for freeing Hugo and Willy. He thinks he knows of a good lawyer who might represent them both and should be in a position to free them, although it won't be easy, since most lawyers shy away from any confrontation with the Gestapo.

It should be easier to defend Hugo, since he is the authorized representative of a big company that is in the process of being Aryanized and desperately needs all of its non-Jewish employees, especially those with Hugo's knowledge and language skills. It could be more difficult for Willy, since he has been careless enough to take some of the young men for rides in his car. But as vice-president of the Verband Österreichischer Strassengesellschaften (Federation of Austrian Road Companies) Willy has good connections, and the Nazis likely won't keep someone in his position locked up for too long.

Exi has been cautious, has avoided the public baths and toilets since the beginning of the year, and therefore isn't personally up to date on the latest developments. But some of his colleagues at the Volkstheater have very good connections to the new rulers, and through them he has learned about all the arrests that have delivered high-ranking men and their lovers into the hands of the Nazis.

Muschler, he tells her, is the one who has been the most drastically affected. A fifty-year-old businessman and men's tailor from Königsberg, he came to Vienna at the end of 1937 and took up residence at Hotel Sacher. In early '37 he had been arrested in the Reich and sentenced to nine months in jail because of Section 175. The moment he was released, he headed for Vienna, determined to enjoy life to its fullest. Many young men came to appreciate his generosity, and he quickly got the nickname "Exzellenz" at the Römische Bad. Everyone he invited to accompany him on outings to the nearby city of Baden was delighted to be included in what always turned out to be a big carouse. But when he was re-arrested—by the very regime he had fled the previous year—it had been too much, and while still on remand, he hanged himself.

But Egon doesn't actually know anything about how Willy is faring in jail, and Sidi leaves after two hours with a lot of background knowledge but little information for Grete.

Grete, for her part, has already spoken to two lawyers who have agreed to take on Willy's defense, though both suggest that it might be a while before anything can be done.

Willy and the young men who denounced him are thoroughly investigated and interrogated while in detention, and all the details eventually emerge and are recorded.

It was a man named Rudolf who first called the wealthy Willy to the attention of his friends Günther and Friedrich, Willy's blackmailers. Willy had first encountered Rudolf in October 1938 at the public toilet in Resselpark. He later recounted that when that dark-haired "Gypsy type" young man had first eyed him, his whole spine tingled. He invited Rudolf to go for a ride to Prater where, on a remote pathway, they did what the police later describe as "reciprocal touching of their male members and reciprocal masturbation."

On his next business trip, Willy took Rudolf along as his driver. First, they stopped at Hotel Bahnhof in Köflach and checked into one room. Both admitted having had sex there. Looking for further proof, the police interrogated one Rose Rossmann, the hotel's maid, who said she remembered the two men from Vienna very well, even though it had been several months since their visit. She had noticed that the older man was very attentive to the younger one and also spent a good chunk of money on him. As she remembered it, the younger man looked like neither a gypsy nor a Jew but was a very handsome guy.

The next morning they drove on to Graz, where Willy bought a trench coat for Rudolf and promised to buy him a suit and shoes the next time, and then went on to Klagenfurt, where Rudolf decided to visit a friend in Maria Saal, and Willy continued on his business trip to Vorarlberg without his driver. During the next month, Willy took Rudolf on another business trip, to St. Pölten, and often met him in Resselpark and at cafés or movies.

By December 1938 Willy had lost interest in Rudolf, and in early 1939 he picked up young Friedrich on Kärntnerstrasse. Soon Friedrich was the one being taken for rides in Prater and invited to dine.

He told me he was hustling and that he knew why I had been looking at him. Then he suggested that I do it to him. Today I can't imagine why I agreed to it. We drove to Prater in my car. In order not to attract any attention, I turned off the lights and parked in a side alley by the Lusthaus. In the car we caressed each other's member. He told me that he had been called up for Arbeitsdienst (Reich Labor Service). Sexually, I enjoyed this encounter. In all the instances where I committed an offense in Prater, I parked the car in a side alley and turned off the lights. The car doesn't have any blinds.

The next day the two had a date in Resselpark, followed by a meal and the movies. At Willy's suggestion, they checked into a room on the fourth floor of Hotel Apollo. Foolishly, Willy had taken his camera along and photographed his latest conquest, which obviously angered the young man. Soon after Willy had satisfied him sexually, Friedrich choked the engineer until he was almost unconscious and then, before disappearing with the camera and Willy's wallet, he threatened to denounce Willy to the Gestapo. But instead, the blackmail started a few days later—first via threatening notes left under the windshield wipers of Willy's Imperia-Adler, then with the demand for the two tickets to Munich.

It isn't difficult to guess the Gestapo's methods for making the young men talk. In the end, Günther and Friedrich said that it was the "Gypsy"—Rudolf's nickname, thanks to his Hungarian family name—who gave them the idea of blackmailing Willy.

Rudolf does not deny that he'd brought up the subject of blackmail but maintains that it wasn't his idea but his colleague Karl's. He knows

Karl from the table tennis club at Theobaldgasse; they'd been hustling together in Resselpark since the spring of 1938.

The only arguments these young men can offer in their own defense are the general social misery, their youth and their poor economic situation.

> … I have committed these crimes in order to acquire the means for a better life. I didn't have an apprenticeship. I was just hanging around and that's how I ended up going wrong. The Amon dancing school in Meidling was my ruin.

They don't have a lawyer. Nothing they say can rescue them. All three are handed over to the Gestapo, and the chances are good that they will be sent to a concentration camp.

Willy, Hugo and other johns who can afford to hire expensive lawyers can ward of the worst and eventually will get themselves out of their disagreeable situation.

Hugo's lawyers write letter after letter to the officials. They mention his service at the front lines during World War I, how necessary it is for him to be at his workplace, which is in the economic interest of the Reich, since his company's considerable wealth is at stake and his presence as an "Aryan" is imperative. His lack of a previous criminal record, his education level and current position all weigh in his favor. On April 28, 1938, Exi's friend Hugo is granted release after posting bail of 10,000 Reichsmarks. He immediately departs for Prague. In September 1939, when he is sentenced to three months under Section 129 I b, the police ask the University of Prague to rescind Hugo's university degree. This takes effect on January 19, 1940.

Willy's lawyers take a different approach. After three months in detention, on June 19, 1939, he goes to trial in City Court, where he is portrayed as a sick, broken man who strayed from what is right only because he had so overextended himself in service to his country that he had entered a state of extreme nervous exhaustion.

They point out that their client had been buried alive during World War I and has suffered from various ailments, including insomnia, ever since. In addition, he is very hot-tempered and has repeatedly suffered attacks of madness in the presence of his ex-wife. He used to be a heavy smoker but stopped in 1937 on the advice of his doctor. This has led to serious withdrawal symptoms and psychological problems. Given all these circumstances, the defense asks that the accused be put under psychiatric care. The district attorney agrees and supports the doubts about Willy's soundness of mind.

In his favor, it is also noted that Willy's "racial background is purely Aryan on both sides" and that he is from a well-known Viennese family, his father being a technical engineer and wholesale merchant. During the difficult years from 1931 to 1938, Willy had kept his company afloat and had thereby supported countless, at the time illegal Nazi party members in several ways. After the political change, the company has employed about 2000 workers; and since 1934 he has also built relationships with road construction companies in the German Reich.

Willy testifies in his own defense. He can't explain why he committed his sexual offenses. Neither before nor afterwards had he felt such desires. He despises his deeds and is convinced that his period of weakness—most likely caused by his extraordinary exhaustion at work, his overall nervousness and the resulting state of confusion—is definitely a thing of the past.

On July 11, 1939, Willy is released from jail and ordered to live at his parents' flat in the Thirteenth District. His sister lives in the same building. The trial concludes on July 27. Willy is found guilty and sentenced to five months in jail. He also has to pay the costs of the trial. The sentence is conditional, however, and is suspended for three years. The Gestapo does not oppose this. Willy's time on probation will be over in August 1942, when the case will be closed for good.

Sidi follows Willy's case closely in her role as Grete's supporter and counselor, and she finds the eventual outcome alarming and disquieting. As a Jewess and—even though hidden—a lesbian, she could be next.

Willy's arrest took her circle of friends completely by surprise, and the political situation has by now immobilized everyone who hadn't been in favor of the new regime from early on. They are frozen in place; nobody dares to move or to say anything against the Nazis, even though they all know what has been going on. Anything could shatter the fragile stasis. Almost every family is divided between those who are more or less engaged in activities supporting the National Socialists and those who strictly oppose them. And everyone has friends or family members who are endangered and have already emigrated or yearn to do so. One of Grete Weinberger's former teachers commits suicide—her husband is in jail, and when war breaks out, one of her sons will be among the missing. An old friend of Sylvie Dietz no longer dares to leave his house, and she will end up looking after him until his death; and her best friend, Trudl Rosenfeld, has already emigrated. The Imhofs, for example, with whom Sidi and Ed had once enjoyed playing bridge, are opposed to the Nazis, but they, too, remain silent and turn away from the destroyed businesses. They bite their lips in dismay when someone jumps out of a window, cry when one of their friends goes into exile. Their own lives demand so much attention, so much energy; the children have to be protected; it will be over soon; one doesn't want to endanger oneself. There is a lot one doesn't know—doesn't want to know.

THINGS GET EVEN TIGHTER

ON JANUARY 1, 1939, THE MERCILESS LAWS AGAINST JEWISH CITIzens are expanded. Jews have to liquidate their businesses and properties and/or must sell them to Aryans at well below market value. Jews are not allowed to buy jewels or any art, are denied access to theaters, movies, concerts, exhibits, sports events, spas and public baths. They may not have a driver's license or own a car, are barred from universities and public libraries.

On February 21, 1939, non-Aryans are ordered to turn over to the government all the precious metals (with the exception of wedding bands), gemstones and pearls in their possession.

By March 1939, it becomes clear for the first time that there is a shortage of food, and everything containing fat is rationed. The National Socialist daily, the *Völkische Beobachter*, reports in May 1939 that over 100,000 Glaubensjuden (religious Jews) left Ostmark during the preceding year.

On September 1, 1939, the German Wehrmacht attacks Poland, opening the sluices of war.

With the arrival of 1940, rent control protection no longer applies to Jews, and contracts with Jewish renters are no longer honored. (Jews who are in privileged mixed marriages are excluded from these special regulations.) Flats occupied by Jews have to be marked by a "Judenstern" (Star of David) on the entry door. Hermann Göring insists that "increased Jewish emigration should continue, despite the war," but with the caveat that Jews who can be drafted and/or are able to work should not be allowed to emigrate to other European countries, particularly those that have been hostile to the Reich. This leaves Jews with only two options—emigrate by boat from Italy or take the Trans-Siberian railroad through the Soviet Union. Until the German attack on the Soviet Union on June 22, 1941, many emigrants choose the latter.

To Sidi, these decrees are ridiculous, and she is not afraid of them. With a mixture of contempt, pride and utter political innocence, she ignores whatever can be ignored. She doesn't know how to drive, and Ed has kept the car she had always been driven in. Of course she will continue to go to the theater and to concerts. She considers the public baths disgusting; and the days are long gone when she was a student and needed to use the local libraries.

It is the order to hand over her jewelry that proves to be the last straw, and for the first time Sidi feels she's under personal attacked. It is outrageous that people she considers riffraff want to get their hands on her jewelry. She is not going to relinquish a single item. Her mother has already taken their more prized pieces to France, and now Sidi plans to have an Aryan friend smuggle her valuable pieces to Paris. She'll leave the Nazis all the Rhinestone brooches, little hat pins and silver rings from which she used to choose gifts for her maids.

But soon not even Sidi can continue to shut her eyes to political reality. She finally starts preparing to emigrate, though that is becoming increasingly difficult as German troops continue their advance in the west. In April they occupy first Demark, then Norway. On May 10 they march into Belgium and the Netherlands, and in June the "phony war" with France comes to an end and German troops occupy Paris.

Sidi receives agitated phone calls from her mother and brother, who feel safe in France for the time being but are considering joining the two Csillag brothers who are already in Cuba. They urge her to leave Vienna as quickly as possible.

In the spring of 1940, Sidi tries on her own to obtain a Cuban visa and a ticket on a steam ship that can take her there. She doesn't want to appeal to the Jewish or Christian refugee organizations because she detests the idea of having to register somewhere. Being on the record means being controlled, then ending up filed away somewhere by some bureaucracy or other. She is a free woman who will decide for herself what happens and when. Perhaps she truly has no idea how constrained and dangerous her situation has become, for she goes on the offensive with the brazenness of the ignorant and proud.

Paying no attention to the 1940 order banning Jews from leaving their place of residence without written permission from the local police, Sidi buys a sleeping car ticket to Hamburg, where she plans to organize her passage to Cuba. One of the shipping companies is sure to have room on a boat to Cuba, particularly if she slips the right person some money in an envelope.

One evening in late April, carrying only one small suitcase, Sidi boards the train and the sleeping car attendant takes her to her assigned seat without hesitation. She's still using the identity card issued to Sidonie Weitenegg. It sounds so very German. The elegant woman already in the compartment smiles at her, and Sidi thinks a long talk with her might be a charming way to pass the time. But the woman launches into a monolog. She comes from the Old Reich, has just spent a few days in Vienna, didn't see much evidence of the many Jews supposedly living there. Most likely the Führer has already cleared them out. Maybe she could tell her a bit about the mood in Vienna and the city's "Jewish problem"? It's really terrible. Vienna, the pearl of the finally reunited Reich and yet at the same time all those foreign people from the East. At least one has defeated Poland, and Russia will be next ... As she goes on and on Sidi keeps a smile on her face and says she doesn't know, she doesn't know any Jews, she doesn't travel in such circles. The words fall from her lips like lead and leave a metallic taste in her mouth; she says them in order not to betray herself. Soon she pretends to be dreadfully tired, calls the attendant to unfold the beds and feigns sleep. Anything to still that terrible voice. After a light and fretful sleep, she is awakened shortly before reaching Hamburg. The stranger has already left the train.

With a delighted sigh of relief she leans out the window to look at the docks, the cranes and cargo ships, the brick buildings of the warehouse district. This will be her departure point. She fills her lungs with air that smells of the sea, and great distances, and newness.

But there is no berth to be had, no passage to purchase. All access to the west is closed off. She'll have to approach Cuba from the east, across Russia, Siberia, Japan It's the more difficult, more adventurous route; and in one corner of her heart Sidi feels a budding thirst for adventure. Having accomplished nothing in Hamburg, she returns to Vienna bitterly disappointed but determined.

She now accepts help from the religious charity Gildemeester, an organization that primarily helps baptized Jews who are considered "Volljuden" under the Nazi racial laws. Gildemeester's only role will be to provide help with her baggage, while Sidi—as before, all on her own—will arrange her train travel to Berlin then on to Königsberg and from there by plane to Moscow. In Moscow she will take the Trans-Siberian railroad.

Her emigration will take place under cover of night, and none of her close friends, not even her beloved Wjera, is to know about it. Wjera has been coming to Vienna more frequently lately, since she is still part owner of the Gutmann's house on Hasenauerstrasse and is therefore affected by the complex Aryanization process.

With all her documents and tickets finally in hand, Sidonie leaves Vienna on August 12, 1940, right after the spectacle celebrating Baldur von Schirach's appointment as Vienna's Gauleiter and Reichsstatthalter. It's the last time she'll have to be a passive bystander at such an event. Once Vienna is behind her, she'll be free as a bird, won't own anything, will have no home, no homeland, no roots. Gildemeester will transport a single trunk to Cuba for her. That is it. She'll write her farewell letters from Berlin. Only her ex-husband knows about her departure.

Effective September 19, 1941, all Jews will be ordered to wear a black bordered, yellow, palm-sized, six-pointed star with the word Jew stitched on it in black letters. At that point Sidonie will have been in Cuba for nearly a year, but surely no one could have forced her to wear such a thing.

FOR THE LAST TIME: LEONIE

IT'S ED WHO TAKES SIDI TO FRANZ-JOSEFS-BAHNHOF, THE DEPARTURE point for night trains to Berlin. Though the pain of leaving her beloved city is immense, there is also a certain joy in thinking about the freedom that's to come. She hugs Ed tightly and feels overwhelmed by her emotions. It feels good to cry on the shoulder of someone she had once loved. Stepping back, she sees that her eye liner has left rivulets like little spider legs on his linen suit jacket. She rubs at it and mumbles apologies, but for once Ed forsakes vanity. He caresses her hair and wishes her God speed. Of course he'll stay in touch, of course this is all pro forma, of course he'll look after her belongings, of course he'll wait for her. When this is all over, they will be together again, there will be a time for love again.

Sidi nods and boards the train. It seems like she has seen this film before, this pushing down the window in the corridor and blowing kisses. It's as awkward as it had been with her mother, and maybe just as genuine. Then the train pulls slowly out of the station, and Sidonie Csillag leaves forty years of her life behind her.

In true Sidi style, she has made plans for how she's going to spend the few days she'll be in the Führer's city. For the past sixteen years, Sidi has associated Berlin with Leonie, and since she hasn't heard from her in all those years, it is time to make contact again.

She arrives the morning of August 13 and checks into a pension. The Nazis had started their air campaign against Britain the previous month, and that first evening, Sidi experiences the Royal Air Force's ongoing response. She puts together a jigsaw puzzle as she waits out the attack in the pension's air-raid shelter; it calms her nerves and helps to pass the time. She also consults the phone directory she borrowed from the reception desk, and there she is, "Puttkamer, Leonie von."

Sidi's heart isn't hammering because bombs are falling but with ela-
tion at finding Leonie. After the air-raid and a few hours of sleep, and
without further reflection, she finds a phone booth, dials and hears a
woman say "Puttkamer." It's still the same melodious, dry and slightly
mocking voice. Sidi's reaction, too, is almost unchanged: there is still
the joy, the little jump of her heart, the expectation. Sidi gives her
name, but instead of the joyful greeting she anticipates, there's a nervous little cough on the other end of the line.

"Sidi Csillag died years ago..."

"No, no, she's alive and talking to you. I'll be in Berlin until the six-
teenth, then I have to take the train to Königsberg. I'd like to see you."

Leonie's skepticism persists, and she starts a question-and-answer
game to be on the safe side: "Where did we meet? To whom was I married then? What was the name of my dog? If you can answer these questions, then I can be sure that you are the Sidi I used to know."

For a second Sidi is deeply hurt, but then she recognizes that distrust reigns in times like these, and, like a student taking an exam, she
begins a detailed report of their past. When she gets to her admiration
for Leonie's beautiful hands, the baroness starts laughing and the ice is
broken.

"We don't want to stay on the phone for your whole stay in Berlin.
What's the name of your pension? I'll come there."

Sidi is so nervous she almost trips as she hurries to answer the knock
on her door an hour later. There she stands, older but still very beautiful, still very enticing. For a short eternity the two women look at each
other in silence, then they move into a long and tender embrace. Still
that wonderful smell, Sidi thinks, still that muscular body beneath her
clothes. How did I live without her all these years? If only I had been
more daring!

The baroness suggests lunch at a small Italian restaurant, because a
reunion after sixteen years has to be celebrated properly. There is no
need for food coupons for an Italian meal; and despite the food shortage, Italian wine is available always and everywhere, thanks to the
brotherhood with Il Duce. And French champagne has been flowing all
over Berlin since the Nazis occupied France. There is still a reasonable
night life and good music in many bars.

Sidi smiles with amusement; obliviously Leonie is sticking to her old habits.

On the way to the restaurant she admires the forty-nine-year-old Leonie: her posture is upright, her gait supple, and her hands are still delicate and so characteristic of her. She can only congratulate her seventeen-year-old self for having had the taste to choose this woman, who really had been worth all that adoration and cosseting.

After a delicious meal and a bottle of Lambrusco, Leonie looks at her watch. Her current source of funds is teaching English to prospective emigrants, and she has two lessons scheduled. Generous men, she remarks with a mischievous smile, are no longer part of her life. The two women head buoyantly out into the afternoon. Looking deep into Sidi's eyes, Leonie gives her her address and suggests the she come by later that evening. She can meet her girlfriend then; a wonderful woman, with whom she has been living for several years.

With a coquettish wink, Leonie—her flower-print summer dress hugging her waist most becomingly—disappears around the corner.

Around 8:30, Sidi rings the bell at Leonie's and it's answered by a tall, very blonde woman in a state of some disarray. She's wearing a bath robe and her pale, flat face seems to be accustomed to lots of make-up.

"Oh my, I should have known," Sidi thinks, "still such terrible taste when it comes to women." But she smiles and extends her hand.

Two women who adore the same woman, one looking particularly elegant, the other particularly sloppy, stand in the same door frame. This won't do. Embarrassed and with a certain air of distrust, the blonde takes Sidonie's hand.

"I'm Magda. Sorry, didn't know you'd show up so early. Come in. Leo's still teaching," she says in a very broad Berlin dialect.

"Leo," Sidi smiles to herself, "how long has it been, since I heard all those ... women ... calling her Leo."

Magda invites Sidonie into the kitchen—the living room is used for lessons—then disappears for a few minutes to "pull something on," as she puts it.

Sidi sits at a simple wooden table and looks around at the battered white cabinets, the piles of dishes in the sink, the two-tiered porcelain coffee pot. The small window in front of her frames a withering parsley plant and looks out on a Berlin backyard.

They are not exactly leading the wild life, she thinks as Magda returns, all made up. Her beige dress and shrill lipstick don't really do much to help. Sidi knows poor Magda is trying to keep up with her, and Madga does indeed think she's facing a powerful opponent. She starts talking fast and loudly about her activities in films but doesn't reveal her actual role. Sidi is pretty sure she's not an actress. Well, maybe an extra, she thinks condescendingly. At that moment Leonie enters, wearing a blue silk dress and obviously ready for a night out.

Leonie takes Sidi's face in her hands and plants a loud kiss on her mouth. When all three are seated at the kitchen table, Leonie shakes her head in disbelief and beams at Sidi. "That it's you, and that you're here …!"

Noting Leonie's elegant outfit, Magda goes to change her clothes and to escape, however briefly, the open display of delight and mutual attraction.

Leading Sidi toward the living room, Leonie tells her that when Magda is dressed, they will all go to one of the elegant bars where Berlin's ladies meet.

"I still just want to devour her with my eyes," Sidi thinks but restrains the impulse and takes a seat on the couch next to the baroness, who suddenly starts kissing her. As simple as that, after sixteen years, and with the girlfriend in the next room. As if time had stood still, the charged atmosphere of the old days is back, and the feelings they had for one another are still there—unchanged.

Then, inevitably, a door opens and Magda, now wearing a black suit, stands frozen for a second before she starts shouting.

She has had enough, this can't continue. Sidi should go back to where she came from. This is her house; Sidi is only a guest and she should keep her hands off her girlfriend. If she doesn't disappear instantly, she'll report her to the Gestapo.

Sidi has actually enjoyed the scene up to this point, but this last is too much, and she stands and prepares to leave.

Leonie, too, was quite relaxed until Magda mentioned the Gestapo. Now she tells her partner sharply to leave the room.

"Sidi, it's better if you go. All hell is breaking loose, and it will take me a good two hours to calm Magda down."

She scribbles an address on a scrap of paper and asks Sidi to meet her there the following afternoon.

The address, the home of a couple Leonie knows, is quite far from Sidi's pension and requires a long ride on the S-Bahn. Sidi is somewhat agitated by the time she finally arrives. She needn't have worried, the welcome is friendly and relaxed, and the flat is as elegant as the couple who live in it. They entertain Sidi with tales of everyday life in Berlin until Leonie arrives.

For months now, one can bathe only on the weekend, since hot water is no longer available during the week. Their eating habits have changed a great deal. When they eat out, it's usually oysters, because one doesn't need food coupons for them. But one never feels full … At home they eat lots of yoghurt, they hardly ever have milk; they don't like yoghurt all that much, but it kills the hunger.

As for fashion, one can only say: the times dictate how women dress. Only hats and ties don't require coupons; and since they do not want to give up the habit of shopping for clothes and dressing up to go out, their closets are full of hats and ties. There are plenty of opportunities to show off the ties, for they dress as garconnes when they go to bars. People get together at the Adlon, the Eden, in the Ciro-Bar, and there are plenty of private soirées.

Leonie arrives while they are arguing about which actress in *Mädchen in Uniform* is more their type, Hertha Thiele as Manuela or Dorothea Wick as the teacher.

In Leonie's presence, the rest of the afternoon passes quickly, and Sidi even forgets about her imminent emigration. At some point, Leonie's friends withdraw discreetly and no doubt leave the flat. For the first time in many years, in these times of war and destruction, in this city where the Nazis have their headquarters, Sidi and Leonie revel in their kisses and in their bodies amid prickly pillows on a velvet-covered couch. Both know that each moment is precious and that their situation is exceptional—and that helps them push everything else aside and devote themselves to lust. Tomorrow there will be no demands for an accounting, no pay back required for today's emotions and experiences—

tomorrow everything will be over. This gives both women permission to be free, exuberant, heartsick and very loving.

The day after tomorrow Sidi will begin her journey to the other side of the world.

This time, when Sidi and Leonie say farewell, it really is forever; and both women must sense it. There are a few kisses, a few hugs, they hold each other's hands, but there are no reassurances and no promises.

Sidonie carries the memory of Leonie's beauty and their shared experiences with her on her travels. Staying in contact by mail will soon no longer be possible; by 1942 international deliveries grind almost to a standstill. The letters she will write to Leonie after the war remain unanswered, and the package of Leonie's favorite tea that she sends to the old Berlin address is never acknowledged. Many years later, she learns that Leonie survived the war in Berlin and died there in 1953.

THROUGH SIBERIA AND ACROSS THE PACIFIC

SIDI LEAVES BERLIN ON AUGUST 16 AND ARRIVES IN KÖNIGSBERG with barely enough time to catch her plane for Moscow. It's her first time in one of those little sheet metal machines, and there's room for just a dozen passengers. She is sweating with fear but also full of joy as she peers through the small window at the landscape below and the towering clouds nearby—she feels like a bird.

Her twenty-four hours in Moscow leave her with the impression that it is a city of beggars. Her hotel has remnants of Czarist pomp— her room boasts full-length mirrors in ornate gold frames—but only the second floor has functioning toilets, and in the evening there is no water.

She's shocked by how shabbily people are dressed. All the women wear worn out cotton dresses and seem to look at her as if she were from another planet simply because she's wearing a neat skirt and blouse. She's also the only person wearing leather shoes; everyone else is either barefoot or wears cotton socks and cloth shoes, or galoshes, or even house slippers. They stop Sidi frequently and use agitated gestures to suggest that they are willing to buy everything she's wearing. Feeling pressured and embarrassed, she escapes into the Underground, whose lavish marble stations let her flee both the summer heat and the crowded metropolis.

It's a relief to board the Manchuria Express the next day and leave behind the jarring contrast of decaying splendor and human misery. The Trans-Siberian Railroad leaves Moscow for the Pacific coast twice a week, once via Manchuria and once to Vladivostok. Before the war of 1914, travel on the Trans-Siberian Railroad had been heavily promoted, and it was considered glamorous to let the Compagnie des Wagons-Lits whisk one past taiga and tundra in style. During the Russian Revolution and in the twenties, these luxury trips ceased, only to be revived in the mid-thirties by Intourist, the state-owned Soviet travel agency.

The timetables are subject to erratic changes and the quoted prices are not guaranteed, but Sidi is happy just to find the right train in the right station, despite the Cyrillic signage, to have a valid ticket and to be leaving Nazi Europe behind.

At five in the afternoon on August 18, 1940, it's mostly older people who get on the train with Sidi. The younger ones, if they had the means and the opportunity, have already left Nazi-contaminated Europe behind.

The non-aggression pact of August 22, 1939, had postponed military conflict between the German Reich and the Soviet Union, and a similar pact with Japan secured peace at the Soviet Union's border with China. And so, until Hitler invaded the Soviet Union in June 1941, the Trans-Siberian route was one of the two remaining possibilities for Jews to escape Europe. The other was via Lisbon.

Sidi has reserved a single compartment in first class in one of the re-activated old Compagnie de Wagons-Lits carriages. Second and third class passengers traveled in USSR-built carriages. All classes are furnished with beds, mattresses and linen, but only first class provides a lavabo. She'll be quite happy for this in the steaming hot days to come.

As soon as she gets into the compartment, Sidi tests the bed. It proves rather hard, and the linen is of poor quality—over the next eight days, it will be changed only once. She also finds it difficult to communicate with the conductors—there are two per carriage—who

Departure station for the Trans-Siberian Railroad, Moscow

speak only their own language. Their greasy, worn-out uniforms make them look impoverished, but they are obliging and disciplined and are doing their best.

Before departure everyone's luggage is thoroughly inspected. Sidi is unhappy when her small camera and some of her books are confiscated and sealed, to be returned only upon leaving Soviet territory, and she is surprised that the officials don't take her cigarettes. Clearly, they are tolerated in smaller quantities, and there may be times during the trip when it will be useful to have a foreign cigarette to offer.

For eight long days there is little to do but sit in one's compartment or in the dining car. Sidi prefers the latter, but not because of the food, all of which has been brought from Moscow. Though there is plenty, the quality is terrible, and the meals are carelessly prepared. Nothing fresh is taken on board at stops, and the meat gets worse every day. There are no vegetables other than the occasional chopped white cabbage in a meat broth. Instead of potatoes, big, coarse pieces of macaroni are prepared like porridge. For Sidi, it is all hideous sludge and she eats only as much as is absolutely necessary, sticking to the only menu items that appeal: the appetizers.

Salmon and Russian caviar, which Sidi loves, are available at any time during the first four days, and she eats little else. However, these special appetizers cost her dearly, as they can only be purchased in rubles at an exorbitantly high exchange rate.

Sidi also declines dessert, which is always a kind of farmers' cheese cookies. She tried them once, and the taste and smell reminded her of what babies spit up after drinking too much milk. Sidi doesn't like anything having to do with babies.

Even more disturbing are the table clothes. When she sees them for the first time, they don't look right, because they started out grey. They are never changed, and soon grow black with soot particles and sticky with smeared food. Sidi's sleeves stick to them if she rests her arms on the table. As a precaution, she uses a few sheets of the toilet paper she brought from Vienna to clean her plate and utensils before using them— some of her fellow travelers use their napkins, but she finds this unappetizing.

So, it is definitely not the food that draws Sidi to the dining car but the opportunity to sit for hours among other people and watch fascinating new landscapes pass by. But there is no one with whom Sidi can share her enthusiasm. Most of her fellow travelers seem to be interested in only two topics: visas to the United States and their digestion.

On the morning of August 20, the train stops in Swerdlovsk in the Urals, geographically the last stop in Europe and the beginning of Siberia.

The vast plain of western Siberia's lowlands rises gently then reverts to endless flatness, and Sidi devours the passing scene with her eyes as the train passes by many villages with small, grey wooden houses and well worn, muddy paths, and then cities that take up a lot of territory. The cities seem to date from the end of the previous century, and their railway stations are beehives of activity. Whenever the train stops at one, Sidi presses her face to the window to take in the many souvenir shops, the political posters and the huge portraits of Stalin, Molotov and other Soviet leaders. Outside every station there's an identical, pale grey statue of Lenin decorating a meadow.

When it gets dark and her eyes grow tired and she has seen enough for the day, Sidi returns to her compartment. The mid August nights are hot and sticky, and Sidi wants to keep her window open, which triggers an ongoing battle with the conductor. Gesticulating wildly, he tries to explain that an open window lets in soot and dust that will ruin the walls and the carpet. She doesn't really care about that but acknowledges that the conductor's concerns might well apply to her dresses. So she gets used to the idea that she needn't wear something different every day and from time to time opens the window secretly and enjoys a cool breeze that allows her to sleep wonderfully well.

The real problem is that there is no cold water. Since neither coffee nor tea has agreed with Sidi for years, ice cold water has become her favorite drink. The tea that is available from a samovar any time of the day or night is an impossible substitute. The water shortage is such that travelers who didn't purchase enough of it before boarding in Moscow end up brushing their teeth with tea. Only the Russian travelers had known to bring containers so they could buy boiled water at the stations. Sidonie gave the conductor a bit of money to find her a somewhat decent container so she could buy water, but unfortunately, it's always hot water.

The farther to the southeast the train travels, the more varied the scenery becomes and the more lively the villages. Sidi sees lots of gardens with beans, cabbage and even currants, as well as an occasional apple tree. People here seem to own some animals, and a calf or a goat can often be seen tied to a fence post. Sometimes vendors or children board the train at a station to sell hot piroshky and even blueberries or raspberries.

The train reaches the Manchurian border station of Manchuli at midnight on August 26, and the next day arrives at the station in Harbin, where Sidi is unexpectedly pulled off. The representatives of an aid organization for refugees have noted that she hasn't booked passage on any ship, and they are concerned that this may cause a big problem in Japan. Her papers only allow her to stay in Japan for a week, which isn't enough time to secure passage across the Pacific. The organization promises to take care of the problem as quickly as possible. They take her papers and house her temporarily with a doctor who specializes in venereal diseases—an émigré like herself.

While in Harbin, she can once again walk in a town unaffected by war and food shortages. In Manchuria there is no rationing, and many items offer colors and smells that Sidi finds new and delightful. Her host can even feed his cat sardines. Yet, like a dark echo from Europe, even here they are preparing for a possible war, and there are frequent blackouts and air-raid drills.

One evening, out of boredom and maybe with a certain schadenfreude triggered by the fact that she has escaped the Reich, Sidi attends a concert at the German embassy. Afterwards, she can't understand what had provoked her to endure such provincial, colonial entertainment. The Lieder had been peeped out by a young soprano who had come to this faraway place to please the Nazis. At the reception afterwards, Sidi introduced herself to an embassy official as an Austrian, then went on to comment that since the Austrians had gotten rid of the Turks centuries ago, they wouldn't find it difficult to rid themselves of the Germans now. Left speechless, the official will later try to convince his superior that this woman should be prevented from continuing her journey—but it will be in vain.

After less than a week, Sidi takes an evening train from Harbin to the harbor, where she continues on by boat to Shimonoseki in Japan, where the train to Kobe is waiting. In Kobe, Sidi is taken in by the same refugee organization that looked after her in Manchuria.

She finds this whole situation annoying. The organization has usurped her ability to continue this trip on her own. She's also been left without money or papers and has to share a room at a refugee center with fourteen other Europeans, none of whom are used to Japanese sleeping arrangements involving futons laid over tatami mats. There are no showers or bathtubs, and the refugees crowd around the few available faucets. They are fed lots of rice and some vegetables, but life there is quite monotonous. Though free to leave the center anytime, Sidi, like the others, sits around just killing time, waiting to continue the journey. She doesn't like Japan and has no wish to explore it.

It will be over a month until this group can move on. The delay makes everyone nervous—they fear Japan will declare war on the United States, thus closing off their routes into exile—but Sidonie ends up finding the wait rather agreeable. In addition to her food, she receives a small allowance, enough to buy cigarettes anyway, and if she doesn't have enough left over to buy additional food, the other emigrants help her out.

In October, Sidonie finally receives some money from her brothers in Cuba, and with the help of the refugee organization, she buys passage on a small Japanese vessel heading to the west coast of the United States and then on to Panama. It is allowed to carry only up to 10,000 tons of cargo and has just twelve first class cabins. Sidi and some of the other emigrants embark on October 24.

Even though the fall winds make the sea rough and many passengers are sick in their cabins, Sidonie enjoys every minute of the long crossing. She often stands at the bow until late into the night—regardless of the weather—and lets the cool breeze blow through her hair. If a storm rises, she takes advantage of the noise to shout her happiness and love of life into the wind. She even feels just fine when she's in her cabin, which she shares with a woman who has papers for Honduras.

One other thing makes the voyage unforgettable. At the beginning, while strolling on deck, she encounters a good-looking man with curly dark hair who throws meaningful glances her way. He introduces himself as Carlos. They easily agree to speak French, as he doesn't speak German or English, and she doesn't yet know a word of Spanish. He is on his way home to Peru and invites her to dine at his table. After dinner, casually carrying along a bottle of wine and two glasses, he leads her to a row of deck chairs where they can sit under the star studded Pacific sky and he can propose a small adventure. A beautiful woman like her must have had lots of lovers. It would be wonderful if, now, on the spur of the moment, riding the rough sea on the tropic of cancer, he could hold her in his arms and love her. Electrified by the proposition, and even a bit in love, Sidonie is afraid that it will end as it always does when the deed is over and done with. She tells him that she has been married but has never had male lovers, and besides, she lacks experience and doesn't really care to acquire any.

Carlos isn't prepared for this response and, somewhat rattled, beats a retreat. When Sidonie continues to treat him with a certain reserve during the days that follow, he turns his attention to a busty young Pole who is less inhibited about having a fling on the high seas.

All that will remain of the Carlos episode is a little sketch Sidonie did of him when they were both sitting on deck. He hadn't found it half bad. A few months later, already in Havana, she will draw him again from memory, and this is how she'll think of him—frozen in time and place—every so often until the end of her days.

On November 7, the ship docks in Honolulu, and on November 16 it reaches North America, docking first in San Francisco and then in Los Angeles. The European emigrants are not allowed to disembark at either port. After a stop at Manzanillo in Mexico, the ship finally docks in Balboa, Panama, on December 4. Most of the passengers go off in different directions from there. Carlos heads directly for Peru, but Sidonie must spend a great deal of time in Panama looking for passage and securing the necessary papers so she can continue on to Cuba.

After the weeks of fresh ocean breezes, Panama City's tropical climate is hard to get used to—the thermometer never falls below 28 degrees Celsius. Sidi takes a somewhat run down room in a city center hotel that has bright blue shutters and hosts a variety of insects, most of which she doesn't recognize. But there is no lack of water and she can take three cold showers a day, which bolsters both her mood and her blood circulation. Finally, on December 24, 1940, Sidonie boards her final—a bit rusty this time—means of transportation into life as an émigré. It's painful to face Christmas at sea, in the tropics and so far from Europe, and it brings up many emotional memories from her child-

Entrance to the harbor, Havana, Cuba

hood—of snow and her kind father on skis. The Latin American Christmas celebration starts as soon as the boat leaves Colon's harbor, but it is not to her Central European taste. Retreating from the loud drumming, the dance music and the din of tipsy passengers and crew, she stands between decks looking at the tirelessly glittering stars and finds herself thanking something or someone she doesn't know and doesn't believe in that she is still alive, that her flight has been easier than she had anticipated, and that she has been granted more than she ever dared to dream about.

The boat enters Havana's beautiful harbor in the late morning of December 27. Moved and overwhelmed, Sidonie stands at the rail letting Cuba welcome her with bright sunshine and a warm tropical wind. She has done it! After nearly circumnavigating the globe in almost five months, she has arrived. She has left terrible things behind and seen wonderful new things, and history and circumstances have tumbled her and her partly reassembled family out into this wonderful city. She will start a new life.

9

CUBA, MI AMOR

ROBERT AND ERNST CSILLAG HAVE BEEN PACING BACK AND FORTH for two hours at Havana's harbor, glancing now and then at the telegram giving the arrival time of the boat from Panama. If it weren't winter, they'd already be dead from heatstroke. But what does "winter" mean when its 25 degrees Celsius? It is still hard for the brothers to believe Sidi will really arrive, given the long build up to her emigration and how difficult her travels have been. They often had no contact with her at all, and both had secretly been afraid they wouldn't ever see her again.

The waiting crowd begins to stir, then to shout and point at something that Robert, despite his glasses, can't quite make out. Ernst's eyes are better—yes, there's a ship on the horizon. It finally reaches the pier a good half hour later, triggering much waving of handkerchiefs and shedding of tears, both on deck and on the dock.

Even for those who've done it often, entering Havana's harbor is something special—and it is particularly so for Europe's refugees, who arrive with their diverse destinies in their luggage, seeking safe harbor in more than one sense. Sidonie has watched Cuba's dark green vegetation and white sand beaches come slowly into view, eventually resolving into individual palm trees—she knows them only from postcards—and the outline of a city that she immediately opens her heart to. Upon first seeing Cuba in 1492, Christopher Columbus proclaimed it "the most beautiful place in the world" and added, "I heard the birds sing that they will never ever leave this place."

Standing on deck, Sidi watches the sailors throw the heavy mooring lines to black longshoremen, who wind them around iron bollards. She hears the anchor hit the water with a loud thump and realizes that the ship's engines have gone silent. Now just two meters from Cuba's shore, she spies her brothers in their light-weight summer suits, shielding their eyes against the sun's glare as they try to locate her.

Checking herself one last time in one of the ship's mirrors, Sidi grips her hand luggage more tightly, holds her head high and walks down the gangplank with a delighted smile on her face. The crowd propels her towards buildings where bored young men in uniform check everyone's papers at a snail's pace. When it is Sidi's turn, her beaming smile and intense stare are of no help whatsoever. To be sure, the young men's eyes light up and they grin, but their pace doesn't change, and they take their time leafing through her passport and finally stamping it. She shrugs off the delay. After all this time, a few minutes more or less just don't matter.

Once outside the customs building, she walks the few steps to the barrier, and there is Robert with his characteristic squint and his increasingly high forehead glistening in the sunlight. He is holding a spray of yellow-orange heliconia—a flower she will forever associate with the island. Behind him, Ernst—casual, grinning and still more dashing than his elder brother—opens his arms, and Sidi falls into them, laughing and crying with joy. After a few kisses, it is Robert's turn ... quieter, more tender. Sidi holds him tightly for a long time, murmuring in his ear that he has always been her darling. He makes a joke in order to hide his emotions. It has been over an hour since the boat docked.

Soon the siblings revert to the distanced behavior that characterized their childhood. Since Sidi doesn't have any other luggage—it could be months before the trunk that Gildemeester sent will arrive—they head for the line of taxis on Avenida del Puerto, where every driver calls out the advantages of his vehicle. The Csillags get into a big red Dodge for the short drive to Pension Sophia in La Habana Vieja, where Robert and Ernst have been lodgers since arriving in the city. Though somewhat overwhelmed, Sidi is also euphoric as she soaks up her first impressions. There's life on the streets; the old houses remind her a bit of Italy, the walls surrounding them are covered in flowers; the people are dressed so colorfully and seem so animated and friendly. She's almost relieved when the huge car—it reminds her of a Hollywood movie—stops on a side street off the Parque Central near the theater. Finally, she can give her eyes a rest.

Pension Sophia's doors open, and an obliging young mulatto comes out to take Sidi's luggage and lead her to a quiet room with a view of the backyard, which is filled with cascades of bougainvillea. The bed is big and soft, and in the coming months, this room will be her first and most important homeland in Havana. Sparrow song is the last thing she hears before falling into an exhausted sleep.

Her first days in Havana are devoted in part to rest and relaxation, but she is also determined to explore the old town and refuses all her brothers' offers to show her around. She prefers to go out on her own. The moment she leaves the pension, she's caught up in the pulsing life of the city, since there is always something going on in Parque Central. Among the majestic king palms and big frangipani trees, women vendors offer everything one could possibly want or not want from small carts. Most are young, beautiful and dark skinned, and they try to tempt Sidonie to buy flowers, mangoes, bananas, straw hats or cheap jewelry. Yet again, she finds that she has to set aside one of her many prejudices, and she lets a broad smile spread across her face as one of the women peels a mango with slow, erotic strokes and hands it to her with a grin. Black women are beautiful, and from now on mangoes will be her favorite fruit.

Walking on, she admires the pompous neo-baroque Gran Teatro with its ionic pillars, arched windows, plaster of Paris embellishments and three gigantic bronze angels perched on three wedding cake towers.

Exhausted by the time she reaches the Plaza Vieja, she enjoys a glass of pineapple juice in one of the lovely, peaceful arcades called portales. She will come to think that this is the city's loveliest square. Beautiful Creole palaces sit shoulder to shoulder with classic buildings reminiscent of Europe; balconies grace each floor, and through the intricate cast iron shutters one can glimpse colored glass windows and large wooden doors. And for the icing on the cake, every roof sports low balustrades decorated with everything from urns to busts of the important men who are somehow connected to the history of the house or the country.

During those early explorations, Sidi always has the feeling that the Capitolio is following her, like an ever-present companion. She thinks it's a hideous building, and subsequent explanations that it is an exact replica of the Capitol in Washington, DC, and a symbol of Cuba's democracy, do nothing to change her opinion.

Soon, her brothers invite her for an evening out to celebrate her arrival and show her Havana's night life. They'll also have a surprise for her. And so Sidi lets herself be surprised. The evening begins with a stroll to the famous Cine Teatro Fausto movie theater. It's been so long since she's seen a film! This is the best time of day for a stroll. The Csillags join many other elegantly dressed people ambling between the double row of laurel trees that flanks the Paseo Prado, which is inlaid with mosaics and ends at the Cine, an art deco palace painted pink and gold. Sidonie is bored by the movie and won't recall the title a few days later; though she knows it was some kind of love story. She doesn't like the stars and is disgusted by their constant kissing.

But the subsequent dinner at Hotel Sevilla makes up for it. Famous for its Arabic-Moorish decor, this is one of the city's smartest restaurants, and it makes Sidi feel as if she's entered "A Thousand and One Nights." Delighted and rather in disbelief, she sits in a beautifully tiled, green inner courtyard listening to the chatter of a pair of parrots and the splash of a fountain. She feels as if she's landed in paradise and greedily soaks in the aura of luxury and wealth that seems to prevail everywhere.

This splendor rests on a shaky foundation, but she doesn't know that yet. Though Havana is one of the most exciting cities in the world and seems to pulsate with life, it is also thoroughly corrupt. Since Army Sergeant Fulgencio Batista declared himself president in the fall of 1940—he had been pulling strings behind the scenes ever since a military revolt in 1933—Cuba has been nothing but an outpost and puppet of the United States. This situation has been years in the making. The USA began keeping a greedy eye on Cuba in 1898 and got involved in the final battles of Cuba's War of Independence, helping to rid the island of its

Spanish colonial rulers. The USA declared itself Cuba's liberator and since then, the island's extensive concessions have included letting Washington dabble in its internal affairs, establish several marine bases, and veto any commercial or monetary dealings with third-party countries. Cuba also became a locus for everything that was no longer allowed in the States and found itself deeply entangled with the Mafia.

When prohibition was being rigidly enforced in the United States, Cuba openly promoted the pleasures of "personal freedom"—men could hop on a boat in Florida, cross the 90 miles to Cuba, drink until they dropped and openly buy sex. Nightclubs flourished and rivers of rum flowed to the rhythms of rumba and Son Cubano. Batista was quite lucratively connected to the Mafia through the flourishing enterprises that purveyed liquor, prostitution, drugs and gambling. In 1938 he invited US Mafia boss Meyer Lansky to run a few casinos and night clubs in Parque Oriental, and since those did very well, Lansky took over all of Cuba's casinos and hotels, paid a share to Batista and could operate nation-wide with impunity.

The elegance and wealth that Sidonie encounters on her Havana walks are the product of speculation and corruption and reflect only one of Cuba's many, huge social and economic contrasts. People in the countryside live in great poverty; 60 percent of the land is owned by people from the States, as are most of the sugar industry, always the mainstay of Cuba's economy, and the oil industry.

Nevertheless, here in the prosperous capital, the rum is delicious, and Robert raises his glass of daiquirí to announce the surprise: he is extremely happy to have Sidi here, it is so important to be reunited with a part of the family, and in honor of this, the new unity will soon move into their own home. Shortly before Sidi arrived, the brothers bought land in the suburb of Miramar—everybody who is anybody is moving there now—and two young architects are building them a villa befitting their social status. The foundation has already been laid, and they'll all go there tomorrow morning.

Sidi breaks into applause. To own a house with a garden where she could keep some animals is more than she ever dared to dream about. Now nothing stands in the way of an idyllic life in an island paradise.

To top off the evening, the brothers take her to one of Havana's most popular hangouts. El Floridita is just a simple bar-restaurant with a wooden counter, a few ceiling fans and a three-man band; but somewhere along the line, it become famous. When they are in Cuba, Hollywood stars such as Spencer Tracy, Ava Gardner, Marlene Dietrich, Barbara Stanwyck and Robert Taylor enjoy their mojitos or daiquirís here. The locals like it, too, and it has developed an infamous reputation, as it's also the meeting place for lesbians and gays.

In the sultry fug of too much liquor and heavy, aromatic cigar smoke, Sidonie enjoys many a glimpse of beautiful, dark women and coquettish, erotic young men who swing their narrow hips to the beat of the band.

After breakfast the next morning, the siblings take a cab along the Malecón, the grand avenue bordering the sea, toward the construction site. Sidi is riveted by the brightly painted houses, the way the waves send up sprays of water. They cross the Almendares River, then leave the Vedado neighborhood on Havana's outskirts behind and enter an almost rural setting, where Robert tells the driver to stop next to a small, old house. This belongs to a Cuban poet who will be their neighbor, otherwise there's nothing but green shrubs, flowers, trees, a few cows in a pasture and the foundation of the Csillag's house.

It hadn't taken the brothers long to find this site; the land was affordable, and construction materials and labor are plentiful and cheap. They will be able to build a quite spacious house.

Vedado and Miramar didn't become truly fashionable neighborhoods until the end of the 1940s, by which time many recent immigrants, particularly Jewish refugees from Europe, had achieved a standard of living that allowed them to leave old Havana and build in Vedado, or, if even more successful financially, to settle in Miramar. By the mid-fifties, only old and poor members of the Jewish community hadn't yet moved to one or the other of these neighborhoods, which, until the Cuban Revolution in 1959, were absolutely the most fashionable places to live or to frequent as a tourist.

Sidi threads her way through a maze of bricks, wooden planks and large rocks to examine the foundation. Robert and Ernst talk proudly about the floorplan, plumbing and garden—now just a big expanse of mud—as if they had a profound understanding of construction. Sidi doesn't really care, she is only thinking of the future cannas, bougainvillea and mariposas, the white ginger lily that is Cuba's national flower.

All of a sudden, a strange woman comes mincing along the wooden plank that spans the foundation. She hugs Robert, kisses him on the mouth and behaves as if she were also on very familiar terms with Ernst. An obviously embarrassed Robert introduces her to Sidi as his fiancée, soon to be his wife. Sidi has never heard a word about this woman, but she isn't surprised, given how fickle Robert is with regard to women. Stiffly taking the stranger's outstretched hand, Sidi greets her rather sourly.

Robert had left Austria with his then wife, the singer Herta Glaz, with whom Sidi had been acquainted. Obviously, they have since split up. Herta stayed in New York, embarked on a career at the Metropolitan Opera and would later give singing lessons there. Robert has been living with this new woman—also a singer—since before Sidi's arrival, but he hasn't found the time to marry her. But they will tie the knot soon, since they are all going to share this new house, and he would feel uncomfortable living in "concubinage" in the presence of his older sister.

Sidonie has been wondering how her brothers can afford all this. She doesn't know much about money matters, doesn't really like to think about such things, but building and maintaining a villa must cost a pretty penny. When she brings up the topic a few days later, both brothers explain how difficult it has been to settle in here and invest the inheritance they had been able to take out of Europe.

With a deep sigh, Robert says that for the past year and a half, Cuba has been none too gentle with its Jewish immigrants, erecting a lot of bureaucratic as well as anti-Semitic hurdles.

THE LIFE OF JEWS IN CUBA

JEWISH IMMIGRATION TO CUBA, MAINLY FROM EASTERN EUROPE, started in the early 1920s and added to the island's than very small Jewish community made up mostly of families that had left Spain during the Inquisition. The idea was to use Cuba as a steppingstone to the States, but in 1924 that option was cut off by new US immigration restrictions, and many European immigrants of all creeds had to stay in Havana. By then, at least a third of Havana's population had been born abroad. About 5,000 East European Jews stayed in Cuba, though many others emigrated legally or illegally to the United States. In the following decade, an additional 5,000 immigrants from Eastern Europe arrived in Cuba, among them a disproportionately high number of single men, who slowly began to bring over the brides their families and friends had selected for them.

In mid-1939, when the first wave of Jewish refugees from Nazi Germany to Cuba came to an end, Sidonie was still in Vienna and Cuba was no longer willing to issue immigration visas. Indeed, in many cases even existing visas were no longer recognized. The influx of refugees was stopped precisely when the chance of survival was dwindling for Central Europe's Jews and help was needed more urgently than ever; this was largely a result of Cuba's own political and economic realities.

As at other classic immigration destinations, Cuba had its share of Nazis and Nazi sympathizers. In the twenties and thirties, many Germans and Austrians emigrated to Latin America, where some of them joined local Nazi organizations. Thanks to its Fascist Spanish and German immigrants, sympathy for the Falange and the Nazis reached a high point in Cuba in mid 1938. Germany's rulers had a spy ring in Cuba that was supervised by the managers of the Hamburg–America shipping line. At one point, the US embassy in Cuba counted 500 Nazis who were active on the island, where Nazi Party membership was not illegal and members could openly wear their Hakenkreuz badges.

In October 1938, the Cuban government legalized the local Nazi and Falange organizations, each of which had an estimated 5,000 members. The Falange was active in three areas: commerce, the elite schools and the newspapers. With this as their backing, they pressured the government to stop Jewish immigration. Although the government was ostensibly pro-American and anti-National Socialist, it gave in to the pressure.

Until mid 1939 immigration visas were only issued to those who could pay, but at that point the system changed and the only prospective immigrants who had a chance were those with relatives in Cuba who could apply for a visa for them. After the attack on Pearl Harbor in December 1941, even this avenue was no longer available.

Since mid 1936, about 100,000 refugees had come to the island, though many used Cuba only as a transit point. As the situation in Europe worsened, the number of immigrants to Cuba increased, and by January 1939 an average of 500 new refugees reached its shores every month. Those with relatives in the United States were allowed to go there—though they first had to wait an average of three years—the others had to stay in Cuba or eventually settle elsewhere on the North or South American continents.

For those who stayed—or rather, against them—in 1939/40 a new constitution was drafted that would make their lives more difficult. It prohibited the new immigrants from working as doctors or lawyers, made access to the labor market generally more difficult and—before the above-mentioned border closing—banned the entry of political or religious refugees. This constitution was passed on September 15, 1940, just as Fulgencia Batista took over as president. Publicly, Batista never took a stand against the rising tide of anti-Semitism, but at the end of 1939 he banned both the Nazi and Falange parties.

As an added burden, the German-speaking refugees on the island—they numbered about 10,000—carried the extra weight of being German as well as Jewish. The problem of being a German speaker arose from the authorities' reality-based precautions. During World War II large numbers of Nazi spies operated in the Caribbean, particularly in Cuba and the Dominican Republic. They were in touch with German submarines, airplanes and telegraph installations, and Gestapo agents were on hand to kill any agent who turned away from the Nazis. Cuba didn't want such people on its soil and therefore eyed all German speakers with suspicion, including refugees. After the attack on Pearl Harbor, all Germans who were not of Jewish descent were arrested, and the US State Department suggested that Cuba not take in any more German Jewish refugees because too many spies had mingled among them. Today, one must question whether this advice was based in reality or simply reflected the anti-Semitism that prevailed in the US State Department.

Both Robert and Ernst Csillag had had an unpleasant introduction to this atmosphere of mistrust.

In the language of the Nazis, Robert's new fiancée was an Aryan, and her marriage to a Jew would not be valid according to the Nazi laws. They were far from the German authorities, and nobody could hinder their marriage under Cuban law, but the Nazis could still make their lives difficult, as both were German citizens and needed to go through the German embassy for official matters.

Before her "race-defiling" relationship was made official, Robert's fiancée had been invited to all the official receptions at the embassy as a "German" singer. Robert and all her friends advised her not to accept any of these invitations, but one day she decides that doing so could build useful bridges. Soon it was common knowledge that she had participated in an official reception, and malicious gossip maintained that Robert had been there as well. Both brothers were immediately suspected of being Nazi sympathizers.

Robert sent a Cuban friend to the Cuban authorities to find out what was going on, and a few hours later the friend informed him with a laugh that the word was that neither Robert nor his siblings were of Jewish descent.

This was the other big problem for German-Jewish immigrants: the Cuban authorities either couldn't or wouldn't understand that people who had a Christian baptism certificate could be persecuted as Jews in Europe. The Csillags had Catholic baptism certificates and knew more about Catholicism than about Judaism. When Sidi was asked about her religious affiliation, she would answer Protestant. If asked, "and before?" she answered Catholic. These answers were perfectly correct, but German bureaucrats didn't want to hear them, and Cuban bureaucrats didn't understand them. A Catholic couldn't be a Jew at the same time, and it wasn't supposed to work the other way around either.

This peculiar ambivalence and the Cuban officials' distrust regarding their identity as Germans and as Jews had landed the brothers in a strange no man's land and had complicated their lives in Cuba. Robert still had his music company, but for the above-mentioned reasons his reputation had suffered, and therefore he was giving lessons in harmony and composition while trying to be hired as a teacher at the conservatory or the university. Ernst was giving English lessons to immigrants waiting to go to the States.

The money for the house would not come from their current earnings but from the capital of their father's inheritance. As long as Heinrich was able to stay in touch with them from Paris, he continued to give Robert solid financial advice; but Robert had always had a carefree attitude toward money, and he was convinced that things would work out and Sidi wouldn't need to worry about her future.

EVERYDAY LIFE IN CUBA

AFTER THE FIRST EXCITING WEEKS, SIDONIE SETTLES INTO A NEW kind of everyday life: the brothers go to work; she is more familiar with Havana; things have normalized, and she has to and wants to find something to pass the time. The first thing—and this makes sense—is to enroll in a Spanish language course at the school where Ernst teaches. She goes to the Avenida del Belgica near the railway station every day to sit and study, with stamina and discipline, in a run-down colonial building. She knows French extremely well and a bit of Italian, and so Spanish, with its similar-sounding words and expressions, poses no problems. She'll never master it as well as Ernst, who speaks like a native after only two years, but after a few months, she can read, write and hold a simple conversation in Spanish and is ready to dive more deeply into everyday Cuban life.

In the language course, she meets a pretty, dark-haired French woman who affects flashy sunglasses and big, colorful bracelets and rings. Jeanette has followed her husband into exile and, probably to make good use of her free time, decided to learn German and ended up at the language school. Sidonie takes a liking to the capricious young woman and offers to teach her German or at least to supplement the language course with German conversation. Enthusiastically, Jeanette offers to pay, which Sidonie indignantly refuses. The meetings for German conversation soon expand to include private social encounters, and Jeanette will soon be Sidi's best friend—a sort of Ellen-in-Cuba.

Jeanette has been in Cuba much longer than Sidonie and knows how two pampered European women can best pass their time. Since Sidonie is going to move to Miramar shortly, Jeanette takes her to the Vedado Tennis Club and signs her reluctant friend up for membership. This is where Sidi will get to know all the local families one must know if one wants to enter Cuban society. Sidi is a terrible tennis player—she considers all that running back and forth on a red clay court silly, exhausting and ruinous of one's shoes—but she's well aware of the club's social implications. She does like the shade of the tall palm trees in the gardens near the sea, and the substantial clubhouse surely offers a good hunting ground for new acquaintances, so, sighing, Sidi purchases a tennis racket and a white outfit and courageously agrees to meet Jeanette twice a week to bat a white felt ball back and forth.

Jeanette is also an enthusiastic swimmer and regularly takes her new friend to the Beach Club, located right on the Malecón on the way to

Miramar. Long, low buildings with arcades to protect visitors from the sun had been built atop the coral reefs along the shore, and long piers stretched into the sea to give swimmers access to the water without having to climb over the sharp reefs.

Sidi and Jeanette have a little ritual. They arrange to meet for a late breakfast at the Hotel Nacionál, which is on the way to the Beach Club, and then they spend half a day on the beach. The Hotel Nacionál has been a city landmark and its most elegant hotel since the late twenties. It is a big art-deco building with two symmetrically-arranged towers and a distinctive roof—a replica of a hotel in Palm Beach, Florida. The garden is the most beautiful part, offering lots of shade in which the two women can enjoy their breakfast of various breads and rolls, always a bit of caviar and the most delicious fruits—mangoes, guavas, sweet little bananas or pineapple slices so aromatic and ripe that juice runs down Sidi's arms and stains her summer dresses.

Well nourished and ready for sensual delights, the two women prepare for the little ceremony of vanity and flirting that accompanies them whenever they approach the sea in their two-piece swimsuits— the height of fashion, imported from the United States. They attract everyone's attention, but in particular that of every male. Sidi is forty-one and projects an elegant but unattainable beauty. Jeanette, the perfect younger edition, is much more open to the men's compliments. Nevertheless, both women enjoy lounging on their towels for hours on end, spending lots of time in the water and rebuffing the aroused men. They always leave the club trailing an air of cool elegance.

In the summer of 1941, earlier than expected, the Csillag's villa in Miramar is ready. The two architects had created a pretty, modern, two-story house in the fashionable California style, but built more solidly. The ground floor is of rough-hewn natural stone and the south face has a long arcade that shades tall doors that lead into the house. A large terrace tiled in terracotta serves as the house's focal point. Robert claims a big room on the ground floor for composing; Sidi takes two rooms on the second floor, one of them with a small terrace; and Ernst, as long as he remains single, will have a room next to hers. A couple of small rooms facing the street provide the pampered Csillag siblings with staff accommodations.

Jeanette and Sidonie at the Beach Club

Sidi feels comfortable in the new house from the very beginning, and the soon-to-be-planted garden will become her grand passion. In addition to all the trees, bushes and flowers she plans to put in, the Csillags buy a few bantams from the neighbors, simply because they contribute to everybody's amusement with their pretty feathers and excited cackling. They also acquire three dogs to guard the house but spend a good deal of time preventing them from eating the chickens before the birds acquire an aviary. Sidi loses her heart to one of these dogs, an endearing, light brown mutt with a white tip on his tail and white paws. She names him Petzi, and he'll be her most faithful companion for many years to come.

Cuba's vibrant colors remind Sidi of her former interest in painting, and she purchases an easel and some oils. Years ago in Vienna she had taken lessons, focused mostly on portraiture, with Otto Friedrich, who studied at the Vienna academy and was later a member of the Secession. In 1917 he gave lessons at the Viennese Women's Academy, where Sidi considered him her favorite teacher and he considered her one of his most talented students. She would like to have him looking over her shoulder now and commenting and advising her as she struggles to recall everything she once knew about landscape painting techniques. Soon, she sets aside the barely remembered theories and just starts to paint, practicing almost every morning in the garden.

During these quiet but animating hours, her thoughts weave their way back to Europe. First, she tries to decide to whom she could someday, upon returning, give the paintings she is working on. Then she starts to worry about how her friends in Vienna are faring; and she ends up thinking about her mother and Heinrich in Paris.

The news she gets here is both sparse and one-sided. From time to time she listens to the radio, but its news reports are influenced and colored by the United States, and despite the worrisome headlines, the content is superficial and meaningless. Being in business means that the brothers have to stay well informed, and so they have a subscription to the English-language daily, the *Havana Post*. Sidi prefers *Bohemia*, the magazine with the widest circulation.

She is particularly interested in *Bohemia* because rumor has it that its publisher, Miguel Angel Quevedo, is a gay man who is proud that no woman has ever set foot in his house. He throws big parties every week, inviting not only all the well-known artists but also the political elite. These invitations are in high demand, not only because there is plenty of food and drink but also because of the opportunity to establish and nourish important contacts.

As of 1942, mail to and from Europe comes almost to a standstill, cutting Sidi and her brothers off from any personal source of information about their family and friends. During her quiet hours in the garden, Sidi often finds herself in tears when she looks at the abundance all around her and despairs about the hardships her loved ones in Europe must be experiencing.

Such emotions aside, the Csillags lead very comfortable lives in their new house. Robert has been made director of the Philharmonic Choir and is now also a professor of harmony, composition and music history at the Conservatorio Nacionál de la Habana; which is to say, he holds an important position in the world of classical music in Cuba.

Ernst is no longer tutoring languages. His first step towards independence, founding a small spice company, doesn't fare very well, so he has turned his hand to diamond cutting. In between those two ventures, he found time to marry a pretty Cuban, Rosa, but the union only lasted a few months.

The profession of diamond cutting wasn't practiced in Cuba before a group of Polish Jews who had been cutting diamonds in Antwerp for years managed to buy immigration papers for Cuba in 1941. Only a few small machines are needed to cut diamonds, and they got back into business quickly, using machines imported from Brazil.

Diamond cutting requires extraordinary precision, and in Cuba the task was split into several production steps, each of which was paid at a different rate. By 1942/43 there were already 24 production sites in Cuba with over six thousand employees, among them many Jewish refugees but also a fair number of native Cubans. After the war ended, most of the refugees in the diamond business returned to Belgium and the Netherlands, some emigrated to Palestine. The Cuban government would have liked to retain the diamond cutters, but the island was too far off the beaten path for the dealers, who preferred to return to their old places of business.

Just as the Csillag's domestic life has its daily rhythms, their social life, too, has a consistent, steady beat.

At least once a week, one goes to Reisman's on the corner of 21st and K Streets in Vedado. Reisman's is frequented by German-speaking emigrants, most of them from Austria, and Wiener Schnitzel, desserts with whipped cream and coffee are always on the menu. The guests hang out there, speak their own language and complain a bit about their destinies. The Csillag brothers esteem the quality of Reisman's coffee, Sidi favors the excellent desserts. On Mondays, the family goes to the Cine Gris in Vedado, because on those days one can see films in German or French.

But Cuba's real social life takes place in clubs, and the siblings usually frequent the famous Tropicana. Friday evenings after dinner, the men don their dinner jackets and the women their finest attire and everyone takes a cab to Alturas de Belen, south of Miramar. Built in 1931, the Tropicana offers the best and most expensive of everything. It is Cuba's best-known cabaret, if one understands cabaret to mean a dance and variety show.

The Tropicana offers a nice mix of North American jazz, European music and the Cuban rhythms that feed Robert's enthusiasm. Not only

Havana in the 1940s

do Salsa, Son and Rumba entice him onto the dance floor, they also in-spire his own compositions. After returning from the clubs, he might spend days letting the sounds reverberate in his mind before embedding the motifs in his classical compositions.

Sidonie doesn't much enjoy the regular visits to the Tropicana—too much nudity and liquor for her tastes—so she has found an alternative that is much more to her liking. The Zombie Club is the temple of ev-ery bridge-besotted person on the island and the meeting place for Cu-ba's best players. Not someone to be trifled with when it comes to bridge, she spends many hours there several times a week. She is known to forget her manners on occasion. If one of her partners leads incor-rectly or doesn't follow her strategies and thus loses the game, Sidi can turn mean, refuse to continue playing with that foursome, even throw the cards on the table and leave the room. But such outbursts are quick-ly forgotten and forgiven, and soon afterwards Sidonie is eagerly in-volved in the next game.

A major topic of conversation in all these clubs is Cuba's all-perva-sive corruption. Most of the Austrian immigrants refer to the "greas-ing" and "oiling" with a certain ease and compare it to attitudes they are familiar with from the Balkans. But the German immigrants find it more difficult to accept and consider the practices morally and politi-cally dubious.

One day during lunch, Robert suggests to Sidi that she might con-sider getting a paid job. She reacts with indignation. She loves her inde-pendence and having free reign over how she uses her time. She doesn't understand how her brother could suggest such a thing.

Angrily she announces, "You can be sure that I won't consider it as long as I have a dry piece of bread to eat."

Robert responds calmly and says that she should just leave it be then. He doesn't tell her that they are not in the best situation financially. Ac-customed to spending generously, in the past the Csillags had been living off interest but were now dipping into their capital, which might very well run out one day. They had all reckoned on a faster end to the Third Reich and had happily been eating into their inheritance. Sidonie's broth-ers were earning money, but Sidi's share would soon be gone; and be-cause of the war, no money has been coming from Heinrich in France.

Robert doesn't bring up the issue again. Heinrich probably would have explained to Sidonie that she was going to go into debt—a prospect neither of them could find comfortable—but Robert is accustomed to living beyond his means and going into debt, and he thinks his sister will figure things out when they get bad enough.

AMOR IN CUBA

JUST SO HER LIFE WON'T GET TOO PREDICTABLE AND DULL, SIDI DEcides to see more of Gisela, a woman she met at Robert's wedding. Since that event they had encountered one another several times at private parties as well as in clubs, and Sidi has noticed that Gisela responds to her gentle wooing. Gisela is a Jewish émigré from Germany who is beautiful enough to meet Sidonie's aesthetic criteria; so despite her vocal dislike for everything Jewish, Sidi is willing to make an exception. Also, unlike most émigrés, Gisela doesn't bore her with incessant talk about the affidavit that will allow them into the United States. She doesn't understand people who dream about the US and can't wait to get there. She likes Cuba far too much to think about moving elsewhere. It has plenty of sunshine, warmth, help and even money—why give it up?

Gisela's light brown hair, agile gait and pale skin are too lovely to ignore, so Sidi arranges to meet her more frequently. Gisela is slightly younger than Sidi, frequents intellectual and women's circles where the enthusiastic talk is of art, music and politics, and when with her, Sidi is exposed to a whole new circle of acquaintances. Gisela also has a small second-hand Ford in which the two women go on excursions. Their drives are usually undertaken in the morning and always have a new and exciting destination. On one such trip—this time to visit the famous Cuban historian Lydia Cabrera—Gisela regales Sidi with stories about life on the Rive Gauche in Paris in the twenties and the many well-known women she met there.

Sidi doesn't believe many of Gisela's tales, but since she tells them in an amusing way, she accepts them, thinking that a bit of fantasy can go a long way.

But Lydia Cabrera, who had indeed met Gisela in Paris, tells them the same stories, and they correspond to Gisela's versions. Born into a wealthy Cuban family in 1894, Lydia got interested in African art when she lived in Paris from 1927 until 1939. Then she returned to Cuba with her companion, Maria Teresa de Rojas, and started writing and publishing about Afro-Cuban art. Her book *El Monte* is one of the most important works ever published on the topic. Her house is filled with African masks, statues, some furniture and textiles—and Sidi finds these things, like the woman herself, somewhat eerie.

It is much more pleasant to play bridge with Gisela, go to the Beach Club and from time to time drop by El Floridita, where they meet up with others in their crowd. But despite Sidi's efforts, these encounters never develop into anything more intimate. She is too cautious to try to cultivate Gisela more intensely, and for her part, Gisela seems to be one of those effusive women who are fully aware of their appeal and enjoy flirting with men as well as with women—playing with fire while making sure they don't get burnt. So nothing progresses beyond intense glances, meaningful remarks and seemingly accidental touches. Sidonie sublimates her attraction by painting Gisela's portrait; for hours on end she can stare undisturbed at her beautiful model. The portrait turns out to be quite good, and encouraged by the praise, Sidi starts to paint all the women in her growing circle of friends.

Gisela is extremely enterprising. Soon, she proposes expanding their itinerary in the Ford and taking the road to Pinar del Rio, Cienfuegos or Trinidade, each of which she describes in glowing tones. Since Gisela will organize everything and Sidi doesn't have to lift a finger, she agrees to go along.

In the months that follow, Sidonie gets to know a few of Cuba's wonderful old cities, and Trinidade, an architectural gem on Cuba's south coast, becomes the women's favorite and most frequent destination. While they sit in Trinidade's Plaza Mayor gazing at the beautiful old wooden balconies and the intricate window screens called Rejas that grace the palacios, Gisela, the storyteller, conjures up the love stories that must have played out here over the past centuries. Sidonie doesn't seem to understand Gisela's hints. At a very late hour, music erupts in the middle of the street, and the two women can't refuse the invitations to dance. Sidonie would never have danced with strangers in Europe, but the rules are different in Cuba, and she wants to enjoy life. Most Cubans are not what she considers beautiful, but the way they move to the Rumba makes for heavenly dancing.

Then one evening when visiting at the Csillags, Gisela stretches out comfortably on Sidi's bed and purrs that she almost feels as if the house belongs to her. This should have been left unsaid, for as far as Sidi is concerned it offers proof that Gisela combines the worst German and Jewish characteristics. It's an unforgiveable blunder that angers Sidi so much that she responds dryly, "I don't have that feeling, because I only own a share." She had been thinking for some time that she and Gisela were getting too close, and this is the perfect excuse to cool off the relationship. Gisela is relegated to the bottom of Sidi's social list.

In the late fall of 1943 she finally finds the right opportunity to end their connection both unobtrusively and elegantly. Robert has organized a benefit concert for the Asociación Austria Libre in the roof garden of the Hotel Sevilla, and afterwards he introduces Sidonie to a friend, a conductor who immediately starts to shower her with flattery. Sidonie loves to attract the admiring glances of men and women, but she dislikes it when she detects a certain erotic gleam in a man's eyes.

Shortly thereafter, he sends her flowers accompanied by a card with an invitation to a rendezvous, and she starts to spin her web. She is worried that she might hurt her brother's career if she doesn't please his colleague, so she accepts the invitation but will have Gisela in tow. Gisela prefers women, but she is not averse to men. "The most important thing is good sex," she once said to Sidonie; and since theirs is certainly no good, this matchmaking could be a relief for all concerned.

Two days later, in the bar at the Hotel Nacional, Sidi feigns absentmindedness while watching each little move the conductor and Gisela make. At first this man, who she finds particularly uninteresting, had tried to woo her, but getting nowhere, he shifted his attention to Gisela, and she has responded to his invitation to flirt. After all, she hasn't gotten anywhere with Sidonie. Two hours later, Sidonie finds a flimsy excuse to leave and feels an exhilarating sense of relief. She has gotten rid of both Gisela and the conductor and the two of them can take care of each other now.

But a new love waits just around the corner. While still with Gisela, Sidi met another couple—Hélène, whom everyone refers to as "the little Belgian," and Marie-Louise, the daughter of a Cuban diplomat who met his French wife in Paris. The little Belgian managed to escape from Europe with her two children, though her husband stayed behind. In Havana she found consolation with Marie-Louise. In the ever-expanding circle of female couples in Havana, everyone is of the opinion that the little Belgian exploited Marie-Louise, who takes much better care of her girlfriend than any man would. Later, it turns out that Marie-Louise is always very caring and attentive with her lovers, which has led some to think that she is far too naïve, while others consider her the most attractive partner available.

Until her husband also managed to escape and showed up in Havana, Hélène remained devoted to Marie-Louise and had no desire to give up their relationship. But her husband convinced her to drop Marie-Louise and stay with him for the sake of their children. To reassert

Marie-Louise

his claim on his wife, he sent threatening letters to Marie-Louise, telling her harshly that she had taken advantage of Hélène's situation and was no longer allowed to contact her. When Hélène got pregnant again, it was clear who had prevailed.

Marie-Louise didn't remain downhearted for long. When she first encountered Sidi at a reception at the US embassy, she decided Sidi was the most attractive woman she'd ever seen and has been thinking about her ever since. Now, with Gisela out of the running, she begins a months-long courtship.

Sidi doesn't even notice Marie-Louise at first, then all she sees is a sweet but totally uninteresting woman who is too short for her taste, has a bad figure, a broad face and a pug nose. But Marie-Louise is so considerate and dear and has such a wonderful character that one day in the spring of 1944 Sidi gives in. To her great surprise, it turns out to be one of the warmest and most fulfilling relationships that she—with her limited experience and her tendency to intellectualize her relationships—could ever have imagined. Even sex is fun with Marie-Louise—surely a good sign where Sidi is concerned.

On their quiet evenings together, Marie-Louise talks to Sidi about her strong desire to have children—for which she would need a man. Sidonie encourages her to go for it and one day Marie-Louise shows up with a man from North America, whom Sidi doesn't find attractive at all. But it is none of her business, and she is not surprised to learn that a marriage is in the works—just a marriage of convenience, in order to produce children. Nothing will change in their relationship. Sidonie has never been in love with Marie-Louise—for her it is a deep, warm friendship—and she is not the slightest bit jealous. Indeed, she is, as ever, just fine with any arrangement that keeps her lover from getting too close—except in the realm of dreams and fantasies.

Soon, however, Marie-Louise tells Sidi, with indications of disappointment, that her future husband hasn't had any sexual experience with women. They have seen a doctor, who gave them—the man in particular—exact instructions on what to do and how men and women fit together. But despite the tutorial, Marie-Louise doesn't get pregnant. It's all the same to Sidi, who continues to enjoy Marie-Louise's company as before and continues to find it quite incomprehensible that her girlfriend wants to make babies with such a dreadful guy. This is how she keeps a version of Marie-Louise for herself that is whole and undivided.

SIDI HAS TO GO TO WORK

IN THE MIDST OF SIDONIE'S AFFAIR WITH MARIE-LOUISE, THE unpleasant topic that she has always avoided resurfaces one evening at dinner. The family is in a wretched financial state, and Robert's message is clear: Sidi is in debt. True, her debt is to the family, but she will need to pay it back, and she must start to pay her own way. At age forty-five, she'll have to work for pay for the first time. Sidonie always thought that working was the worst thing she could imagine—but being in debt trumps it. There's nothing she can do but swallow the bitter pill and consider something she has always held in great contempt: a life "in service."

At first, she looks for an easier solution and starts by helping out at Ernst's diamond cutting business. She gets up far too early every morning in a sullen mood, eats a quick breakfast of half a mango and a glass of milk, and tortures herself by always taking the same road to his office near the harbor, where she does boring work at the typewriter and sorts through endless files. She hates being forced into a daily routine that can lead to only one thing: becoming smugly bourgeois.

She can't forget an episode during her lunch break on her first workday. She went into Havana's cathedral to escape the heat, and when she came out, a beggar-woman on the steps held out her hand. With a snide remark and vehement shake of her head, Sidi moved on, only belatedly becoming aware of her anger. In the past she had always given a small handout, why had she reacted so differently? She realized suddenly that she envied that woman because she was still in charge of her own time and her own life, while she, Sidi, had had to give up that control.

But Sidi can't earn enough at Ernst's and has to look for other employment. Like all refugees, she doesn't have a work permit, though even without one, small bribes to the right authorities can smooth the way. But Sidonie decides to peruse the ads for nannies, housekeepers and language teachers—fields that require neither a permit nor formal training.

In January 1945, the caretaker of a large sugar plantation in Matanzas province, about two hours southeast of the capital, advertises for a woman to look after his young son. The salary is good, and since she would also have two large rooms in a manor house with a park-like garden, Sidonie applies and is offered the job. To a degree, the prospect even piques her spirit of adventure; she's curious to find out all about grand colonial life in the countryside.

At the end of January she leaves Havana with a leather suitcase and her dog Petzi. She takes the train to a small town not far from the city of Matanzas, where a young mulatto waiting at the station greets her with a polite bow. He says he recognized her immediately—she must be the new Madame—because there are not many European-looking ladies with a dog in this out of the way place. A horse and buggy are waiting for him to take her to the plantation called La Mercedes. After a long trip, they turn onto a narrow, sandy drive that leads through two big yellow pillars, then past a barracks and some cabins—obviously the farm workers' quarters—then through a spacious park to the circular drive in front of the manor house.

A girl takes Sidi's suitcase and ushers her into the foyer, where she is met by Señor Mattacena, who runs this sugar plantation. A tanned Italian, grey-haired and in his fifties, he wears a light jacket, white jodhpurs and leather boots, one of which has a small riding crop stuck into it. He shakes her hand in a friendly but distant way, and his vain and bossy attitude immediately reminds Sidonie of her husband Ed. She takes this as an indication that she needs to be careful around him. She returns his handshake in a similarly reserved way. Obviously used to giving orders, he outlines the situation rapidly: he is responsible for over a thousand workers, and therefore has no time for his son; his wife has to look after a big household, and therefore Sidonie is to take care of his five-year-old son Orestes. Orestes needs someone to play with him, read to him and teach him good manners. From her own childhood, Sidonie is only too well acquainted with the pedagogical tasks that will be required of her, and she indicates with a nod that she understands.

Señor Mattacena and his
son Orestes, Cuba, 1946

Orestes is called in to greet the new Madame. He wears beige over-alls and has wild dark curls; his eyes are narrowed, and his mouth is set in a stubborn line. Shyly, he hides behind the apron of the black maid who brought him in. From the first moment, Sidonie is enchanted; but it is only Petzi, waiting behind Sidi on his leash, who moves the little boy to emerge and hold out his hand—even if only to touch the dog.

Finally, Señora Mattacena is called in to size up the stranger, whose role will be an amalgam of housekeeper and nanny. The Señora is Cuban, a plump, friendly woman, who somehow reminds Sidonie of Empress Maria Theresia. After just a few moments, she returns to the kitchen. Sidi is then taken to her quarters on the ground floor at the back of the building—two bright rooms with red tile floors, rough-hewn ceiling beams and simple furniture built on the plantation. The only thing that reminds her of Europe is the gleaming, black baby grand piano, most likely intended to be used to further the boy's education.

From this point on, Sidonie and Orestes are left to their own devices, and they soon become good friends and accomplices. Sidi has a kind and friendly way with children, lets them keep their individuality and free will and always has original ideas for activities. Before long the little one is so taken with her that the moment she opens her door to go to breakfast each morning, he comes running toward her whooping with joy and demanding that they go out to play. They both enjoy spending their days outdoors, either wandering the extensive grounds or taking Petzi—the boy has also taken the dog into his heart—for strolls around the plantation.

Orestes is a courageous, enterprising child who enjoys people's company and often takes Sidonie to visit the workers' cabins, where life is far more entertaining and lively than at home. Something new is always happening there—a little goat has been born, some chickens have hatched, the women have made new baskets or shoes or cooked something they'll offer for a taste.

But the thing that's dearest to him in all the world is his friendly little black pony, which he visits in the stable several times a day. Every afternoon after his nap—he masters the lesson of going to sleep thanks

Orestes on his pony, accompanied by a housemaid, Cuba, 1946

only to considerable pedagogic effort on Sidonie's part—the pony is outfitted in the same style as the vaqueros' horses. Like the Cuban cowboys', his saddle has a big knob in front, the horn, which Orestes uses to support himself while holding the reins, and behind are two leather saddle bags and even a small lasso. This is in keeping with his riding outfit—wide pants decorated with appliqués of horses, a tight-waisted jacket and a round straw hat. Thus equipped, the little one rides— proud and erect—through the park. And even though he is only allowed to walk the pony, so Sidonie can keep up, he often prods the pony's flanks until it starts trotting, and sometimes he even gallops until they disappear behind the bushes. If father knew about this, he would punish Orestes severely.

The boy is afraid of his father, and he has Sidi's sympathy and protection, since she had also feared her father. Señor Mattacena turns out to be jealous of his child's intimacy with and love for the foreign Madame and demands that she treat Orestes more sternly. He listens in on their conversations and wants to dictate what she and the child can talk about.

But the Señor is not her father, and she enjoys resisting someone so macho, so she has no problem deciding not to respect his orders.

Mattacena embodies everything Sidonie doesn't like about men. He is Italian, which in her monarchical, old-Austrian mind is connected to the loss of Austria's territories in northern Italy, and she holds him personally responsible. His vanity and his sharpness with his child make her furious. Sometimes she's convinced that he must actually be related to Ed, particularly when, in the morning before leaving for the plantation or the sugar mill, he stands in front of the mirror and once again parts his perfectly parted hair. He places great value on dressing to perfection and knows how to harry his wife on this point, which leads to stormy scenes with her and the child. Because of the heat, the little one prefers to run around naked, but his father insists that he dress like a little gentleman when in his presence.

Sidonie often thinks that the couple had their child too late in life. They could be his grandparents; indeed, Señora Mattacena, who has grown children from a previous relationship, is already a grandmother.

The relationship between the Señor and the Señora is not the best. She often makes fun of his vanity, which hurts him deeply and leads to fights. Sidi, who grew up in a family where the parents never showed any weakness in front of their children, is appalled by the loud nagging that takes place in front of everyone. When especially angry, Señor Mattacena often simply picks up his hat and disappears to Havana for a few days.

That's the best for everyone. In his absence a great pressure is lifted and there is suddenly space to enjoy life. When on site, the Señor insists that formal dinners be served in the dining room by black maids wearing white aprons and gloves. As soon as he is gone, everyone eats together outside. Even Sidi sits with the staff under the big plane trees and enjoys the simple meals of rice, beans, bananas and chicken.

When the Señor is away, the Señora sometimes takes a glass too many. There is no shortage of rum; the farm workers distill their own, and it is of excellent quality. They gladly provide it to the Señora, who quite likes her rum. If she drinks herself tipsy, her speech starts to slur, which the staff finds quite amusing, but she'll also open her heart and indulge in tearful outbursts of emotion. Even little Orestes can't get the gist of what she's saying, but when that happens, Sidonie just goes to him and explains that his mother is suffering from a terrible toothache and hopes that he will fall asleep soon. She spends many hours with the Señora, who complains and sighs and says she can no longer endure life with that man; but the next morning, everything will have been forgotten.

The workers usually celebrate the end of the sugar cane harvest with an all-day feast. Sidonie has never in her life heard so many drums or seen such exuberant high spirits—despite the harsh working conditions. In the early morning the workers' wives cook up a storm and produce delicious stews with beans, plantains, and all kinds of potatoes and manioc, as well as lots of meat dishes from animals that have been fattened for the occasion. Many piglets, calves, goats, chickens and ducks end up in the cook pots. All friends and family members are invited, and happy, open generosity reigns supreme—the landowners could learn a lesson or two.

In the evening, the feast is laid out, much home-distilled rum is drunk from big glasses or gourds, and eventually the revelers forget their harsh conditions and let their zest for life spill out in dance. Drums, the primary instruments, are accompanied by rattles, rhythm sticks and a notched scraper made of gourds or bamboo called a guiro. Only at daybreak do the exhausted macheteros and vaqueros lie down under the bushes to sleep it off. This is far too wild an affair for Sidonie, who always keeps other people at a distance and cannot give in to the frenzy. She's also simply too tired to enjoy the festivities. Keeping an eye on Orestes all day, every day leaves her little time for herself or even for her beloved Petzi.

She chooses to take her extended walks with the dog at night, when everything has grown quiet and a kind of magic settles over the countryside. That's when she can finally take some time to dwell on her thoughts and give in to her emotions. The Cuban nights are mild and fragrant, the starry sky pulls her into another world, and the owls' hooting can make her laugh. The peace is interrupted only once, when the *señal* sounds briefly to indicate the change of work shifts.

Word has gotten around that Sidonie walks alone at night for hours, but the Señora spreads the rumor that Madame carries a revolver, and nobody dares to approach her. After her walks, Sidonie finds it hard to get up at seven to look after Orestes; sometimes she falls asleep sitting under a palm tree in the afternoons, and the unexpected freedom rather delights the little one.

During her stay with the Mattacenas, Sidonie rarely leaves the plantation and doesn't yearn for life in the big city. She hardly ever goes to Havana when she has time off, but sometimes visitors from the city come to her. Jeanette wants to see how her friend is faring, and Marie-Louise, that good soul, often shows up on the weekends. Marie-Louise is introduced as Sidi's best friend and stays in her second room. Sidi enjoys showing her the plantation, the most distant corners of which can be reached on a small train installed years ago. During the week it transports workers to the cane fields or the cattle herds. On the weekends, guests who want to tour the vast estate have access to its salon carriages with wooden benches and billowing curtains—much more beautifully decorated than the carriages the workers use. Marie-Louise loves this train because, aside from the engineer, she and her love are alone and can hold each other close and talk about everything that has happened since they were last together.

Sidonie and Petzi on the La Mercedes plantation, 1946

That Sidi enjoys such privileges often causes jealousy and conflict with the other staff. The Señora has ordered the staff to treat Madame like a lady of the house, but many do not accept the idea that an employee like themselves must be treated differently. And why is she allowed to receive private visitors and live in the house with her dog? Some take out their resentment on poor Petzi in secret, aiming occasional kicks at his shaggy brown haunches and driving him out of the house with harsh words when Sidi is not around. When confronted about this, they claim that Petzi has been peeing in one of the corners and show evidence. Sidonie cleans up after him, advises him on his behavior, and at times even hits him. Then one day she sees one of the employees peeing in that corner. He is fired, Petzi is rehabilitated, and from then on nobody dares to say anything against the dog.

World War II comes to an end during Sidi's stay at the sugar plantation—she barely takes notice.

Over the two previous years the media had reported many terrible things in addition to news that gave Sidi hope. In July 1944, the radio crackled with stories about a failed attempt on Hitler's life. This put the emigrant community into a state of extreme agitation; if only the crazy house painter really was dead, then the war would be over and they all could return to a "normal" life.

The Allied landing in Normandy in June 1944 and the liberation of Paris had also let everyone breathe a sigh of relief. Sidonie's brothers greeted this news with great enthusiasm: Paris was liberated, it would finally be possible to get news from Heinrich and Mother. Robert immediately contacted the Red Cross and asked for information, but as it turned out, he would have to wait for it for several more months.

In the spring of 1947, Señor Mattacena informs Sidonie that he and his family will be moving to Havana after the next harvest and her services will no longer be required. She is relieved to be given notice, because it means that she is free to execute her secret plan to return to Europe as soon as possible—to see her mother and Heinrich, to be in Ellen's cheerful presence and to rekindle her love for Wjera. It has been impossible to save much from her plantation salary, and she will have to find the money for passage on a ship; but in this, too, as with everything she really wants, she'll find a way. At the beginning of June 1947 she leaves the plantation behind with a light heart.

FAREWELL CUBA; HELLO USA

BACK IN HAVANA, SIDONIE INFORMS ROBERT AND ERNST THAT she is thinking of returning to Vienna soon. The brothers, who know that it is no use trying to talk their sister out of anything, warn her not to return to Austria unless she has a new passport and new citizenship. She was born in Lemberg, now part of the Soviet Union, and she can't be sure that the Russian occupiers won't consider her one of theirs. She could end up in the Soviet Union in her next involuntary exile. As communists are not her cup of tea, she realizes that in this case it would indeed be better to wait a while.

For most of the refugees, the general situation had grown far less tense since the end of the war. Those who want to leave Cuba are now free to do so, and even though Cuba offered most German-speaking

Jews a "peaceful paradise," there is a mass exodus to the United States. Those who choose to stay encounter no difficulties when applying for Cuban citizenship.

Heeding her brothers' warnings, Sidi decides she should at least acquire the security of a Cuban passport and applies for the necessary papers.

But she doesn't want to return to Europe empty-handed, and the journey itself is going to be expensive, so she has to find another job, something more lucrative than the one at the hacienda. She doesn't think it's possible to earn a higher salary in Cuba, however, and so decides to accept a long-standing invitation from Marie-Louise, who has recently moved to Connecticut with her North American husband and writes glowing accounts of the wonderful job opportunities there. Once again, Sidi's stay in a new country will last longer than expected, and she'll spend almost a year in the United States.

Finding even halfway acceptable work in the land of unlimited opportunities turns out to be anything but easy. Returning soldiers are given preference on the job market, women are expected to go back to the hearth rather than keep or take away men's jobs, and for weeks Sidonie answers want ads without success. She learns in the process that she has one serious problem: Petzi. In contrast to Havana, where she could take him everywhere, here, dogs are not welcome in the homes of prospective employers. She will have to leave Petzi at home when she goes to work.

Home now means the pretty, white New England-style house in New Haven where Marie-Louise lives with her husband. On the weekends, when she can no longer stand him because their marriage has been in crisis for some time, Marie-Louise retreats to a nice little house in the countryside. Marie-Louise assures Sidi that Petzi can stay with her while Sidi is working, and Sidi knows she will look after him with affection.

Naturally, Sidi has noticed that the prospect of having Petzi around, and in particular the efforts Marie-Louise makes on the dog's behalf, don't sit well with the husband. But her little darling's well-being is more important to Sidi than her friend's marriage.

Sidonie eventually finds a job in Brooklyn, New York, taking care of an elderly Jewish lady during the week. Weekends are spent with

Marie-Louise in her little country house, where the two can enjoy each other's company far from the suspicious and jealous eyes of the husband.

Sidonie's new work environment in Brooklyn is an unfamiliar one, and the caregiving is exhausting. The old woman can hardly do a thing for herself, and Sidonie has to handle everything. She actually had had a choice between two jobs: caring for the old lady or for two young Jewish children in a wealthy household on Manhattan's Upper East Side. Very consciously, she chose the more difficult and unattractive job. On their first weekend together, Marie-Louise asks her why and gets a seemingly absurd answer: it would be unfair to Petzi if she enjoyed a good day with the children, while the poor dog had to be without her. The unpleasant job would not only be more fair to Petzi but in the end would be easier on her, since she'd feel less guilty.

Sidonie would have preferred to work for a non-Jewish family, but having no access to New York's posh Protestant circles, she had to accept a Jewish employer. The old lady's husband lives in the same house and is still in good shape. He treats Sidonie well and with courtesy and teases her about her *goykopf*. His parents had come to New York from the Bukovina region and risen from being poor scrap dealers to running a thriving hardware store. The youngest of five siblings, he had studied law and earned a nice living at a big New York firm. His two children are doing their best to emulate him. When the day is over and the lady of the house has been put to bed, Sidi often sits with him for a while and they talk about the past. He has always been proud to be Jewish and tearfully reminisces about the seders of his childhood, where, as the youngest, he was allowed to ask the questions. His family had never been orthodox, but they kept certain traditions, including going to temple for Rosh Hashanah and Yom Kippur and sending the boys to schul to be prepared for their bar mitzvahs. It never occurred to them to deny their Jewish origins or their religion, and the old man simply will not understand that Sidonie comes from a family that never kept the traditions of their faith. He decides it is about time for her to learn about them.

If being Jewish means eating bagels with cream cheese and adding lox on special occasions, Sidonie likes the idea. Every Friday she is sent to the bakery in the morning to buy challah and then is free to leave at noon—before the beginning of Shabbat. On the weekends, the children and grandchildren come to help with the old lady's care, and Sidi doesn't have to be back until Monday morning.

On Friday afternoons she hurries to the station to catch the next train to New Haven, where Marie-Louise and Petzi are waiting for her. On one of those trips—she must have dozed off—she suddenly feels a hand on her knee. Was that what woke her? Awareness of its presence shoots through her like a bolt of lightning: this is a kind of pure indulgence that she hasn't experienced in ages. She keeps her eyes tightly closed and pretends she's still asleep. How long can she prolong this moment? She doesn't want to see whoever this hand belongs to, doesn't want it to make another move, just remain where it is so this feeling of delight will never ever end. She makes a small move and the hand

Marie-Louise in her Jeep, Connecticut, USA

creeps a bit higher. Sidi doesn't mind. Then she's startled by the conductor's voice announcing her stop. She turns and without speaking looks at the man whose hand was just on her thigh. An average face: not beautiful, not ugly. But his hand is slender and agile. What more could it have shown her, if there hadn't been so many deterrents—the approaching station, the rules of decorum, one's upbringing …?

But she takes the sensation with her, buries it deep inside and carries it like a treasure well into old age.

She leaves the compartment without saying a word but with one long last glance. On her way to Marie-Louise's house, she has to laugh out loud. She wishes she had the courage to rest her hand on the thigh of a woman who pleases her and somehow transmit this superb, free and secretive feeling. How many would react as she does, with pleasure and in silence?

Later that evening, snuggled up against Marie-Louise, she tries to explain why her experience on the train was something special and more erotic than deliberately planned sexual contacts, which do little for her. But her girlfriend doesn't want to know, shakes her head, wants to kiss away the experience and pretend that all is well between her body and Sidonie's. She doesn't want to hear that Sidonie might have experienced more from a stranger's brief touch than she had in all the seemingly secure moments they have spent together. But she's too good-natured and too repressed to continue questioning Sidonie, who realizes that she should hold her tongue—some experiences belong only to one's self and cannot be understood by anyone else.

While enduring her monotonous everyday life commuting between New York and Connecticut, Sidonie prepares for her return to Europe. As soon as ships began carrying mail across the Atlantic regularly, she had written to everyone in Europe who had been close to her. The replies are deeply troubling. Even in letters, Europe comes across as a field of rubble, on the inside as well as the outside. From Vienna, Ellen scribbles strange and alarming notes describing the terrible headaches for which she needs to take morphine. Sidonie should get some for her; it would be much easier to find it in the United States. Wjera writes short messages from Munich that barely fill a page. Her husband has died, the

Nazis tortured him in Dachau, she can't write more—maybe one day she'll have the strength to talk about it.

Heinrich's letters from Paris are equally brief. Hints the he was in hiding from the Nazis for years, somewhere in the French countryside; he has survived and out of decency has married the woman who hid him ...

Sidonie opens each letter with a shudder and is always confronted by news of something traumatic. She reads them all with a feeling of dismay and great compassion.

Many goods that are—and always were—available in both Cuba and the United States are now such distant memories in postwar Europe that they're the stuff of dreams. Sidonie consoles herself by sending regular packages containing staples, cigarettes, liquor ... and she never forgets to include some sugar and sweets.

The only recipient who seems to take Sidi's packages for granted is her former husband. In their exchange of letters, the subject of Petzi takes up lots of space. Sidonie has informed Ed that she plans to return to Vienna and move into the flat that used to belong to her and is still filled with her furniture. Back and forth across the Atlantic they discuss resuming their life together, and Sidi makes it clear that she is going to bring Petzi along. Ed wants to know where the dog is going to sleep. In her bed, at her feet, the place he is used to, is Sidonie's response. This provides Ed a perfect opening to respond that the dog is clearly more important to her than he is, and she won't be welcome if she brings the mutt.

More angry and disillusioned letters are exchanged, and Sidi soon realizes that Ed hasn't changed a bit and still thinks only about himself. His offensive missives are additional nails in Ed's metaphorical coffin.

Everything is going to have to change. No living together with Ed, Sidonie decides while she's still in New York. She will retrieve all the things that rightfully belong to her and her family, and she'll tell Ed, who had been nibbling away at her family's wealth, how much he owes her for the years she has been abroad.

The winter of 1948/49 seems to go on forever. By February, when Sidonie has enough money to pay for her passage to Europe, she resigns from her job and starts preparing.

Sidonie and Petzi in Central Park, New York City, 1949

It isn't easy to book a ticket. Ships already go back and forth regularly but with nothing close to pre-war frequency, and some of them are still being used by the military to transport goods and troops. Regular passengers have to wait.

But by April it is settled: at the end of May, Sidi will have a berth on a ship to France. She fantasizes arriving at Cherbourg, well rested after a wonderful week at sea, and then going on to Paris, where she'll see Heinrich, meet his courageous wife and finally embrace her Mama again.

From Paris it will only be a short trip back to her beloved Vienna, which she longs for with every fiber of her being.

Soon she has to face the most difficult and painful part of her plans: parting from Marie-Louise. Both women know that this will be good-bye for good, that when the ship sails, their shared years in Cuba and Connecticut will drown in its wake. It is terribly difficult for Marie-Louise to let Sidonie go—she is the best and most beautiful woman with whom she has ever had a relationship. She cries often during the final weeks, and in contrast to her usually sunny disposition, grows irritable and hypersensitive. There are arguments and tears, and a renewed, even more painful truce as the departure date approaches.

In order to make their farewell easier, the two women decide to spend the last few days in New York. During the day they shop in the elegant department stores, filling Sidi's luggage, and the nights are spent in Greenwich Village bars.

The final day dawns grey and sad. Sidi wakes early and moves restlessly around the room, checking her luggage one last time. Far too early, she wakes Marie-Louise, who immediately starts to cry. Sidi sits on the bed and strokes her friend's face, then takes off her sapphire ring—a beautiful old family piece she's kept with her throughout her exile—and moves to slip it onto Marie-Louise's finger. Sobbing, Marie-Louise rebuffs this most intimate gesture saying, "I want to keep you and not your ring!" Sidonie is upset and hurt, and another round of fighting ensues. Finally, they give in to their pain, lie in each other's arms and can truly say good-bye.

The cab arrives at midday to take them to the Hudson River piers where the ships to and from Europe dock. Sidonie and Marie-Louise get out of the taxi; Sidi's luggage is taken by a porter and disappears into the ship's hold. There's one last embrace, two quick kisses, and, almost nine years after debarking in Havana, Sidonie walks down yet another pier. Accompanied only by her dog, she'll leave this continent behind and finally complete the circumnavigation of the globe that history has forced on her. Marie-Louise waves until the ship is just a dot on the horizon.

10

LEADEN TIMES

In June 1949 Sidonie stands on the Pont Neuf pensively watching the sluggish gray Seine flow beneath it. In front of her are the splendors of the Tuileries and the Louvre, behind her stands Notre Dame—faith in God enshrined in stone. Why has she never been to this beautiful city before? Probably because a young woman from a good family would never have been given permission to go there alone; and such a trip was out of the question during her marriage, because Ed couldn't be persuaded to leave Austria.

If only such beauty didn't also cut her to the quick. She can't help weeping, and she imagines that the Seine could carry her tears to the Atlantic and much, much later they would reach Cuba's beaches and the warm, perfumed abundance she longs for. Here, everything is fragmented, ruptured; the war has destroyed people, burnt them out.

After several days at sea and a train journey from the harbor at Cherbourg, Sidi reached Paris only a few days ago. Onboard the *De Grasse*, a large, adequately-elegant ship, everything had still been all in one piece, whole, and she'd been full of joyful expectation, secretly nourishing a childish belief that some kind of triumph was imminent. She, Sidonie Csillag, was returning from adventurous travels in faraway lands after having been gone for many years ... there would be a grand reception.

The Cherbourg dock was crowded with arrivals in a hurry to pick up their luggage, but no one met her with flowers or waved a handkerchief; no familiar face lit up in happy recognition upon seeing her.

*Sidonie and Petzi aboard
the* De Grasse, *May 1949*

Only Petzi gave a friendly wag of his tail and seemed to say, "I'm always here for you."

Heinrich picked her up at the railway station in Paris, their mother hadn't come along. The shock of seeing him again instantly stifled whatever joy she might have been feeling as she realized what he must have gone through. He looked shrunken, haggard, much older than his years, and he obviously was no longer capable of feeling joy. Almost mechanically, the siblings embraced, then he mumbled something—something like "good that you are here"—and that was that. At the family flat in the 12th Arrondissement—not a very elegant neighborhood—she experienced for the first time a feeling that would become almost second nature over the years: between her zest for life and her pain, something fragmented and gradually turned to leaden apathy. This oppressive feeling would overwhelm her everywhere she went in Europe, but particularly in German-speaking countries.

It was so strange to be in France, to see Heinrich and Mother again. Like so much else in her mother's life, the war had more or less passed over her without leaving a mark. She still had the doll-like façade of a woman who had been willing to sacrifice everything in order to foster her ideals of beauty and social position, to have others arrange life for her so she had to do only whatever she was told to do. Her welcome upon Sidi's return had been so superficial that it rekindled her daughter's old, painful feeling that she simply was not important.

On Sidi's second evening in Paris, the three Csillags finally started to talk about the years they had been separated, and as had always been the case in their childhood, Heinrich at first kept silent, but once he began to talk, everything poured out. His story of the past several years was chaotic, out of sequence and delivered in disjointed segments, as if he could bear the horror more easily that way. Mother sat and listened, nodding. Heinrich's wife also kept silent. Sidonie wondered how he could tolerate the woman, then instantly took it back, knowing that he owed her his life.

When, after talking for hours, Heinrich finally took a break, Sidonie said simply, "I could not have endured it."

HEINRICH'S WAR

AT THE BEGINNING OF THE WAR IT HAD STILL BEEN POSSIBLE TO correspond with Mama and Heinrich in Paris, and Sidi, still in Vienna, had known that they were faring quite well. As a woman, and because of her age, Emma had been too unimportant to have been considered an enemy alien and wasn't bothered. Heinrich had been living in Paris since 1928 and had become a French citizen. His business was doing well, and he was prudently saving for the future.

Those of his letters that had reached her during her first months in Cuba had hinted that Germans and Austrians in France were being put into camps for enemy aliens. But why should Sidi have worried? As a naturalized French citizen, this hadn't affected Heinrich, and anyway, having been born in Lemberg, he was considered Polish.

The French referred to their "phony war" against the Germans as "drôle de guerre." Paris had nightly blackouts, gasoline was rationed, but life continued to be most amusing. The restaurants, movie houses and theaters were full every night of the week. Mama had even had a few admirers, and she was as jolly as she'd been when she used to go to Karlsbad.

And then the great disillusionment—the Wehrmacht overran Europe and nothing could stop it. One country after the other fell and was occupied, including, in June 1940, the northern half of France. By mid June the takeover in Paris was complete and Marshal Pétain took over from the previous government. In desperation, émigrés who had fled to France from previously annexed European countries tried to flee once again.

The German–French armistice was signed on June 22, 1940, and German emigrants—and this included Austrians—were suddenly without any legal protection and were subjected both to the arbitrariness of Pétain's collaborating Vichy Regime and to persecution by the German occupiers.

Like thousands of other French citizens, immigrants from many nations fled to the south of France. Heinrich had been in the south on business at the time of the armistice and decided to wait there to see how things developed. After a few days, he was able to get in touch with his mother in Paris. She seemed a bit confused and didn't quite know what to do, but she assured him that the Germans had been acting quite humanely and correctly—so different from how they had behaved in Vienna. Maybe things would not be so bad after all.

Sidi remembered that this was just how her mother had sounding in the last letter she received from her before leaving Vienna. But because no mail had crossed the Atlantic from Nazi-dominated Europe after 1942, she has known little about the years Heinrich is reliving.

Continuing to bide his time in the south of France, the reports Heinrich heard from refugees escaping northern France hadn't been encouraging. A new law revoked the French citizenship of everyone who was naturalized after 1928, and since he belonged in this category, it was best to be careful. Mother had a residency permit but had to report to the police regularly in order to extend it. He had tried to explain to her that she needed to come south as quickly as possible, but she hadn't been able to manage it, so he decided to risk returning to Paris.

No trains were running at all, and he had to make his own way north. Peasants gave him rides in their horse- or ox-drawn carts; he slept in hay mounds and on really hot nights, under the stars with cicadas singing him to sleep. It was summer, and if one could put everything unpleasant out of mind, it was possible to pretend to be in paradise.

The southern peasants were a pugnacious, headstrong lot who despised old Marshal Pétain as a weakling and never gave the German soldiers the time of day. They used rude gestures and upright pitchforks to accentuate what they thought of the "old man" who was in no position to save their country. And as for the German Nazis—blond milksops all of them—they would never win the war because they were only interested in buying up everything they could find in the French shops and having it gift wrapped and sent back home.

After walking for weeks, Heinrich arrived in Paris and immediately set a plan in motion. Thanks to his good connections and small bribes, he arranged for two residency permits for Casablanca. But Emma Csillag, naïve as ever, was enjoying life in occupied Paris and was in no hurry to go to North Africa. Again and again Heinrich stressed the urgency of their departure only to founder on the shores of his mother's delaying tactics. In May 1941 he issued an ultimatum; but two days before their scheduled departure, Emma Csillag came down with the flu, and again their escape was thwarted.

Then, at the end of May, Heinrich was caught up in the first big anti-Jewish raid to take place in Paris. Emma had no news of her son for a long time before finally learning that he was being kept in a camp in Pithiviers, a small town about hundred kilometers south of Paris.

The camp had been unbearable; but it's amazing how quickly one can get used to the unbearable, and in that terrible first war, he had grown accustomed to enduring almost anything. In Pithiviers he had been crammed into a barracks with men of all nations, social backgrounds and worldviews. The days went by slowly; after getting up from their cots in the morning and reporting for roll call in the dusty square between the barracks, there wasn't much to do but go back to the barracks. Heinrich would almost have preferred to be called up for work duty just in order to escape the oppressive confinement and the almost tangible air of aggression between the camp's different factions. But the French were hardly as effective as the Germans in exploiting their prisoners' manpower—or maybe the Nazis just hadn't been in the country long enough to pass on lessons in efficiency. For whatever reason, they contented themselves with just keeping the men imprisoned.

What made co-existence with his fellow prisoners nearly unbearable was the shortage of water. There was barely enough to drink, let alone even consider using it to wash, and this brought Heinrich close to a state of frenzy. Sometimes he wanted to kick or strangle the prisoners near him, or simply take them into a meadow and force them to roll around in the grass in the vain hope that it might mask the stench of stale sweat.

There were lots of Viennese in the camp, among them some excellent musicians who tried to pass the time by making music. There was also a group that played the French card game Tarot day in and day out—some even tried to play bridge. There were a few writers, and they spent all day discussing the value and meaning of what they penned. Only the orthodox Jews retreated as a group into a corner, praying nearly constantly and preparing kosher meals as best they could.

Of course, there had also been political arguments, often between the Prussians and the Austrians, who reproached each other viciously for their allegedly differing approaches to the world. Among the Austrians, verbal battles were waged between the monarchists, among them Heinrich, and the communists. Heinrich was a great fan of the writings of Joseph Roth—this would have earned him a few points among the writers—and he pointed out that during Roth's later life, he not only sympathized with Catholicism but also defended the House of Habsburg, and thus Roth's political beliefs eventually corresponded perfectly with Heinrich's. Leo, a young communist who bunked next to Heinrich and coincidentally also loved Roth's novels, would try to walk an impossible tightrope by drawing a distinction between what Roth wrote and what he said in other contexts. These discussions brought Heinrich and Leo closer together, and despite their disagreements, they ended up bring friends. Thanks to this friendship, Heinrich was able to escape the camp—alive and in the nick of time.

At first it had still been possible for people in the camp to stay in touch with their relatives. Heinrich worried constantly about his mother, wanted to make sure that she was taken care of, and was able to arrange false papers for her that would provide a measure of security.

Naturally, the inmates kept the German Wehrmacht's war maneuvers under close scrutiny, always anxious to learn what the consequences would be for them. In June 1941, Germany attacked the Soviet Union, and a month later Goering ordered Heydrich to evacuate Europe's Jews. This news spread fear throughout the Pithivier camp and convinced many inmates that it was time to try to leave by any means possible. Heinrich had spent weeks pondering how to arrange his escape, but it seemed futile until Leo came to the rescue.

Leo and some of his comrades were part of the camp's internal organizational structure, and he was responsible for collecting the outgoing mail. Leo wanted to establish contact with a young woman who worked at the post office. She had smiled at him coquettishly, indicating her probable inability to resist his sparkling eyes and dashing charm, and his instinct told him this was an opportunity worth following up on. He was generous enough to include Heinrich in his plans, which included the strategic imperative that Heinrich make this young woman's acquaintance.

Leo arranged for Heinrich to accompany him the next time he went to the post office to pick up the mail. Two dusty figures in battered grey pants and worn out shirts weren't exactly dressed for courting, and the guard shoving them along with the barrel of his gun didn't improve the situation; also, they wouldn't have much time to win her over.

They arrived to find that the woman they sought wasn't working that day. Instead, it was her younger sister, who grew painfully shy in their presence and didn't know what to do with her hands or where to look. Heinrich didn't learn until later that this was not the targeted post mistress, and he couldn't fathom why Leo was supposedly attracted to such a shy person. But with their survival at stake, such concerns could be set aside.

Leo always slept late in the mornings—an ability Heinrich envied because that meant Leo could sleep through the barrack's hideous wake-up noises, among which the coughing was the "best" and the loud nose blowing and farting the most repulsive—and only operated at full speed at night. So it was the evening after their trip to the post office before he and Heinrich whispered together for a long time, trying to come up with a plan: both sisters had to be convinced that their help was desperately needed and that the men were putting their lives in their hands. With typical male self-assurance, they were certain the sisters wouldn't fail them.

Leo managed to make the arrangements, and the following Friday was chosen as the day to implement the plan. As soon as they entered the post office, the elder sister took them out the back door, where the younger waited with a horse cart. The guard had grown bored with escorting Leo and Heinrich on their daily post office runs and didn't think to wonder why it was taking them so long this time because the sisters had thought to send a few of their female friends to distract him. The guard remembered his charges only after half an hour of being playfully cajoled to go with the pretty young women to a friend's birthday celebration—they simply didn't have enough dance partners. By then the "closed for lunch" sign hung neatly on the post office door. So why not celebrate with the young women and invent some explanation later? Nobody would care about two inmates more or less.

By then, Leo and Heinrich lay panting with fear and excitement beneath a layer of straw in the back of the cart. They had reached a safe distance from the camp when the young woman, who introduced herself as Mathilde, suggested that they take a short break. Keeping a competent hold on the reins, she turned the cart into a corn field, where the escapees would be hidden by the tall stalks. They could stay there until dusk; it would be better if they got to her parents' house on the other side of Pithiviers after dark. Despite their jangled nerves, the two men managed to stretch out for a few hours' sleep.

If they had known that they wouldn't see the outdoors again until after France was liberated, they might have chosen to spend those hours consciously breathing in the fresh air and looking closely at the clouds, birds, trees and fields.

The parents of the three sisters—there was an even younger one—took them in and assured them that they could stay as long as there were camps in France. They were simple, good-natured people who knew how to distinguish between right and wrong and had the courage to act according to their beliefs, even if that meant endangering their own security. With warm smiles they assured the fugitives that not only did they have a big garden with lots of fruits and vegetables, they had a grocery store as well and there would always be enough food for everyone.

Heinrich found all this acutely embarrassing and tried to convince his host that he was a wealthy man and would reimburse the family for its hospitality once all this was over. Finally, the paterfamilias put a hand on Heinrich's shoulder and with a broad grin told him to shut up and not put too much of a strain on French hospitality.

Heinrich stops briefly in his narrative to caress his wife's hair. "I owe you my life: you know I'll never forget that."

Heinrich's account has tumbled out in short bursts, and Sidi can see in his gestures and tensely balled fists how much pain he is in and how hard it is for him to relive the endless monotony of two years in hiding in a partitioned-off section of a fruit cellar. The two men read a lot, carried on endless discussions, and were always hoping the war would end soon. The first year, things looked very bad. They learned that the French police were collaborating with the Nazis and diligently supported the mass deportations of Jews from France to Auschwitz. Once, an overzealous neighbor infected by "brown fever" had denounced the grocer's family to the police after months of observing unusual activity in the house. One day a gendarme appeared in the little store with a search warrant in hand and demanded entry to the living quarters. But his search proved fruitless; Leo and Heinrich had been well hidden inside an enormous pile of the previous year's russet apples. But after that, they had to be even more careful. Then in November 1942, they were joined by a third refugee, a quiet young man, also from Vienna, who Leo and Heinrich quickly learned to appreciate for his fine sense of humor.

In 1943 they started to have hope. The Wehrmacht was defeated at Stalingrad in February and the Warsaw Ghetto Uprising in April showed that resistance was possible. When the Allies landed at Normandy in June 1944, the three men dared to put their heads out the window for the first time, and when General de Gaulle entered Paris in

August 1944, they came out of hiding and looked up at the sky. Their nightmare was finally over.

While in hiding, Leo's flirtation with the post mistress had turned into a glowing romance and the shy younger sister, Mathilde, had developed a fancy for Heinrich. At first, he had not been willing to get involved, after all, he was over forty and she not yet twenty. But he learned to appreciate the delicate, restrained and persistent way she showed her affection for him, and in the end, he loved her in his own way.

And now she's his wife. Deep inside, Sidi sighs heavily. Heinrich had had several beautiful women in his life, but there was never any talk of marriage. Now her. Because she saved his life. Because he wanted to be decent and show his gratitude. That she loves him was obvious. But what about him?

The passage of time, the suffering, the cruelty of history, the processes of humiliation, none of these have altered Sidonie's arrogance when it comes to matters of beauty and what is of benefit to one's social standing. Mathilde doesn't match her standards, and Sidi would have wished for someone better for her brother.

One evening, after Heinrich has finished the last of his many tales and after Mathilde has gone off to bed, Sidonie can't restrain herself any longer. "What do you see in her?" she asks.

A bit put out, he squirms a little, knowing that this is his Achilles' heel. After a few reasonable explanations about her having saved his life and the nature of responsibility, he extricates himself by remarking that regular facial features are boring, and his wife has her own qualities.

Sidi bites her tongue and swallows a nasty rejoinder—"In that case, you're certain never to be bored." On this matter the siblings will never come to an understanding, and at least Sidonie has learned by now that if she doesn't want to cause pain, it's worth it to keep her mouth shut.

Now, almost four years after the war, Heinrich is doing well again. Both his health and his finances have recovered. A reliable managing director did an exemplary job of running the solid paraffin factory in his absence. Everything is running smoothly now, he has a guaranteed income, and he can sit back and relax a bit. The money Antal Csillag had invested in Amsterdam also survived the war, and it is now under Heinrich's control. Only the company the family had had in Vienna in 1938, which Heinrich took over after Papa's death, had been liquidated, but Heinrich soon realized it would be uselessness to insist on any rights of ownership at this point. All the family's stock from Poland and Hungary had also become worthless, and he certainly was not going to ask the new Communist rulers for restitution.

After a week of post-reunion happiness, the old family patterns begin to reassert themselves. Her mother is cool and dismissive, Heinrich grows distanced, and soon Sidi can't stand it anymore. Before the emotional storm clouds can darken her mood, she'll get on a train to Vienna. It had been her home for so many years, and she wants with all her heart to make it so again.

VIENNA AGAIN

A few days later, as Sidonie's train approaches Vienna's bombed-out Westbahnhof, she literally can't believe her eyes. Where is the railway station? Where did it disappear to?

As the train pulls up to the platform, she feels as if time has been disassembled and all the images from her past reassembled in a distorted way. Where is the beautiful statue of Kaiserin Sisi that used to greet her in the vestibule? Wasn't it just yesterday they'd seen her mother off from the platform two tracks over? Even some of the same people are on the platform—as if this were all part of a play. There are the shining faces of Grete and Muni Weinberger, Sylvie Dietz and Christl Schallenberg, only Ellen is missing—but, of course, she must be in great pain and has stayed at home. They focus on the passing carriages, looking for their friend. They've all grown older and are looking rather impoverished; the war has left its mark on their faces and their wardrobes—Sidonie only hopes she doesn't come across like that, too. But, no, that wouldn't be possible, because she spent those years in a warm paradise wrapped in security and peace. Her beauty will have been better preserved.

With tears in her eyes she descends the two steep steps from the train, and after nine years she's back in Vienna. She pauses for a moment as if to thank her feet for bringing her back here across time and continents.

What's different this time is that as her feet touch her new/old homeland once again, so do Petzi's four paws.

Muni Weinberger embraces Sidi tightly for a long time. "Not even my mother hugged me like that," Sidi thinks, "but this might not mean anything." Then it is Grete's turn, followed by Sylvie and finally Christl. All of them show the same affection, the same intimacy as before, and they make her feel that their friendship has remained unchanged.

There are flowers for Sidi, homegrown bouquets of what Vienna's gardens might yield in early June: daisies, a few roses, larkspurs.

They are all going to the Weinbergers, where the friends have prepared a little buffet. It will be very modest, Muni whispers in her ear, but they will have a bit of champagne to celebrate. The ladies catch the Number 58 streetcar on Mariahilferstrasse—everyone sharing the burden of the suitcases. Nobody has a car these days, and it is too expensive to take one of the few cabs. On the Ring they change to the D line, which will take them to the Fourth District, where the Weinbergers still have their large flat at Schwindgasse 10.

Here, time really does seem to have stood still. Sidonie moves among the familiar furniture and the well-known rooms feeling tenderly nostalgic.

As it does everywhere in Europe now, the talk soon turns to the war, as if people are just waiting for the moment they can unburden themselves and tell outsiders about the horror.

Sidonie already knows most of what they tell her. She has read between the lines in the letters she received ... the aerial attacks on Vienna that started in the fall of 1944, the bombing of the opera and St. Stephan's cathedral in March 1945, the advance of the "Russians," the occupation of the city by the four victorious powers.

Soon, however, the talk turns to personal issues. Grete says she no longer exchanges a word with former friends who made "arrangements" with the Nazis, and she never will again. She lost her son to people like them. This is the first time Sidi has heard that Grete's darling boy Peter had gone missing in the war. She thinks of Grete's brother and father and their enthusiasm for the Nazis and doesn't know what to say—most likely they have all learned something.

"Your Ed also got into some difficulties," she hears Grete say. "He was really clever. Never joined the Party and got his old comrades to help him. But that's over now and he's hard up, is the Herr Major."

Sidi shivers at the sharp bitterness in Grete's voice. But Ed's opportunism is nothing new to her.

What is new soon follows: "Soon after your departure he started flirting with me. But he wasn't very clever about it. I think what he wanted was to continue coming to Katzelsdorf on the weekends. But I have one ironclad rule: Hands off my girlfriends' husbands. Others aren't all that particular about it."

Sidi tries to evade her friend's nattering and indiscretions, which may be because she's tipsy, and turns her attention to dear Pussy Mautner-Markhof, who has just come into the room. With Pussy she can revel in telling tales about Cuba, the wonderful years she spent there, the opulence of nature in the tropics, how it can easily be compared to Brioni. But she learns that not much is left of Brioni aside from memories. It has been lost to Yugoslavia, and summer vacations there are no longer possible. Indeed, travel to anywhere abroad is now beyond the means of the women gathered in this room.

Christl Kmunke shows up in the late afternoon. She has remained boyish and still has an offensive way of kissing, but Sidi is happy to see her. Petzi finds Christl irresistible, most likely because she carries the smell of her sheepdog, and he finds himself a cozy spot at her feet.

Then comes the relationship gossip. Everyone makes fun of Christl Schallenberg's third attempt at marriage, there are smiles about Grete's affairs, and even Sylvie seems to be taking the relationships with men in a lighter vein.

It grows late, and Sidi wants to make her way to Sylvie Dietz's around the corner in Wohllebengasse, where she'll be staying for the next couple of weeks. She needs to rest a bit, because tomorrow she wants to get up early and go to visit Ellen, and that's going to be difficult. The need to embrace her best friend is nearly unbearable, but so is the fear of holding a very sick person in her arms.

Eventually, the much-anticipated highlight of her return, the reunion with Wjera, will be a reality, but Sidonie plans to prolong the expectation. She will do so with great pleasure, because it is what will keep her going. Fantasy is what has always kept her going in matters of the heart, and Wjera has held the most special place in her heart and her mind for years. Just thinking about her makes Sidi shiver, and she understands that she feels much more secure in this state than she does when looking reality in the face.

A while ago, the Ferstls moved to a luxurious villa on Felix-Mottl-Strasse, in the neighborhood called Cottage, and from the moment she starts to get ready to go there, Sidi is so tense and uncertain about what she'll encounter that she can't concentrate. Paul, Ellen's husband, answers the door when she rings. Silent and serious, he embraces her before saying, "Go to her, she's in the bedroom. She's in a lot of pain today."

Sidi slaps on a bright smile, heads toward the indicated bedroom door, and encounters Ellen tottering towards her. Sidonie feels as if she's been lashed by a whip, that's how deeply the sight shocks her. Her girlfriends have warned her that Ellen is faring badly, but this exceeds her anxious expectations. She looks at least ten years older than her age. Her mouth is tight with pain, her eyes shadowed and strained, the round cheeks bloated, and her already broad nose is almost shapeless. Where is her vibrant Ellen, whose gaiety had been so infectious and whose laughter seemed to reach to the sky? Sidi's eyes burn as she embraces her friend for a long time and with all her heart, but she has to compose herself quickly. She can't let Ellen know how frightened she is … frightened to death. Frightened of death?

Ellen has prettied herself up for the reunion and clearly wants to show her best side to her best friend. Still holding Sidi's hands, she murmurs quietly, "I'm overjoyed that you are back … finally. I'm not feeling all that well today. I'm in a lot of pain, but now everything will get better. In a few days we will go for a walk and pick flowers."

Sidi kisses Ellen's hands, her cheeks, and can't restrain her warm but painful feelings. She wants to do something good for Ellen, take away all her pain if she only could. But knowing that she can't, she urges her to go back to bed, to take care of herself.

A memory surfaces of an afternoon on Kobenzl, in the late thirties, not long before she had to leave Vienna. Ellen had showed her the palm-sized bald spots on her head and how she could pull out her hair by the handful. It had grown in again, but the headaches Ellen had already been complaining about had grown increasingly worse.

During lunch with Paul and their two daughters, Ruth and Lotte, Sidonie hears that sometimes the headaches literally drive Ellen mad, and then she stays in her room and screams in pain. She also has spasms. A medical examination has revealed that a fall she'd taken on the ice in the twenties had left a fine crack open in her skull, which allowed air to enter slowly. If it had been discovered back then, it might possibly have been fixed, but after so many years, it's no longer possible to save her. Ellen had turned to stronger and stronger medications to stop the pain, finally morphine, to which she is now addicted, though it brings only temporary relief. An x-ray had revealed the crack in 1946, and there had been an operation that they hoped would mean she could stop the pain-killers. She had even gone through a rehabilitation program, but the terrible pain never abated.

She does have pain-free days when her radiant smile and sparkling disposition are just as they used to be. On those days, it's as if strength were coursing through her like hot water through long-empty pipes. Then she bikes into the forest, goes for long walks and even—in the right season—goes mushroom hunting.

Paul says quietly that he's glad Sidi has returned; he has high hopes that her visits will have a good effect. Ellen almost never leaves the house anymore and sometimes can't endure anyone's presence except that of Lotte, her younger daughter, and so it is very important, perhaps vital that the person dearest to Ellen since childhood can be at her side once again.

Sidonie leaves hours later feeling that she is going to need a great deal of strength in the coming months, though in the back of her mind she also senses that this strength isn't going to be of any use.

Wjera ... yes, it is Wjera who is going to save her from all this, from the collapse of her former world. In just a few weeks she will finally see her again, somewhere in the countryside in a very intimate setting—

everything has been arranged by mail. The thought of this meeting consoles Sidonie—if touched on every day, it works like medicine to help her see the world from a more positive perspective.

But before she sees Wjera, she has to clear another difficult hurdle: meeting Ed again. Sidonie has been in Vienna for a while but still hasn't seen her ex-husband. It just hasn't worked out. Once he cancelled a pre-arranged meeting for professional reasons; the next time she used Ellen as an excuse. She was of the opinion that after their exchange of letters about Petzi, he should be made to wait for a while. But the inevitable is finally unavoidable.

The apartment they once shared in Weyrgasse is unchanged, but Sidonie has the absurd impression that she has entered a doll's house. Everything seems strangely distanced and unreal. Ed has turned into an old, ossified relic of his times and its artificial manners—in other words, he hasn't changed a bit. They face each other like strangers. He embraces her mechanically; she automatically pats him on the back. Petzi's hackles go up as he makes it clear that he doesn't like Ed. As they walk through the apartment, Sidi sees everything as if she's looking through the wrong end of binoculars. She sits down on the old living room couch, accepts something to drink, and is certain—has been from the very first moment—that living here is out of the question.

During their distanced and stiff conversation, Ed tells her about his life during the past nine years. She nods, seeming to be engaged, but in reality, she is growing increasingly disgusted with every word she hears.

ED WEITENEGG'S WAR

THROUGHOUT THE WAR, AND THANKS TO HIS CONNECTIONS AND some obviously smart moves, he kept his post as director of the Institute of Pictorial Statistics. A party member named Jahn had been appointed as technical director, and as such had taken care of all the interactions with the National Socialist Party, but Ed had been the real director. Orders from above dictated another name change for the Institute, which became the Institute for Exhibition Technology and

Pictorial Statistics. Except for Ed, who pretended that he couldn't join the Party for personal reasons, all the functionaries joined the NSDAP.

The Institute prepared several exhibits during the Nazi period, with "Soviet Paradise" having been one of the largest. In October 1944, probably because of the impending collapse of the Nazi regime, there were personnel changes at the Institute, but Ed remained on as managing director.

By May 1945, all the functionaries save Ed Weitenegg had disappeared, and once again he became the Institute's only director. He reactivated the organization that had existed between 1934 and 1938, and this organization asserted its right to reclaim the Institute's assets. The office was moved to the Neue Hofburg, the Institute itself was housed in several rooms in the Am Fuchsenfeld council housing blocks in Vienna's Meidling district.

Soon after the end of the war, some of the Institute's original members returned to Austria, among them Franz Rauscher, who had founded the Austrian Society for Economic Statistics in 1947 and was Otto Neurath's rightful successor.

But over the years Ed had started to enjoy his work at the Institute, and he defended his right to retain his position, even taking the matter to court. When the lower court ruled against him, he appealed; but the appeal was denied, and Ed had to give up his "rights" and surrender all the Institute's remaining assets to Franz Rauscher and his organization. As a countermove and to demonstrate his new/old backbone, Ed offered to collaborate with the Institute on its antifascist exhibit "Never Forget."

By this point, Sidi is thoroughly disgusted and in order to torture him a bit, she asks how, along with all his professional success, he has been faring romantically. Grete Weinberger has already told her about his attempted flirtation, and Sidi can be certain that Ed won't mention that. He doesn't like to talk about his failures, but he certainly doesn't stay quiet about his success with another of her friends. In the years Sidi was away, he spent a lot of time on her nice estate outside Vienna, letting her console him when times were hard. It isn't difficult for Sidonie to guess which friend this is, and her growing disgust approaches the level of nausea. How could he have dared...? And with such an unattractive woman?

She can't refrain from asking Ed if he had asked this woman, too, not to wash too often. During their marriage, she had found it incomprehensible when Ed asked her to wash less "down there" because doing so had a dampening effect on what he thought of as "erotic emanations." Had this helped to increase the other woman's otherwise limited appeal?

He squirms a bit, but he no longer seems to have any concept of what is decent or indecent, what constitutes good manners or good taste, and he goes on chatting cheerfully about his years without Sidi.

Sidi simply disconnects. He really does seem to be a type that is found everywhere in Austria at the moment—the conformists, the new social climbers, the old-school diehards. There are so many like him, right up to the highest levels of government.

POST-WAR AUSTRIA

In July 1949, around the time Sidi first reconnects with Ed, the Austrian government institutes the reinstatement of 550,000 so-called "minimally incriminated" (former) National Socialists. This is just fine with the many Austrians who want to put the past behind them and don't want to waste time thinking about National Socialism. Even though they had been loyal to it, they now refuse to take any responsibility for it, and all those reproachful voices were getting to be rather a burden.

At first there had been a rather ambitious war crimes law, passed in June 1945. Then there were actions such as the one in January 1946 that cleansed all Austrian libraries of Nazi literature. Nonetheless, a month later the British House of Lords criticized Austria for its slow and tepid process of denazification, and with justification. The process had fallen prey to the icy winter, because 1946 was a hunger year and all everyone was thinking about was their next foraging trip.

In early summer 1946 a comprehensive law was drafted that was meant to be both unifying and enduring. All National Socialists had to register and were to be divided into two groups—those to be punished and those who had to atone. The latter were further divided into the incriminated and the minimally incriminated. The proposed atonements were to be higher income-, wage- and property taxes.

The Allies had to sign off on this law, but they were divided as to whether or not it was strict enough. The USA and the Soviets asked for a stricter law, the British considered it too strict and the French supplied a list of changes. These internal differences among the Allies allowed the Austrian government to distance itself from the proposed law and eventually put the blame for its wording and the responsibility for its implementation on the occupiers.

The law finally passed the National Assembly in February 1947. Again, the dominant theme was hunger rather than denazification.

In spring 1948 everybody's ears pricked up when they heard that US politician George Marshall had proposed a comprehensive aid program for Europe. It formally began operation at the beginning of July, but the general climate had been nervous since early June when the embargo of Berlin began, and in addition, barbed wire barriers were being erected only fifty kilometers east of Vienna. Relatively soon, they would become the historic reality generally referred to as the Iron Curtain.

In April 1948 the National Assembly—with its eye on the upcoming elections—dared for the first time to pass a law granting amnesty to minimally incriminated National Socialists.

Sidonie's arrival in Austria in June 1949 coincides with the height of the election campaign. As a Cuban citizen, she is not allowed to vote, in contrast to the half million soon-to-be-reinstated former National Socialists, the 400,000 returned prisoners of war and the 100,000 German-speaking refugees from Eastern Europe who have been naturalized. None of these groups had participated in the general elections in November 1945, but now they represent a large pool of potential voters, and all the political parties want to woo them. One must adapt to the times.

Each party has its own way of canvassing for votes: the ÖVP (Austrian Peoples' Party—Christian Democrats) opens a path for the Nazis; the KPÖ (Austrian Communist Party) demands the destruction of the Gauakte—the district personnel files on NS-Party members, then in storage at the Ministry of the Interior; and the SPÖ (Austrian Socialist Party) ostensibly turns its back on its 1946 proposal to exchange Nazis in Austria for prisoners of war held by the Allies. The Verein der Unab-hängigen, VdU (Association of Independents, founded in Salzburg in February 1949) is not only courting the votes of former Nazis but also considers itself the only opposition to the dominant ÖVP and SPÖ.

The October 9 election results will surprise everyone: the ÖVP loses its absolute majority; the SPÖ also loses many votes; the KPÖ gains one seat and now has five; and the VdU gains sixteen seats. The ÖVP and SPÖ will react by forming their first coalition and cementing a tradition of what might be called party-based proportional representation, in which even jobs and flats were evenly apportioned. This practice will weave through the history of the coming decades like red and black threads—red representing the Socialists, black the Christian Demo-crats—and eventually will result in the return of that which had been suppressed.

Sidonie has heard enough. Stiffly she gets up from the table they once had shared, puts Petzi on the leash, regretting that he hadn't vomited on Ed's carpet on her behalf, and takes her leave—for good.

She'll avoid all contact with her former husband in the future, and in doing so will escape having to listen to all kinds of unappetizing sto-ries about him.

Later, Petzi does vomit—on Sylvie Dietz's carpet. Sidonie is beyond embarrassed, and in order to avoid being any more bother, she accepts Ellen's offer to move in with her. Ellen's house is big, Petzi will enjoy the garden far more than Sylvie's cramped apartment, and the two women can make up for the lost years.

The day finally draws near that will bring Wjera Fechheimer back into Sidonie's arms. Everything has had to be planned both well and discreetly. In Paris, Heinrich and Sidonie had agreed that she would spend summers with her mother in the Austrian Alps. With their first such sojourn in mind, she has rented rooms for July and August in a nice hotel in the town of Lofer, at the foot of the Steinberge. She isn't sure how she is going to endure her chilly, difficult mother for six weeks, but at least she is going to have a beautiful diversion.

Sidi's plan focuses on the week when Heinrich and his wife will be in Lofer for a vacation and will spend some time with Mother. Wjera will be coming by train from Munich, and she and Sidi have arranged by mail to meet mid-way, in Golling in Salzachtal, and spend a weekend together. Wjera agreed to this only after some hesitation and has sworn her friend to absolute secrecy. From Vienna, Sidi rents two rooms in a nice inn and the preparations are complete.

As it turns out, Sidi doesn't actually mind being alone with her mother for the two weeks before Golling. Things are easier because, since Emma's darling sons are not present, she doesn't refer to them constantly; in their presence she still forgets that her daughter exists. When mother and daughter are alone together, Emma has to deal with Sidi, and Sidi continues to do the best she can.

In part, this isn't so hard, because Mother is crazy about sweets. In her youth, Sidonie indulged her mother with flowers, chocolates and hand kisses, and she is relying on the effect of edibles once again. Her mother's favorite sweets in the past were chocolates called "cat's tongues," but now she prefers "sprinklers," round chocolate discs decorated with small red and white streusels. Once seduced by these and other culinary pleasures, Mama can turn into a quiet, friendly person for several hours. Therefore Sidi accustoms herself to the heavy meals that are served locally, and a few times a week she takes Emma to the inn on Lofer's main square for her favorite dish—semolina dumpling soup.

The prospect of meeting Wjera makes her mother's every painful barb and blast of unfair anger endurable until, at the beginning of August, she takes the Postbus to Golling. Even Petzi has to stay behind—this reunion should take place without any possibility of a disturbance.

Sidonie is the first to arrive at the little pension right at the foot of the Hohe Göll on the outskirts of Golling. She's immediately enchanted by the pretty, fin-de-siècle-style house with wooden balconies and green and white shutters. According to the schedule, Wjera's train has only just arrived at the station in Salzburg, so after unpacking, Sidi takes a seat beneath the linden and fir trees beside the house and keeps a restless eye on the narrow dirt road where Wjera will first appear, after having walked the kilometer from the Postbus station. Sidi enjoys the excitement and anticipation but can barely stand the tension.

After more than an hour, a dot appears in the distance and slowly resolves into a tall, slender figure. Sidi stands and with utmost concentration watches a beautiful, serious woman, slim and unpretentious, calmly putting one foot in front of the other. Wjera hasn't lost a millimeter in stature, Sidi thinks, her heart racing. She is wearing a simple, flowered summer dress, white socks with heavy shoes, and a thin wool jacket; a small leather suitcase is in her right hand. The years have pared her down to her essence, to a beauty and serenity that take Sidi's breath away. Then Wjera notices that she

Wjera Fechheimer, Golling, July 1949

is being watched. She stops, drops her suitcase and after that, everything is easy—the two women run toward each other and half laughing, half crying fall into one another's arms and twirl around.

Ten years have passed and yet not a moment. Sidonie runs her hand through Wjera's hair, rests it briefly and tenderly on her neck, and is happy. She hasn't been so incredibly happy in ages. Wjera is radiant and says softly, "You are back, back in one piece, what a gift."

Arm in arm, they go into the house. In the evening they walk to the Golling waterfall and sit on a boulder beside a large pool, where the sound of the falls almost drowns Wjera's words as she talks about the last few years.

WJERA'S WAR

WJERA SURVIVED THE WAR IN MUNICH. SHORTLY AFTER THE END OF the war, her husband died as a consequence of his treatment in Dachau. Her parents-in-law perished miserably in Theresienstadt. Her mother, who was in Vienna, suffered a stroke during the war. Sidi knew of this collection of horrors through letters she'd received in the States. Today she hears all the details, and both women are frequently moved to tears.

Wjera and her husband, Hans Martin, had left Nuremberg in 1935—probably a life-saving decision, since they likely would not have survived National Socialism in a city the size of Nuremberg. Munich afforded anonymity, and that made many things easier. In 1939 her in-laws also moved to Berlin, where their daughter married an aristocrat who looked after his wife and her parents with affection. But by the end of 1942 even the son-in-law's noble origins couldn't prevent the old peoples' deportation to Theresienstadt. He used all his connections, and he was promised that his parents-in-law would be treated well, but even "good" treatment by the Nazis led older, ill people to a quick death. Over 141,000 people had been imprisoned at Theresienstadt; of these, 88,000 were later transported to one of the extermination camps in Poland. About 35,000 people died a "natural death" at Theresienstadt. When the Red Army liberated it on May 7, 1945, just 17,000 inmates were still alive. But by then Wjera's in-laws were long dead.

At first Hans Martin Fechheimer had been protected by his "privileged mixed marriage" to a "non-Jew," and until 1940 they didn't feel they were in any danger, but then things got increasingly difficult and walking the tightrope grew more precarious. The Nazis were trying to get their hands on everything that belonged to Jews, in particular flats and everything in them. Using a combination of threats and recently minted laws, Jewish flats were Aryanized, and the few thousand Jews still living in Munich after 1938 were forced to move into the so-called Jewish Houses located in Goethestrasse, Ainmillerstrasse, Galeriestrasse, Hohenzollerstrasse and Maximilianstrasse.

The Fechheimer's lovely flat in the Bogenhausen neighborhood had attracted the attention of a representative of the Gauleiter, but since the rental contract was in Wjera's name, the Nazis couldn't pounce, since she was a so-called Aryan.

The Jewish population had been urged to build its own settlement in Milbertshofen, but everyone forced to live there was eventually deported. At the end of 1942 only 645 Jews were registered in Munich, more than half of them still protected from deportation by "Aryan" spouses. In January 1943 the number of Jews was reduced even further, and the Gauleiter rejoiced that Munich was "free of Jews."

After the defeat at Stalingrad and the actions by the Scholl siblings and their friends in March 1943—they dropped leaflets protesting the Nazi regime into an air shaft at one of Berlin's university buildings—the harassments increased. After a few of the Jewish men in the Fechheimers' circle were arrested by the Gestapo, Hans no longer left the house, and soon an untreated lung infection began bothering him. The confined living conditions literally took his breath away, but he and Wjera didn't dare endanger him even further by leaving the city without permission—even though fresh mountain air might have saved him. Wjera went to the countryside on her own, not for fresh air but in a desperate search among the clandestine rural markets for some strengthening food for Hans.

When her mother had a stroke in the summer of 1944, Wjera traveled to Vienna in a state of high anxiety. But soon Helene Rothballer was out of danger and was being well taken care of; she fully understood that Wjera needed to return to Berlin as quickly as possible.

The Fechheimers heard from those who dared to listen to foreign radio transmissions that the Allies were approaching Germany from France and Italy, and they began to breathe more easily—the war would end soon. After January 1945 it was nearly impossible to make contact with family and friends in other cities. Hans and Wjera were locked in. Wjera was deeply concerned about her mother, as she'd heard about the bombing of Vienna and the approach of the Red Army (which would occupy the city three months later).

It happened in early February 1945—Germany had just about lost the war, but the Nazis pushed on in their determination to exterminate Europe's Jews. The last Jews residing in Munich were ordered to report to the Gestapo. Hans and Wjera talked it over at length and decided to ignore the order. That would have worked if a particularly zealous neighborhood Nazi hadn't reported him. Literally at the very last minute, the Gestapo arrived at their flat. Wjera braced herself against the door, shouting and arguing that they were not allowed to take a person so sick and weak. The Gestapo agents shoved her aside, pushed their way in and took Hans away.

Wjera dared to go to Gestapo headquarters the next morning to try to find out what had happened to her husband. She endured a barrage of the vilest abuses, and still had to leave without having accomplished a thing. Utterly desperate and with no idea what to do, she went back home to Bogenhausen. Standing in the hallway with tears running down her face, she encountered a neighbor who had always greeted her in a friendly way. Aghast, she asked Wjera what had happened, and putting aside all the distrust and caution that had by now become second nature, Wjera unburdened herself.

Just a few hours later this neighbor knocked on Wjera's door with the news that Hans was still being held by the Gestapo but would be transferred to Dachau within the next few days. She had also learned who had denounced Hans and promised to give the miserable cur a tongue lashing.

Wjera never had the courage to ask how this Good Samaritan got her information, but she was deeply grateful that someone was looking after her.

On her next visit to Gestapo headquarters Wjera tried to bribe various functionaries with valuable works of art, but she was always refused. Nothing worked. At least she was allowed to leave food packages for Hans and later found out that he really was receiving them.

Somehow, Hans managed to stay in Dachau rather than be sent on one of the death marches. At the end of April 1945 he was witness to the US Army's liberation of the camp. The helpful neighbor with the special connections organized spiriting him out of Dachau, despite the fact that it was under quarantine because of epidemic typhus. Hans got immediate medical attention—his tuberculosis had gotten worse—but he died just two weeks after he and Wjera were reunited.

Wjera's courage in the face of the Nazis had managed to protect her beloved partner for so many years, and then, when all that was over, his life had been taken.

Wjear's whole world collapsed, but she barely had time to mourn before taking up the next burden. She gathered up her pain into a small dark fleck and stowed it deep inside, and she was only aware that it was there when her bitter hatred of everyone who had been so submissive for all these years welled up. Immediately after Hans died, she had to go to Vienna to be with her now seriously ill mother, but because the few functioning trains were full to bursting, she had to walk most of the way. For the past four years she has been immersed in caring for her mother, with little time for anything else. The emergencies and shortages made the usual problems of caregiving even more stressful, for even if one had money or something to barter it was impossible to get everything that was needed. Perforce, Wjera had become a good businesswoman, and some of her jewelry had helped to procure the things her mother needed most.

Night falls while the two women talk; cold, moist air blows over from the waterfall and dampens their skin. Wjera falls silent, wiping away water droplets and tears, and Sidonie starts to curse Europe, Austria and the incredible sorrow that she is encountering everywhere, all the time.

If only she could protect Wjera in retrospect, make up for everything. Tenderly, she takes her friend's hand, pulls her to her feet and pulls her into her arms.

In a close embrace, they walk back to the pension in the dark.

The days that follow far exceed Sidi's imaginings during all her years of fantasizing. It is as if the sky had opened up and showered the two women with joy, with ease and desire. Wjera has grown soft und gentle, full of love and able to open her heart. Having gone through the worst, now she wants to be happy, to indulge in love. Convention and false morality had stopped her twenty years ago; they no longer matter.

Sidonie can't really understand what's happening to her. At night, attacks of desire she's never felt

Wjera Fechheimer, Golling, July 1949

before keep her awake until dawn watching the woman who is surrendering herself to her, putting herself in her hands.

The lovers spend all the daylight hours together. They hike into the high alpine meadows and forests—to be undisturbed, to make up for the lost years with talk and in companionable silence, just looking at one another as if they were tuned to exactly the same note. When Sidi's eyes and heart are both so full that she can't even speak, she takes out her little camera to capture the magic that is Wjera in her summer dress, Wjera at the fountain, in the meadow, on top of the mountain, in front of the pension, Wjera at dusk, and always her warmly teasing eyes and unruly hair. Sidi hasn't brought enough film.

The planned weekend turns into ten days, the brief encounter becomes a honeymoon, and for the moment at least, both women know that they belong to each other and it will be forever.

And yet, in the wee hours when Sidi is too agitated to sleep and lies staring, besotted, at Wjera's naked back, she finds herself overwhelmed by fear. How is she going to keep this woman she has carried in her heart for so many years, who means everything to her? How is she going to be able to bear so much fulfilment of something so splendid?

She suddenly understands that being in love—this wild, anarchistic, very new love—can generate a terrible, fearful state of being. She feels small, insecure and insufficient. And what tortures her most is the memory of that poisonous little gagging feeling that, sooner or later, always wells up in her—her disgust with sexuality. At the moment, every curve of Wjera's sleeping body still excites her; at the moment, the strength of her feelings can overcome the strangeness of Wjera's moans, her wetness, her mortal transience. But in a month, in six months? How, for heaven's sake, will she be able to hold on to Wjera without disappointing her terribly?

Separating after ten days proves incredibly difficult. They agree to meet from time to time in Vienna; Wjera has to go there anyway to see her mother. Other than that, everything remains open, is given over to the certainty of emotions and the uncertainty of spontaneity.

After the wonderful days in Golling, Sidonie finds everyday life in Vienna terribly drab. She moves into Ellen's in the Nineteenth District and will spend nearly a year there as her close companion, bearing witness to her ever-increasing pain. The elder of Ellen's two daughters, Ruth, is expecting her first child when Sidi first moves in, and Ellen asks Sidi to accompany Ruth to the hospital in her stead when the time comes. Sidi has decided to be the best mother substitute imaginable, but she doesn't anticipate that her dislike of everything physical will be an insurmountable hurdle. In the delivery room, she whimpers in sympathy with every contraction and makes Ruth so nervous that she asks Sidi to go home. She wants to concentrate on giving birth, not on a highly-strung aunt. Sidi gladly agrees, but before leaving reminds Ruth to take her time so the child will be born on Sidi's fiftieth birthday.

The baby, a delightful girl, brings both Ellen and Sidi great joy, but soon Ellen's pain grows so acute that it often leaves her semi-conscious, and Sidi is increasingly wrapped up in taking care of her. This makes her so unhappy, however, that she starts making plans to leave the Ferstel household.

During this time, Sidi finds she must endure yet another unpleasant Ed Weitenegg story. The Ferstel's housekeeper is close friends with Lina, Ed's housekeeper, and one day at tea time the former trots out some gossip for Sidi.

Ed Weitenegg's first family has surfaced unexpectedly. Ed had a daughter with his first wife, who married a Hungarian count after the divorce, and all three moved to Hungary. But the count has died, and the daughter, now thirty-one years old, is married and has two small children. Recently all five of them appeared on Ed's doorstep—they found him in the Vienna directory—and demanded to be taken in.

After a few weeks, Ed's first wife moved in with a woman who was an old friend, and the daughter, Hanna, made plans to move with her family to Carinthia. But Hanna was having such a good time in the company of her rediscovered father, and he with her, that she kept postponing her departure. One day Hanna's husband issued an ultimatum: either they all leave for Carinthia the following week or he'd take the children and go without her.

Ed wants to keep Hanna in Vienna. He enjoys her company and likes the idea of being the head of a small family again. He takes advantage of the situation to get a little too close to his daughter.

Lina now has to take a back seat, after years of enjoying the status of a lover, and she does not like this new development. Sidi had always suspected that Ed started carrying on with Lina after she was out of the picture. A laughable and tasteless situation, but Sidi could have remained indifferent if Lina hadn't been such a gossip monger and sent letters to Cuba revealing details better kept private.

The longer Hanna stays on, the more jealous Lina becomes, and she lets it be known that Ed's interactions with his daughter go beyond the boundaries of a "normal" relationship. She hasn't filed charges yet because she feels sorry for poor, lonely old Ed, but soon …

The scandalized ladies at the Ferstel's tea party find it grotesque that Hanna prefers her father's company to that of her husband and small children. But that a "domestic"—the disloyal cow—would spread such monstrous tales … well, one simply can't keep someone like that in one's employ. So, rather than denounce Ed, they recommend to him, through various channels, that he fire Lina.

Once again, Sidonie feels nothing but disgust and congratulates herself on her decision to give up on Ed altogether. Wanting to wipe the slate clean, she asks Heinrich if he's still sending Ed regular monthly payments. Receiving a positive reply, she tells him to cancel them immediately; it's high time to put an end to that pre-war arrangement.

Soon, Sidi receives a phone call from her enraged ex-husband demanding to know if she has revoked the payments.

With relish she replies, "Yes, I did it. We don't need to keep financing your messes."

He adopts his "I give the orders" persona, but this attempt at intimidation fails. Then he tries pleading, but Sidi's decision is irrevocable.

"There are no decent humans left in this world," he whines.

"No, you are the only one."

This reply ends the discussion and permanently closes the book on Ed Weitenegg.

New Year's Eve 1949 holds the promise of a beautiful new decade and the hope that the horrors of the war and its aftermath will finally recede into the background. Maybe the Austrian government's negotiations with the four Allies will bring some results. The end of the Berlin blockade the previous May had brought new hope.

Initially, life was on the upswing. A wider range of goods was already available, the railway stations and the buildings on Ringstrasse were being restored, travel within Austria as well as to other countries was getting easier, and maybe there would be a treaty with the Allies. But in June 1950, the Korean War begins, with strong repercussions in Austria. There's a further tightening of the already tight markets for raw materials and commodities, food markets experience shortages worldwide and US financial aid is reduced. Food prices in Austria go up between 30 and 50 percent. Negotiations regarding the withdrawal of Allied troops from Austria come to a standstill, and in September there are massive protests against the escalating prices.

But when Sidi celebrates New Year's Eve at the Ferstel's, all this is in the future. The family's financial situation is still quite good; the festive dinner features a succulent saddle of venison, a gift from an acquaintance who had gone hunting. For dessert, there is raspberry ice cream, which the cook has churned for hours in the old fashioned way and has kept frozen between two blocks of ice in the pantry—Austrian households don't yet have refrigerators. There are even some fireworks in the neighborhood. Ellen is not in pain, and for a few hours she seems like her old self, kissing and hugging everyone as if wanting to share her love as generously as she can for as long as possible. The world seems to be in order.

By early February, however, the heavy, gray days have taken their toll on everyone's mood, and Wjera suggests that since she is in town, she and Sidi should find a place with some sunshine for a few days.

Sidi phones Grete Weinberger and Sylvie Dietz—after all, it would be nice to play some bridge in the late afternoon—and they all agree to go to Maria Taferl on the south slope of the Wachau, which has clean air and lovely views as well as the pilgrimage church. Wjera takes care of all the arrangements and finds a pension that allows dogs, because Petzi, her only real competition, has to come along as well.

One sunny winter day, the ladies take the train that saunters along the Danube's left bank to Marbach, and from there they decide to walk—like the countless true pilgrims to this site—up the hill to the basilica of Maria Taferl and its surrounding village.

Sylvie Dietz, Grete Wein-
berger and Sidonie Csillag
in Maia Taferl, 1950

Most of the pilgrims won't come until summer; only particularly devout Catholics and a few locals are visiting this winter day. The ladies lunch at the village's best pub, and afterwards walk along the terraced hillsides above the Danube. It is a bright day; the brown fields lie idle, and the bare trees reveal a splendid panorama of snow-covered Alpine foothills. But the heavy grey clouds gathering in the west will bring more snow overnight.

At a pastry shop, the ladies order Linzertorte and begin the most important task of the day. Sidonie is fifty now, Wjera a bit older, Sylvie and Grete a bit younger and all four are dedicated bridge players. As they sit there playing cards—Sylvie in her little green loden hat, Sidi in her turban—an outsider might have seen the personification of old Austrian respectability, never dreaming that in a few hours Sidi and Wjera will express their mutual love in each other's arms. Sylvie and Grete know but will be as discreetly silent as the grave.

The next day the women trudge through the snowy village in their heavy fur-lined boots for just long enough to be able to say they took a walk. Petzi burrows enthusiastically into the new drifts. Sidi is uncommunicative and pays attention only to the dog. Wjera is tense and fails to attract the focused attention she wants from Sidi. Dark clouds are hovering over their relationship. After one more lengthy bridge game, the weekend is almost over. They will return to Vienna the next morning, and Wjera will continue on to Munich.

Wjera's mother dies in the late fall of 1950, and after all the formalities are taken care of, she no longer has any obligations in Vienna. Even the legal proceedings granting the restitution of the Aryanized Gutmann possessions—Wjera still has a share in them from her first marriage to Ernst Gutmann—have concluded. What is left to bring her and Sidi together except for an open declaration of their love? Wjera seems ready for it. She promises to spend the summers with Sidi and her mother in the Salzburg mountains or the Tirol.

Sidi vacillates between deep happiness and the fear that she'll be torn between her real obligations to her mother and the imagined ones to her lover and it will wear her out. When the three of them meet in August in Walchsee, Mama stays in a single room down the hall, and Sidonie and Wjera dare to share a double room.

But there is a new sense of alienation growing between them. In contrast to Marie-Louise, who had taken to Petzi and looked after him with great pleasure, it annoys Wjera that Sidonie pays so much attention to the dog. She sometimes snaps at Sidi that she should find someone to look after the mutt for a few hours, so that they can be alone. Sidonie feels pressured but also guilty, because Wjera is right, she does transform her fear of intimacy, her panic that she will fail Wjera and lose her, into exaggerated tenderness for Petzi. With increasing frequency, she avoids opportunities to be close to her lover, comes up with excuses when physical tenderness and sexuality seem to be in the offing. She ends up walking halfway around Walchsee late at night, ostensibly because Petzi needs the exercise, while a tearful Wjera waits in the pension.

When confronted, Sidi says that when she's with Wjera, she doesn't want to have any regrets, and she would indeed regret being without

Petzi. Wjera is hurt and feels both unimportant and exposed. After all, she has put her whole heart into this relationship, which for years was simply unimaginable and is still outside the bounds of every social norm. She has risked a lot for Sidi and wants to feel loved and secure in return, but Sidi seems to be retreating like a more and more nebulous shadow.

The quarrels get bigger and bigger, and Petzi is the peg on which they hang their desire for closeness and their pain. Wjera accuses Sidi of treating him more like a lover than a pet; but as soon as she mentions Petzi, Sidi closes down, starts to cry and, obdurate, finally storms out of the room.

One day Wjera issues an ultimatum: it's either the dog or her. Sidi doesn't even need to think about it; offended, she leaves the room with Petzi following in her wake.

The rest of the vacation is a painful and dramatic back and forth between the desire for love and deep fear on both sides. Sidi is desperate, and she thinks about Wjera constantly—one moment wanting to throw herself into the lake and in the next wanting to shower Wjera with gifts, take her in her arms and forget about everything else. In a panic she realizes that her fears are going to materialize: Wjera will leave her.

Sidi returns to Vienna. Wjera returns to Munich, continuing to assert her valid demand for a relationship and consistency. Sidi still hasn't decided; she can barely eat and smokes far too much. She's grateful that there's no shortage of cigarettes now, because otherwise she'd be in a bad way indeed.

And then Wjera sends Sidonie a short letter saying that she doesn't want to see her again. She has waited too long, loved too intensely, cried too much. Sidi should keep her distance, stop sending poems and flowers, leave her alone.

Shocked, Sidi feels her world crumble and fall apart—the worst has happened. She lets a month pass before daring one last attempt. Wjera is in Vienna to close out her mother's apartment and is staying at a little pension in the center of town. Sidonie stakes everything on a single card. Feeling only an ardent desire to talk to Wjera, look into her bright eyes, stroke her wild hair and be happy just for a moment, she walks up the pension stairs and knocks on Wjera's door. When she identifies herself, the door remains closed, and instead of open arms there is only a tired voice saying, "Please, go away."

Sidi is stunned. What a power play! What humiliation not even to open the door but dismiss her and refuse to talk to her! Sidi feels like a fool. Drowning in her own tears, she needs to walk and to cry and then walk even faster all the way back to the Nineteenth District. At home she finally starts to realize how deeply wounded Wjera must feel, and how deep her love must be to have to finally, decisively sever the relationship.

And yet ... doubt, deep pain and anger still sweep through Sidi like autumn storms: Wjera never loved her, was just toying with her and then—the thing she's least able to pardon—let her go without a word. In the coming weeks, she will have to learn to accept this most terrible fact.

She hears nothing more from Wjera, who has left Vienna and returned to Munich for good. After many months, Wjera contacts her one more time, writing to ask Sidi to return all of her letters. It's yet another attack on her aching heart, and Sidi bitterly crams all the paper that once conveyed so much love into a large envelope, watches the postal clerk cancel the stamp, and decides furiously that that chapter of her life is closed for good and Wjera is banished from her heart—but that never proves to be true.

As the pain dulls and the memories fade, what remains, beneath it all, is an abiding love that has been peeled away from its unavailable object like a delicate old transparency. For the rest of Sidi's life it will survive as a relic in her museum of unrealized love.

Years later she will paint one of her best portraits for this museum: Wjera, untouched by time, with her sensitive mouth and bright eyes, watching as the world goes on.

Portrait of Wjera Fechheimer by Sidonie Csillag, 1958

And even later, during a stay in Munich, out of old habit Sidi opens the phone directory and moves her finger down the names starting with F, but Wjera withholds even this tender, second-hand gift. There is no entry under her name; and who knows, perhaps all worldly traces of her have been erased.

Soon after things come to an end with Wjera, Sidi decides it's best to leave Ellen's house and find new, very modest and provisional housing. She can't take any more misery and doesn't want to watch Ellen's inexorable deterioration. She finds a sublet on Hasenauerstrasse in the Eighteenth District, just a small room under the eaves—a bed, a closet, a few old rugs she wrests away from Ed. That's all, and it's enough. She's still devotes herself to Ellen almost every other day, and during these visits she is often the only person, the only medicine, that can calm the dying woman.

On Christmas day 1952 Sidonie answers a phone call from the husband of Ellen's daughter Ruth. Overriding his hesitation and her own surprise that he's called, she quickly asks after Ellen.

He says only, "She died this morning."

Mechanically, Sidonie dresses in a black suit, and soon the Ferstel's driver arrives to take her to the family's house, where she learns that her radiant, beloved friend simply hadn't been able to take it anymore. Ellen, who understood what freedom and love of life are all about, had made use of her freedom one last time. That morning, after everyone had left the house and the cook was out shopping, she moved the mattress from her bed into the kitchen, closed all the doors, settled into the corner next to the stove, and turned on the gas.

As Sidonie approaches the body, now formally laid out, she is suffused by a feeling of deep calm. The soft smile on Ellen's face recalls the radiant woman she used to be, and Sidi knows that her friend has done the right thing.

After the funeral, this envelope of calm and certainty deserts Sidi, and she is left with only a great, dull ache. Losing Wjera has made her old, but losing Ellen has torn out her roots, the last vestige of a feeling of belonging.

The darkest years in Sidi's life descend. She curses the times; she curses Europe, which has brought her nothing but destruction and loss, and its rapid reconstruction means nothing to her. Everything is hideous, everything is a torment. No matter what the season, when the morning light shines into her attic room, she wants it to be dark again, to experience the long evenings that are so much easier to bear than the days.

She drags herself laboriously through the ensuing months and years and often thinks about following Ellen's example. But she already tried that three times in her youth, and it never worked out—obviously she isn't meant to leave life by her own hand, and besides, she lacks the necessary courage.

She assesses the world around her with distrust and repulsion. She finds the music, the movies, the fashions, the consumerism of the 1950s disgusting. Everything is cheap, superficial, made of plastic for the masses; everything that is exclusive, individual and elegant has disappeared. This perspective might also be attributable to the fact that she can no longer afford the latter. The once rich and pampered Sidonie Csillag has become poor and déclassé and has to live according to her means, but she does so with poise and elegance.

When she looks in the mirror—which she generally avoids, even to the point of keeping the treacherous piece of glass covering with a cloth—she sees an older woman with deep furrows around her mouth who smiles even less than before. Eventually, she even cuts off the long hair she always wore in a bun at the nape of her neck—the grey has taken over and it no longer pleases her.

During these leaden years, Sidonie embarks on a pattern of living that she will maintain almost to the end: she becomes a vagabond. Her world has fallen apart, so what is the point of making attachments? She doesn't rent a flat—not unusual in 1950s Vienna, which was still short about 200,000 flats—and doesn't maintain a household of her own; instead she sublets or stays with women friends. Sometimes she has kitchen facilities, most of the time she lives without them and doesn't really care. She doesn't drink coffee or tea, only cold water, and for breakfast she always eats yoghurt and fruit. As a single woman, she sees no reason to invite people to visit and prefers to go out. Her women friends often invite her for lunch, and when she does agree to meet someone, they go to a restaurant.

Once or twice she tries to retrieve some possessions from the household she shared with Ed—possessions she feels rightly belong to her.

But he puts huge stumbling blocks in her way, and she backs off, though she does mention the problem to her friends. Ellen's husband gets so indignant that he personally gives Ed a piece of his mind, after which Ed forks over some of the furniture, the silverware and parts of the famous set of china that once belonged to the actress Katharina Schratt. The silver and china soon find their way to the Dorotheum auction house, where Sidi's father bought her the china as a wedding present. Sidi needs money more urgently than she needs to possess things that she no longer uses.

When this money runs out, she has to go to work again. Having always refused to learn a trade, she can only consider jobs she might be good at without any professional training. For some time she tries being a sales representative for books and wine. But she has no talent for sales and doesn't like trying to persuade someone she neither knows nor wants to know to buy something. She soon gives up on this activity.

Some of her friends ask her to tutor their grandchildren in one or another of the languages she speaks, and according to her needs she gives lessons in English, French or Spanish. She does it because she likes her friends and she likes their children, but she suffers from perfectionism, and in her opinion she herself hasn't really mastered all the rules of grammar.

One day, a friend spots Sidi while she's painting, likes what she sees, and suggests that a little money could be made by painting portraits. Though Sidonie's self-esteem isn't well developed, particularly where her paintings are concerned, she's in urgent need of funds and just hopes that her friends don't have well-tutored eyes for art. Initially, her most important contact is Ellen's husband, who holds an important position in Austria's sugar industry and commissions her to paint all the branch managers. Most of them are quite taken by the quality of their portrait—such an amazing likeness—and soon there are more commissions than she can handle from acquaintances and friends of all ages. Night after night Sidonie agonizes over the details, getting the perspective just right, the eyes at the same height—nothing is simple. And what if they don't like her choice of colors? Sometimes she destroys a half-finished picture in anger and desperation and starts again. To relax in between, she daydreams herself back to Cuba and paints landscapes from memory.

Eventually, portraiture earns her enough money to provide a certain degree of stability and security, but that doesn't make up for the suffering caused by her rigorous perfectionism. And she regrets having to do professionally what she had previously done only for pleasure. One more pleasure is gone from her life, another obligation has been added.

Throughout the dark fifties, and after all her losses, the only thing that can still move her is her great love of animals, specifically Petzi. All her feelings focus on him, she can love him without risk and revel in his trusting cheerfulness. Since the beginning of the 1940s, smart, kind, uncomplicated Petzi has been her most important companion. Though once used to the tropics, he has adjusted well to Viennese winters, though he doesn't like having to wear a muzzle and walk on a leash any more than his mistress does. Those of Sidi's friends to whom he has taken a dislike dread seeing him because he snarls at them in a most unfriendly way and tends to bite if they come too close or tread on his tail even accidentally. Sidonie defends him fervently—the human is to blame—and eventually, they all steer clear of the dog.

Petzi has accompanied his mistress almost everywhere for fourteen years, and that's getting to be a more and more awkward process. He is too fat and can't move very quickly; he is often tired and doesn't eat well. At first Sidonie doesn't want to acknowledge this, but on Sylvie's recommendation she takes him to a vet, who determines that Petzi suffers from nearly every ailment an old dog can have. He is full of tumors that have grown so large it is only a question of time until his organs fail. As long as he isn't in pain, there is no need to do anything, but if Petzi should start having pain, then it would be best to put him to sleep. Sidi is taken aback and can no longer deny another inevitable loss.

In the spring of 1955 Sidonie again moves in with Sylvie Dietz for a while. The Fourth District is still occupied by the Soviets, and every day she crosses Schwarzenbergplatz, officially still Stalinplatz, and also passes the House of Industry, where Allied Headquarters is housed. Shortly after her arrival in Vienna, Sidi had been very concerned about living here, but since Stalin's death in March 1953, the "Russians" have seemed less scary. Nikita Khrushchev, the man who'll soon be in the Kremlin, appears to be more conciliatory, and he knows how to win peoples' sympathy.

That May, the hopes and dreams of thousands of Austrian citizens come true at last: the treaty that will reestablish Austria as a sovereign state has been brokered and is ready to be signed. As with most of the major political events in her life, Sidonie is a witness by accident. She becomes part of the grand May 15 celebration in front of the Belvedere only because she is taking Petzi for a walk at the time, and the only reason she knows what's happening is because it has been the only topic of conversation for weeks. But basically, she just doesn't care. The only detail she remembers, and it's one that makes her uneasy, is that a clause regarding co-responsibility has been deleted from the treaty. She's disgusted that the people responsible for her and her family's expulsion, for the terrible suffering within her circle of friends, are going to have their complicity whitewashed.

Therefore, she can't feel particularly joyful standing there on the periphery of a jubilant mass that reminds her, with a shudder, of previous jubilant masses. And there's also no joy in October at the reopening of the Burgtheater and the withdrawal of the last Allied troops, or the first performance in the reopened Staatsoper in November.

Society might be trying to return to the "old" world, but Sidonie Csillag knows that the old world is gone. So many of the people who were part of it and made it possible are dead, and without them this world seems lifeless and frozen.

For a while now Sidonie has been following the same routine. She works as a governess for the son of the French ambassador, a job she finds easy because she has taken the boy into her heart. After spending the day at the ambassador's residence, she rushes home to walk Petzi around Schwarzenbergplatz. On one such outing, Petzi suddenly disappears. Terribly worried, she calls and calls for him, and when she finally sees him running towards her, she's so happy that he is still capable of running, he gets no reprimand. But after this escape, there's something different about Petzi. One terrible night Petzi grows much sicker and weaker, and the following morning he's no longer able to hold up his head or control his bodily functions. With a heavy heart, Sidi calls the

vet; and when the syringe goes into Petzi's fur and his body grows limp her arms, it's as if a piece of her has been excised.

Despite all her fervent passions, despite all her intense and painful love affairs with women, she has never experienced anything else on this scale. In the weeks that follow, she endures a pain so deep it takes her breath away. This being, which never hurt her, which always lived with her in friendliness, trust and irrepressible vitality, is no more. She gets through the pain, and soon the sharp edges are rounded off, but Sidonie is lonely: there's no longer anyone—no human being and no animal—by her side, and this is how it will be for years to come.

11

MONIQUE

Rio de Janeiro, April 15, 1972

If I had a little corner all to myself, I really might try to write a book. Wouldn't you like to play a role in this book (whether under your real name or a name I'd choose for you)? The book would be dedicated to you. In particular, I'm thinking of writing my memoirs, which would be in three parts: my first great love, my second great love and my last great love!

As Sidonie writes those lines, it is already night in Rio. Sugarloaf Mountain looms dark violet against the sky, and the city's thousands of lights are reflected in the sea. The windows of Sidonie's room offer one of the world's most beautiful views, but she has no interest in it when writing to Monique.

On the fifteenth of every month, exactly, she pulls her chair up to the desk in front of the window, opens her little portable typewriter and writes to a woman she has seen on only a few occasions, many months ago and many thousands of kilometers away, just before she left Europe for Brazil.

Her letters are to a woman a generation younger than she, the mother of a grown son, the partner of a wealthy vintner who is lord of a castle in rural France. Typed in an archaic font using a fading ribbon, they are really only short summaries of the uninterrupted train of thought that she directs across the Atlantic toward this newest infatuation and obsession on a daily basis.

Shortly before Christmas 1970, during a stay in Paris, she had visited Jacqueline and Jean-Pierre Costa, French diplomats with whom she had become close friends during a stay in Bangkok in the early sixties.

They had been making small talk in the drawing room during one of those never-ending receptions or dinners that diplomats have to organize when a woman entering the room immediately captured Sidi's attention. She knew how to make an effect and had obviously staged her entrance. Slender and tall, she was dressed in ecru silk—narrow trousers, a sleeveless top and shawl A charming smile, a graceful turn of the head that moved her long blonde curls just enough to expose her neck, an almost gossamer touch on someone's upper arm, shoulder ... clearly she had mastered the art of moving among guests with elegant coquetry! The diplomats' wives were mute with envy, their husbands and Sidi held their collective breath in the presence of such beauty, such charisma.

Sidi was introduced to the stranger, a cousin of the lady of the house, only when good-byes were being said. She had shaken Sidi's hand and purred *au revoir*, à *bientot* in a soft, erotic voice, but then continued her on-going conversation. When she again took Sidonie's hand to say good-bye a second time, the die was cast.

Passion hadn't burned in Sidi since losing Wjera, and she thought it had been doused forever. But since that night, Sidonie, at age seventy, can think only of Monique, who is perhaps fifty and has rekindled her dreams and her imagination.

Sidi has by now been in Rio de Janeiro for four months, since December 1971, having accepted the Costas' invitation to join them during their diplomatic mission to Brazil to take care of their small son and be their housekeeper. She had consented to this plan because the Costas made her an alluring promise: at the end of their stay in Brazil, she could live with them in their castle in the south of France. Monique lived nearby and oversaw her partner's vineyards.

But time in Brazil passes with tortuous slowness, spoiling Sidi's stay—or at best making her indifferent to it. This is unfortunate, because she's in quite comfortable circumstances here in the official residence in an elegant flat in the Leme neighborhood, one of Rio's best locations. From her window on the building's twelfth floor she has a view of the Bay of Guanabara and Sugarloaf Mountain; the domestic staff looks after everything, and life could be as easy and self-indulgent as it was in the far distant past.

Yet she can't really enjoy herself in the moment and so withdraws, leaves diplomatic and social events early, sequesters herself in her room and travels to Europe in her imagination.

Sidi is actually deeply grateful to Monique, who hasn't the slightest inkling of her feelings and has done nothing to earn her devotion. Once again Sidi had built a pedestal upon which she's installed the object of her adoration, someone who makes her life easier and allows her to feel alive. She loves feeling as if her emotions are intoxicated, however unrealistic it may be, and she loves the obsessive perseveration of her thoughts.

Recalling the past fifteen years, Sidi has to admit that they have been hard, maybe because they had lacked all passion. After losing Wjera in the early fifties, her heart had simply been a barren landscape where other human beings were concerned, and she spent many months just trying to avoid going crazy. With an iron will, she had disciplined her inner self not to get carried away and topple right off the planet. But an even worse phase followed when she recognized that it was impossible to sustain a state of active mourning, and at that point, all the love and pain evaporated into a great empty silence that made what went on in the past seem ridiculous and childish. She had almost longed for a return of the earlier pain, because the stagnant silence, which adjusted everything to fit into a terrible normality, had robbed her of her illusions. Wjera would never be Wjera again.

Throughout the fifties in Vienna, Austria's climate of bourgeois respectability made her furious, and her own poverty was humiliating. She no longer felt free, and so clutched eagerly at an eventual offer of escape.

THAILAND

IN 1960 SIDI'S FRIEND RUTH, ELLEN FERSTEL'S OLDEST DAUGHTER, invited her to live in Thailand with her family for three years. Ruth had married for a second time, to a Dutch diplomat named van der Maade, and she wanted the help and support of someone trustworthy.

Jeanette, Emma Csillag and Sidonie, Kitzbühel, mid 1950s

As a diplomat's wife, she'd be very busy with official duties and wouldn't have time to look after her young daughter. Sidonie had been her own perfect "auntie" for decades and could be something of a mother or grandmother substitute for young Andrea. She would have a comfortable life in a beautiful, exotic country and would even be paid a salary.

It wasn't a difficult decision in light of the long list of defeats she'd endured in the previous, leaden decade. She could count the positive events on the fingers of one hand: her friend from Cuba, Jeanette, had offered a ray of hope when she moved back to Paris and entertained Sidi with letters and visits. And there had been a brief flirtation with Elisabeth, a young woman from Rotterdam she had met in Kitzbühel; she had brought some cheer into Sidi's life. But that was about it.

She had contemplated returning to her brothers in Cuba but was horrified by Fidel Castro and the Cuban revolution that kept the whole world enthralled in 1959. She had even renounced her Cuban citizenship and reassumed her Austrian nationality, and after 1961, she would be glad not to hold a passport from a Communist state.

Accepting the Thailand offer would mean she wouldn't have to keep on half-heartedly considering such options as Cuba just because she was short of money.

Her brother Heinrich and his wife, Mathilde, were less than enthusiastic about her plans. Since her return from Cuba, Sidonie had spent two months each summer with her mother in the Austrian mountains. The rest of the year, Heinrich and Mathilde took care of that aging and increasingly difficult woman, whose tyranny would be focused on them year-round if Sidi were gone. Sidonie couldn't and wouldn't take this into consideration.

Sidi made a short stopover in Paris to say good-bye to her family and Jeanette and then continued on to Rotterdam to see Elisabeth before meeting Ruth and her daughter to embark for Thailand—Ruth's husband would follow later by plane.

Ever since her long journey to Cuba, Sidonie had loved traveling by sea. The vast expanse of blue waters gave her a feeling of infinite independence, and as before, she spent most of her time in a deck chair—dressed for whatever the weather—reading or just watching the waves and the gulls. The ship crossed through the Suez Canal, made a few short stopovers, and after a month docked in Thailand.

Wide-eyed as the big passenger ship approached Bangkok's harbor, Sidonie, Ruth and Andrea watched the throng of little wooden boats that surrounded their last enclave of life in the European style. Ferrying great hands of bananas, mounds of sweet potatoes, baskets of rice and fresh fish to market, the slim, bare-chested boatmen paddled with great skill through the crowd of other small boats, tugboats and the occasional steamer.

One of the small boats transferred the three European women to shore, just as they did the thousands of other people who needed to go upriver in Bangkok every day. Soon, they were installed in a large, newly built house on Bangkok's embassy row. Its enormous living room had tall glass doors that opened onto a large, roofed veranda that was the focal point of the house. The family and Sidi spent most of their time there or in the cool shade of the adjacent tropical garden, which was enclosed by high walls. Soon they acquired a much beloved

Sidonie in the walled garden with two Gibbons and a dog, Bangkok, 1961

menagerie—two big shepherd-cross dogs, a cat, a cock and three Gibbon monkeys named Chico, Benjamin and Hexi. Two domestics were on duty day and night to make sure everything ran perfectly smoothly.

Nobody was in a hurry to get up in the morning. Depending on the weather, Sidonie and Ruth breakfasted together on the veranda or in the garden under two large banana trees. The animals, always keen for something to eat, would encircle the dining table, the dogs on the floor and the monkeys on the backs of the chairs. After breakfast Ruth talked through the menu with the cook and checked to see whether a cocktail party, a small informal dinner or a big reception was on the schedule. Sidi looked after the animals. She combed and brushed the dogs and, with the monkeys' help, devotedly picked the bugs from their fur. If necessary, she took them to the vet. But most of her love and attention was lavished on the monkeys, with Chico her absolute favorite. He had the lightest colored coat and a radiant corona of fur around his dark face. He had arrived as a baby and couldn't yet climb. This stirred Sidi's maternal instincts, and she tried to help with his first attempts at ascent by twining his long, thin arms around a tree trunk and pushing him up from behind. She carried him around for hours while he clung to her neck, and he often sat next to her on a bench or in her lap, his little black paws quickly and cheekily snatching food from her plate. This brought a delighted laugh from Sidi, though Ruth would point out a bit sourly that the animals brought in a lot of vermin. Undiscouraged, after lunch Sidi would fill a basin with warm soapy water and scrub the little monkey in the garden.

Among Sidi's other tasks, also one of her pleasures, was to go to the market with Ruth. The vibrant colors of the goods offered there—be it food or handicrafts—enchanted her every time.

At noon, Sidonie went to pick up Andrea from school. She had learned to drive by then but preferred to be chauffeured. She didn't like to use the bicycle rickshaws, because she found it embarrassing to watch a panting, sweating person pull her weight. She preferred Bangkok's so-called tuk-tuks, small, motorized vehicles that smelled terrible and made an extraordinary racket but moved one about quickly, cheaply and somewhat comfortably. They had the added advantage of making a little sightseeing tour possible.

When Ruth was busy in the afternoons and evenings, Sidi looked after Andrea and tried diligently to help her with her homework, which the girl considered unnecessary and boring, since she was an excellent student and already at the top of her class. She preferred to hang out with her friends and not be dictated to by the old woman she had always called "Aunt" but found rather tedious. She feared Sidi's authority, had no sympathy for what she'd gone through in life—which seemed light years in the past—and couldn't understand why she enjoyed such peculiar, dull activities as card games, puzzles and painting.

In a diplomat's household, there was no shortage of partners and models for Sidi's "peculiar activities." The van der Maade's villa was a stopping off point for many international visitors and she enjoyed the cosmopolitan society that gathered there. She organized regular late afternoon bridge games, and soon the Dutch embassy had a reputation in the international community for its high-class card parties that were on a par with those anywhere in Europe.

Shortly after arriving in Bangkok, the van der Maades and Sidonie applied for membership in the Royal Bangkok Sports Club. It offered delicious snacks, a nice swimming pool and plenty of children for Andrea to romp around with after school. Andrea also rode daily at the

Riding and Polo Club, where she kept her own horse, and Sidi liked going to the stables with her afterwards to hold the friendly little mare and press her lips to the soft, fragrant muzzle while Andrea finished the grooming chores.

Sidonie discovered that she and some of the ladies she encountered shared a passion: painting. One of them suggested that they all get together to paint, since that would make it easier to find and share a model. At first the European women were keen on painting Buddhist monks and the female dancers whose graceful movements and colorful costumes had fascinated them at folkloric performances. For a small donation, one could pick them up on the streets and take them to a garden or parlor for a sitting.

Soon there were weekly gatherings of ten to twelve painters, and though Sidi enjoyed sitting alone in the garden while painting, she also appreciated the company of other talented dilettantes. While waiting for the oils to dry, one had a fine opportunity to chat about the latest affairs, wardrobes, even the tidbits of world politics that the diplomats' wives gleaned from their husbands.

Vacations and weekends were generally spent outside of town, usually on one of the beautiful white sand beaches on the west coast. In the early sixties there was no mass tourism in Thailand, and farmers and fishing families lived in the villages close to the beach. Lacking other options there, the Europeans rented simple bamboo or wooden houses, often built on poles. Sidonie particularly appreciated the animals found in the countryside and could spend hours watching buffalo working in the fields or crocodiles splashing in the lagoons. She only regretted not seeing more elephants.

When Ruth's husband was recalled from Bangkok and the family had to return to Europe, Sidonie decided to stay on with Chico. The Costas, French diplomats who were among her large circle of friends, agreed to hire her as their housekeeper.

But in the spring of 1964 Sidonie received a note from her mother that more or less forced her to say good-bye to her beloved Chico and book passage back to Europe. Emma Csillag had moved to southern Spain with Heinrich and his wife, and she was nearly blind and so ill that more than two people were needed to take care of her.

Sidonie with Chico, Bangkok, 1961

Sidonie prepared to leave with a heavy heart, not because she was attached to any people but because smart, funny Chico almost tied her to Bangkok. She could have taken a dog with her, as long as it had the necessary vaccinations, but a monkey used to living in freedom had to stay where it could enjoy that freedom.

A Swiss couple, business people who had lived in Bangkok for a long time and also kept a Gibbon monkey, agreed to look after Chico as if he were the apple of their eye. A few days before her departure, Sidonie bought a little lidded basket and lined it with a towel to transport her darling to his future keepers. They passed muster, and Chico seemed to get along well with the monkey of the house, a lady Gibbon, but the parting was hell for Sidonie, who turned and ran from the house in tears while Chico was busy chasing through the bushes in the garden. Once again, she had loved an animal above all else, and once again she had lost it...

ALGECIRAS

Sidonie docked in grey, rainy Barcelona in November 1964, and the prospect of looking after her callous but nevertheless needy mother did nothing to improve her mood. She immediately took a cab to the train station and went straight to Algeciras.

While she was still in Thailand, Heinrich had written that he was through with life as a businessman and longed for a warmer climate. Having vacationed in Algeciras and liked it, he and Mathilde had decided to buy a little villa there, with room for Emma and possible guests.

After they moved to Spain in early 1964, Emma Csillag's health rapidly declined. She couldn't be left alone, which made life for Heinrich and Mathilde almost unbearable, and they hoped that having Sidi there would make things easier.

Heinrich picked Sidi up at the railroad station in a light blue car so tiny she had to pull up her knees and rest them against the dashboard in order to fit in the seat. Her suitcase rode awkwardly on the back seat. Unbelievable. Heinrich folded himself in behind the wheel and they whirred along to his new house, which he raved on and on about and which Sidi didn't like from the moment she first saw the small, flat, whitewashed box with a grey lid. It perched on a plot of sunburned land that was distinguishable from the surrounding steppe only because of the surrounding chain-link fence. Inside the fence was what Heinrich obviously considered to be his garden, just one measly little palm tree. Clearly, Heinrich had been forced to curb his lifestyle considerably.

Later, Sidi asked herself repeatedly why her brother had chosen Algeciras of all places—there were far more lovely cities in Andalusia. Maybe it was because it was by the sea, which reminded Heinrich of his youth on beautiful Brioni. Maybe it was the chance to live cheaply in a warm climate, which had attracted many other retired people from northern Europe. And Heinrich valued the political stability of the Franco regime and felt safe in Algeciras. In this he and his sister were in agreement for a change: a conservative government, though preferably a monarchy, was the best of all systems.

Gradually, Sidonie got used to the household's prevailing frugality, but she couldn't get used to dealing with her mother. Now a tiny, stooped old woman with a sparse, light grey fluff of hair and hands disfigured by gout, Emma Csillag constantly needed to have someone near at hand. Having escaped all responsibility for her mother while in Thailand, Sidi felt obliged to unburden Heinrich and Mathilde as much as possible.

Mathilde Csillag in front of the house in Algeciras, Spain

Besides, Heinrich provided a room in his house and discreetly took care of all the expenses, even though his life was no longer a bed of roses.

When Sidonie first arrived, Emma Csillag was still relatively spry. Despite old age and temporary bouts of confusion, she insisted on taking a daily walk in the late afternoon, and she wanted to go on her own, since she would be meeting one of her admirers. Unable to live without her flirtations, if there were no real men around, Emma dreamed one up, and Sidi—still seen as a rival—was forbidden to accompany her. Emma still didn't want a daughter along on an amorous adventure. For Sidi this was as crazy as it was painful. To be pushed away again, and now because of some chimera, was as bitter as ever, and it triggered the old wounded feeling of being unloved.

On returning from her walk, Emma preferred to sit at the window or on the patio and stare into the distance with watery eyes and a toothless smile, making sure she wouldn't miss her admirer's arrival. She knew the train schedule—that it was the old one from Vienna to Semmering made no difference—and she always wanted to be dressed properly to receive her guest.

When her mother was lost in such dreams, Sidi endured her easily, but by evening, when the admirer once again hadn't shown up, Emma turned moody, anxious and fearful, and with age her fears had become almost uncontrollable. During Sidonie's childhood her mother had primarily been afraid of diseases, to this were now added fire, flood and animals. In the grip of her fears, Emma would sit like an anachronistic pile of misery on a tubular steel patio chair webbed with poisonous looking plastic that cut into her thighs and back, until, in tears, she would ask to be taken to her room. Once there, she would quickly lock the door and not reopen it that day.

By early 1966 Emma had grown so weak she could no longer leave the house and sat on the terrace wrapped in a dark blue shawl, staring silently into space. She died that March.

Robert arrived from the US shortly before his mother's death, but Ernst refused to travel all the way to Europe. He hadn't visited Mother in many years and didn't want to see her when she was old, weak and dying. Heinrich, ever practical, thought it best to buy a burial plot in Algeciras; later, he and his wife could also be buried there. Thus, the farewell to Emma Csillag took place on a very small scale, and when the light red soil of southern Spain pattered onto her simple wooden casket, Sidonie was too exhausted after months of caregiving to mourn and felt almost nothing—or rather, she nearly felt relieved. Perhaps the pain of being an unloved daughter could be buried along with her mother.

At any rate, the loss she endured nine months earlier had been so very much harder.

At that time her world had been reduced to caring for Emma and the small, dry piece of land fronting the patio. Only the letters she wrote—always overtired, always late at night—and the answers she received from friends all over the world made her recall that she was still alive. She exchanged many letters with the Swiss couple who had taken Chico, and one day in mid June 1965, they wrote that the little Gibbon had suffered a knee injury and could no longer climb. In the next letter they reported that both his legs were paralyzed and asked if it would be okay to have him put to sleep. That terrible question triggered sleepless nights, and when, after crying for hours, she dozed for short periods, it was only to dream of Chico, tortured by pain, looking at her beseechingly. She knew she ought to make a quick decision, but also knew that it would send the dearest thing to her on the planet on to the other side. Chico relieved her of her anguish by dying in February 1966.

Sidonie broke under the weight of this news, even though she had been prepared for it. She was also enraged. What kind of a cursed God

Robert, Sidonie and Heinrich Csillag with their mother, Emma, Algeciras, 1966

would let Chico die? Full of bitterness, she decided never to set foot in a church again and stayed defiantly at home when all the pious Spaniards went to church on Sunday. Whatever belief she had carried around the world with her all these years was gone for good. Wherever God was, He should stay there.

LIFE IN THE SUBURBS

AFTER TWO DIFFICULT YEARS, SIDONIE HAD HAD ENOUGH OF SPAIN. Her mission there was completed, and her relationship with Heinrich and Mathilde wasn't so close that she would have wanted to stay on.

Sidonie's youngest brother, Ernst, clearly harboring a guilty consciousness for not having done anything to take care of their mother, tempted her with an offer to live with his family in Florida. He, his second wife, a Cuban, and their two children had moved there before the Cuban revolution, and he was now a naturalized US citizen. He said he'd file immigration papers for Sidi, and she could move from chilly Europe to sunny Florida. Having no desire to return to Vienna to scratch out a living teaching languages and painting portraits, Sidonie accepted.

She arrived in Florida for a joyful reunion in June 1966, but after a few weeks, it was clear that she couldn't stay on in Ernst's home. He had become a pedantic bookkeeper who talked about nothing but numbers, and besides, she didn't like Florida. Images of New York's crazy beauty and the freedom she'd felt there began to loom large in her imagination, and she gently told Ernst that of all cities, that was where she preferred to live—though it meant she would have to look for work when she got there.

A few days later, Sidi was on a northbound train. Girlfriends from her Cuba years and her previous stay on the East Coast helped her peruse the classifieds until she found an attractive offer in one of the wealthy New York suburbs: one Miss Herbert was seeking a housekeeper and lady's companion. With a pounding heart she took the train from Grand Central Station to Scarsdale for the job interview. This time, she very much wanted to secure the best possible job, make money and eventually retire on her savings.

If appearances were any guide, she seemed to have made the right decision. Miss Herbert lived in a grand wooden house on a gorgeous estate. A butler answered the bell and ushered her into a large, round foyer with art deco-style windows, then disappeared. Soon, an elegant woman of around sixty, dressed in a perfectly tailored pants suit, emerged through a side door and offered a friendly handshake.

Miss Herbert and Sidi took to one another at first sight. Miss Herbert explained that she needed someone to cook for her and keep her company in this large house she had inherited from her parents. Sidonie had never cooked, the very thought of doing so was anathema, but she decided not to mention this detail to Miss Herbert. After all, cookbooks could provide instructions, and it would not be easy to find another work situation like this one.

For her part, Miss Herbert was fascinated by Sidonie. This was not a professional housekeeper but a woman of the world, and it was not her business to question why, at an obviously advanced age, she would be willing to keep her company in exchange for a decent wage.

Sidonie had never before lived in a suburb and she found that life quite boring at first. Why would anyone want to live where one grand house and garden abutted the next in a monotonous expression of noblesse? Somewhere there was also a shopping mall, where faintly annoyed, well dressed ladies passed their time scurrying from store to store with apparent purpose. The bustle, noise, smells and freedom of New York City were at a safe distance, to be consumed by Scarsdale matrons in measured doses on the weekends.

Still, given the past few years, life at Miss Herbert's was rather like a stay in a sanatorium for Sidi, and for three years the two women lived by a daily routine that suited them both. A cleaning woman and the butler took care of the house, there was a gardener, and everything anyone needed—from groceries to light bulbs—was delivered to the door.

Sidi never saw Miss Herbert before late afternoon and could do as she pleased in the mornings, which she spent reading, solving puzzles or, weather permitting, sitting in the garden. Her only morning task was to put a breakfast tray in front of Miss Herbert's door. Her real workday started in the early evening, when she began preparing dinner. At first, this caused her to break out in a cold sweat triggered by anxiety and perfectionism. A classic standard, *The Joy of Cooking*, was her primary teacher. Every day she chose another, relatively simple meal and followed the instructions to the letter so that absolutely nothing could go wrong.

To be sure, Miss Herbert was not particularly demanding, for she ate Sidi's offerings with great appetite and complimented the cook.

Soon it became clear that Miss Herbert had a crush on Sidi. Initially stiff and seeming older than her years, she started to blossom and began to scratch at Sidi's ladies-companion facade with a chummy kind of charm. This made Sidonie's work easier, but she sensed that she needed to carefully avoid letting Miss Herbert get too close—her neediness was somewhat frightening. Sidi intuited the woman's boundless loneliness and had no wish to add it to her own, and while she found Miss Herbert sympathetic, she did not think her attractive. The only thing beautiful about her was her hands, which clearly had never known work—they offered a pleasing contrast to her heavy-set body and too-puffy face.

What Sidonie found truly appalling about Miss Herbert was her outspoken racism, which, usually after reading the daily paper, she aimed indiscriminately and with fervor at "colored people" and Jews. She often wondered how Miss Herbert would react if she found out that her beloved lady's companion had Jewish origins. To avoid any such suspicion, Sidi acted the good Catholic and pretended to go to church each Sunday morning, but once out of sight of the house, she turned in the opposite direction and used the time for a long walk.

Sidonie found it a bit surprising that Miss Herbert, who strove for conformity, didn't go to church. Obviously, the only god she prayed to was money, of which she certainly had more than enough. She subscribed to all the business magazines and several daily papers, and shortly after waking would don her dark green robe and spend several hours leafing through these publications, mumbling and studying the stock market reports. One day, wearing an expression of utter horror, she told Sidonie that she had just discovered that the bank in which she had placed her trust for lo these many years had done business with the Rothschilds. Reason enough to withdraw her money from that bank and invest it where, in her opinion, it would be safe from Jewish bankers.

When Sidonie first started working for Miss Herbert, she had surmised that she and her employer were about the same age. To be sure, Miss Herbert had made a few remarks that led Sidi to question that assumption; but it was one of Miss Herbert's rare visitors who set the matter straight.

One day a very well-groomed woman, perhaps thirty-five to forty years old, arrived unannounced and asked to see Miss Herbert. A bit put off by the unexpected visit, Sidi asked who she should announce and had stifle incredulous laughter when the lady gave her name and added that she was Miss Herbert's friend from school.

Not long afterward, Sidonie discovered the reason for Miss Herbert's accelerated deterioration. She had already noticed that her employer stayed up until the early morning hours. Whenever Sidi took a turn in the garden before going to bed at midnight, she could see Miss Herbert in her room, either sitting in an armchair or pacing restlessly. Then by accident one morning, she discovered a large number of empty sherry bottles in the garbage can. This unsettled her, because to the best of her knowledge, the grocery deliveries didn't include liquor.

Sidi almost never drank alcoholic beverages and had no idea that in many US states, including New York, liquor could be purchased only in specially designated stores. Those stores also made discrete home deliveries, and apparently Miss Herbert had made a high-proof pact with the butler to spirit each case up to the second floor, where he was given one of the bottles and kept his silence.

Sidi began to pay close attention to the evidence of Miss Herbert's alcoholism, and with the guarded compassion of the truly detached, she noted how the sherry embedded itself in her employer's face, body and speech and left its traces.

At about the same time, Sidi made another discovery. In the USA, it seemed, the garage was used mainly to store items that, for sentimental reasons, one didn't use but had a hard time being parted from. Sidi had noticed several boxes jumbled in a corner of Miss Herbert's garage and found that they were full of paperback books, many with covers showing half-naked women in suggestive poses. Fascinated and horrified, she found that the titles said it all: *We Walk Alone through Lesbos' Lonely Groves*; *Libido Beach*, subtitled *A modern Isle of Lesbos—a sun-drenched*

Sodom just an hour from Manhattan where love has many faces; Perfume and Pain, with the particularly arresting subtitle, *Could she have been born a lesbian? She knew no desire but that for another woman.* Though it felt both embarrassing and forbidden, Sidi rummaged through all the boxes, but she couldn't muster the courage to take any of the books to her room. So she crouched in the garage, reading quickly, short of breath, simultaneously scandalized and worried that she'd be discovered.

Now she understood what connected her to Miss Herbert, understood the many compliments and awkward hints. Of course she would take care not to say anything, but Miss Herbert's loneliness and the many sherry bottles now made more sense, given this wealthy yet barren puritanical environment.

Once a week, Sidonie spent a day in Manhattan doing errands, going to a museum or meeting friends. She occasionally longed for a bridge game, but her time in the city was too short for a satisfying one.

One day she went to the Social Security Administration's office with a routine question, and since she wasn't used to the jargon and the requirements of that particular bureaucracy, it took a while. Looking through her papers, the clerk noticed her birth date, raised an eyebrow and asked if she was really still working. In response to her outraged "of course," he pointed out that like everyone over age sixty-five who had worked in the US and paid into social security, she was eligible to collect benefits. This was both music to her ears and a huge shock. She had been paying in intermittently since 1945, and most recently it has apparently been unnecessary. Seeming delighted by Sidonie's strange mix of European femininity and complete naiveté, the clerk gave her the required paperwork, explained the formalities and told her to get in touch with him anytime if she had questions. She didn't plan to tell Miss Herbert about this until she was sure that it was going to work out.

In the spring of 1969 Sidonie learned that her monthly social security check would be for 69 US dollars. At the time, the exchange rate was 25 Austrian shillings or four Deutschmarks to the dollar. In the states, a gallon of gas cost 25 cents, as did a hamburger. Nevertheless it was, as one said in Austria, "too little to live on, too much to die."

When the time came, it was easy to tell Miss Herbert she was planning to quit, though Sidi did feel a bit of compassion for the lonely woman she had taken something of a liking to. She knew there wouldn't be another companion and Miss Herbert would be even lonelier. She promised that she would stay in touch; and in the years that followed, whenever she was in New York she took the train to Scarsdale to pay a visit.

SPAIN AGAIN

WHILE WAITING FOR AN ANSWER FROM THE SOCIAL SECURITY AGENcy, Sidonie had been thinking rather frantically about what to do with her new-found freedom. She didn't want to stay in the States, neither New England nor Florida had triggered particularly positive feelings in her. She knew there wouldn't be enough money to live comfortably in Vienna, and if she thought about it, she no longer felt any particular longing for that city. If Chico were still alive, she would have gone straight back to Bangkok, but without him it was just a hectic, unpleasant, empty shell. Maybe she could go first to Elisabeth in Rotterdam and then to friends in Paris ... and if Spain was still as cheap as it used to be, she could try to live there. Her mother had always needed her, so she hadn't had time to explore that country, now maybe she could travel spontaneously and indulge in its people, the warmth and the colors.

In the summer of 1969 Sidonie returned to Algeciras and with Heinrich's help located a small house that was just perfect. The rent was so low she could even afford to hire a local housekeeper. In the summer, with southern Spain at its warmest, Sidi realized that she hadn't felt such a sense of well-being in a long time. Once again mistress of her own time, she could put up her easel when and where it pleased her, get up in the morning when she felt like it, meet with people if the urge struck her. Soon, she'd gathered a small coterie of bridge players.

On warm evenings, and "evening" began quite late in Spain, Sidi often strolled through the streets of Algeciras, thinking that there was still so much travelling to do. But Algeciras held her. It was full of beautiful young people from all over the world—the women in gauzy summer dresses and bikinis were particularly attractive. The Spanish women were too short for her taste, but among the tourists she often saw women whose appearance—or more particularly their bearing—reminded her of Leonie Puttkamer or Wjera Fechheimer. She recalled with longing the years when her passionate obsessions had kept her life in motion, kept her alive. It had been years since a woman had touched her heart, and the great interior stillness she'd harbored for so long had begun to resemble boredom. She wanted to feel that all-consuming fire once again but didn't know how; and since it wasn't available on demand, and since at the age of sixty-nine she felt too old for such infatuations, she tried to keep her heart in check.

In September faithful Jeanette visited from Paris, and being in her company doubled the pleasure Sidonie got from gazing at women in the city's small pubs and bars. Jeanette had a sharp eye and never missed a beautiful dress, erect carriage, a good pose. And, rather anachronistically, the two aging ladies frequented the places favored by young locals and pleasure-seeking tourists, where everyone enjoyed the fine Spanish cooking and on-going Flamenco performances.

Sidi found Jeanette's enthusiasm for the music contagious, and when they patronized a different bar every evening, she felt young and daring—though the unaccustomed late-night hours made it hard to get out of bed, and both women felt their age the next morning.

Elisabeth, Sidi's Rotterdam flirtation, arrived after Jeanette left. She had driven down from Holland and wanted to visit several of Andalusia's cities with Sidi. When they discovered Ronda, a beautiful medieval town surrounded by a mighty wall, Sidi knew she had to paint it.

Cursing softly, Elisabeth had to park outside the city walls, and Sidi quickly gathered up her painting materials and ran on ahead. The perfectly maintained old town was built around a castle, and they spent the afternoon exploring, tripped over the bumpy cobblestones of each new lane that Sidi found enchanting, and taking in the spectacular view from the city wall. Eventually, an exhausted Elisabeth pointed out to Sidi that they hadn't seen a hotel, pension or even a restaurant anywhere. But when Sidi took a liking to something, she either had no interest in reality or she adjusted it to fit her needs. In this case, she started asking women in the streets if there might be a room to be let and found one in half an hour.

Sidonie arranged a price for a three day stay, and that turned into a week, but when she wanted to add a second week, Elisabeth went on strike. She got into her car and promised to return in a week. When she did so, she hardly recognized her friend, who couldn't talk about anything but her paintings and had made four sketches, the second of which was evolving into a "true" oil painting that was almost finished. She had painted it by the light of an oil lamp, because the town was so prone to power outages that people were used to relying on such old-fashioned lighting. The local children usually stayed up past midnight and often played in the streets if the moon was bright enough—this was the scene Sidonie had been able to capture. Elisabeth liked the painting a great deal. Perhaps feeling the need to assuage a bit of guilt, Sidonie gave it to her, though she did so with a heavy heart as she was particularly proud of it. It became Elisabeth's favorite painting and for many years was displayed prominently in her Rotterdam flat.

It was usually warm and comfortable in southern Spain until mid December, when the weather turned wet and shockingly cold. The winter Sidi had spent in Algeciras taking care of her mother had been unusually warm and dry, and in addition, Heinrich's new house—despite its ugliness—was much better insulated than Sidi's small old one, where the inescapable, creeping chill make her bones and joints ache. Some days it was so cold and damp that Sidonie simply chose to stay in bed. One of her neighbors noticed that this strange foreigner had nothing with which to defy the chill and brought Sidi a *brasero*, a small coal brazier designed to fit underneath a table. But the *brasero* still did not make it warm enough for her to paint, so she continued just to stay in bed on rainy days. Just a bit of sunshine, however, was enough to make a day quite pleasant, and Sidonie would set up her easel in the garden and make herself believe that the rainy season was over, which actually wouldn't happen until April. But then, within days, it grew warm, the air filled with the smell of blossoms and Sidonie was again delighted that this little spot on Earth allowed her to lead such a pleasant life.

Sidonie remained relatively carefree until November 1970, when, once again, she was confronted by the fact that she had used up all her savings. She had a hard time believing it, having saved quite frugally while at Miss Herbert's and spent little in the past year. Where had all those dollars gone? Her social security wouldn't be enough to live on, she was sure of that.

She might have been able find a job in the tourism industry during the summer, but now, at the beginning of winter, that was impossible. Then, at the most opportune moment, a letter from Vienna informed her that a friend's son had opened a small agency that sold theater and opera tickets, and he was desperate to find reliable employees. Sidonie replied that she would be willing to help out during the coming winter; she had no desire to experience the previous year's cold and damp ever again.

En route to Vienna, Sidi stopped in Paris, primarily to visit Jeanette, but when she learned that her beloved Ruth would staying in Paris with the Costas at the same time, her heart did a little dance. The Costas, their mutual friends from Bangkok, lived abroad most of the time and they wanted to use their limited time in Paris to see all their friends and relatives, so they were giving dinner parties two or three times a week.

Sidi attended one of those parties shortly after she arrived in Paris, though she had had reservations about accepting the invitation—she was still travel weary but also, she now endured large crowds less and

Sidonie painting a portrait in France

less well. She knew only a few of the twenty or so guests from her time in Thailand, and it took some effort on her part to mark their reunion with an appropriate display of pleasure.

And then Monique came on the scene, and that event would occupy Sidonie for years to come.

In the days that remained before her departure for Vienna, Sidi did everything humanly possible to arrange a meeting with the unknown beauty. Immediately following the dinner party, she dared to telephone Jacqueline Costa early in the morning. When Sidi, a famously late riser, dropped Monique's name, Jacqueline understood which way the wind was blowing, but she nonetheless readily answered the insistent questions about her cousin.

Jacqueline explained that Monique had a grown son, who was as beautiful as his mother, and a companion who was a well-known playboy—which was about all one could say about him. At that point, Sidi heaved a great sigh. Why, she wondered, did she always fall for women who were already with men? Monique would be in Paris for a few days before returning to her partner's estate in the south; if Sidi wanted to see her again, it could surely be arranged.

When she and Jacqueline met Monique at a small restaurant two days later, Sidonie was wearing her most elegant suit and all the jewelry she still possessed after so many lean years. She stared incessantly at Monique, and after taking just a few bites, put down her knife and fork and hardly touched her food again. Monique, who must have noticed the fervent way this peculiar woman had hung on her every word at the Costa's party, found her behavior at the restaurant inhibiting and almost aggressive. What did this stranger with the cultured speech and the piercing gaze want from her?

On the way home, Jacqueline told her cousin that Sidonie had always preferred women and obviously found her fascinating. Monique shrugged this information off with a nervous, dismissive laugh and quickly suppressed the hint of that flattered feeling she always got when someone admired her. She was used to this from men ... but from a woman! Is this what things had come to?

So it was best that she didn't have an inkling about the internal and external machinery Sidi had already set in motion. The two meetings were sufficient to guarantee that for years to come, Monique would be installed—persistently and unrealistically—in the role of Sidonie's third great love.

Sidi arrived at Vienna's Westbahnhof after the Christmas holidays and found that the grey and bustling city felt like a strange place indeed.

She quickly found a sublet, met with old friends and acquaintances and sometimes wondered if it has really been ten years or only ten days since she was last here. In no time she was back in her old familiar circles; and if a member of her generation had died, she found that the next welcomed the old auntie into its midst in the very best Viennese tradition.

The theater and opera ticket agency did indeed have work for her, and for the first time in her life, she genuinely enjoyed her job. It was not difficult; all she had to do was speak with people in different languages all day long. She didn't earn much, but it was enough to live on.

In the early summer of 1971, Jacqueline Costa sent Sidonie a letter asking if she could imagine going to Brazil for two years. The situation would be similar to when she cared for Ruth's daughter in Bangkok; Jacqueline's son Laurent was now ten and needed someone like Sidonie to look after him when his parents were busy. Sidi was touched that Jacqueline had thought of her, but she was also concerned about being responsible, at her age, for a boy soon to enter puberty.

She noticed the postscript only when reading the letter a second time: "If you want to talk about the details, join us this summer in Carcassonne."

Of course she would go to Carcassonne—not on Jacqueline's account but just to see Monique again. She did indeed see Monique several times during her three-week stay, and each encounter had been the highlight of her day. The two invitations to visit Monique's castle had been especially thrilling, and afterwards she flatly refused to acknowledge that the conversation had been superficial, the object of her admiration artificially charming and the visits quickly terminated.

Before returning to Vienna, Sidi made a promise that she would return to Paris in November 1971 to sail for Rio with the Costas. She had, however, set one condition: when the Costas returned to France after two years, she would accompany them to their castle as their permanent housekeeper, family friend and live-in companion. Their castle was so conveniently close to Monique's.

Sidi's friends in Vienna were surprised to hear that she would take her leave again after just a short stay. At afternoon teas and bridge parties, all agreed that it was rather unusual for a lady her age to take employment in Brazil. Sidi thought it quite normal, because the fuel for this adventure was named Monique, but nobody needed to know that.

She quickly gave away or packed up most of her remaining belongs. Her friend Christl Kmunke had a small room in her flat where she agreed to store the few pieces of furniture, the boxes of photos and memorabilia and the rolled canvasses with Sidi's oil paintings. Sidi might have stored these things elsewhere had she known that Christl would die the following year and a friend of hers would clear out the flat. Relatives of that friend looked after the furniture, but the paintings, the embodied memories of many years, all disappeared.

BRAZIL

Rio de Janeiro, August 19, 1972

One always says that one is only as old as one feels, but this isn't true. It's a misfortune if one has feelings that do not correspond to one's age! For the first time in my life, I regret not being younger.

Excuse me for saying this to you, but if I were twenty years younger, I'd do anything to conquer you! But since this isn't the case, I have sworn to myself, from the first moment on, to do nothing! I'll always be content to see you, to hear your voice; but you have to feel a certain sympathy towards me and experience my presence as something pleasant!?

Once again Sidonie sits in her room high above Rio's waterfront and dreams of a castle amid vineyards where her third great love resides. Everything having to do with Monique is unstable terrain through which she builds safe paths for her regular letters to follow, in the hope that they'll create real access to her beloved. But Monique doesn't reply to her letters, doesn't communicate and remains a vague image that mingles hope and anxiety.

Sidonie finds her everyday life in the reality of Rio de Janeiro increasingly gloomy. As agreed, she takes care of Laurent, but even though she likes the boy, dealing with a boisterous eleven-year-old who is rapidly moving towards puberty is more a burden than a pleasure. He doesn't listen to reason and certainly isn't going to listen to an old woman who has been set up as an authority figure. He impresses this on Sidi quite forcefully: when she wants to do his homework with him, she can't find him—in addition, she can no longer keep pace with some of the things he has to learn for school. When it's time to put him to bed, he hides in the garden. And when he is supposed to eat breakfast, he won't even sit down but grins at her brazenly, takes something out of the fridge that is intended for his parents, and disappears.

Sidi is no longer strong enough to control him, and such episodes stretch her to the limit. Increasingly, she questions the wisdom of remaining in Rio. Already overextended by her duties as diplomat's wife, Jacqueline hardly bothers with her son at all. In addition, her poor circulation means she can't tolerate Rio's hot, muggy climate, and she often spends consecutive days in her room, where the noise from three fans gives the illusion of cooler air.

For his part, Jean-Pierre is constantly away on diplomatic missions and is no help at all with Laurent. If he does happen to be at home, he's obliged to host hordes of guests at receptions or dinners. Sidi attends these receptions, but in her heart she hates to spend her evenings with people she doesn't care about. They drain her energy, and she usually retreats early, puts on her nightgown, thinks about Monique and falls quickly into a light sleep.

She can't even muster the energy to paint. The only thing she enjoys when she has time to herself is listening to the radio. When carried away by the rhythms she hears on some of the music programs, she understands the notion of *saudade*. This difficult to describe sentiment combines longing and desire, and it has been her life's companion—though she only learned the right term in Rio. She thinks wistfully of the days when she both desired and was desired, but they are gone along with the beauty of which she had always been so proud. Now, she must resign herself to being the modest observer. Nevertheless, fate has sent Monique, and this new passion allows Sidi to forget her age from time to time.

Sidonie lives from day to day, joining the family if there is a weekend excursion to the cooler mountains around Rio; but she has no eye for the lovely scenery, tires easily and remains self-absorbed.

On one such trip, in January 1973, Sidonie finds that she likes the little baroque cities in the state of Minas Gerais so much that she considers staying there for a few days to paint, but instead she journeys on to the capital, Brasilia, with the Costas.

At one of the many evening receptions in Rio, Sidonie meets Catherine, who reminds her quite astonishingly of Monique. When they shake hands, twice, when saying good-bye, there seems to be evidence of a special connection. Catherine soon realizes that Sidonie had taken a liking to her, and her subsequent behavior indicates that she is not entirely reluctant, but Sidonie is embarrassed and remains very cautious. She doesn't understand why a woman who has given birth to five children, once worked as a model and is on her second marriage, would be interested in her. She adroitly evades Catherine's personal invitations at first, but in November she writes to Monique:

> I know that there is a big difference between the effect Catherine has on me and the effect you have on me. I'm always most delighted to see Catherine, but she doesn't excite me, and I never have a problem falling asleep after I have seen her. When I have been together with you, I am excited and cannot sleep.

Having originally promised to stay in Rio for two years, Sidi thinks more and more often of making an earlier return to Europe. It torments her that Monique hasn't gotten in touch in a year and a half. She harbors no illusions, but nevertheless, she continues to write to her with clockwork regularity—despite reality, or maybe in an attempt to create a new one.

> I wish I were in Fifi's place so I could sit at your side and put my head on your knee. And if I were Fifi, would you pat my head softly with your small, graceful hand…? But unfortunately, I'm not Fifi!!!!!

On a woman friend's recommendation, she goes to see the film *Harold and Maud*, and the way it portrays the conflict between love and age both shocks and envelops her. She has to report this to Monique:

> For sure the actress wasn't eighty; she must be around sixty. I could understand if a young man fell in love with Catherine. But she is fifty-three and a very attractive woman who comes across as being quite young. I want to show you how objective I am: I'm not yet eighty, but surely at an age when it is no longer possible to kindle love. Once I read something about this that impressed me: "Old age is the most terrible curse in this world. It takes away all one's pleasures; one gives up all desires and allows free rein to suffering." I don't think one can apply this generally, but for the person who said it, it must have been true, and for me it holds true as well. I have feelings for you that do not correspond to my age, but I don't deny them, and I'd be more than happy if I could secure your friendship, which is independent of age. In my thoughts, I embrace you with all my heart. I'm already quite restless, because I want to see you again and hear your voice again.

When she finally makes up her mind to leave Brazil earlier than planned, she's in inner turmoil: it means she'll soon see Monique again, but at the same time, she fears the reunion, because she expects it will decide her future. Will she be able to stay in the Costa's castle, paint, laze about, actually live in that neighborhood—at least as a well-tolerated friend—and meet with Monique once a week?

At the end of June 1973, Sidonie flies from Rio to Miami to visit Ernst and Robert. In her last letter to Monique, written before her departure, she again draws comparisons with Catherine:

> When I left, you didn't ask me to write to you, and during my long absence you haven't written one word to me. I'm sure that Catherine would have responded to each of my letters.
>
> Sometimes I ask myself if I do not love Catherine more than you, but unfortunately there is no doubt that I'm much more in love with you!!!
>
> But soon! I feel a bit like a defendant waiting for her verdict. And you are the judge!!!

After the visit with her brothers and a brief stay in New York, Sidonie arrives in Paris at the beginning of August, and once again the familiar restless, unhappy mood sets in—there's nothing to keep her there. She immediately boards a train to the south, then takes the bus to her final destination. Sidi finds the reunion with the woman she has adored from afar for two years overwhelming. As attractive as ever, graceful and elegant, when they meet, Monique grasps Sidi's hand and says with a radiant smile, "Bonjour, Aunt Sidi." "Aunt Sidi" has become an accustomed form of address in recent years, and Sidi ignores it, as she does Monique's nervousness and superficiality, her complete lack of any joy at this reunion.

In the weeks that follow, Sidonie rides an emotional roller-coaster. She regularly sends flowers and little cards to Monique but never receives a thank you. Then she makes Monique a present of an inscribed gold ring. This is graciously accepted, and Sidonie is invited to visit over the weekend.

She is not the only guest; every room in Monique's house is occupied, and the hostess doesn't exchange a single private word with her.

When she returns to the Costa's after this disturbing weekend, Jacqueline—who is in residence for a few weeks—takes her aside for a serious talk. It has been tearing her apart for some time now to watch her besotted old friend chase around the world like a fool just in order to be near her pampered and totally disinterested cousin. Jacqueline knows her cousin very well and tries to make it clear to Sidonie that Monique is only toying with her, that she ridicules Sidi behind her back.

But facts have never held much sway with Sidonie. She sighs, and says that considering Monique's beauty, there's not much she, Sidonie, could do to address such observations anyway. Besides, in the course of her long life she has had plenty of experience dealing with pampered women.

And anyway, she doesn't care; she just wants to see Monique's slender, elegant figure, smell her perfume and listen to her voice.

In the late fall, after several weeks of chasing after her destiny in France, Sidi has to acknowledge, to her great disappointment, that nothing is going to come of her dream of living in Jacqueline's castle. Not because Jacqueline is unwilling to fulfill her wishes, but because the castle doesn't have a heating system, and one simply can't live in it during the winter. But maybe that's alright. Monique doesn't have the slightest interest in being in touch with her, why should she freeze unnecessarily in an icy castle because of an icy heart. She can make a life for herself in Vienna.

Nevertheless, her infatuation with Monique will dominate Sidonie's thoughts for several more years. During her frequent visits to France, she is always ready to drop everything and do whatever is necessary to be close to her. Plans with friends are cancelled at the last moment, and they must be very patient with her in the face of an unexpected opportunity to see Monique—even only for a few hours.

And then, one day, the fire is simply extinguished. Sidonie and Monique are at the same party; it is getting late, and Sidonie no longer feels that anything is keeping her there. She leaves the salon, goes to bed— and it is over.

IN VIENNA AND ABROAD

SIDONIE RETURNS TO VIENNA FROM FRANCE WITH A HEAVY HEART. She will have to start all over again. When she hears that Sidi is looking for a place to live, her old friend Countess Stürgkh suggests that she contact Countess Kuenburg, who still lives in a beautiful large flat in the Third District near the Donaukanal. After her husband's early death, she had decided to rent out a few rooms.

The situation turns out to be ideal. Inge Kuenburg, a good-looking woman in her mid-fifties, already rents two other rooms to ladies of her social class—now there will be a perfect constellation for frequent bridge parties. Sidi won't be living on her own, which she would prefer, but neither does she have any obligations. Her large room, where she feels quite comfortable, is cleaned twice a month, and there is a shared kitchen, though Sidi uses only the refrigerator, where she keeps her yoghurts and tomatoes. She doesn't even consider cooking for herself; there are so many nice restaurants that provide better and more inexpensive meals than she could create. Besides, she's almost always invited somewhere for lunch; and she accepts all invitations with great pleasure.

Sidi also has the pious countess to thank for her return to religion. After Chico's death she had bitterly renounced her belief in god, but her friend's quiet ways, her constant worry about Sidi's salvation and her questions about the meaning of life—"What will happen to you, when you die?" is her favorite—convince Sidi that it might be useful to placate Christianity's long-neglected god by going to church once again and thus secure herself a place in the hereafter.

In early 1976 Sidi gets the urge to travel again. She has enough time and a bit of money and wants to visit friends all over the globe.

Her first destination is Thailand. The real reason for this trip, which nobody is allowed to know about, is Chico. That wound still hasn't healed, and Sidi at least has to visit the place where her little monkey is buried. Maybe then she will be at peace with him. Her old friends in Thailand have urged her to visit, and she doesn't let on that they are taking a back seat to her Gibbon. Once she has seen the little sandstone slab in her Swiss friends' garden and shed a few tears, she's content and reassured. She has said good-by and can leave Thailand behind her.

Her next trip will also be in the interest of finding closure and a certain peace of mind. She wants to go to Cuba. On a visit to her brothers in Florida, she sees a good offer for a flight via Mexico City and a one week stay in Cuba. With her Austrian passport, she has no visa problems, and soon she is on Cuban soil again after more than twenty-five years.

She is both overcome with emotion and utterly shocked. Her feelings tell her that this is a homecoming; her eyes tell her something very different.

On the drive from the airport to the city center she has already noted the miserable state of her beloved, once rich Havana. The old buildings on the Malecón and in Habana Vieja are half decayed, the colors faded, the plaster crumbling. This sad picture is rounded out by a row of ugly, Soviet-style plattenbau apartments in which the residents are forced to live cheek by jowl.

Inwardly, Sidi curses Fidel Castro, who in her view is the one responsible for this obvious decay.

But maybe she'll still find corners where her heart will feel at home. She'll have a whole week here; that isn't much, but it's better than nothing.

Castro's Havana

What she wants most is to locate some of the paintings she left behind in Cuba. In particular, one that Rosa, her younger brothers Ernst's first wife, has and Sidi doesn't have a copy of. She knocks on many doors and makes many inquiries, but though everyone is generally helpful, she's unsuccessful.

Her search for the painting is, to a certain degree, also a search for a piece of herself, something to bring back the lovely feeling of life in the forties, and eventually it takes her to the house in Miramar where she lived with her brothers.

She has been warned that the house will be unrecognizable. She dismissed the warning, but it proves true. What were once single-family houses are now crowded collectives shared by multitudes of people, chickens and goats. Sidi can't even locate her former house until the children she asks point to a wild green square that she recognizes as her former garden. She fights her way through the wall of greenery to the entrance, where the plaster is crumbling away, but traces of the house's soft charm remain. Though if something isn't done soon, this ruin will be lost. But most of the houses in Havana, even those built only ten years ago, are already in need of repair.

She climbs the decaying stairs to her former rooms; each step still feels familiar, but the rooms themselves are a battlefield of cracked flooring and sagging wallpaper. Feeling nostalgic, she steps onto the terrace and looks out over the splintered railing into the garden, whose once well-contained tropical greenery she had so enjoyed painting. But she is neither angry nor bitter—not any longer. It is over. Like everything else in life, Cuba has changed, and there is nothing here to hold on to. She is simply grateful that during times that were so much more her times, this country offered both security and joie de vivre.

After some hesitation, Rosa finally agrees to meet her, but with constant warnings that Sidi must be careful not to say anything during their reunion that could cause trouble. Everywhere the walls have ears, and Rosa doesn't want trouble with the authorities.

Convinced that there is no way Sidi can be careful enough, an extremely nervous Rosa visits Sidi at her blocky, Soviet-style hotel, where they sit in the lobby to talk—hotel guests are not allowed to take visitors to their rooms. Rosa keeps glancing around the room and speaks only in whispers.

She tells Sidi about the government's possible plans to offer the Csillags' former home to an embassy, explains how difficult it is to lead a normal life in today's Cuba, but talks mostly about Marie-Louise. After Sidi left Cuba, Rosa had been her successor with Marie-Louise, who had died a few years earlier and left Rosa feeling very lonely. She lives with her sisters now, who she loves a lot, but although they know Rosa and Marie-Louise lived together, and they accepted her into the family as Rosa's best friend, the true nature of their relationship had always been hidden behind a veil of knowing silence. Since Marie-Louise's death, Rosa hasn't dared to approach other women. In the forties and fifties, everything had been so much more nonchalant, but now there's a chance of being denounced, and at her age, she has no desire to be sent to a reeducation camp.

At the end of the week, while drinking a last fresh mango juice at the Havana airport before boarding the plane to Mexico City, Sidonie understands that this is her final farewell to her beloved Cuba. She doesn't ever want to return and spend money that will benefit that bearded trailblazer for communism. Cuba is a beautiful memory, another chapter she can close for good.

Back in Vienna she returns to her routine of lunch with friends, bridge parties and occasional excursions until, in 1980, her landlady, Inge Kuenburg, dies suddenly at the age of sixty-five. Sidonie had moved in with the countess convinced that she would stay there for the rest of her life. Now she has to look for a place to live and worry about practical things she finds fundamentally distasteful. She's eighty years old and doesn't want to waste time on life's ridiculous, everyday banalities.

Ellen Ferstel's younger daughter, Lotte, is a friend with whom Sidi can talk about such worries. Determined and full of good will, Lotte starts calling various institutions that might offer a lady a suitable place for her retirement. After a brief search, Lotte locates a women's residence run by the Catholic charity Caritas—apparently, Sidi's attempt in recent years to reconcile with god via regular church attendance has borne fruit. Lotte and Sidonie go to inspect the residence and the bourgeois women who reside there, and in just minutes Sidi decides to take one of the rooms.

12

"NOT ONE DAY GOES BY WHEN I DON'T THINK OF HER..."

SIDONIE'S HAND SHAKES AS SHE TRIES TO FIT HER KEY INTO THE lock on the door that leads into the garden that gives her access to the big yellow building on Frauenheimgasse. She never succeeds on the first try, and one of these days she's afraid she simply won't make it home because she can't unlock this door. She presses her hand firmly against the door frame and the key cooperates. These infernal tremors! It's also gotten hard to drink from a glass, and that is embarrassing. Today, during dinner with her young friend, there was almost a fiasco. Since her head wobbles in time with her hands, but in the opposite direction, if she didn't always request a straw, the ice-cold tap water she favors would spill across the table, onto her lap, onto the floor. The doctors have told her she's in perfect health, not a trace of Parkinson's.

One shouldn't get old, not as old as she is now. Until she turned ninety, she felt much as she had all her life—ageless, untouched by limitations or weaknesses. But now, at ninety-six, she has started to curse her very existence.

The door finally opens; a final wave to her young friend, who has driven her home from their dinner together; a gentle smile. The door closes behind her. It has gotten late, and that signals the start of the most pleasant part of the day for Sidonie. In the hours between midnight and four, the darkness and silence create an expanse of space in which she can travel through her thoughts and memories, free of her body.

She still has plans for tonight. She'll pull the wooden board on which she does jigsaw puzzles out from under her bed and continue with the one that has commanded her attention for days: a Spanish frigate with two thousand pieces—a few got left out at the factory, but that's always the case, and this ship must embark on its great voyage minus two or three elements. The picture is all in muted brownish-yellow tones that tire her eyes and make finding the right piece more difficult, but it's almost complete, and she'll finish it tonight.

Sidonie walks slowly to her small room on the mezzanine level. It has a view of the now-flourishing garden, a closet to the right, two armchairs with a table between for her guests. To the left is a dresser, behind it a bed and, half hidden behind a screen, a fridge. All of these items merit the adjective "small." On the walls are a few photos of family members and also of Kaiser Franz Josef and the revered Kaiserin Sisi, some of her paintings from Thailand, and her portrait of Wjera. There is a huge stuffed dog on the bed. She doesn't want and doesn't need any more than this.

Sidonie has liked living in this residence for seniors from the very first day. Everything is taken care of, she has no obligations, and she is still grateful to Lotte for discovering it.

The idea of founding a residence that would suit the needs of ladies from the aristocracy and high military circles first came up in 1881 in the salon of Auguste von Littrow-Bischoff, and soon afterwards, together with other wealthy ladies, she started to bring it to fruition. She had inherited a beautiful villa and garden from her father, and after making some adjustments, she opened it for twenty pensioners in 1883. In 1906, the villa was enlarged to make room for a total of twenty-seven ladies, each of whom had her own room, furnished with her own possessions.

Erzherzogin Marie Valerie, Kaiserin Elisabeth's youngest daughter, supported the institution for many years; a plaque in the foyer continues to honor her memory. Charity was considered an obligation not only for the women of the royal family but also for everyone belonging to the high aristocracy. This revenue source supported the residence for many years, and ladies from those circles still take on charitable tasks there. Today, this institution for old women continues to flourish due to the ongoing support of Caritas, the official Catholic charity, and of private Catholic benefactors.

A renovation in the mid-1980s added an in-house nursing ward so that residents who become dependent on care would no longer need to relocate. During the renovation, Sidonie was offered a larger room, which she could have furnished a bit more luxuriously, but she declined. It wasn't just a lack of financial resources that prompted this decision. Rather, despite, or perhaps because of the fact that she had grown up in luxury, Sidonie didn't really care about material possessions. They were there to be enjoyed and used, but why have more of them than necessary? Why the need to own them?

Despite her life-long disinterest in financial matters, Sidi is aware that the residence is far more expensive than her retirement income can cover. She is currently receiving a monthly social security payment of 357 US dollars, plus supplemental money from the Austrian government, but this does not cover the monthly fees at the residence and never has. She didn't think it was right to take a more expensive room when she couldn't even pay for her small one. True, she still has some of the money she saved from the sale of her father's former factory in France, but she guards it as if it were the apple of her eye.

Thanks to Lotte's good advice, Sidi recently applied to the Austrian National Fund for Victims of the Holocaust and received 70,000 Schillings (the equivalent at the time of about 5,000 Euros). She has no idea what to do with such a large sum at her age, and though she listens to the ideas her friends propose—telephone all her girlfriends who live abroad, treat herself to taxi rides—she rejects them as unnecessary and wasteful.

At half past three in the morning Sidi gives the Spanish frigate a final satisfied perusal and puts it back underneath the bed. She only needs a few hours of sleep and will soon get up at her regular time to start another day. However, waking up has been accompanied by a weary sigh for quite a while now. "Again; once again, you are awake," is her first, almost angry thought before getting out of bed. She has had enough. What's the point of getting older every day when the next generation is also getting old and sick and is dying before she does, leaving her even more lonely? This unnecessarily advanced age doesn't suit her. Her spirit remains far too alert and is no longer in tune with her body, which is getting weaker and weaker. The resulting rift feels increasingly painful: it cuts her off from any joy in life. She'd just like to go to sleep and not wake up.

But as day dawns once again she takes her usual breakfast of yoghurt and fruit—an orange this morning—out of the fridge and sits on the edge of her bed to eat. She washes up in her bathroom, chooses a nice dress, puts her imitation pearls around her neck and in her ears ... and the day can begin.

The midday meal will be served in the common dining room, but until then, Sidi has nothing to do, no plans, and no appointments until the afternoon. She no longer has any wish to move much or walk, only sitting doesn't tire her. So she sits in her light blue armchair and takes her time going through the latest issue of *National Geographic*. She loves the reports about distant countries, and her heart is especially touched by articles in which beautiful color photos tell the story of little-known species.

At noon—an hour she would have found inconceivably early in the past—a bell rings to convene the diners. Generally, she's content with the food that's always served by friendly young women, though occasionally she wishes it were more varied and a bit heartier. But, oh horrors, today's menu features Topfenknödel (cheese curd dumplings) ... again. Something sweet as a main dish! Sidonie can't bear the idea. The other day they served pastries with a vanilla sauce—she doesn't like vanilla sauce, she detests Kaiserschmarren (sugared pancakes) as a main course. But she can only choose her own menu on her birthday, and she always asks for asparagus and for chestnut puree with whipped cream for dessert, dishes that are never served otherwise.

Today, she has to endure the sweet, easy-to-chew dumplings yet again, and her mood is set accordingly. It is even more difficult than usual to endure the other old women at her table who either sit in silence, or are demented, or have an overwhelming need to talk while they shovel food into their toothless mouths. She often finds that she can hardly bear this. Constantly comparing herself to them, she frequently checks her reflection in the mirror and finds that she comes off much better than they do. Others at age ninety-six are pushing a walker or using a cane; they can't hear or see anymore or are absent mentally. She doesn't want to have anything to do with such human wrecks.

Nonetheless, Sidi has recently become the doyenne among the residents. Only one woman, at a hundred and two, is older than Sidi, but she has been confined to the nursing ward for a long time. The physiotherapist recently introduced the two and asked Sidi if she wouldn't like to talk with the older woman. Sidi's defensive reply was, "No, why? I'm old myself!" Then she fled to her room, where she could be alone and didn't need to witness an incarnation of her own decline.

Only once has Sidi taken a fancy to a fellow resident, a Norwegian former dancer who had been married to an Austrian baron and moved in after his death. Sidi remembers her as a delicate woman who was not really pretty but held herself in a certain way that aroused a certain ardor. While the dancer was alive, Sidi tried to anticipate her every wish and fulfill it; since her death, she regularly puts flowers on her grave.

After eating, Sidi takes her obligatory siesta, trying to make up for the hours of sleep she loses at night. She wants to be in particularly good form for her weekly bridge party this afternoon at her friend Lotte's in Grinzing.

She'll take public transportation to get there. She likes to get around that way and prefers a cab only for very long distances, if several transfers are involved, or if it's late at night. The city of Vienna provides a special cab service for old and disabled people. It costs the same as public transportation, and Sidi uses it occasionally, but she doesn't like it all that much, because she sometimes has to wait as much as half an hour for the driver to arrive.

If she is only going a few stops on the underground or by tram, she chooses not to pay. It's silly to spend money to go such a short distance. And although she's ticketless, her demeanor is so self-possessed that she is never caught. A friend of hers can't stand this and admonishes her because it's so transgressive. She wants to buy Sidi an annual pass, but her daughter forestalls that rather expensive undertaking, explaining that Aunt Sidi actually enjoys dodging the fare, and one shouldn't deprive her of that pleasure.

At the bridge party in Grinzing today, Sidonie is going to encounter a woman who turned her head at one time but is now out of favor. Dora is attractive, she worked as model in her youth, seventy years old, and the former wife of a well-known Austrian industrialist. At one time, she had caused Sidi's heart to beat a little faster and she'd been flattered by the older woman's attention. For quite some time, the two had met regularly at bridge parties and often for dinner á deux.

Then Dora invited Sidonie to her home, ostensibly to discuss what to wear to a forthcoming reception. Sidonie asked Dora to model the evening gown under consideration, but after leaving to change, to Sidonie's horror Dora returned topless and wearing only pantyhose. Sidi could still remember, with a thrill of indignation, that she had avoided looking at Dora. What did Dora want from this old woman? An old woman who is an aesthete and whose personal standards about her bygone beauty meant that anything physical was now absolutely out of the question.

A few days later Dora asked Sidonie on the phone why she had refused to look at her. When Sidi responded, "Because you are already seductive enough when dressed," Dora just laughed and assured her that she would never do such a thing again.

After that incident, Sidi rather fixated on Dora. She learned that Dora and a woman from the aristocracy with whom she had an intimate relationship were planning to vacation in the same place in Turkey at the same time. When questioned, Dora denied it. Why, Sidi obsessed, were they concealing the trip, which, in her opinion, had to have been arranged in mutual collusion? Why did Dora lie about it to her? A big minus on Sidi's scale of values. The only question Sidi couldn't bring herself to pose was whether Dora also presented herself to the other woman topless?

Nonetheless, from time to time Sidonie sent Dora flowers in the time-honored tradition. One day, when Dora wasn't at home, the delivery person left a card asking her to pick up the exquisite orchids at the flower shop.

For Sidonie, orchids had always been the most beautiful possible symbol of her admiration and adoration, and she had no idea that Dora didn't like them. At the shop, Dora asked if she could choose different flowers instead and indicated a marvelous arrangement of tulips.

When Dora telephoned to thank Sidi and let her know about the substitution, she was unprepared for the nasty tirade that followed. Aghast that Dora could choose flowers as vulgar as tulips over the most noble and expensive blooms available, Sidonie announced, "I never want to have to deal with you again," and hung up.

For weeks the scandalized Sidi told everyone who would listen that Dora had so embarrassed her at the flower shop that she would never again be able to set foot in there, that Dora had rejected her gift of love and devotion, that she felt deceived and betrayed. She became increasingly convinced that the vain Dora had come to her only because she enjoyed being admired or as a favor to a poor old woman. She decided to cut Dora out of her life—barring the occasional encounter at bridge parties.

Sidonie also has plans for the day after the bridge party, a Sunday. Once a month the Imhofs invite her for lunch. Though the Imhofs of her own generation are now long dead, she still socializes with their children and grandchildren. She remembers how she, Ed and the Imhofs would play bridge for days on end in St. Gilgen. That was in the thirties, when Vicki was a fat, happy boy who impressed her with his charm and intelligence. Today he is an old man who has been married to the vivid Helga for many years and is proud of his two grown daughters and his grandchildren. It worries her that Vicki now has diabetes and is almost blind. What kind of justice is that, at his age, so much younger than she is?

But today good cheer is, as usual, also a guest at the Imhof's table. Helga has served a fine pork roast and the grandchildren talk about their adventures. Vicki cracks jokes, and the big black Labrador wags its tail while consuming the leftovers. Sidonie loves this family and admires the fact that Vicki and Helga are among the few couples she knows who still have a happy married life and caring, self-confident children.

Content, she begins a new week, which will include a meeting with two young friends. Several years ago, one of them—the granddaughter of Sylvie Dietz, now long dead—started to tape record her memoirs. A couple of years ago, she brought along a friend, who asked the same questions all over again and then so many more. She wanted the details about things Sidonie has long since forgotten or never knew in the first place. Did Leonie Puttkamer really try to poison her husband? Which films did she see in the thirties? What did she make of politics in the fifties? And had she known that the actress Dorothea Neff had also been "one of us?" For some reason, Sidonie enjoys this questioning, and what she doesn't want to tell, she doesn't tell. She knows that her life is being documented; and she is proud, even a bit vain, that others find it so interesting.

But what are all these little vanities compared to the daydreams about her great loves that she can elaborate on without restraint during these discussions? Those women with unforgettable hands and a matchless gait who had given her life its special stamp. And whenever she meets with her young friends, she talks about Leonie Puttkamer; sometimes unfurling the complete story of the relationship, sometimes only selected elements. But with every reiteration she emphasizes that still today she is proud that as a young, innocent girl she chose someone like Baroness Leonie Puttkamer.

With a dreamy smile, Sidi sits in her pale blue armchair and relives for the hundredth, probably the thousandth time, how she first took Leonie's hand and kissed it. She remembers Professor Freud with a mixture of rage and contempt and gloats rather maliciously about having given him such a tough time. He was a jerk, and that's all there is to it!

The more Sidonie acknowledges that her own beauty is a thing of the past, the more the faces and bodies of her great loves resurface and with them, inevitably, the topic of sex. With a show of aversion that masks her unspoken regret, Sidonie talks of physical love. She knows that she has lost out on a lot of pleasure. What did that doctor say, the one who treated her in the Wiener Neustadt hospital? He treated her after her third failed suicide attempt, when the bullet missed her heart by just two centimeters, and he had understood how it is with her. "You are a classic asexual," he had said. She could only agree with him, and still does. She had been so much more aroused by the touch of a hand, a body as it turns, even a glance than by those body parts that are designed for lust. She found those hidden parts and the threatening "thing" between men's legs quite terrible; a woman's dampness was frightening, though slightly better; and the feel of a strange tongue in her mouth had been so disgusting.

"And then, when things did click, it was all over," she says with a loud sigh. "I ended up like this because of my mother," she notes soberly. "Every woman was her enemy. She was nicer to me only when she discovered that something about me wasn't right. She was really nice only at the very end, when she took pills; then she even told me that I had beautiful eyes."

Only beauty—her mother's, her own and that of many other women—has moved her and brought out her strongest feelings.

"I have always been in love with beauty. A beautiful woman is still a pleasure for me, and this will be true until I'll die."

And so the linked associations carry her forward into the present. She still can't refrain from telling certain women that she fancies them. Conveniently, the president of the women's residence is close at hand and very much suits Sidi's taste, though regrettably, she sees her only rarely.

But recently, after a gathering, she had finally let this woman know how much she liked setting eyes on her, how doing so brightened her day. These words brought a glow to the president's face, and Sidonie was delighted that her remarks were so well received, so successfully flattering.

The tape recorder is switched off; the room is bathed in early evening twilight, and it is finally time to go out to dinner. The two friends have planned something special that Sidi has been anticipating for days— they are going to a type of pub she's never been to before and in her youth would have been considered "demimonde." Even today, no one she socializes with would ever set foot inside Café Willendorf in the Rosa-Lila-Villa.

When Sidonie enters the café, her eyes light up with pleasure. All heads turn in her direction, most likely because no one ninety-six years of age has ever crossed the threshold before. As soon as the three women take their seats, Sidi begins to survey the room. There's so much she wants to know, and she listens, unbelieving, to the answers to her questions. Marveling, she registers the patrons—those she can "know just by looking" and those who don't fit the pattern at all. She doesn't like the rough-looking women, and she can't believe that the more feminine ones are actually lesbians. She's delighted by the graceful, campy men, and she simply doesn't understand the transsexuals. Tonight, food is totally unimportant, and for a few hours, smiling shrewdly and clasping her glass between shaky hands, Sidi is a guest in a world she might have liked to inhabit seventy years ago.

The next time the two friends visit, they all go to Sidi's favorite pub, the Wienerwald chain restaurant right across the street from her residence, where she can order roast chicken with waffle fries. She finds waffle fries particularly inventive. They taste so much better than the boring roast potatoes served at lunch in the residence, and she eats them with gusto. After ordering her drink of choice, ice-cold tap water, she carries on a lively discussion about her diverse loves, not noticing that a family at a nearby table has been watching her the whole time. They pay a flower vendor making his rounds through the pub to present Sidonie with a few roses. She initially refuses to take them, but he assures her with a broad smile that they have been paid for. Sidonie is thoroughly taken aback. Who would give her flowers?

The mother from the nearby table comes over to explain that her daughter has taken a fancy to Sidi and wanted to give her those flowers but is too shy to do it in person. A few minutes later, the girl, who is about fifteen years old, dares to come over to offer some shy compliments and express a few words of admiration before leaving the restaurant with her family. Sidonie's always dignified presence can still make an impression.

If someone has the time to take her, Sidi enjoys going to the movies. Sometime in the late fall of 1998, her two young interlocutors collect her, and they take the underground to go see *The Horse Whisperer*—a corny Hollywood production with lots of superb animals, shots of beautiful scenery and, hopefully, not too much sex. Judging by the previews, it seems to have all the components of a film Sidi will enjoy.

Whenever Sidi gets on the underground, she receives impressed and respectful glances that take note of her excellent posture, neat appearance and posh diction. She looks around with curiosity, comments on what she sees, notes the details of the fashions and talks loudly about them. She does this in such a way that everyone is pleased.

This time she sits opposite a young woman whose elegant suit has a short, quite revealing skirt. With great delight, Sidi scrutinizes her long legs, and after a third inspection, she turns to her companions and says loudly, "She really has lovely legs." The woman and half the people in the car can hear this, of course, but nobody finds it offensive. Obviously pleased by the compliment, the young woman smiles and repositions herself on the seat the better to display her legs. Sidi makes a few more appreciative remarks before they reach their stop, and she only takes her mind off those legs when they arrive at the theater.

She sits waiting for the film to start, alert and curious, her head shaking from side to side and the seats in her row shaking with it. No one seems annoyed; rather, everyone appears to be pleased that someone so old has joined them. The film suits Sidi, at least at first. Superb shots of Colorado and wild horses trigger complacent sighs, and the scenes of romantic infatuation make her smile. But then—love scenes, kissing and eventually, sex. When the kissing starts, she yells "Outrageous," and all heads turn. By the time the bedroom scene fills the screen, she has fallen asleep. Still, the film will stay with her, and she will tell every friend she meets in the coming weeks all about it.

Those friends are the ones who support and, if necessary, advise her—Lotte and Ruth chief among them, followed by Ruth's daughter, Andrea. With them Sidi can talk about everything, get counsel, pour out her heart. They are more concerned and more supportive than any relative would be, and this is something Sidi knows how to appreciate. Lotte phones her every day, sometimes just to ask how she's doing, sometimes for a long talk.

Sidi gets invited everywhere during holidays, and she has spent summers at hunting lodges in Styria, in Salzburg with Andrea, in Paris with Jeanette. When she was younger and stronger, she vacationed with her youngest brother in Florida. She has only recently given up travelling, afraid she might get sick and become a burden on her hostesses. Or she might die, and she doesn't want to trouble anyone with that. Besides, even many of her younger friends are now ailing or frail themselves and can no longer host her. This makes Sidi feel both bitter and lonely. Her contemporaries are long since dead and gone and now the next generation is going as well. Once again, she curses her advanced age, her clear mind that registers everything. She wants to die.

Then, at age ninety-eight, she is seized by a reawakened thirst for adventure and fantasizes about taking a big, final trip. By chance she learns that diplomat friends of hers are in Lima, Peru, and that brings back old memories. It's been more than fifty years since her voyage from Japan through Panama to Cuba, but she can still see her fellow passenger Carlos, the handsome Peruvian to whom she took such a fancy. He had proposed an affair in such a charming way as they stood together at the ship's rail. She can still feel a slight shiver when she thinks about that never-realized opportunity, and she convinces her diplomat friends to make inquiries about the object of her long-ago crush.

Carlos is still alive, and armed with his address, Sidi immediately dictates a letter—even she can't read her own shaky handwriting. Not too long afterward, she receives a reply—not written by Carlos, whose eyes are too weak, but by his son.

She books a flight to Lima, and her friends there assure her that she can stay with them. But Carlos asks her to delay her trip for six months, because at the moment his health won't allow him to receive her. In her reply, Sidonie includes a picture of herself and asks Carlos to reciprocate. "He sent me one of him, and there was nothing in it that I liked. I returned it, because he looked like an athlete to whom I never would have taken a fancy."

The dream was over, the fantasy fizzled out: Carlos was a vain old man who wanted to impress her but only disillusioned her. Sidi is glad she will never make the trip; most likely the reunion would have been a huge disappointment. Relieved, she closes the book on men ... once and for all.

Her relationship with Wjera is the only one Sidi apparently cannot resolve. Most likely her most intense and most important love, Wjera is never far from her thoughts, and she often repeats the sentence: "Not one day goes by when I don't think of her." But the pain and disappointment, whether her own or what she inflicted, also lie close at hand, and it's almost as if she wants to repress this dark side.

And so Wjera remains the one person who is never mentioned by name, who has been draped in a mantle of protection and silence. With Wjera, it truly would have been necessary to put social conventions aside and dedicate herself to love. Sidonie hadn't managed it, and that failure lives inside her as a deep pain until her final day.

She still owes Wjera something.

At the end of April 1999 Sidonie enters her hundredth year. On her birthday, her room is a sea of flowers, and the many large and small parcels remind her that people love her and are thinking of her. But she doesn't really feel like celebrating. She has felt tired, dead tired, for months and has started to forget appointments and people—this has never happened before. She doesn't want to go out, is impatient and grumpy, and only wants to sit and stare. As her world becomes ever narrower, she'd prefer just to fall asleep and not wake up.

One day in early May, she takes the first step on that path. Catching her foot in her carpet, she falls and breaks her hip. The usual procedures follow—she's taken to the hospital, operated on, confined to a bed. The days are hot, and she lies like a helpless animal, pale and transparent, her arms at her sides, in a high-tech hospital bed in a high-tech hospital. There is not much left of her body—flaccid skin, a bit of meat on bones and joints that seem much too big. Her hair is a fine, white fuzz, her mouth toothless and shrunken.

She speaks softly, if at all, doesn't complain, stares at the ceiling and slips farther and farther away.

Then one of her two young friends brings a picture of Leonie Puttkamer to her bedside, the only personal item in this white limbo, and Sidi's body reanimates. Her eyes widen, there's a smile on her lips, and she whispers, "I used to love her so very much."

After some time, the medical necessities have all been dealt with, and Sidi is returned to her residence. At first, she's put in the nursing ward; then she returns to her own room, where her sense of dignity, which she can no longer maintain for herself, is restored to her through

Sidonie Csillag as an old woman

loving care. She's taken to the hairdresser in a wheelchair, wears a clean, colorful dress every day, is fed regularly, sits in the garden.

But she has almost stopped talking. She endures what is unavoidable, smiles at the few things that still strike her as beautiful and pleasant.

Then things go quickly. The days get hotter, and Sidi weaker. No more outings in her wheelchair; the hairdresser comes to her bedside; helpless acquaintances bring her ice cream and spoon it into her tooth-less mouth until she starts to complain. She develops dark spots on her legs from poor circulation, an indication that the end is nearing.

Her young friend arrives when Sidi is already poised at the very edge of this world. Her breathing has almost stilled, her body is barely warm. A hand rests on her shoulder, in her hand, it caresses her. A voice reaches her from very far away. Then she pushes herself over the border of this existence into another one. It is easy ...

BIBLIOGRAPHY

Translator's Note: The first German edition (Vienna: Deuticke, 2000) contained an extensive bibliography of 175 works, the great majority of them in German and many available only in archives. The abbreviated Bibliography below lists all the English-language entries in the original, a selection of the German-language entries, and all of the archives.

ENGLISH-LANGUAGE BIBLIOGRAPHY

Allen, Janik. *Wittgenstein's Vienna*. New York, 1973.

Benstock, Shari. *Women of the Left Bank: Paris 1900–1940*. Austin TX, 1986.

Faderman, Lillian. *Odd Girls and Twilight Lovers: A History of Lesbian Life in Twentieth-Century America*. New York, 1991.

Garcia, Christina. *Dreaming in Cuban*. New York, 1992.

Gerris, Lisa. "Aspects of the Image of Vienna (1910–1933) in North American Fiction." PhD diss. Vienna 1990.

Havana Post, 1940–1945.

Hicks, Albert C. *Blood in the Streets*. New York, 1946.

Kater, Michael H. *The Twisted Muse: Musicians and their Music in the Third Reich*. New York, 1997.

Levine, Robert. *Tropical Diaspora: the Jewish Experience in Cuba*. Gainesville FL, 1993.

Marting, Daine E., ed. *American Women Writers*. Westport CT, 1990.

McCagg, Willain O. Jr. *A History of Habsburg Jews 1640–1918*. Bloomington IL, Indianapolis IN, 1989.

Menaker, Esther. *Appointment in Vienna*. New York, 1989.

Messick, Hank. *Lansky*. New York, 1971.

Michaelis, Karin, with Leonore Sorsby. *Little Troll*. New York, 1946.

Morton, Frederic. *Thunder at Twilight: Vienna 1913/1914*. New York, 1989.

Rothschild, K.W. *Austria's Economic Development between the Two Wars*. London, 1947.

Sapir, Boris. *The Jewish Community of Cuba*. New York, 1949.

Smith, Lois M. and Alfred Padula. *Sex and Revolution: Women in Socialist Cuba*. New York, 1996.

Sterba, Richard. *Reminiscences of a Viennese Psychologist*. Detroit, 1982.

German-language Bibliography

Andics, Hellmut. *Das österreichische Jahrhundert: Die Donaumonarchie 1804–1918*. Vienna, 1983.

——— *Die Juden in Wien*. Vienna, Munich, 1988.

Bei, Neda, Wolfgang Förster, Hanna Hacker, Manfred Lang, eds. *Das lila Wien um 1900: Zur Aesthetik der Homosexualität*. Vienna, 1986.

Berger, Peter Robert. "Der Donauraum in wirtschaftlichen Umbruch nach dem ersten Weltkrieg." PhD diss. Vienna, 1979.

Bettelheim, Peter, Silvia Prohinig, Robert Streiel, eds. *Antisemitismus in Osteuropa*. Vienna, 1992.

Binder, E. "Doktor Albert Gessmann". PhD diss. Vienna, 1950.

Bruckmüller, Ernst, Ulrike Döcker, Hannes Stekl, Peter Urbanitsch, eds. *Bürgertum in der Habsburger Monarchie*. Vienna, 1990.

Brunner, Andreas and Hannes Sulzenbacher, eds. *Schwules Wien: Reiseführer durch die Donaumetropole*. Vienna, 1998.

Carsten, Francis L. *Geschichte der preussischen Junker*. Frankfurt am Main, 1988.

Czeike, Felix. *Historisches Lexikon Wien in 5 Bänden*. Vienna, 1997.

Das Interessante Blatt, 1918–1925.

Eldorado. *Homosexuelle Frauen und Männer in Berlin 1850–1950: Geschichte, Alltag und Kultur*. Berlin, 1984.

Fischer, Lothar. *Anita Berber. Tanz zwischen Rausch und Tod 1918–1928 in Berlin*. Berlin, 1988.

Freud, Sigmund. "Über die Psychogenese eines Falles von weiblicher Homosexualität". In *Gesammelte Werke aus den Jahren 1917–1920*. London, 1947.

[Quotations in this edition are from: Freud, Sigmund. "The Psychogenesis of a Case of Female Homosexuality." *International Journal of Psycho-Analysis* 1, no. 2 (1920).]

Gay, Peter. *Freud: Eine Biographie für unsere Zeit.* Frankfurt am Main, 1989.

Gessmann, Albert. *Das Fremdvolk.* Drama. Gewidmet Herrn Bürgermeister Dr. Karl Lueger. Vienna, 1904.

Gessmann, Albert and Otto Kämper. *Neues Bauen: neue Arbeit! Bauwirtschaftliche Massnahmen zur Behebung der Arbeitslosigkeit in Österreich.* Vienna, 1932.

Garnichstaedten-Cerva, R, J. Mentschl, G. Otruba. *Altösterreichische Unternehmer: 110 Lebensbilder.* Vienna, 1969.

Hacker, Hanna. *Frauen und Freundinnen: Studien zur weiblichen Homosexualität am Beispiel Österreich 1870–1938.* Weinheim, 1987.

Karlsfeld, Serge. *Vichy-Auschwitz: Die Zusammenarbeit der deutschen und französischen Behörden bei der Endlösung der Judenfrage in Frankreich.* Nördlingen, 1989.

Kos, Wolfgang. *Über den Semmering: Kulturgeschichte einer künstlichen Landschaft.* Photographien von Kristian Sotriffer. Vienna, 1984.

Kraus, Karl. "Bericht und Brief von Anita Berber." *Die Fackel* 601 (November 1922).

Mauntner-Markhof, Manfred. *Haltestellen.* Vienna, 1978.

Meyer, Adele, ed. *Lila Nächte: Die Damenklubs der zwanziger Jahre.* Cologne, 1981.

Morgenbrod, Birgitt. *Wiener Grossbürgertum im Ersten Weltkrieg.* Vienna, Cologne, 1994.

Mutzenbacher, Josefine. *Die Geschichte einer Wienerische Dirne, von ihr selbst erzählt.* Höchberg by Würzburg, 1991.

Neues Montagsblatt, 1924.

Neue Freie Presse, 1924.

Niel, Alfred. *Die k. u. k. Riviera von Abbazia bis Grado.* Graz, Vienna, 1981.

Österreiches Biographisches Lexikon 1815–1950. Graz, Cologne, 1959.

Pass, Walter, Gerhardt Scheit, Wilhelm Svoboda. *Orpheus im Exil: Die Vertreibung der österreichischen Musik von 1938 bis 1945.* Vienna, 1995.

Reutter, Lutz-Eugen. *Katolische Kirche als Fluchthelfer im Dritten Reich.* Recklinghausen-Hamburg, 1971.

Schoppmann, Claudia. *Zeit der Maskierung: Lebensgeschichten lesbischer Frauen im Dritten Reich.* Berlin, 1993.

Stadt Chronik Wien. Vienna, Munich, 1986.

ARCHIVES

Österreiches Staat Archiv (Austrian State Archive)

Stadtarchiv Stadt Nürnberg (Nürnberg City Archive)

Wiener Stadt- und Landesarchiv (Vienna City and State Archive)

Sigmund Freud-Privatstiftung, Sigmund Freud Museum, Vienna. Depository of Margarethe Csonka-Trautenegg's estate, including many of the photos in this biography and the tapes and transcripts upon which it is based.

SOURCES OF PICTURES

Sigmund-Freud-Privatstiftung (Private Archive): front cover, xii, 6, 13, 15, 22, 30, 31, 39, 41, 52, 94, 108, 110, 112, 119, 121, 135, 139, 140, 141, 150, 153, 163, 168, 174, 178, 183, 187, 189, 192, 195, 200, 247, 249, 257, 261, 262, 266, 270, 273, 276, 296, 300, 305, 308, 314, 318, 320, 323, 325, 327, 336
Direktion der Museen der Stadt Wien: 8, 128
Bildarchiv Österreichische Nationalbibliothek Wien: 26, 35, 44, 70, 148, 172, 207
Helfried Seemann: 88
Wiener Stadt- und Landesarchiv: 101
Josef Otto Slezak: 229
University Press of Florida, Herbert Karliner Archive: 234
University Press of Florida, Norbert Adler Archive: 252
Philip Abbrederis: 346
Gudrun Stoltz: 362

NAME INDEX

Names in brackets are the real names of individuals who have a pseudonym in this book